TORTURE AND ENGLISH LAW

Contributions in Legal Studies
Series Editor: *Paul L. Murphy*

The Promise of Power: The Emergence of the Legal Profession in Massachusetts, 1760-1840
Gerard W. Gawalt

Inferior Courts, Superior Justice: A History of the Justices of the Peace on the Northwest Frontier, 1853-1889
John R. Wunder

Antitrust and the Oil Monopoly: The Standard Oil Cases, 1890-1911
Bruce Bringhurst

They Have No Rights: Dred Scott's Struggle for Freedom
Walter Ehrlich

Popular Influence Upon Public Policy: Petitioning in Eighteenth-Century Virginia
Raymond C. Bailey

Fathers to Daughters: The Legal Foundations of Female Emancipation
Peggy A. Rabkin

In Honor of Justice Douglas: A Symposium on Individual Freedom
Robert H. Keller, Jr., editor

A Constitutional History of Habeas Corpus
William F. Duker

The American Codification Movement: A Study of Antebellum Legal Reform
Charles M. Cook

Crime and Punishment in Revolutionary Paris
Antoinette Wills

American Legal Culture, 1908-1940
John W. Johnson

Governmental Secrecy and the Founding Fathers
Daniel N. Hoffman

TORTURE AND ENGLISH LAW

An Administrative and Legal History from the Plantagenets to the Stuarts

James Heath

Contributions in Legal Studies, Number 18

Greenwood Press
Westport, Connecticut • London, England

Library of Congress Cataloging in Publication Data

Heath, James, 1920-
    Torture and English law.

    (Contributions in legal studies; no. 18 ISSN
0147-1074)
    Bibliography: p.
    Includes index.
    1. Torture—Great Britain—History. I. Title.
II. Series.
KD8225. T6H4   345.41'077   80-24552
ISBN 0-313-22598-2 (lib. bdg.)

Library of Congress Catalog Card Number: 80-24552
ISBN: 0-313-22598-2
ISSN: 0147-1074

First published in 1982

Greenwood Press
A division of Congressional Information Service, Inc.
88 Post Road West, Westport, Connecticut 06881

Printed in the United States of America

10 9 8 7 6 5 4 3 2 1

To
the Memory
of
David R. Boult, M.A., B.C.L.,
Fellow and Dean of New College, Oxford

CONTENTS

PREFACE

This book concerns a long period in English history. Its subject is the occurrence—and, where remarkable, the non-occurrence—during that period of interrogatory duress in governmental contexts.

The lesson of world history is that recourse by public agencies to such duress may aim at the discovery of judicial proof, or at the acquisition simply of intelligence, or at both; and that there will usually be aspects of technique, not only in the procedure immediately adopted, but in the construction for it of an administrative or juridical framework. Thus not only historians but many others—lawyers, political scientists, sociologists, penologists, police scientists, military scientists—may regard this sad topic as worthy of investigation.

For historians, the familiar large issue will arise between explanation in terms of evolution —social, political, economic—and explanation in terms of accident, and on such a broad interpretative plane, questions deserving scrutiny will easily be discovered. For instance, was medieval English resistance to the Continental example of judicial torture due to only some mere falling together of pieces confined within the area of judicial procedure? Or was it based in peculiarly English features of the political balance struck between the interests of Crown, Baronage, Church, and Towns? Or even under the Plantagenets, was a significant factor something more mysterious, such as the persistence of an Anglo-Saxon Volksgeist?

The legal historian, of course, has here the usual duty to ascertain the actual development of a particular system of law. From his standpoint, moreover, the repulsiveness of torture does not exclude useful comparative perceptions regarding a range of less horrifying, yet not necessarily less threatening, practices. One such practice is so topical in the United Kingdom that I mention by way of example its English history.

The obvious, if not the only, mode of torture is by painful physical aggression. Beyond the lowest levels of legal development, such aggression is usually penalized if it causes death or a listed form of physical injury; at higher levels, a broader basis of liability is provided by reference to insult or to trespass. Therefore, where a government has used torture, its agents generally either have been able to ignore the law, or have been provided, actually or at least arguably, with special exemption by the law itself. In England, writs of trespass to the person became available under the Plantagenets. From then on, if torture in a crude form appears to have been practiced, the question arises why the law did not operate as a deterrent. On the other hand, the English Common Law still has not embraced any general rule of liability for interference with personal privacy. Some judicial dicta, indeed, have favoured the existence of such a rule, but others have denied it. As yet, broadly speaking, legally protected privacy does not prevail among us. Since World War II, this state of affairs has been perceived to work importantly within our unwritten constitution. The story, however, begins much earlier.

A regular postal service was first established in Britain by a Commonwealth Ordinance of 1657, which expressly assumed that mail committed to it would be open to official surveillance. After the Restoration, an Act of 1660 confirmed the provisions of 1657. On the 25th of May, 1663, a proclamation announcing the appointment of a Postmaster-General contained the command that no officer or other person should open any letter or other packet in the mail, not addressed to himself, except upon "the immediate warrant of our Principal Secretary of State". The *Post Office (Revenues) Act*, 1710, made it an offense to open, detain, or delay letters or packets in the mail "except by an express warrant in writing under the hand of one of the Principal Secretaries of State for every such opening, detaining, or delaying". This provision was substantially reenacted in a consolidating measure, the *Offences against the Post Office Act*, 1837.

Under the *Telegraph Act*, 1868, it came to extend to telegrams delivered to the Post Office. By the 1900s, the practice of intercepting and examining mail under a Secretary of State's warrant had continued for nearly two centuries and a half. The view emerged, and gained the acceptance of some constitutional lawyers, that such a warrant legitimized in a general way the opening of mail. This effect might be attributed to the Post Office statutes, or the Prerogative, or a mysterious operation of the Common Law. If a relevant power, other than statutory, existed, it plainly might extend to interception of telephone messages;

the telephone service was being developed by the Post Office, but no statutory offense of interference, with an exception for cases where there was a Secretary of State's warrant, had been created regarding it. At first, telephone interception was carried on without warrants. However, in 1937, by arrangement between the departments concerned, the warrant system was extended to that business also. After World War II, by the *Crown Proceedings Act*, 1947, it was provided that generally "anything done or omitted to be done in relation to a postal packet" and "anything done or omitted to be done in relation to a telephonic communication" by a person "employed as a servant or agent of the Crown" should impose tortious liability neither upon the Crown nor upon the servant or agent involved.

In 1951, the Home Office produced a memorandum setting out general principles which it proposed to implement regarding interception warrants. In a criminal case, an interception warrant would be issued only if the crime was serious, and normal methods of investigation had failed or were unlikely to succeed. The *Post Office Act*, 1953, provided, once again, that it should be an offense for an officer of the Post Office to interfere with mail, but not where he acted in pusuance of an express warrant in writing from a Secretary of State.

In 1957, the report was published of a Committee of Privy Councillors appointed "to inquire into the interception of communications." The committee had been headed by a respected judge, Lord Birkett. It did not deny the possible correctness of the view that the warrant system was backed by some legal power other than statutory or at any rate not confined to exclusion of liability for particular statutory offenses. However, objections could be seen to the view that such a power existed. The *General Warrant* cases of the eighteenth century were authority that the Executive did not acquire title in law to a power, simply by pretending over a long period of time to possess it. Interception warrants were issued by one minister to another; a claim by the Crown to confer authority upon itself was plainly anomalous, so as in law to seem to require a statutory foundation; Post Office legislation that referred to such warrants did not expressly contemplate more than the restriction of specific statutory criminal liability.

The committee reported an alternative view that outside the express scope of legislation, interception of communications was not made legal by warrants, but did not in law need support: it was not illegal, anyway. At the same time, the committee accepted that few interceptions were authorized by the Home Secretary, that his personal control over interception was effective in each individual case, that what was happening was reasonable and desirable.

By the *Post Office Act,* 1969, the Post Office ceased to be a department of state. However, immunities to tortious liability were conferred under the new act, corresponding to those that had existed under the *Crown Proceedings Act,* 1947. The provision of the 1953 Act on interception continued in force, but moreover the new act contained a vague provision that, whilst it did not expressly mention either interception or warrants, was capable of being construed as conferring upon the warrant system, so far as might turn out to be required, a broad legalizing effect.

In February, 1979, in *Malone v. Commissioner of Police of the Metropolis* (No. 2), the legality of telephone-tapping under a Secretary of State's warrant at last became a matter for judicial decision. Amended pleading claimed declarations: a kind of remedy which in England has attained great Public Law importance. The hearing was by Vice-Chancellor Sir Robert Megarry, who held that existing practice, as described by those responsible, was lawful. He reached this conclusion on various grounds, but laid most stress upon a finding that to listen to another's telephone call simply was not contrary to English law. In July, 1979, in *R. v. Sang* , the House of Lords (although dealing with a different form of abuse) put beyond doubt that a judge would be wrong to exclude evidence simply because it was obtained by *opening* mail *without* a warrant.

In April, 1980, a White Paper on "The Interception of Communications in Great Britain" was presented to Parliament by the Home Secretary. It provided some statistics; for example, that in 1979 four hundred and eleven warrants had been issued in England for telephonic interceptions. It assured that everything was still being done as the Committee of Privy Councillors had been satisfied it was being done in 1957. Warrants were being issued in favor of the Police and of the Customs and Excise and the Security Services, but only upon principles identifiable with those endorsed by the Home Office memorandum of 1951. This complacent publication would hardly have served to allay anxiety that arose from allegations published by the *New Statesman* in January, 1980, regarding the scale and organization of the official telephone-tapping enterprise. However, on the 2nd of April, following the presentation of the White Paper, the Home Secretary told the House of Commons that a senior judge was to be asked to monitor official practice in that matter. Further, in March, 1981, a report that the Prime Minister had invited was published on (again) "The Interception of Communications in Great Britain". The author was Lord Diplock, the chosen senior judge. He is one of the most distinguished lawyers among the English judiciary. Occasionally, he has appeared as a juridicial pragmatist; in December, 1967, in *Chic Fashions (West Wales) Ltd. v. Jones*, he seemed to suggest that the *General Warrant* cases, to which I have referred and which English lawyers regarded with special pride, had become largely irrelevant to modern conditions and so of little legal weight. In his report, the only legal matter upon which he touched came to the possibility that some care might be needed to show the accordance, in the business concerned, of United Kingdom practice with the *European Convention for the Protection of Human Rights and Fundamental Freedoms*, a.8. So far as concerned the facts, he was brief, but firm. In his investigations, he had received due cooperation. He was satisfied that what was being done was required in the public interest, and carried out in accordance with the procedure officially laid down.

On the other hand, in *Malone v. Commissioner of Police of the Metropolis* (No. 2), the learned Vice-Chancellor, whilst affirming the present lawfulness of telephone-tapping, had described it as a "subject that cries out for legislation." He now proved to have the agreement of Members on both sides of the House of Commons. The *British Telecommunications Bill*, (on course through Parliament at the time of writing this preface) is designed to allow some denationalization of mail services and of telecommunications. In the House of Commons committee stage, against the wishes of the Government an amendment was adopted that would have given the Courts some control over telephone-tapping. The Commons' report stage of the bill began on 1 April, 1981. Already, the media had carried reports of extraordinary pressure exerted by the Government upon Members of Parliament who, although belonging to its own party, had supported the amendment.

A further amendment was proposed in the House that would have controlled the interception of mail; new allegations were made as to the real scale of what was going on. A compromise amendment also was proposed on telephone-tapping. The amendment accepted in committee was rejected; both the new amendments were defeated. The Home Secretary's argument, presented to the House early in the debate, was juridically fascinating. If the interception business were regulated by law, litigation in various individual cases would probably ensue. As a result, there would be offers of and demands for evidence. Evidence could not in such matters be given and secrecy at the same time maintained. Secrecy, however, was here essential to combat terrorism and drug-smuggling and to protect the lives of innocent people. On the other hand, an effective safeguard against abuse was afforded by Executive self-regulation, where legal protection of individual privacy would be a public bane.

Whilst by contrast an entirely extra-legal context (a situation in which lawfulness resulted from an entire absence of law) could never have been claimed for it, torture also is a subject which possesses topicality in the United Kingdom. Recent events in Northern Ireland showed that some Crown agencies had supposed forms of interrogatory duress to be legally at their disposal. Contagion might well have spread the resulting practices to Britain. Almost miraculously the supposition, which had seemed capable of easy acceptance even by lawyers, was dispelled. However, we had back-pedaled only just in time. For this reason, in particular, the time seemed opportune to recall the history of torture examinations in England prior to the Revolution of 1688, when their illegality probably was felt to have been placed beyond question, and of the relevant juridical climate as it evolved during that earlier period.

A standard work has been, for many years, David Jardine's *Reading on the Use of Torture in the Criminal Law of England previously to the Commonwealth*. Jardine delivered his *Reading* in 1836 to students at New Inn. The following year, he published it, with an appendix setting out the principal sources in the Council Book—the Register, or Acts, of the Privy Council—and among the State Papers, upon which he had relied.

Previously, Protestant opinion seems to have been that in England the use of torture had occurred as a brief aberration, hardly started before a rise in the sense of national danger at a critical point in Elizabeth I's reign, deprived of impetus as soon as the crisis was over, and entirely ended by advice that in 1628 the judges tendered regarding Felton, who had murdered the Duke of Buckingham. Such is the view that was expressed already under Charles II, by Baron Weston in *Mrs. Cellier's Case*, later by William Blackstone in the fourth book of his *Commentaries*, and then by Francis Hargrave in a *State Trials* note to the *Countess of Shrewsbury's Case*.

Jardine made such complacency impossible. His research did not permit him to establish when the use of interrogatory torture by the

English Executive began, or —with complete certainty—when it ended, but showed it to have been established under Edward VI and to have occurred as late as 1640. Also, he argued that John Rushworth's account, upon which reliance had been placed, of what had happened in Felton's case might well be misleading.

This ought to have created an immediate stir. I have not discovered whether it did. Yet certainly, with the passing years, the *Reading*— although copies were becoming hard to find—received recognition. In 1845 Henry Hallam added a note mentioning it to his *Constitutional History*. Later, reference was made to it by the American historian H. C. Lea and in England by L. Owen Pike, James Fitzjames Stephen, S. R. Gardner, and William Holdsworth.

On the other hand, it has serious shortcomings.

Jardine did not carry his investigation beyond 1640, and he offered, on events before the accession of Edward VI, remarks that were at once desultory and reckless. Yet no clear break in either legal or administrative history exists to recommend a beginning of exposition in the present matter only with Edward VI, or an ending earlier than 1688. Negative findings would have been as interesting as positive. The appearance of lack of concern, which I am sure was occasioned really by the extreme difficulties of his nobly undertaken research, is to be regretted.

The same difficulties explain his having overlooked, within the period to which he attended, some relevant conciliar records.

But then, regarding the interpretation of events, some errors are harder to explain. One, in a reference to the Masters of Requests, was castigated by I. S. Leadam in the Selden Society volume, *Select Cases in the Court of Requests*.

Whilst, even more serious, in my view, is a certain impetuosity and anachronism in Jardine's juridical explanations.

It was not until my labors were nearly complete that I saw a copy of John H. Langbein's unusual and valuable book, *Torture and the Law of Proof* (1977), but it afforded me comfort by tending, in various ways, to confirm my impression that the *Reading* possessed considerable weaknesses.

My first plan was to produce an enlarged and corrected edition of Jardine. However, I soon perceived that what was emerging contained so much new material that I ought myself to accept full responsibility for it. The main continuing effects of the way in which I set out are a division of each of the central chapters into parts—the first part related mainly to texts, drafts, or records of particular torture warrants—and the inclusion of an appendix setting out the principal sources and indicating, inter alia, which of them were published in the *Reading*.

My research on the present subject started some years before I came to write this book, and I received help from many institutions and individuals, both within and without the United Kingdom. I have special indebtedness to the British Library, Cambridge University Library, the Library of the University of Newcastle upon Tyne, the Public Record Office, and various officers of the Tower of London, but I take this opportunity to express my gratitude to all who have sustained my efforts.

My thanks are also due, and offered in full measure, to my wife for reading and correcting typescripts and proofs.

JAMES HEATH
Faculty of Law
The University of Newcastle upon Tyne

TORTURE AND ENGLISH LAW

INTRODUCTION

I. "TORTURE"

In the arts and the social sciences, the task of definition commonly proves frustrating to those who attempt it and the product wearisome to those to whom it is addressed. Still, having used the word *torture*, on account of its familiarity and its impact, in the title of this book, I had better try to define it *ad hoc*.

By *torture* I mean the infliction of physically founded suffering or the threat immediately to inflict it, where such infliction or threat is intended to elicit, or such infliction is incidental to means adopted to elicit, matter of intelligence or forensic proof and the motive is one of military, civil, or ecclesiastical interest.

The topic so selected corresponds, essentially, to that contemplated by Maître Alec Mellor's definition in his book *La Torture*.[1] Except that it extends to extra-judicial practice, it further corresponds, broadly, to juridical usage of the European penal *ancien régime*.[2]

Yet I must acknowledge different concepts that juridically have been given the shelter of this word in modern times.

A.17 of the third of the Conventions, which were signed at Geneva on 12 August, 1949, relating to armed conflict, provides, inter alia, that "no physical or mental torture . . . may be inflicted on prisoners of war to secure from them information of any kind whatsoever." I have excluded some methods that might be described as "mental torture."

Also, my definition, by referring exclusively to interrogatory proceedings, and by containing no reference to the degree of suffering inflicted or the full advertence of the party inflicting it, differs from the interpretation of the word *torture* recently adopted, in a particular context, by the European Court of Human Rights. The Court was seized of proceedings that had been brought by Ireland against the United Kingdom. The Republic alleged that by way of an "administrative practice,"[3] procedure had, in the Belfast area, been adopted for the

3

interrogation of suspected terrorists, which contravened the *European Convention for the Protection of Human Rights and Fundamental Freedoms*, a.3. The latter article (repeating, almost verbatim, a.5 of the *Universal Declaration of Human Rights*, which was proclaimed by the General Assembly of the United Nations on 10 December, 1948) lays down that no one shall be subjected "to torture or to inhuman or degrading treatment or punishment." Plainly, this list is such that a narrow emotive definition of *torture*, as included in it, may yet leave adequate protection by virtue of the other terms. Besides, to represent *torture* as a word of almost infinitely dire implication, so that its use with reference to modern police and military interrogations is an unfair exaggeration (a position that had on several occasions been adopted or suggested in French official communications[4] was, apart from questioning of the facts in particular instances, perhaps the only argument that could be used for relief of the beleaguered United Kingdom Government, relentlessly pursued in an international forum on account of events that, domestically, it no longer aimed to defend. Whilst, as an argument, it was fortified by a declaration in Resolution 3452 (XXX), a.1, adopted by the General Assembly of the United Nations on 9 December, 1975, that "torture constitutes an aggravated and deliberate form of cruel, inhuman or degrading treatment." At any rate, the Court obliged by holding that whilst there had been an administrative practice constituting an infringement of the Convention, a.3, *torture* was not the right word for it. Referring to what it regarded as a distinction embodied in the article, between the notion of *torture* and that of "inhuman or degrading treatment", the Court said that "this distinction derives principally from a difference in the intensity of the suffering inflicted." It concluded that although "as applied in combination," certain techniques employed "undoubtedly amounted to inhuman and degrading treatment," although "their object was the extraction of confessions, the naming of others and/or information," and although "they were used systematically," still "they did not occasion sufficient suffering of the particular intensity and cruelty implied by the word torture as so understood."[5]

Whether, in any particular case, the fact that the proceedings were interrogatory could have any weight at all regarding the description of associated duress for the purposes of the article was not made clear. On the other hand, the Court, citing the General Assembly resolution to which I have referred, did seem to suggest that deliberateness in the infliction of suffering might here be a factor for consideration, if a minor one. For the purposes of legal historical exposition, it is obvious that such subtleties would be unmanageable. Moreover, I think the work of a historian in this area will be facilitated if he responds to the older juridical tendency to identify torture with interrogatory duress having a physical base. Interrogatory severity, being an apparently distinct phenomenon from penal severity, may deserve separate treatment; whilst, regarding interrogatory procedures, it may be convenient to deal with physical measures, or the threat of them, but to keep clear of any entanglement with the fact—which may intrude, if there is reference to "mental torture"—that examination can itself be a source of much mentally based suffering, especially if the examinate is suspected and in custody. Confinement of investigation to physically based suffering does not, on the other hand, exclude measures such as starvation or deprival of sleep, although Judge Frank, during his important judgment in *U.S. ex. rel. Caminito* v. *Murphy* (1955),[6] described the latter as "psychological torture."

II. *"LAW"*

By "English" law, in the title of this book, I mean law in England, or in England and Wales, which was appreciated there as deriving from the national social or political order. So I exclude from the description law transported from England elsewhere—say, to the Irish Pale or North America—and law observed in England on account of an order regarded as universal—for example, law regarded there as depending directly upon the authority of the Holy See.

The word *law* itself is unlikely to excite curiosity from many lawyers. Still, in philosophy, battles continue to be fought over it, and I must offer legal theorists a confession of the artlessness with which it is here employed.[7]

To have varied, in the sense attributed to it, from conservative lawyerly thought would have been to court confusion, even had there otherwise seemed something to be said for its different employment. So I have gone along with Mr. Justice O. W. Holmes's celebrated aphorism: "The prophecies of what the courts will do in fact, and nothing more pretentious, are what I mean by law."[8]

If a more formal approximation is desired, I would venture the following: *Law* here describes normative matter that a Judicature (or less specialized magistracy, in a judicial function) would appear likely somehow to observe, in appropriate circumstances, as containing or implying a rule for its own conduct, respect for which is necessary to the validity of its acts.

Law, in this humdrum sense, is distinct from rules simply of established morality and often from self-regulatory provisions of an executive branch of government.[9] According to some authorities, however, when associated with penal sanctions it is capable of reinforcing or modifying moral sentiments.[10] Established non-legal norms may of course be transmuted into law, replacing parts of the existing fabric or at least affecting their operation.

Since familiarity often breeds non-recognition, it may be well to remind ourselves of some of the causes for anxiety that ought to afflict a legal historian when he seeks, by aid of a traditional concept such as suggested above, to determine what was the law at a given time and place.

1. As Mr. Justice Holmes stated the criterion, it is essentially subjective and admits a kind of objectivity in the contemporary context only because lawyers find that they often share the expectations, regarding judicial conduct, of other lawyers. Now the legal historian does not so intimately share the ambiance of the profession actually at work at the time and place that he brings under review. Yet he must accept the negative Holmesian inference: no prophecy, no law!

2. Particularly in the past, a multiplicity of systems of law may be encountered, some of them in conflict and accompanied perhaps by a corresponding multiplicity of courts, also in conflict.[11]

3. The legal historian also shares problems with analytical jurists, working on the systems of their own time. Notably, for present purposes, it may be difficult to gauge judicial reaction to the moral pressure of established executive practice. Where the Executive has arrogated a power to itself, the fact of its having continued in exercise of that power for a considerable time will increase willingness to believe the behavior concerned is necessary and may directly promote willingness to believe that what is being done is legal. The latter attitude will be strengthened further if the Executive by self-regulation in the matter, establishes the sort of conditions that might well have resulted from legislation. Further, if the courts let pass openings to refer, although obiter, to what is going on, this will encourage the idea that were they compelled to pass upon

it, they would uphold it; all such impressions may well be reflected back onto, and influence, the Judicature itself. Yet the weight they will carry is no more than matter of speculation. If and when the question does arise forensically, much may depend upon the particular occasion and the particular judges.

III. WEAKNESS AND STRENGTH

Jean Bodin observed[12] that the message of a thesis is best brought home by spelling it out at the beginning.

This book, however, was written with purposes mainly of conflation and revision and the hope that every kind of specialist concerned would make, of the material it presented, whatever his or her own science or art dictated or allowed. Thus I shall here offer upon that material only a few broad reflections.

First, aside from all legal questions, some of the information collected does affirm the use of torture and so recalls William Godwin's remark:[13]

Though the evils which arise to us from the structure of the material universe are neither trivial nor few, yet the history of political society sufficiently shows that man is of all other beings the most formidable to man.

On the other hand, regarding law, what will be reviewed may seem suggestive in one place of weakness and in another, of strength.

The cautionary catalog with which I ended the last section conveys that the emergence of executive practices, at the outset illegal or within a legal hiatus, may create or heighten uncertainty—which is weakness— in the fabric of law. If we attempt the feat of forming impressions about probable judicial behavior out of our own time, we may perhaps think that such for a while was the effect of a practice of torture, which we shall encounter, by the Executive in England.

To provide in advance a certain basis for comparison, it may be well to recall here a more recent experience, to which the proceedings above noticed before the European Court of Human Rights formed an epilogue.

During 1971 the troubles of Northern Ireland brought within the United Kingdom an army interrogation practice that had been developed elsewhere. Concerning its application overseas since World War II, there had been complaints, official denials, inquiries.[14] In terms of public relations, the matter was sensitive already, and when in August, 1971, reports were published in the press that suspected terrorists had been maltreated during interrogation in the Belfast area, the Home Secretary promptly appointed a committee to investigate them under the chairmanship of Sir Edmund Compton. The language employed for this purpose proved significant: the committee members were to look for "physical brutality". It transpired that the United Kingdom Staffs had from time to time issued, and revised, a "Joint Directive on Military Interrogation in Internal Security Operations Overseas", the latest revision having been in 1967; this, apparently, had been regarded as an apt guide for interrogations in Northern Ireland. Before the Compton Committee, it was officially claimed that rules there applied—rules contained in the Directive—followed the "broad principles" of the 1949 Geneva Conventions, a.3.[15] They did, indeed, contain like a.3 a prohibition of, inter alia, "torture", and "outrages upon personal dignity, in particular humiliating and degrading treatment." However, they added not only that subjects were to be treated humanely, but that they were to be subjected to "strict discipline"; the Directive was not understood to exclude "restricted diet" or "isolation".[16]

For what must have worked as interrogatory duress, the expression "strict discipline" was one let-in. The Compton Committee found in the word *brutality* its own let-out. Its members decided that "brutality" did not exist in the absence of a disposition to inflict suffering, coupled with indifference to, or pleasure in, the victim's pain; and that it meant "an inhuman or savage form of cruelty".[17]

There was no denial before the committee that measures adopted with detainees had comprised "wall-standing", "hooding", subjection to continuous noise, and a bread-and-water diet supplied at six-hour intervals.[18] Complaints from detainees included assertions that wall-standing had for them involved being placed facing a wall, hands high above the head, legs spread apart, and being so kept for days, being lifted up in case of collapse; that they had been prevented from sleeping, without or almost without respite, over periods of two or three days; and that denial of food went beyond what officially had been admitted.[19] As far as official admissions went, where the justification advanced was not "discipline", it was "security".[20] The committee was able, in the end, to spare the morale of those with or on the side of authority, because nothing it found to have been proved satisfied its concept of "brutality".[21]

However, liberal anxiety was not appeased; accordingly, a committee of three privy councillors was appointed to consider "authorized procedures for the interrogation of persons suspected of terrorism." Its chairman was a former Lord Chief Justice, Lord Parker of Waddington; another of its members was a former Lord Chancellor, Lord Gardiner.

Lord Parker and the third member, Mr. J. A. Boyd-Carpenter, concluded that the techniques, use of which was revealed by the Compton Report, were, if not carried to extremes, in accordance with the Joint Directive and acceptable: although, for the prevention of excess, it would be desirable to supplement the Directive with "guidelines" about the degree to which, in particular circumstances respectively, those techniques might with propriety be applied (guidelines, only, because "it may sometimes be impracticable to comply fully with them").[22]

On the other hand, Lord Gardiner not only expressed[23] dissatisfaction with the mode in which the Compton Committee had understood "brutality", but simply and firmly asserted[24] one fault of the "authorized procedures" under review to be that they were illegal. The impact of this cool pronouncement proved immediate and, as far as concerned official opinion, for the present decisive.[25] But in terms of the prospective judicial appreciation of the Common Law, it may have been a close-run thing.[26] Modern experience can illuminate the past.

Evidence supporting the conclusion that, for the period embraced by this book—if torture did prevail—we may say, "the opposite is also true", regards the practice of the Judicature itself. There, English experience over many centuries proves that doctrine and institutions may be excluded from a national legal system with great tenacity, in the teeth of close foreign example, and in conditions the relevant difference of which, from those that have nourished different legal ways, may not be easy to ascertain. The English Common Law rejection of the Continental system of legal proofs,[27] and its embodied practice of judicial torture, presents an interesting anomaly for those who seek to establish, in broad anthropological terms, a pattern of evolution in judicial praxis.[28]

chapter 1

TWELFTH CENTURY: THE SHADOW

I. CIVIL LAW AND COMMON LAW

Our occidental society has now achieved such a rate of scientific and technical advance that we seem to be responding with chronological isolationism: we may study the past, but we have little sense of dependence upon it. Yet this represents a deep change of outlook, only very recently approaching completion.

Belief that the extant product of classical antiquity had some fundamental cultural importance for us lingered, in many places, until the middle of the present century. Even now, its shade may be perceived in some academic curricula. Moreover, it was itself a residue of earlier attitudes, which included the assumption that classical institutions could themselves be adopted or transmuted to improve the quality of life centuries after their first decay.

When the theme of classical revival is presented, we of course think first of the historical phase that we call the "Renaissance"; the possibility will later be noticed[1] that the ethos of that phase had some relevance to the use of torture in England. However, in various spheres, texts derived from the ancient world—including, what concerns us, those of Roman Law—became objects of high regard during the Middle Ages.[2]

In the eleventh century, study of Roman Law was revived at North Italian universities; this "Civilian" learning spread, under ecclesiastical patronage, reaching Normandy before, in 1066, the Norman Duke William conquered Britain. Lanfranc, who under William became Archbishop of Canterbury, had been a student at Pavia and subsequently had founded what became an important law school at Bec.

11

The main source of Roman Law, from the Middle Ages to the present, has been found in the work of consolidation and amendment achieved in the sixth century under Justinian I. This *Corpus Iuris* consists of the Digest, comprising the conflated and revised work of many jurists; the Code, a compilation and revision of imperial constitutions, some from as early as the Severi, although most derive from Diocletian or later emperors; the Novels, subsequent legislation by Justinian; and the Institutes, borrowing very considerably from earlier material, but designed as a coherent introduction to the law. For determined students, the core is provided by the Digest and the Code, of which only the Digest offers something like a continuous treatment of each topic. Yet the latter compilation was largely unknown to medieval lawyers until a complete text of it was discovered, at Amalfi, some time in the second half of the eleventh century. Seized and carried off to Pisa, this text was copied, and its content thus reached Bologna. The Digest's reappearance was, of course, a powerful stimulus; at Bologna a grammarian, Irnerius, began the work, which was continued by his successors until the mid-thirteenth century, of glossing the texts of the whole *Corpus Iuris* with cross-references and paraphrastic explanations.[3]

To the medieval learned world, the *Corpus Iuris* seemed an illumination, a monument of rational striving after justice, a demonstration of divine beneficence. Its contents, accordingly, were felt to have inherent, universal validity, justifying its direct application wherever lack of opposing custom existed and encouraging the displacement of such custom wherever established.[4] Further, once changes or additions made by the Novels had been duly noted, the rest was apprehended—in accordance with Justinian's own intention—as homogeneous and as though coeval: thus numerous inconsistencies, which Justinian's compilers had failed to exclude, were regarded as posing problems for simply analytical, not historical, solution.

In England the new wave of Civilian learning was introduced, as would appear, by Vacarius. The evidence regarding him and his work has been explored by Felix Liebermann[5] and by Francis De Zulueta. If we venture to make the most of references in medieval literature and of what may be inferred from contemporary records, the following account may recommend itself.

Vacarius was brought to England in the mid-1140s to join the household of Archbishop Theobald of Canterbury. The original purpose was to employ his recognized Civilian talent on the Archbishop's behalf in a controversy over the legateship with Henry of Winchester. However, he started—or, at any rate, participated in—the teaching of Roman Law at Canterbury; in 1149 he produced an important book, which became known as the *"Liber pauperum."* In its prologue, he declared that its purpose was to offer an adequate selection of texts, from the Digest and the Code, the relative brevity of the whole facilitating quick mastery of essentials and ensuring that copies would be within the financial reach of poor students. In the ordering of material, broadly he followed the first nine books of the Code, although drawing much upon the Digest and interjecting a high proportion of Digest titles. His teaching was suspended by a decree of Stephen, which prohibited Civilian instruction and commanded the destruction of Civilian books.[6] After the accession of Henry II, this decree ceased to have effect. By that time, Vacarius had entered into Orders, and for the first decade of Henry's reign, he held a prebend of Northwell. During the reign, he found professional employment in ecclesiastical causes, and works attributed to him, which are supposed to be of later date than the *Liber pauperum*, have an ecclesiastical character: one is a short tract on the human aspect of Christ's nature; the only other, a Canonical *summa* on marriage. Still, he was also called to teach at Oxford and there concerned himself at least partly with the Civil Law. The *Liber pauperum* was established as the prime source for students of the latter subject and continued to be so, at any rate well into John's reign. By then, students of law at the university had gained from its use the nickname *Pauperisti*.

The labors of the glossators of the *Corpus Iuris* were enormous and by general character deeply academic;[7] yet they were not, and could not have been, supported by a supine acceptance of every letter of every text. Indeed, before the end of the Middle Ages, Roman Law had begun to assume in various areas a new appearance. The Digest itself recommended liberal interpretation of laws,[8] in accordance with their spirit; and extension by analogy, sentences or phrases being prized out of context, became part of Civilian technique. Nonetheless, it is said that the manipulation of Roman material to make it fully relevant, in a practical way, to medieval life came only later, after Accursius—who died in 1260—had crowned the glossators work by collecting it all in what came to be called the *Glossa Ordinaria*: that then, and particularly in the middle and later years of the fifteenth century, a new kind of juridicial effort produced a modernized Civil Law.[9] This is no doubt accurate, regarding private substantive law. Seemingly, as far as con-

14

cerns the attainment of practical effect before Accursius's time, care should be taken not to read too much into it.

In Canon Law, dramatic practical development occurred before the middle of the thirteenth century. Its stimulus and material clearly derived in considerable measure from Civilian learning, and here again there was an early rather academic phase. The first major step was the publication in 1151 of Gratian's *Decretum*: a compendium (more complete than others that had preceded it, but like them published without special authority) of decrees of general councils and synods, and of papal decretals, genuine or forged. Following publication of the *Decretum*, Canon Law quickly acquired a place as a distinct university discipline, but the contents of the *Decretum* were often not apt to meet directly twelfth-century practical needs. The response to these by Canon Law, which soon followed over a wide range of topics, was the work of the Popes.[10] To promote forensic investigation of offenses, they approved recourse to inquisitorial procedure starting from public suspicion.[11]

As far as concerned the secular scene, the Civilians themselves had for the purposes of constitutional and forensic development a good deal to offer that would not need much sifting or adaptation.

The *Corpus Iuris* contained a broad political-ideological suggestion that, in some quarters, was bound to be welcome. For centuries—in Britain, well back into the history of the Anglo-Saxon kingdoms—a political balance of power had reflected a deep conflict of ideas. The confrontation may perhaps here be sufficiently expressed as between two stereotypes: limited monarchy, harmonizing with feudalism in the broad sense, and unlimited, centralizing monarchy. Until the eleventh century, the primary doctrinal base for the latter concept was an ecclesiastical view that, all authority deriving from God, a king was one upon whom a plenitude of legitimate power had—through sacerdotal agency employed at the vital moment—divinely been conferred.[12] From the eleventh century, ascendency of the royalist star is increasingly apparent, but the presumption of monarchs did not invariably meet with acquiescence on the part of their magnates. We may suppose that some importance attached to the boost inevitably given to the morale of royal governments by acceptance of political absolutism that permeates the *Corpus Iuris*.[13] The Civilian viewpoint must moreover have had added charm, because it ignored the ultimate sacerdotal hegemony implied by ecclesiastical thought.

Moreover, anything that made royal government more aggressive was capable of influence in the matter of legal procedure, and the broad political implication of the *Corpus Iuris* must to some extent have been apt to promote adoption of the forensic methods it depicted.

As far as concerned grave offenses, in twelfth-century Europe, the traditional process of justice broadly depended upon accusation followed by ordeal, unilateral or bilateral: if the latter, usually battle.[14] The ordeal, occurring before final judgment, had several aspects; an outcome favorable to the accused purged him of suspicion.[15] At the same time, since it led to human judgment, it may appear to us in retrospect a kind of proof, and it was itself viewed as a judgment of God[16]—according to some ecclesiastical doctrine, on the broad question whether the accused had hidden sin.[17] As far as concerned discovery of the truth, these methods may have worked somewhat better than we readily would expect,[18] but it can hardly be supposed that they failed to allow the escape—whether through non-accusation or acquittal—of many who were open to severe suspicion or the conviction of a fair number against whom more rational evidence was largely wanting. Of course, in Judicature, discovery of the actual truth is not everything. Indeed, it may not be the main thing, but there must be confidence, or at least willing acquiescence, in the results.[19] By the thirteenth century, the old methods were under scrutiny.[20] Now a monarch of high ambition—especially one who, or whose advisers, had drunk of the Civilian well and believed that not only the peace but the laws themselves were his—would not easily be reconciled to the idea that offenders, whether of high or of low estate, were cheating justice: his justice.[21] He would want to attack them, to bring them down.[22] If, therefore, he looked directly to the *Corpus Iuris* for an alternative, he would find evidence of a system rational in general tone and assuming positive, vigorous magisterial involvement. Proof had been by evidence—though the prevailing sense was that a single witness had no standing—and by inference. The magistrate had interrogated witnesses[23] and accused.[24] Accusation by private party had been the general rule, but the magistrate might proceed instead upon information from his own agents.[25] In fact, when accepting inquisitorial procedure, the Papacy may have found Civilian learning an encouragement; doubtless the introduction, which soon occurred, of secular procedure recalling the Roman imperial pattern was (at any rate, in some places) due directly more to the ecclesiastical example than to Civilian teaching itself.

However, any medieval tribunal that sought to found its judgments only upon such evidence as we ourselves would be prepared to employ must have been gravely hampered by want of efficient police organization and technique. Our own solutions leave plenty of room for cynicism, but the complexity of our police machinery helps, perhaps, sometimes to hide its shortcomings. One medieval response to judicial difficulties was the erection of a large doctrine of (legal) proofs,[26] invocation of which might supply needed comfort and camouflage, but this doctrine referred, inter alia, to another, less sophisticated means of solving the judicial dilemma: in fact, to "torture".

The doctrine that emerged specifically concerning torture had a tripod base. One foot was firmly placed in the Corpus Iuris; another rested upon ecclesiastical principle, of an earlier age, that confession should be free; a third stood within the new, wider doctrine of proofs.

The *Corpus Iuris*, whilst it does offer one warning against the unreliability of torture as a touchstone of truth,[27] by and large grants it a fairly strong commendation. The Roman texts have much more to say about interrogation under torture for evidence of persons other than the accused than about torture of the accused for confession[28]—which, in the new doctrine, was to have greater importance. Again, whilst relevant passages are scattered in the Digest and Code, in each the most important source on the matter is the title, *De quaestionibus*.[29] Therein we have an ambiguity, which Justinian's compilers to some extent exploited, so that the most realistic translation might be something like: "Concerning interrogations, and especially interrogations under torture, and notably such interrogations of slaves for evidence." Still, at whatever human target a medieval tribunal was looking, Justinian had clearly bequeathed enough to provide both an encouragement and some guide to torture praxis. Nor can one fail to imagine the appeal of such a method for a medieval monarch undertaking a campaign against crime, with a sense of having a personal stake in the outcome.

There may, therefore, seem little cause for surprise that, before the end of the thirteenth century—indeed, by early in its fourth decade—judicial torture was certainly again being used.[30] It is thought that secular authorities then copied ecclesiastical use of inquisitorial procedure and—ahead in some places of Canon Law and under Civilian influence—embodied torture in it;[31] this pattern may well have been illustrated in Sicily, regarding which in 1231 the *Constitutiones regni Siciliae* of the Emperor Frederick II provided, inter alia, that where a general inquisition concerning a murder threw suspicion upon a person of low standing, but proof was lacking, the suspect should be tortured to confess.[32]

Yet during the first two decades of the century, Azo was already at pains to explain away a Digest fragment prima facie at variance with the view that he had espoused concerning the amount of proof required against an accused to justify torture;[33] such tendentious doctrinal preoccupation may seem unlikely to have occurred in a practical vacuum. Again, the *Liber Iuris civilis urbis Veronae,* of 1228, suggests in the present respect a transitional phase of forensic history in which the judge had some sort of choice between using torture and using trial by battle or by individual ordeal and does not represent such a state of affairs as a novelty.[34] It is thus possible that the resumption of torture had already begun in the twelfth century.

*   *   *   *

I shall postpone to the next section notice of Civilian and Canonical literature of that earlier period. As far as concerns what was then transpiring, the point has come at which to recall the emergence of what was to be in England the most important kind of law, neither Civil nor Canon.

The very crucial time, in the latter respect, was surely the reign of Henry II. He, using means within (although not entirely peculiar to) the administrative practice established by his Norman predecessors, so far enlarged the judicial activities of his court in the private law area that a considerable national body of substantive custom emerged, encapsuled in its practice.[35] In or about 1187, that custom, wearing its procedural garb, was expounded (with analytical discipline, although little else, probably owed to Civilian jurisprudence) in the treatise *De legibus et consuetudinibus regni Angliae,* which came to be attributed to Henry's justiciar Ranulf de Glanvill. The latter work, as its *Prologus* makes clear, was intended to invalidate Civilian condescension.[36] It contains the core of what, in the following century, was to acquire in England the name of "Common Law"[37] and would come to be regarded as embracing also developments upon Henry's planning in the area of criminal justice.

Problems, there, evidently presented themselves concerning the prosecution of suspects, the due conduct of trials, and modes of proof.

To promote the due conduct of criminal proceedings, two expedients were adopted earlier, under Henry I: the appointment of local justices, to act alongside the sheriffs, and the appointment of itinerant justices with authority, wherever they might go in England, extending to the conduct of criminal trials. Under Stephen, the employment of itinerant justices eventually lapsed. However, Henry II resumed it in 1168.[38]

There may have remained a difficulty in obtaining prosecutors. According to the custom brought from Normandy, an individual accuser, or appellor, was required, and trial ought to be by battle.[39] We can see only dimly much of this passage in procedural history. However, for whatever reason, Henry in reestablishing order apparently imposed the rules that local jurors should be required to present to royal justices any cases in which individuals were suspected of appealable offenses, yet had not been appealed, and that any individuals thus named as suspect were to go to the other widely current mode of proof in grave cases, the unilateral ordeal,[40] and suffer maim if they failed thus to purge themselves. It appears that ordinances in this behalf were promulgated, most importantly, at a Council held at Clarendon in 1165-66 and a Council held at Northampton in 1176.[41] It also appears, from "Glanvill", that such a system was known, another decade later, in cases of high treason;[42] if it was not fully operative by that time, in respect of other appealable crimes, it became so under Henry's successors.

Especially if the key idea was one of popular accusation, this way of going about things may have had its roots in Anglo-Saxon practice: perhaps, particularly, in that of the Danelaw;[43] some will think more plausible the explanation that the presentment jury was charged, upon the model of a Norman administrative practice,[44] with the task of offering conclusive evidence:[45] in this instance, evidence concerning the state of public opinion and held apt to confer upon the Crown a right to any suspect's purgation. Language in "Glanvill" suggests that a broader precedent was discovered in general ecclesiastical inquisitions after public ill-fame, leading to a requirement of purgation by all whose ill-fame they established.[46]

Given the system of jury presentment, dependence on the old modes of proof remained, and the unilateral ordeal seems to have been under question in England even before this period.[47] However, according to the received text of the ordinances promulgated at the Clarendon Council, it was laid down that those whom the unilateral ordeal acquitted, but who were shown by the testimony of many respectable men to be of the worst reputation, and publicly and gravely suspect, should suffer exile.[48]

Now, if indeed this represented Henry's policy, he may seem to emerge—not the only time[49]—as in penal attitude inclined towards Social Defense[50] and as in matter of possible political ideological conflict inclined towards compromise on lines for which some conservative base could be adduced.

In any case, nothing, either in what the sources indicate about his general concept of criminal procedural improvement, or in English criminal procedure as it emerges in the following century, suggests that he introduced use of torture for confession, or for evidence, as a judicial expedient.[51]

II. THE LIBER PAUPERUM ON TORTURE

Piero Fiorelli remarks that a *tractatus criminum*, which has been attributed to Italian authorship in the 1130s, contains a large number of passages from the Digest and Code and includes, under the title *De quaestionibus*, thirty-five such passages on torture.[52]

Soon after that decade, Vacarius's *Liber pauperum*, of wider scope, appeared also with a title *De quaestionibus*,[53] under which Vacarius collected a number of passages, mainly on torture, derived from the same title in the Digest or in the Code. Moreover, Vacarius used a few passages on torture from other *Corpus Iuris* titles, placing them under corresponding titles in the *Liber pauperum*.[54]

His prologue explains that he will offer a selection of Digest and Code passages, supplemented by further such passages, which will be distributed in the place appropriate to the gloss: they appear in the margin. A minority, but not an insignificant one, of the passages selected on torture are presented in this way as supplementary. The work, however, as it has reached us, has a true gloss, distributed in a complex way and in part consisting of still more *Corpus Iuris* passages. Modern scholarship has sought to distinguish a contribution to this by Vacarius himself,[55] but here would not be an appropriate place in which to broach so intricate a question. Fortunately, of the passages requiring our notice, only one appears in the gloss, and since it imports material from a Novel out of line with the principle suggested, on the same particular topic, by the selection of passages from elsewhere in the *Corpus Iuris*, I shall relegate it, at an appropriate point, to a chapter note.[56]

Otherwise, the following is a broad interpretation of what, expressly or by implication, the *Liber pauperum* offers with direct or indirect relevance to the subject of torture.[57] I shall point out parenthetically the *Corpus Iuris* passages employed and which among them finds only a marginal place. Vacarius abridged some of his source material, altered words—sometimes probably having regard to the new, medieval, context—or word order; omissions may be encountered, of a sort due obviously to a scribe's error. However, such features, as they occur in the passages bearing upon our subject, are not for our purposes important.[58]

The Purposes of Torture

For evidence, witnesses may be tortured, but not, if they are freemen, unless they are said to have been accomplices of an accused, or appear to vacillate, or—perhaps—the case is one of treason.[59]

Slaves may not be tortured against their masters in pecuniary causes; in other causes, the same is true, except where the charge is of treason, adultery, or "fraud upon the census", but the vice may be cured by subsequent corroboration.[60]

Accused persons may be tortured, before or after conviction.

Freemen may be tortured, somehow on account of their own debts or those of others.[61]

(D.XLVIII.xviii.10[1]: in the margin; 15[pr.]; 18[3]; C.I.iii.8[pr.]; IX.viii.3; 4: in the margin; ix.31; xli.1; 16[pr.])

Special Rule: Age and Torture

A boy under fourteen may not be questioned, under torture or otherwise, against another person on a capital charge.

(D.XLVIII.xviii.15[1].[62])

Special Rules: Privilege of Rank or Calling

Subject to express contrary direction of the Prince in any instance, high rank, including municipal senatorial rank, and military status confer immunity to torture unless the proceedings are for treason: for an "unspeakable offense".[63]

Ecclesiastics who have attained the priesthood or higher dignity may not be tortured as witnesses.

(D.XLVIII.xviii.1[1]: in the margin; C.I.iii.8[pr]; IX.viii.3; 4: in the margin; ix.31; xli.16; 17.)

Conditions for Torture

In capital causes, slaves are not to be tortured for evidence against the accused unless powerful proofs of guilt already appear. In pecuniary causes, slaves are to be tortured only for want of other sufficient proof and only if some, although insufficient, admissible proof has already been adduced.

(D.XLVIII.xviii.1[pr.-1]; 9[pr.]: in the margin; 10[4]; 20: in the margin;[64] C.IX.xli.1.)

The Value of Torture

What is said under torture is prima facie unreliable: yet sometimes it ought to be trusted.

(D.XLVIII.xviii.1[23].)

Guides to the Discovery of Truth, Regard for Which Will or May Affect the Extent to Which Torture Is Required

Inculpations between enemies, and inculpations by accused persons of those who have informed against them, are not generally to be relied upon: yet allegations of enmity must not for this purpose be accepted without investigation; in robbery cases, inculpations of informers by accused should not automatically be discounted.

Voluntary confessions should be scrutinized; they are not necessarily truthful.

Close attention should be paid to an examinate's exact words and to his demeanor, and full weight should be given to his public reputation in his own district.

If several persons are suspected of participation in a crime, and one looks more timid than the others, or because of youth more likely to break down, examination should start with him.

(D.XLVIII.xviii.1[2]: in the margin;[65] [24-27]; 10[5]; 18 [pr]: in the margin.)

Upon a practical judgment, there may seem some inconsistency between the propositions that in capital causes, whereas slaves are not to be tortured at all unless powerful proof already exists against the accused, yet what is extorted from slaves wrongly, because against their masters, can be used as proof only if subsequently corroborated. Why should one look for subsequent corroboration if corroborative matter must beforehand have been produced?

The second proposition, idiosyncratic as far as concerns the *Corpus Iuris*, finds its way into the *Liber pauperum* through Vacarius's importation into his main text of the first entry from the Code title, *De quaestionibus*. Purporting to be of a rescript by Severus and Caracalla, this entry almost certainly falsifies the rescript concerned[66] and is a composite produced by Justinian's compilers.[67] To the *Liber pauperum*, it further contributes the main proposition that slaves are not in capital causes generally to be tortured against their masters, with the exception of cases of treason, adultery, and "fraud upon the census";[68] the proposition that in pecuniary causes slaves are not, even for want of other sufficient proof, to be tortured *against their masters*: although the point of this lies in the rule that, in such cases, slaves may be tortured for want of other sufficient proof, a rule that finds a place[69] only in the margin of the *Liber pauperum*.

The inference that freemen might be tortured on account somehow of debts, would have been hard for twelfth-century readers of Vacarius's main text to avoid, although it arises from incorporation there of another Code entry,[70] *De quaestionibus*, which probably would not have been understood in a like sense by Justinian's contemporaries. What we have is as follows:

> We wish municipal senators ["decurions"] to be exempt entirely, in respect whether of what is owed by them or of what is owed by others, from those punishments which are supplied by ligatures and torments: infliction of such measures will indeed be a capital offence where attempted in contempt, and to the damage, of their Order. Such harsh liability shall remain, to members of the Municipal Order, only if they are accused of treason or as accomplices in or accessories to (quaere, such) unspeakable offences.[71]

Evidently, exemption of the Municipal Order in matter of debt was from a liability to which plebeians were subject.

It is possible, on the other hand, that Vacarius was drawn to include this Code entry by a feeling that reference to the Municipal Order could be related to circumstances in Northern Italy in his own day. It is certainly interesting that whilst the whole selection of texts he made on the present subject is quite brief, he included also the next Code entry,[72] which also referred to the Order.

> No indignation of judges, turning from the path of justice, no mercenary submissiveness to persons promoting the cause, shall be thought to allow

infliction of corporal injury upon those who are protected by innocence or invested with the highest dignity.[73] Devotion proved by the evidence of the discharge of many public liabilities brings this reward of labour. The same is to be observed in the case of a municipal senator who has retired: for he, also, on account of his former dignity, is not to be subjected to a torture inquisition.[74]

If some of what Vacarius here included gives rise to problems regarding his motives, it is also intriguing that he excluded both of two Digest passages De quaestionibus[75] authorizing the repetition of torture, a subject that after his day attracted much attention.[76]

On the other hand, if he was looking for what might prove of contemporary importance, it is comprehensible that he chose to omit many provisions of detail concerning the immunity, or otherwise, of masters to torture of their slaves against them or their interest and some references, in connection with torture, to status, or changes of status, having Roman rather than occidental medieval character.

On balance, therefore, whilst much regarding his motives in choosing torture texts is hidden from us, and mere haste may have played a part in the matter, he may well have looked for material that he thought might have practical relevance in his own time.[77] Fiorelli's sentiment is that such was his preoccupation.[78]

I mention in the next section an obscure event in Henry II's reign that may have involved use of interrogatory torture and, if so, may conceivably have been due in some remote way to influence of the Liber pauperum. It is right, however, first to recall that as far as concerns any doctrinal encouragement of torture, in England during the second half of the twelfth century, Vacarius's work is not alone to be considered. Gratian and his early commentators may have touched educated opinion in the matter.[79]

Gratian himself declared torture of suspects for confession to be against Canon Law.[80] However, the matter he adduced in this behalf was a rearranged Psuedo-Isidorian decretal that qualifies, in an indefinite way, the prohibition even of such torture;[81] elsewhere he included another Psuedo-Isidorian decretal that prescribes the torture of accusers: specifically, of the accusers of bishops.[82]

Whilst Rufino, Bishop of Assisi, in the summa he produced soon after the Decretum's appearance, addressed himself to the Psuedo-Isidorian passages concerned and effected a blend with Civilian doctrine, concluding that the prohibition of torture for confession did not extend to all offenses and did not apply in the case of slaves; and that free persons, unless they were of high rank or priests, might be tortured as witnesses in criminal causes, and slaves might be tortured for evidence even in pecuniary causes.[83]

III. THE CASE OF PETER ADASON

I have suggested that available evidence appears to point away from judicial use of torture under the early Plantagenets. However, some material has been interpreted as showing that in Henry II's reign, recourse did occur, if not judicially, to torture for proof.

According to a Pipe Roll entry,[84] in 1188 one Peter Adason settled his account with the Exchequer in respect of a fine, which had been imposed upon him in Northamptonshire on account of his having taken a certain woman and tormented her, "without the King's license."

The distinguished historian L. Owen Pike inferred[85] that Henry II made a practice of licensing the use of torture. The inference, right or wrong, may seem to have been somewhat precipitate.

The entry pointed out by Pike concerns the completion of payments begun two years earlier. We have other Pipe Roll entries[86] recording previous payments in respect of the same fine. Each states the offense in the same way as does Pike's entry. Like the latter, they do not state that the woman was, for purposes of marriage, in the King's gift.[87] The first of them, however, adds that Adason's liability arose cumulatively on account of an enclosure made by him in contempt of some royal or public right: the exact nature of the wrong here is not indicated. Moreover, a further entry shows that the sheriff paid a small fine on account of Adason's enclosure.[88]

It seems unlikely that the offense of enclosure and the offense concerning the woman formed part of the same transaction, unless, perhaps, the woman was royal niefe, serf; whereas against the latter possibility must be accounted the fact that her status is not mentioned.

That the offense concerning the woman was adequately stated, according to the practice of the time, in Pike's entry is suggested by the fact that the same description was repeated several times before that entry. This indication is valuable. If a woman was in the King's gift, anyone who married her without his leave might be fined. Indeed, as Adason was paying off his fine, one Galfrid Brito is shown by the Pipe Rolls to have been paying off, in step, a fine imposed also in Northamptonshire but on the latter ground.[89] The relevant entries recite, like those concerning Adason, want of royal license, but—unlike those concerning Adason—they explain that the woman concerned was in the King's gift, and that the offense was one of marrying her without license. Thus if only the woman in Adason's case had been stated to be in the King's gift, we should readily have understood that Adason had sought to constrain her to marry him or someone else—perhaps, Brito!—in some way that would have been tolerated had the King first consented to the marriage. Whilst had there been concerning Adason's case but one entry, and without such statement, in the rolls, we might have suspected an accidental omission. However, the repeated entries in the rolls exclude explanation of the case along those lines.

Now, apart from the case of refusal by a woman in his gift to marry in accordance with his decision, at least two occasions may be envisaged on which a twelfth-century king might, conceivably, have been asked to authorize measures of duress between his subjects: where the aim was to obtain money due and where (to return to Pike's approach) it was to promote forensic proof or disproof.

Is it possible that Adason, in his maltreatment of the woman, was seeking to exact payment of a debt? Vacarius, we have seen, had suggested that indebtedness might be visited with torture. The purpose could have been to induce the debtor to discover funds out of which the debt would be satisfied. However, it is somewhat difficult to believe that the Crown authorized torture, for that purpose, in aid of private creditors, without ever resorting to it against Crown debtors; evidence seems lacking of such resort by the Crown,[90] except during 1210 in the (always special) case of the Jews:[91] nor is the evidence, even there, very strong.[92]

As far as concerns proof, it would be easier to believe that torture was fitted somehow into the existing framework than that it was introduced by way of setting that framework entirely aside: after all, the fact that the sort of Crown license envisaged in Adason's case was one action wanting which could occasion a fine payable, in the ordinary manner, to the Exchequer shows that we are confronting a royal claim of right, not an open royal choice to do wrong or open royal disregard for what, on a less elevated plane, would have seemed proper principles of behavior. The following points ought, then, to be noticed, as having been made by "Glanvill" De legibus:

1. In case of proceedings simply upon ill-fame (we may suppose this

to mean, upon jury presentment; the specific reference is to treason) a
thorough magisterial inquisition should occur before it is decided whether
to set the suspect free forthwith, or to require him to purge himself by
unilateral ordeal.[93]

2. A woman may lay an accusation concerning the murder of her hus-
band, or the rape of herself; where she thus appears as accuser, the
accused is entitled to a choice between purging himself by unilateral
ordeal and another course—"to sustain the woman's proof against him."[94]

"To sustain the woman's proof against him" probably means "to
rely upon controverting, by argument, evidence, or both, what the
woman alleges and adduces against him." If, as "Glanvill" tells us,
an investigation was proper, where there was no individual accuser,
before decision whether or not to send a suspect to the ordeal, it must
have been likely where there was an accuser, but she was a woman,
and battle was for that reason not available. Indeed, we have a case of
1206 in which a woman's complaint of rape was subjected to inquiry.[95]
Yet, if a woman who accused a man of rape had satisfied requirements
of prompt recourse to public authority, which "Glanvill" lays down,
some kind of presumption in her favor must have resulted, and—particularly, for that reason—the man whom she accused might have seen
great virtue in an opportunity to test her resolve by torture.

On the other hand, it is perhaps not easy to imagine Adason's obtaining
acquittal of rape by, or at any rate after, torturing his accuser and then
going on dutifully to pay a fine for not having obtained (no doubt, for
an appropriate fee) royal authority in advance, and yet the Exchequer
staff's having been made up of fellows so dry that the dramatic circumstances were left half-hidden in the rolls. But whether or not much
force is felt in this objection, it must be acknowledged that a broader
one, raised by H. C. Lea[96] to Pike's view in this matter, is not necessarily
valid.

Lea's criticism was that use of torture for proof under Henry II would
have been well ahead of praxis abroad. However, we have already
noticed the possibility that torture was resumed on the Continent before
the end of the twelfth century.

Hermann Nottarp, indeed, finds an indication of its use, late in the
century, in southern Germany.[97] Still earlier, possible indications in the
same sense are provided by ecclesiastical sources.

Thus Rufino, commenting in his *summa* on Gratian, C.XV, qu.6,
c.1, says ". . . much depends on who extorts a confession, and from

whom. For, confession is extorted, sometimes from accused persons, sometimes from witnesses. Again, sometimes judges use torture; sometimes others, who have no business, such as violent prosecutors.''

Again, Hildebert—who was Bishop of Le Mans, then Archbishop of Tours, and who died in 1133—wrote a striking letter[98] to a priest. The latter had suffered a theft and proposed to put to torture a man whom he suspected of it. Hildebert advised him that ''to apply suspects to the torture or extort the truth by punishments is a severity of the court, not a discipline of the Church.'' He pointed out that the addressee's calling was not that of the executioner, but one that required of him the display of Christian *mansuetudo*—mildness; he underlined his message by citation of Augustine, Epistle CIII *ad Macedonium*, against the subjection of suspects to unquestionable suffering on account of questionable guilt.[99] From this letter, no suggestion is made that the suspect had somehow come into the priest's power as a serf, nor is any indication given whether the priest possessed special ecclesiastical jurisdiction. But we may suppose, anyway, that he was not purporting to exercise such jurisdiction, or he would surely have been reproved for occupying the roles both of prosecutor and of judge.

It may seem that room for uncertainty exists whether Rufino and whether Hildebert, in thus describing torture as a fact of life, were being realistic or simply speaking from the depths of an academic involvement with the *Corpus Iuris*.

On the other hand, if we return to the Adason case, it is at least an interesting coincidence that, just as there is no hint of Adason's having dealt in an official capacity with the woman concerned, Rufino mentions—although as improper—torture by accusers, and Hildebert's addressee was an accuser.[100]

In the end, regarding that case, I would echo the motto favored by Charron: ''*nescio*''—''I do not know.''

chapter 2

CHURCH, STATE, AND THE
TEMPLARS

I. HISTORICAL CONTEXT

In 1307 proceedings began, in France, that led in 1311 to the dissolution of the sovereign Order of the Temple. The Church, of course, was deeply involved; so, throughout, were the French King—Philip IV, known as *le Bel*, "the Fair"—and various of his servants and clients. Nor could other monarchs and their ministers escape responsibility. But beyond events in France, I shall extend attention only to what happened in England.

In both countries, authority was given for the subjection of Templars to acute torture. In France, it is highly probable that some of them were subjected to it; it is also probable, if not so highly, that a few of them suffered it also in the English Southern ecclesiastical Province. Its being authorized reflected the established practice of the Papal Inquisition.

*   *   *   *

In 1215 the Fourth Lateran Council decreed that heretics should be condemned by the ecclesiastical tribunals and then (having been deprived, if they were clergy, of their orders) should be delivered for due punishment to the secular rulers, or their representatives, who should be in attendance.[1]

Each secular ruler was charged with a duty to assist by the means at his disposal in purging his land of heresy, and some monarchs needed no spurring.[2] The Emperor Frederick II, four weeks before his second excommunication, issued several constitutions regarding heresy that, years after his death, were confirmed by Pope Clement IV, and that

28

later thus came to be included by Bernard de Gui—under Philip IV and his successor, an inquisitor at Toulouse—in his *Practica Inquisitionis Heretice Pravitatis*.[3] Frederick laid down that those whom inquisitors appointed by the Apostolic See suspected of heresy should be arrested by the secular authorities, held in close confinement by them, and in the event of condemnation, visited by them with the punishment appropriate to treason: although condemnation was itself a matter for the ecclesiastical tribunal, and punishment by the secular arm would await delivery of offenders for the purpose by that tribunal. Louis IX's *Ordonnance Cupientes*, 1229, addressed to his barons and royal officers, required them to seek out heretics: it established a secular "inquisition". However, trial was to be left to the ecclesiastical authorities.

Gregory IX had already begun to establish a papal inquisition, directly responsible to himself, through the agency of the Dominicans and Franciscans. It emerged as a standing institution—the Inquisition—after it was organized by districts under Innocent IV.[4]

The latter, by his Bull *Ad extirpanda* of 1252, commanded the secular authorities in the communes of North Italy duly to support the ecclesiastical pursuit of heresy. A particular provision of that bull is discussed below. In 1254, by a bull with the same inception, Innocent extended all of its provisions to the whole of Italy. They were to travel further. By Bulls *Ad extirpanda*, Alexander IV, in 1259, and Clement IV, in 1265, both confirmed them. Responsibility for the ecclesiastical pursuit of heretics lay, in principle, both with the diocesan bishops and, where it was established, with the Papal Inquisition: the inquisitors, however, displayed more vigor than did generally the diocesans.[5] In France, by the mid-thirteenth century, the Inquisition was in the South, where the orthodox campaign extended across the border from Northern Italy.[6]

The Bull of 1252, inter alia, laid down[7] that secular governments had the duty:

> to compel, by measures short of maim or danger to life, heretics under arrest to confess their own errors and to accuse other heretics . . . just as thieves and robbers of temporal goods are compelled to accuse their accomplices and confess the crimes which they have committed.

By Gui's time, the Inquisition's method of securing confession had come to embrace, in considerable variety, modes both of deceit and subterfuge and of physical oppression. Regarding the latter, the inquisitors were fully appreciative of how much could be gained by chronic torture, of deprival and attrition, but they also had recourse to acute torture. Where such recourse seemed to them expedient, it is plain that to have to hand over proceedings—in accordance with the intention of the 1252 Bull—to the secular authorities must have seemed an impediment; however, the difficulty was in fact early removed: in 1256 Alexander IV's Bull *Ut negotium fidei*—confirmed in 1262 by a bull, with the same inception, of Urban IV—gave inquisitors the faculty of mutual absolution in respect of irregularities committed during their work; under this umbrella, torture became, as far as the Inquisition was concerned, Church business.[8]

By Philip's reign, the rigors practiced by the inquisitors in the South of his realm had become a scandal. Having regard to their use of torture, Philip in 1291 went so far as to forbid the Seneschal of Carcassonne to arrest people indiscriminately at their command alone.[9] What was in the air was to use the diocesans as a rein upon their fanaticism; such was the policy adopted by Pope Clement V in a decree promulgated at the Council of Vienna[10] (to which assembly I shall, in the history of the Temple, return).

On the other hand, it would not appear that the contemporary tone of French secular justice was out of harmony with that of the Inquisition's procedure. On the contrary, whilst development of secular process doubtless varied from place to place, some approximation to Canonical inquisitorial procedure seems by the early fourteenth century to have been widely employed by royal officers and use of torture to have been fairly widely imported into their practice.

*   *   *   *

On proof and torture, the doctrine of learned jurisprudence—to which tribunals of the Inquisition, and any tribunals following like procedure, might be expected to respond—embraced the following principles.[11]

1. Condemnation could be founded upon either (a) the evidence of at least two unimpeached eye-witnesses of the offense; (b) complete documentary evidence; (c) voluntary judicial confession; (d) less surely, the existence of more than one kind of factor classified as arguing strongly for the guilt of the accused or suspect, particularly and directly regarding the offense charged or suspected; such a kind of factor might be provided by, inter alia, the testimony of a single unimpeached eyewit-

ness of the offense; testimony, by at least two unimpeached eyewitnesses
that the accused or suspect had threatened to commit the offense, or
was seen running from the *locus in quo*, or subsequently to the offense
fled from his home; powerful *fama*—convinced and widespread public
belief—that the accused or suspect was guilty.

2. Any one of the latter category of strong arguments would allow
the use of torture for confession. So might behavior of the accused or
suspect when under examination: the fact that he seemed to vacillate,
tergiversate. Other arguments, commonly called *indicia*, indications,
and doctrinally classified as of a weaker sort—for example, the duly
proven fact that the accused or suspect was of generally bad character[12]
or low social standing—might do so in combination one with another.[13]

3. If an accused or suspect confessed part of what was charged or
suspected, his confession might be held directly to promote the probability of what he had not yet confessed or merely to indicate that he
was a person of bad disposition. But, either way, it might open the way
to torture.[14]

4. However, confession, if obtained under torture, could not immediately be used to found a condemnation. For that purpose, it had
to be ratified after and away from the place of the torture—at least
desirably, before the tribunal in open session—although if ratification
did not ensue, torture might be repeated.[15]

According to one view, public suspicion—proof of which was needed,
in principle, to authorize inquisitorial process—was itself an indication
for torture.[16]

* * * *

There remains, by way of preamble, the task of sketching the process
against the Templars in its mother country.[17]

In 1305 an Esquieu de Floyran came into France from Spain. He had
laid before King Jaime II of Aragon information of scandalous rumors
concerning the Order. But Jaime had taken no action, and the informer
hoped for more attention from the French. He was not disappointed.
King Philip transmitted to Pope Clement V, at the outset of the latter's
papacy—in November, 1305—news of the reported suspicions. After
that, on several occasions, the King sent to the Pope what purported to
be further information adding to those suspicions. Clement consulted
with the cardinals and with the Grand Master of the Order, Jacques de

Molay; then, on 24 August, 1307, he announced to Philip that he had decided to investigate the matter.

The suspicions alleged were of heresy and obscenity, but the heresy did not consist in attachment to an easily recognizable heretical system of belief. It may be doubted whether the proof of such suspicions, as being publicly entertained, was available in measure that would properly, in principle, have supported inquisitorial proceedings against any individual.[18] Perhaps what Clement had in view was to gather material that would lend a little weight to the case, already under consideration, for merging the Temple and the Hospital.[19]

However, the fact that an entire, internationally operating order was under attack presented a situation not entirely unfavorable to the attackers. A basis might be held to be constituted for lawful ecclesiastical inquisition against any or every member of the Order, in any or every place, if once respectable proof were adduced of suspicion, extending to the whole Order, entertained by responsible members of the public anywhere: such was a juridical conclusion that, if not inevitable, must have seemed possible. Moreover, if an inquisition were anywhere begun, although improperly, against members of the Order, the results, even were they in the short run legally nul, might procure a change of public attitude that would make fresh inquisitorial proceedings lawful.

This was the opening through which Philip—evidently bent upon removing the Order, at least from France[20]—now passed. Whether his advisers had as yet entirely grasped the juridical situation, in all its complexity, may nonetheless seem uncertain.

He secured the support, or acquiescence, of Guillaume Humbert of Paris, who was his chaplain and confessor, but also (by earlier Papal appointment) Inquisitor of France. He represented Guillaume as having himself investigated the matter of suspicions against the Order; and that as things stood, when everything was considered, an inquisition was due against every Templar. He represented, also, that commissioners had been appointed by Guillaume and would assist in the proceedings.[21] However, no pretense was made that what was done would be other, essentially, than an expression of royal authority: an aspect bound sooner or later to raise two questions. The first was whether Philip was entitled to do what Louis IX had not required of his own vassals and officers— to try questions of heresy, and the second was whether, even if so, the Templars—being a religious order—could be tried by him.

Royal commissioners were appointed to handle the affair, from district to district; seemingly they set out with Latin warrants, addressed to royal seneschals and bailiffs, and with each some local notables, in places that their respective districts comprised. Certainly, it appears that such warrants were issued, dated 14 September, 1307, and starting with recitals, aimed primarily to justify the King's action, that contained most of the representations above noticed. Juridically, the key effect here was that Philip had adjudged there to exist the necessary foundations for an inquisition and now delegated its conduct to the commissioners, with instructions that all of the Templars were at the outset to be arrested and confined, their property sequestrated. Directions followed regarding what was to be done, in such initial action, by the addressees.[22]

The commissioners themselves received instructions in French. As far as concerned the inquisition itself, they were to be diligent, and to summon the Inquisitor's commissioners to attend. They were also to use torture, if necessary: *"Il . . . examineront diligemment la verité par gehine, se mestier est."*[23]

The operation was well coordinated, most of the Templars in France being arrested on 13 October, 1307. Many of them, including the Grand Master, confessed: the Grand Master, indeed, obliged by repeating his confession publicly, at the Sorbonne.

On 27 October, however, Clement communicated to Philip his displeasure at what had been done. He hinted that if confessions had been secured, the explanation might well lie in the use of torture: complaints of such use indeed were later advanced on behalf of the Order by some of its members.[24] In any case, Clement set about taking the affair into his own hands. On 22 November, he issued the Bull *Pastoralis Praeeminentiae*, directing that the princes of Europe should in his name arrest the members of the Order and sequestrate its property. Around the turn of the year, he abrogated existing inquisitorial authority in the matter.

Confessions—even the Grand Master's—seemed likely to be retracted; soon, juridical problems began to receive an airing.

Philip addressed a list of interrogatories to the Masters of Theology at the Sorbonne. Their replies,[25] on 25 March, 1308, contained the propositions: (1) that although secular authorities might arrest suspected heretics, they might not, except in great emergency, try them; (2) that the Templars must be considered clergy; (3) that confessions already made by individual Templars created a vehement. suspicion of like offenses, or at least of misprision, against remaining members of the Order: moreover, such confessions had proceeded in some instances from leading members of the Order: these circumstances must have been enough to arouse public detestation of the whole Order: consequently, grounds existed for an inquisition against the Order, as such; (4) that because they were under vehement suspicion, any Templars who would not confess should nonetheless remain under restraint, as a measure of public safety; and (5) that property of the Order should be administered with a view of its application *cy-prè* to purposes resembling those benefactors of the Order had meant to promote.

Answers were also given, by whom is uncertain, inter alia, as follows:[26] (1) that the Grand Master's retraction—it had occurred!—ought to be accounted nul: because, all things considered, it was totally implausible; (2) that if indeed a few members of the Order had at no time been brought, by torture or otherwise, to confess—any *"per tormenta vel alias confiteri non" voluerant*—and no witnesses against them were found, this did not mean that the Order was continuing its existence through them, for they were nonetheless vehemently suspect; (3) that no occasion existed for appointment of a procurator to represent the Order, for no judicial process had been instituted against it, the King simply having besought the Church to take action that the case being so obvious, required no prior ecclesiastical investigation. Anyway, an accuser was not needed to support a judicial process in such circumstances, nor was any defense possible, since the crime was notorious— *"cum rei evidencia reddat rem notoriam."* The Church (here the first point is expanded) was not called upon to proceed against the Order by way of judgment, but by way of urgent governmental remedy, by *provision—"per modum provisionis"*.

However, argument against a judicial solution did not at first prevail with Clement. In the summer of 1308, he with some of the cardinals interrogated seventy-two Templars at Poitiers. Seemingly, they confessed and ratified their confessions subsequently before the full College.[27] Clement issued the Bull *Faciens misericordiam*,[28] announcing that an inquisition was to be conducted, on the one hand against Templars individually and on the other, against the Order collectively; that inquiry was to be made by the diocesans and by any inquisitors whom the Pope might specially appoint: a privilege claimed by the Order, to be subject directly to the jurisdiction of the Pope, was set aside; and that the Pope was in the matter moved by increasingly strong public belief in the guilt of the Order and by confessions in various circumstances received. Philip had refused, on the ground that it would endanger their health, to send to Poitiers the Grand Master and various other dignitaries of the Order, whom he was holding prisoner at Chinon. But Clement sent cardinals there to interrogate them, and they also confessed.[29] The Order, for reasons that remain no more than matter of speculation, had in France entered upon another phase of catastrophe. Clement made amends to the Inquisition by restoring in principle the full measure of its authority. Still, he adhered to the plan of entrusting control of proceedings against individual members of the Order to the diocesans, each of whom was to co-opt two canons, two Dominicans, and two Franciscans, and had discretion also to call upon the inquisitors. To investigate the Order as such, he on 12 August, 1308, appointed a number of commissions, each for a country or large geographical area; they were to report to a Council that would be held at Vienne.

In 1309 Clement issued the Bull *Ad omnium*,[30] which declared his belief that almost everyone knew of the "enormous offenses and abominable heresy" of which the Order and its members were "acknowledged to be publicly believed guilty: not upon light arguments, but upon manifest indications and vehement presumptions." Further, it directed that secular authorities everywhere should arrest Templars still at large, delivering them to the ecclesiastical ordinaries, and forbade, upon pain of excommunication, anyone to aid or protect such Templars.

During the same year, in France, the proceedings he had ordered got under way.

As far as concerned the guilt of individual Templars, at Paris the Bishop issued instructions[31] (apparently also adopted in some diocese) that comprised the following: (1) that members of the Order who had not yet confessed should be kept, as far as their health would allow, under a harsh regime; (2) that if such treatment did not work, they should be taxed with confessions made by others; (3) that if they still resisted, they should be terrorized with the threat of torture and a display of torture instruments; (4) that if even thus they were not overcome, they should—upon the juridical warrant of (seemingly: the existing) indications—be put to torture, starting mildly and progressing to greater severity only if it were needed: the torture being applied in the customary manner, without excess, by a torturer in holy orders.[32]

At Paris also, the Bishop seems to have obstructed the commission appointed to investigate the Order as such. It began to hear evidence only in November, 1309. It seems then to have had some difficulty in explaining to Templars, who appeared before it, the special nature of its own function. It was eager to find a defender, someone to represent the Order before it. No Templar who personally had confessed to participation in corporate misdeeds could well have offered to fill such a role without expressly or by implication retracting his own confession; the commission seems rather to have encouraged such retraction. Morale within the Order in France began again to rise, and numerous of its members did retract. Unfortunately, however, the legal danger in which those retracting placed themselves does not seem in advance to have been explained to them. If they had confessed to the episcopal tribunal, had accordingly been adjudged guilty of heresy, and had abjured, then their past guilt was juridically beyond question and to deny it must be powerful evidence of relapse. The blow, which should have been anticipated, fell. On the 11th of May, 1310, a provincial Council at Sens condemned as relapsed heretics fifty-four of those concerned, and they were duly burnt to death. After this, the commission investigating the Order achieved little.[33]

Nonetheless, when in 1311 the Council of Vienne convened, nine Templars wanted to be heard in defense of the Order. Clement asked the high commission of the Council for advice: whether the Order should be allowed defenders, and if so, whether volunteers should appear for it or whether all of the members should be allowed to meet to appoint a procurator, or whether he himself should nominate defenders for it. He received, in December, 1311, a reply from the large majority of the commission that the Templars should receive a hearing. Philip's representatives thereupon moved in to urge upon Clement that the Order should, after all, be dissolved without judgment, by *provision*: whereupon, they informed him, Philip would agree to the vesting of its property in another order.

Clement advised the high commission and the cardinals that he thought this the only practicable solution; on the 3rd of April, 1312, the dissolution of the Order was publicly decreed.[34] A month later, Clement accorded its property to the Hospitallers.

II. THE INQUISITION ESTABLISHED IN ENGLAND

When Philip in 1307 took the initiative in proceedings against the Temple in France, he wrote to princes and others abroad, communicating the suspicions upon which he claimed to act. Among those to whom he addressed himself was Edward II, who had succeeded to the English throne in July of that year. Edward's response was disbelief.[35] He told Philip that he would seek to inform himself about the matter by having inquiries made on the Continent. He also wrote to Clement, questioning the popular suspicions said to exist against the Order and asking him to resist mere calumny.[36]

Still, after receipt of the Bull *Pastoralis praeeminentiae*,[37] the Templars in England were arrested between the 9th and 11th of January, 1308.[38] (Also, property of the Order was, in accordance with Clement's instructions, in due course sequestrated.[39]) Then the Bull *Faciens misericordiam*[40] reached the realm.

Even so, as far as concerned judicial process, steps taken in England after the Templar's arrest differed considerably from what was done under papal authority in France.

In 1309 the Bull *Ad omnium* was received;[41] in September of that year, Clement informed the English archbishops[42] that he was entrusting the inquisition against the rank and file of the Order, in England, to them; to certain of the diocesans; to one Guido de Vichi (rector of a church in the diocese of London); to the Abbots of Lagny and of St. Germain des Près; and to his own chaplain, Sicard de Vaur, Canon of Narbonne. He described these commissioners as inquisitors of heresy,[43] charged against the Order, and he directed that judgment should be pronounced in accordance with their findings by the provincial councils or, in case of doubt, remitted to him.

The Abbot of Lagny and Sicard de Vaur arrived with these instructions. In what ensued, it was they who were regarded as the Pope's real representatives, and it is convenient for present purposes to distinguish them as "the Inquisitors".

The King intervened regarding the discharge of the inquisition; eventually, it was undertaken by the Inquisitors with, in London, the Bishop; at Lincoln, the Bishop (who had in fact been one of the suffragans appointed to the papal commission); and at York, the Archbishop.

I have encountered no evidence that proceedings were separately conducted against individual Templars on the one hand and against the Order on the other hand.

III. THE INQUISITION IN THE SOUTHERN PROVINCE

Regarding what ensued, it is convenient to begin with the Southern Province.

In London the Templars were lodged at the Tower. They and a number of possible witnesses were examined by the Bishop and the Inquisitors during October and November, 1309, but the results—from the standpoint of the Inquisitors—were disappointing. The only proof obtained of ecclesiastical error lay in the confession of two Templars that they thought proper to confess sins only to such priests as were chaplains of their Order. The Templars were questioned upon an article alleging that they believed their Grand Master, although a layman, to have power to grant absolution, but they all answered that he could forgive offenses only as against the Order itself. On the more scandalous matters alleged against the Order, no confessions were secured. The Inquisitors reported this lack of success to the Council of the Province and evidently advised that the necessary conditions existed for recourse to torture. Whether they had already attempted such recourse but had been frustrated by obstruction on the part of the Constable of the Tower, or other royal officers, does not appear. At any rate, all of the diocesans attending the Council joined with them in approaching the King and petitioning him "that they and others who were the ordinaries of places might proceed against the Templars according to ecclesiastical constitutions; and that he order his officers to render them assistance in this matter."[44]

On the 15th of December, 1309, the King responded by issuing in septuplicate an order as follows.

> The King, to each and every among his officers having custody of Templars . . .
>
> We order you to allow the prelates and inquisitors (to whom authority was delegated, by Papal warrant, to enquire against the Order of Templars and against the Grand Preceptor of the said Order, appointed in England, and likewise against each and every member of the said Order) to dispose and do with the Templars themselves, and their bodies, as often as they, prelates and inquisitors, desire, what seems to them proper according to ecclesiastical law. And for that purpose you are to render assistance to them, prelates and inquisitors.[45]

Nothing appears to have come of the order, for at the end of January, 1310, when fresh examinations were undertaken, upon newly framed articles, again were obtained no useful proofs.[46]

The King was once more obliging. Early in February, 1310, royal orders were distributed in a similar vein to the order of the 15th of December and appointing one William de Dien to help the inquisition.

Indeed, an express reference was made to interrogations under torture. De Dien was to render assistance:

> as much in imposing solitary confinement . . . as in hard-handling, the control of diet, provision of dungeons, subjection of the Templars to torture interrogations . . . as required in accordance with ecclesiastical law . . . until in the conduct of the . . . inquisition the truth can in accordance with ecclesiastical law be known.[47]

Yet still, it seems, the Inquisitors did not get their way. In March, 1310, the King sent to the Constable of the Tower, the Sheriff of Lincolnshire, and finally to all of his officers having custody of Templars instructions repeating the order given on the 15th of December, announcing the appointment of de Dien and directing that there should be certified promptly to the King himself the reason for any failure to render whatever assistance might be required, by either the prelates or the Inquisitors, in committing Templars to solitary confinement or otherwise pursuing the inquisition according to ecclesiastical law.[48]

In April, 1310, and again in May, the Inquisitors were at work in Lincoln; but there, also, they were unsuccessful.[49]

On the 16th of June, 1310, they addressed to the Archbishop of Canterbury a memorandum,[50] which complained of lack of administrative support and suggested eight methods by which they thought progress might be made, so that the inquisition could be brought to an end.

Their complaint, more specifically, was that, despite their urgent and lawful demands, none of the English concerned—the notaries, the royal officers, William de Dien himself—had rendered any real service towards putting the Templars to torture.[51]

They laid the blame, somehow, upon the King himself. Everyone, they asserted, who knew what had been and was still happening, realized that as long as the King retained custody of the Templars, nothing worthwhile would be achieved in the way of coercion.[52] At the same time, they implied that royal officers were restrained from use of torture by fear of popular resentment, and that some juridical opposition had been encountered on Canonical-Civilian grounds.

The means they suggested of bringing the inquisition to an end were various, but the underlying alternatives were simple: it could be ended through torture or without torture; torture might be chronic or acute and might be used, if at all, within the realm or abroad—the proceedings being taken out of the realm, to a more congenial place. By reference to these alternatives, the suggestions advanced in the memorandum may be set out as follows.

1. *An End without Torture*. The Templars should be ordered to canonical purgation[53] (an acknowledgment that their offenses were not "notorious"[54]) and therein not obstructed.[55]

2. *An End through Torture, within the Realm: Generally*. (a) The Templars should be transferred to the custody of persons other than royal officials. (b) Evidence obtained against Templars abroad should be published throughout England, so that use of torture upon the English prisoners might not arouse public resentment.

3. *An End through Chronic Torture, within the Realm*. (a) It being the case that those who, in England, refused either to plead guilty or to accept trial (when indicted before royal justices of felony) were subjected to very harsh imprisonment, with the worst and scantiest of diet, to make them relent:[56] the same should be done with the Templars, until they made all of the confessions required of them in the inquisition. (b) The money allowance made by the Crown for the Templars support in prison should be paid to the ecclesiastical ordinaries.

4. *An End through Acute Torture, within the Realm: Problems of Canon Law*. If individual members of the Order could be convicted of heresy, their conviction should be treated as sufficient to allow condemnation of the Order, which in turn should be regarded as providing a juridical basis for the torture of individual Templars at the tribunal's discretion. Conviction of individual members of the Order in England should: (a) be founded upon confessions (such as had, in a few instances, been secured) to belief that within the Order, sins could be remitted by secular superiors; or (b) be procured (upon more scandalous, and clearly heretical, counts) by aid of witnesses or depositions to be supplied by ordinaries of other realms.

5. *An End through Acute Torture, outside the Realm*. The Templars should be sent to Ponthieu (one of Edward's foreign possessions) or some other place abroad, where they might be tortured without local opposition.[57]

The last suggestion had the support of all of the bishops, although the Inquisitors thought that, as indicating failure faithfully to execute ecclesiastical laws within the realm, it ought to be adopted only with the Pope's consent.

Evidently, the Inquisitors' dissatisfaction was communicated to Clement. He wrote to the English bishops[58] reproving them for failure to render the Inquisitors effective assistance, in efforts to overcome secular obstruction. He also sent Edward a letter, to the following effect: it was reported that he had forbidden use of torture, as contrary to the law of the land, and that the Inquisitors were consequently powerless to obtain confessions; however, no local law or usage could prevail over the provisions of Canon Law for such matters; thus Edward's counsellors and officers were liable to the penalties provided for impeding the pursuit of heretics;[59] Edward should consider whether his own attitude was honorable and safe: if he changed it, he would be rewarded with remission of sins.

Soon afterwards, the King went some of the way towards implementing two of the suggestions in the Inquisitors' memorandum. What he did suggests that what the Inquisitors themselves really wanted was freedom to proceed with as much authority as in ordinary cases the Inquisition possessed in Italy or France: although where it could take any amount of time, they had to hurry. Edward directed that the Templars in the Tower should be delivered, by the Constable, whenever so required by those conducting the Inquisition, into the custody of the sheriffs of London, who were to allow the Inquisitors to do with the Templars' bodies whatever, in accordance with ecclesiastical law, the Inquisitors thought proper; he further directed that the money for their maintenance should be paid to the persons appointed to have custody of them.[60]

On the 22nd of September, 1310, the Provincial Council ordered that the Templars both in London and at Lincoln should be placed in severe and solitary confinement, and that if insufficient results ensued, they should be put to torture, although it added the formula that the torture should not be such as to involve maim, perpetual disablement, or effusion of blood.[61]

In October, 1310, the King—declaring that he was acting out of reverence for the Holy See—gave directions, further to those of the 26th of August, concerning the custody of the Templars, and repeated that the inquisitors were to be allowed to do, with the prisoners' bodies, whatever ecclesiastical law required. Also, he directed that the Templars at Lincoln should, upon the Inquisitors' so desiring, be delivered by the Constable of the Castle into the custody of the Mayor and Bailiffs.[62]

Obstacles, however, continued to be raised. On the 22nd of November, 1310, the King ordered that the Four Gates of London should be delivered by the City to the sheriffs: the latter having objected, to earlier directions for custody of the Templars, that they could not use for that purpose the Four Gates, since possession of them was in the aldermen and the Community of London.[63] Again, either the order for transfer of custody of the Templars at Lincoln had proved impossible to carry out, or for some reason such transfer had not suited the Inquisitors, for on the 12th of December, 1310, the King ordered them to be sent to London, to be housed at first in the Tower.[64]

At this point, the resistance to the inquisition seems to have appeared insurmountable. The Pope came round to the alternative of transferring proceedings to Ponthieu and wrote to the King offering him remission of sins if he would send the prisoners there.[65]

They were, however, retained in England. The arrival at the Tower of the Templars from Lincoln was evidently followed by demands from the Inquisitors that they as well as those originally held at the Tower should be delivered to the sheriffs, and thereupon by a prompt objection from the latter, who said that the Four Gates would be insufficient to hold them all. At any rate, at the end of April, 1311, the King wrote from Berwick to the Mayor, Alderman, and Community of London, ordering them to deliver to the Sheriffs the other gates of the City, if needed to house the Templars, and mentioning that difficulty might otherwise have arisen from the presence in London of the prisoners from Lincoln.[66] About the same time, confirmation of the order for the housing of the Templars, one way or another, within the City, was supplied in an order sent in the King's name to the Mayor and Sheriffs.[67] This communication, which seemingly originated in London, when addressing the Sheriffs was open in its references to torture, although unlike the orders of the 15th of December, 1309, and of March, 1310, it did not seem to require the recipients positively to assist the inquisition in that matter. Its presently relevant passages were as follows:

> Whereas formerly, out of reverence for the Holy See, we licensed the prelates and the inquisitors appointed to pursue an inquisition against the Order of Templars, to proceed and do, as often as they wished, what according to ecclesiastical law seemed to them appropriate, with the Templars themselves, and with their bodies in torture interrogations and other dealings convenient for the present purpose. . . . We command you, the Sheriffs . . . that you allow those to whom the said prelates and inquisitors (or any of them, provided one inquisitor be of their number) entrust the task of ensuring that the incarceration . . . [of the Templars] . . . is duly carried out, to perform that task, and to put the bodies of the said Templars to interrogatory torture and subject them to other

measures convenient for the present purpose, and to do other things which,
according to ecclesiastical law, properly are to be done for the present
purpose.

Then at last, between the 23rd of June and the 1st of July, 1311,
three Templars—Stephen of Stapelbrig, Thomas Tocci of Thoroldby,
and a chaplain, John of Stoke—were induced to confess the more serious
charges of denial of Christ and spitting on a crucifix. By this time, the
inquisitors were able to conduct their interrogations on private premises.
Moreover Thomas Tocci and John of Stoke made their confessions only
upon reexamination.[68] It may thus seem likely that torture was threatened
as imminent or actually used.[69]

Thereafter, the remaining rank-and-file prisoners in London were
persuaded to abjure the errors of which they were suspected.[70] The
Grand Preceptor of the Order in England refused to do so and, reserved
for the judgment of the Pope, died while waiting, in the Tower:[71] his
death presumably relieving everyone concerned of much embarrassment.
The Preceptor of Auvergne, also held in London, likewise refused to
submit, and the Provincial Council ordered him to be kept in double
irons under the grimmest conditions until he relented:[72] his fate is uncertain, but on 6 April, 1313, the King ordered him to be delivered to
the Archbishop of Canterbury, or his deputy, to be dealt with according
to ecclesiastical law.[73]

IV. THE INQUISITION IN THE NORTHERN PROVINCE

The principal sources that concern us regarding proceedings peculiar
to the Northern Province are the *Chronicle* of Walter of Guisborough[74]
and Archbishop Greenfield's *Register*.[75]

Between the 27th of April and the 4th of May, 1310, the Inquisitors
were at York to assist the Archbishop in examination of the Templars
held there. Two examinates asserted that their chaplains had special
powers of absolution; several revealed belief that within the Order, sins
could be remitted by secular superiors.[76]

On the 11th of May, 1310, the Provincial Council convened, and the
Bull *Faciens misericordiam* was read.[77] However, it seems that Canonical arguments, felt to be strong, were adduced against the validity
of proceedings upon the existing charges in the existing state of evidence.
The Council adjourned, and by December, 1310, the Archbishop was

reporting that legal difficulties were foreseen, regarding which advice would be needed.[78]

He sent to all the monasteries and Masters of Theology in the Province a list of questions, which he required them to consider and to be prepared to discuss when the Provincial Council reconvened.[79] Among those questions, the most interesting may seem to have been the following: (a) whether the belief, confessed by some Templars, in the power of their secular superiors to grant absolution, was heretical;[80] (b) whether such confession was nullified by the fact that many other Templars denied the belief concerned, and if not, what should be done with those confessing; [81] (c) what, for the purpose of the immediate proceedings, the juridical effect of the Pope's communication was regarding confessions by members of the Order outside the realm; in particular, whether they: (i) authorized the Council to order the York Templars to Canonical purgation, (ii) on the contrary, excluded those Templars from the benefit of such purgation, (iii) required them, since they refused to make like confessions, to be put to torture—although nowhere in England was such a thing seen or heard of;[82] (d) whether, to protect the bishops from any charge of negligence, if torture ought to be used torturers should be brought in from abroad, for none was available in England.

On the 12th of March, 1311, an order was given for the production by the Sheriff of the Templars, before the Archbishop, to answer new articles that had been drawn up.[83]

Then, on the 24th of May, 1311, the Provincial Council having reconvened, the Bull *Ad omnium* was read.[84] The following day, the Templars were brought in, and a day later they adduced grounds of Canon Law in objection to the proceedings.[85] Reference then was made to the papal instructions regarding trial of the Templars in England. Those instructions had required that—according to the results of the judicial inquisition, which was to be undertaken by the diocesans and the commissioners—individual Templars were by the provincial councils to be convicted or acquitted of heresy: provided that if any doubt existed about which course ought to be taken, the case or matter concerned should be remitted to the papal court. Now, the Council took the view that the Templars had confessed some of the articles, but that they could not be convicted on others; a vigorous discussion resulted whether they ought therefore to be wholly convicted, wholly acquitted, or referred for judgment to the Pope. In the end, the latter alternative was preferred, and the Archbishop, undertaking to report the situation to the Pope, left for Vienne.[86]

However, he had appointed Walter of Pickering as Vicar-General during his absence; the latter, when the Inquisitors at last began to reap a harvest of grave confessions in London, went North with the news and reconvened the Council. Thereupon, the Templars at York were ordered to be loaded with heavier chains, and the Council turned to the question whether what they themselves had already confessed amounted to heresy. Perhaps no conclusion was reached; in the end, it was decided that the Templars should be ordered to Canonical purgation upon all of the articles, and they, admitting themselves unable to comply, submitted to the Council's determination of their penance.[87]

In all of this, there appears no ground for suspicion that acute torture, or even any very savage coercive imprisonment, was employed against members of the Order in the Northern Province. On the other hand, the question raised there—whether torturers should be imported from abroad—may well point to what actually was done in the South.

V. JURIDICAL IMPLICATIONS

If Edward II indeed objected to use of torture, in aid of the inquisition, on the ground that such a proceeding would be against the law of the land, it is very possible that he was raising a question simply of political expediency and just possible, otherwise, that he was attempting a jur-idical argument founded upon the historical origin of torture, by the Papal Inquisition, as a borrowing of secular practice. Yet we ought to consider whether his point may have been that he should not expose any of his subjects to liability at Common Law from which, if they took part in or in any way assisted torture, the Canon Law could not protect them. The question in other words arises, what would have been the response at Common Law had one of the Templars, actually tortured in pursuance of royal instructions and subsequently obtaining his liberty, brought an action against an Englishman who had helped to torture him, or against one having him in custody, who, had been an accessory to his torture?

The following facts may be recalled:

1. At Common Law, there was Bracton's authority that prisoners should not be subjected to painful measures except after lawful judicial sentence and strictly in accordance therewith.[88]

2. More particularly, a jailer or his servant who caused or was party to causing the death of a prisoner by maltreatment, not authorized by such sentence, was guilty of felony; [89] evidently the same would have

been true of one who by such means maimed a prisoner;[90] whilst regarding lesser injury, (a) it had been laid down that jailers, who by maltreatment caused prisoners to escape, should be punished as quasi-homicides;[91] (b) a prisoner who was forcibly maltreated in any unlawful way by a jailer would in principle be entitled to a remedy by writ.[92]

3. Further, any keeper of a royal jail whose maltreatment or neglect of a prisoner or prisoners became a matter of public scandal might have been subjected to punishment and driven from office through royal inquiry following presentation of a *querela*, "complaint," of abuse of office: complaints of official malpractice had been investigated frequently in Henry III's time,[93] and in considerable number by a commission that Edward I appointed for the purpose, following his return from Gascony in 1289.[94]

4. A royal official, other than a jailer, who without lawful justification or special defense inflicted physical injury or imprisonment could be made answerable through ordinary process.[95]

5. Any official who upon royal instructions not themselves supported by law had inflicted physical injury or imprisonment probably would have been regarded as having acted unlawfully and yet as entitled by introducing those instructions to stop Common Law proceedings against him.[96]

6. In English secular criminal process, the verdict of a jury of twelve was emerging as at once the most usual proof and a judgment of peers satisfying the provision (whatever may have been its original sense) of Magna Carta in that behalf:[97] therefore, not easily to be displaced; no provision was made for examination of the prisoner, so no obvious place existed in the trial process for torture to confess: what we learn of transactions concerning the Templars indeed confirms that torture for confession was not at Common Law employed.

7. The Church in England accepted the legislative authority of general councils and popes, who pretended superiority to the emperors: a fortiori, to kings and the institutions of secular kingdoms;[98] Bracton, on the other hand, had adopted[99] the view (in the matter of the Templars, indicated by Philip IV[100]) that there was parity between ecclesiastical and political power, each having its own divinely appointed sphere within Christian society; the attitude towards the Holy See of English secular Government was probably equivocal: where the Church had a strong material interest, rules of Canon Law might yet be rejected in favor of different, Common Law doctrine;[101] both regarding causes and persons, the Common Law

courts asserted jurisdiction beyond what papal decretals would have allowed; Edward,[102] like Philip,[103] resisted papal encroachments of what were claimed as royal rights vis-à-vis ecclesiastical affairs; nonetheless, Bracton at one point[104] had referred to papal law on hereditary bequests; later in Edward's reign there was no resistance to collation pursuant to John XXII's Bull *Execrabilis*:[105] if those administering the Common Law had been pressed to enunciate a doctrine on the matter, they might well have said that where the Church was in any way concerned, they would respect papal decretals except to the extent of any conflict with well-recognized Common Law.

8. Not only did the Common Law treat excommunication as depriving the excommunicate of much of his juridical capacity, but there was an established procedure the legality of which was unlikely to be questioned, and according to which if he failed to submit to the ecclesiastical tribunal within forty days, a royal writ might be obtained, *de excommunicato capiendo*, under which he would be arrested and detained by the secular power;[106] again, although the practice of issuing writs *de haeretico comburendo* had not yet arisen, Bracton had written into the Common Law the existence of a duty, in the secular power, to burn any cleric whom an ecclesiastical tribunal had degraded for apostasy: a fortiori, any layman whom it had found guilty of that offense;[107] thus the Common Law had so developed as to recognize that the King had obligations to implement or supplement the course of ecclesiastical justice.

Returning, then, to our hypothetical suit by a former Templar against one who in England, during the process against the Order, had tortured him: what emerges in the first place is that probably the defendant would have been allowed to resist the jurisdiction of the Common Law court simply by showing that his action had been pursuant to royal instructions.

If so, and if during that process royal resistance to papal demands for torture of the Templars referred at all to Common Law consequences, the reference must have been to illegality that would have been felt to attach substantively (despite the lack of a forensic remedy) to torture used under royal directions. However, would illegality have been felt so to attach? Towards answering that question, arguments possible at the time must be sought and appraised.

Accordingly, it is submitted that in our hypothetical case, a plausible substantive defense could have been constructed by referring, first, to the Canon Law on suppression of heresy and to Clement's bulls, issued in the matter of the Templars themselves. The assertion would then have been that although they referred to new matter, in English experience, this very fact ensured that they should prevail: there could be no positively established opposing doctrine of the Common Law, and in the absence of such doctrine, papal authority must prevail with the Common Law courts. An attempt might have been made on the other side to represent the reference to judgment of peers, in Magna Carta c.39 (John)/29(Henry III),[108] as sufficient to establish the existence of opposing indigenous doctrine. Yet two answers would then have been plain. First, it could have been argued that the torture prescribed by Canon Law—torture short of danger to life and of maim—could not amount to "destruction" of the sufferer, so as to be within the clause.[109] Second, it could have been urged that if the execution (following the expectation of Canon Law) by the secular authorities of an apostate after his ecclesiastical condemnation, if the imprisonment by them of an excommunicate, did not offend the clause, the explanation must be that its use of the expression "the law of the land" created an elastic alternative to the requirement of judgment of peers: there was no reason why that expression should not be found equally accommodating where the Canon Law demanded use of torture. To put the latter point another way: if the Common Law, taking Magna Carta with it, demonstrably adapted to Canon Law in other respects concerning individual liberty, there was not special ground here for opposing a like adaptation.

It must be added that if in our hypothetical case the court had inclined broadly to an argument such as that last put, it might yet, and on the substantive issue, have required the defendant to show that he had acted upon and within royal instructions. It might have done so for either or both of the following reasons: (1) that Canon Law generally imposed responsibility, for assisting the destruction of heresy, upon princes— so, in England, upon the King—and accordingly concerning the Templars, it was to the King as secular authority that both Pope and prelates had addressed themselves; (2) that the established practice, with regard to excommunicates, comprised in each instance the issue of a royal writ.

chapter 3

LANCASTRIANS, YORKISTS, AND THE HENRYS TUDOR

I. LANCASTER AND YORK

Sir John Fortescue was one of the Lancastrians who, in 1463, with Queen Margaret sought refuge in France. He was then titular Chancellor. For nineteen years, until 1461, he had been Chief Justice of the King's Bench. In fact, he was a very distinguished Common Lawyer.

His exile lasted until April, 1471; at some time during its last four years—probably near its end—he wrote his most celebrated work, a book that by the reign of Henry VIII had come to be cited as *De laudibus legum Anglie*—"Concerning the praises of the laws of England." It presents a discourse between a young prince of England and the Chancellor. At the outset, the Prince appears impressed by the support for autocracy, which could be found in Civilian sources, and by claims made for Civilian doctrine regarding, inter alia, the proper forms of civil and criminal procedure. In the end, on all these matters, his view are changed by the Chancellor's arguments.

As far as concerns capital trials, Fortescue observed that whereas the French courts, being reluctant, although able, to convict upon testimony—which he said must indeed be held unreliable—have recourse to torture for confession, the English courts follow the practice—which he said is both safe and humane—of relying in each case upon the verdict of a jury from the accused's locality.[1]

Thus in the matter of torture, English judicial procedure is given a clean bill. Instead of reliance upon legal proofs, proofs classified and graded by learned doctrine, with torture woven into the system, the English at Common Law continued to rely upon the trial jury.

Regarding praxis as a whole—including the pre-judicial phase—a testing time would, however, come when increasing social fluidity, greater sophistication, or both, caused some importance to be attached to the production of evidence and consequently, as far as concerned the jury's verdict, a shift in emphasis from the aspect of proof towards the aspect of judgment. Perhaps the pressures of that change were already being felt; some evidence shows that during Fortescue's exile, torture *was* used in England. But more questions present themselves than may readily be answered: how was torture used—in particular, did it fit into a judicial context of any kind? If it did not, was it in preparation for Common Law trial? When had it started? Did it continue, under the Yorkists, after Fortescue had made his peace with them?

Fortescue's Chancellor mentions[2] among forms of torture used judicially in France, the (stretching) rack,[3] the strappado,[4] and the forcing of the examinate to imbibe large quantities of water.[5] Then he asks:[6]

> Have you not learnt, Oh! Prince! how a certain offender,[7] subjected to such torments, inculpated a knight, noble, honest and loyal, of treason— in which, he alleged, the two of them had conspired—and after he was removed from the torture, lest he be again subjected to it, still maintained the charge: yet, when at last he was near to death from injury caused to him by the torture, and had received the last sacrament, he swore by it, and by the death he expected forthwith, that the knight concerned was innocent, and guiltless in respect of all which he had alleged against him.

He adds that the man who thus recanted explained his having inculpated the knight as having been due solely to the torture he had suffered; moreover, that the man eventually died, not in bed, but by hanging, and that immediately before his execution, he again declared the knight's innocence.

It has been widely supposed that this illustration arose out of a train of events that began in England not later than 1468 and probably in 1467: the examinate thus having been one John Hawkins, a servant of Lord Wenlock,[8] and the knight, a London Alderman, Sir Thomas Cook. If this assumption is correct,[9] it may at first sight appear paradoxical that Fortescue should have used an English instance of torture in developing an argument that the Common Law showed superiority by not admitting torture. However, the Chancellor's résumé of the case, mentioning ratification and fear of repetition of torture in the event of non-ratification, smacks strongly of Civilian praxis:[10] which fact, whether or not those details were a garnish supplied by Fortescue's imagination, harmonizes with the hypothesis that he thought what had been going on was somehow beyond the Common Law pale.

The prime sources on the embroilment of Sir Thomas Cook are the *Annales rerum Anglicarum* of William Butones, of Worcester,[11] and Raphael Hollinshed's *Chronicles*[12] as reflecting some unknown additional record. According to William of Worcester, in 1468:

> One Cornelius, a cobbler in the service of Robert Whittingham, then one of Queen Margaret's companions, was arrested at Queensborough, secretly carrying various letters from the Queen's party to England. One of the letters found on him was from the said Robert Whittingham, addressed to Thomas Danvers: on account of which, the said Thomas . . . was arrested by Sir Richard Widevill, and brought before the King . . . and . . . committed to the Tower of London, to his very great fear and distress. On a like account, Hugo Mill was transferred from the Fleet to the Tower, for suspected treason. In the Tower, Cornelius's feet were burnt, by way of torture, to make him confess much;[13] and he thereupon accused, on the basis of their having received letters from Queen Margaret: Peter Alfrey, a London draper; John Plummer; Sir Gervase Clifton; Hugo Pakenham, Nicholas Huss, Thomas Portalain, William Belleknape, Robert Knollys, Esquires; John Fisher, of the Temple; John Hawkins, a servant of Lord Wenlock, and many others. And the said Hawkins, being under arrest, accused Sir Thomas Cook of treasonable conspiracy with Hugo Mill, and said much to the prejudice of his own master, Lord Wenlock. And the said Thomas Cook was arrested, and committed to the Tower of London.

The chronicler goes on to report that various of Cook's assets were seized when as yet no judgment had been passed upon him; and that later he was tried at a (Common Law) session of Oyer and Terminer, but was convicted only of misprision of treason (criminal failure to report the crime), not treason itself, and further, that Hawkins himself was, on the other hand, convicted of treason and was hanged at Tyburn.

This account at least suggests that Hawkins, like Cook, was tried at Common Law. It does not allege that he was tortured.

No mention of Cornelius, or of the torture of anyone, is made in shorter references to Cook's misfortune by John Warkworth,[14] Robert Fabyan,[15] and Richard Grafton[16] or in the Latin chronicle that was edited by James Gairdner for the Camden Series.[17] Fabyan and Grafton have Cook accused in 1467.

So we come to Hollinshed. He, also, does not mention Cornelius, but he says that Cook, who had been Lord Mayor under Edward IV, had also, before the latter's advent, received favors from the Lancastrian administration; that he was approached by Hawkins with a request to contribute to funds being collected for the Lancastrian cause; and that thereupon—sensible, as one may infer, of his diverse obligations—he compromised by neither contributing as requested nor reporting the request; but that Hawkins, nonetheless, was subsequently arrested, and thereupon: ''was cast into the Tower, and at length brought to the brake, called the duke of Excester's daughter, by means of which pain he shoed manie things, amongst the which the motion was one which he had made to Sir Thomas Cooke, and accused himself so farre, that he was put to death.''

Here we have Hawkins tortured, seemingly, for confession as well as for inculpation of others, and his confession somehow inducing his execution. Popular nomenclature is mentioned, linking the instrument of torture employed[18] with a Duke of Exeter. That nomenclature may or may not have reflected an actual historical involvement of one such Duke. If it did so, then *prima facie* the nobleman concerned may have been either Henry Holland, who succeeded to the Dukedom before the end of March, 1448;[19] or the latter's father, John Holland, Earl of Huntingdon, who was made Duke late in his life; or John Holland, the latter's father, half-brother of Richard II; or Henry Beaufort, a member of the Council during Gloucester's protectorate, after the accession of Henry VI.

*   *   *   *

The fact that we are dealing with what seem to be the first instances chronicled of torture during the fifteenth century may make us readier to credit the responsibility, for introducing the rack, of John Holland, Earl of Huntingdon, or of Henry Holland than of one of the earlier Dukes; we must notice that they were—for a brief period, jointly[20]— Constables of the Tower.

To return, however, to the sources. In Edward Coke's Third *Institute*, written about 1628, it is said[21] that:

> John Holland, Earl of Huntingdon, was by King H.6 created Duke of
> Exeter, and Anno 26 H.6 the King granted to him the office of the

Constableship of the Tower: he and William de la Poole, Duke of Suffolk, and others, intended to have brought in the Civill Laws. For a beginning whereof, the Duke of Exeter being Constable of the Tower first brought into the Tower the Rack or Brake allowed in many causes by the Civill Laws: and thereupon the Rack is called the Duke of Exeter's daughter, because he first brought it thither.

Coke cites Hollinshed and Rot. Parl. 28 H.6 no. 30. The former, as we have seen, mentions the popular name of the rack, but himself offers no explanation of it. The Roll entry is of part of the Commons' bill of complaints, against the Duke of Suffolk, which was presented in 1450. Although various complaints were made against the Duke concerning the administration of justice, he does not seem to have been accused of seeking to introduce Continental criminal procedure. Possibly, therefore, Coke confused him with Humphrey, Duke of Gloucester. Concerning the latter's end, in 1446, Polydore Vergil said:[22]

Divers noblemen conspired against the duke and appeached him of sundry criminall offences, but principally for that he had caused sundry certaine condemned persons to be executed more greevously than the lawe of England appoynted: for the duke being a severe man, because he was skillfull in the lawe which is called civill, and caused malefactors to be sharply corrected, procured thereby against himself the hatred of ungratious people. . . .

Since John Holland was Constable of the Tower under Henry VI until 1448, he must have been involved if Gloucester was responsible for the beginning of torture there.

On the other hand, the candidature of his son in the present respect certainly ought not to be ignored.[23] Henry Holland, in the last days before the advent of Edward IV, served with Fortescue himself on commissions to hear and determine charges of treason, rebellion, and other grave crimes, in London and in the County of Middlesex;[24] it is a curious thought that at the end of his judicial career, the latter may have conducted trials that one of his fellow commissioners was somehow backing with torture. Nonetheless, faint speculative confirmation that introduction of torture at the Tower was the work of Henry Holland may be found in the Towneley *Crucifixion* Play, where a reference, quite probably having (whenever it was written) topical interest, is made

to the "rake" and is followed by a stanza that suggests oblique allusion
to the fate of Richard, Duke of York, at the Battle of Wakefield in
December, 1460. However, the passage is in *rime couée*, which in
itself may hint instead of a fourteenth-century origin and so point—if
anywhere—towards Henry Holland's grandfather.[25]

*   *   *   *

Moreover, before leaving the note cited above from Coke, we should
notice the resemblance between what he alleges against John Holland
and William de la Pole (as well as between the complaint said by
Polydore Vergil to have been laid against Humphrey, Duke of Gloucester) and grievances that—according to some sources—arose against
John Tiptoft, Earl of Worcester.[26]

Tiptoft, having held high office, in 1457 left England for the Holy
Land; on his way back, he stopped for two years in Italy, where it
appears that he absorbed much of the prevailing culture. He returned
to England in 1461 and was welcomed by the Yorkist administration
by then established. He was quickly appointed Constable of the Tower
and Constable of England for life.

There was nothing revolutionary in the terms of his appointment to
the latter office.[27] However, in its execution he showed himself ready
to convict summarily on accusations that treason had been committed
within the realm, even though they were laid against one not produced
as a prisoner straight from the field of battle.

Thus according to Warkworth, the Earl of Oxford, his first son
Aubrey, and Sir Thomas Todeman, being arrested and taken to the
Tower, and accused of treason, were each brought before Tiptoft and
judged by him by "Paduan law"—by "lawe padowe"—his sentence
being that they should suffer decapitation.[28] How much should be read
into the expression "by law padowe" is impossible to say, but it may
indicate, at least, that the prisoners were offered neither trial by battle
nor whichever would otherwise at Common Law have been appropriate:
trial by peers or trial by jury. It is then right to say that whilst Tiptoft's
accepting jurisdiction appears to have been contrary to the law as partly
assumed, partly stated, by Statute 1 H. IV, c.14 (on *appeals*), authority
from the reign of Richard II indicated that the Constable and the Marshall, where they had jurisdiction, ought to reach their judgments upon
testimony if sufficient was forthcoming.[29]

On 24 August, 1467, Tiptoft was compelled to give up the Constableship of England, which was granted to Richard Widevill, Lord Rivers, for life, and when he should die to his son Anthony. The letters patent issued on this occasion[30] are remarkable. They assert that when the office was conferred upon Tiptoft, he was authorized to try cases (without geographical restriction) of high treason and to proceed therein (after the Civilian and Canonical manner) either upon formal accusation or ex officio; moreover, that he was directed to act "summarily and without judicial pomp, fuss or artificiality," an established Canonical-Civilian formula.[31] Then they confer like authority, in like term, first on Richard Widevill and after him on his son.

Tiptoft himself was sent to Ireland, and Richard Widevill duly entered upon the office of Constable, which he held for two years. One curious event, during that time, was the joining with him of a Common Lawyer, Serjeant John Catesby, in an inquiry concerning political offenses alleged to have been committed by one Thomas Taylor, of Northamptonshire.[32] Widevill was put to death by the opposing faction after the Battle of Edgecote. On 17 October, 1469, letters patent[33] conferred the Constableship on the King's brother Richard, to be held, for life, in the same manner as it had been held by Widevill. However, Tiptoft was soon recalled from Ireland, and on 14 March, 1470, he was appointed Constable for a second time, his letter patent[34] authorizing him to exercise the office in as full a measure as it had previously been exercised by himself or any other holder.

Afterwards, in 1470, ships of Clarence and Warwick were defeated by Lord Sales, who took his prisoners into Southampton. According to Warkworth,[35] the King then came there and ordered Tiptoft to sit and judge them; Tiptoft in due course condemned twenty of them to be hanged, drawn, quartered, and beheaded and added a direction for a gross abuse, in each case, of the head and trunk. It may be supposed that he proceeded to judgment, once again, in disregard of Common Law procedure. Warkworth, however, saying that he afterwards became an object of popular hatred, attributes this not to any ouster of the Common Law in respect of accusation and trial, but to "the dysordinate dethe which he used, contrarye to the lawe of the londe": in other words, to the abuse he caused to be practiced upon the remains, after the condemned had been put to death.[36]

Tiptoft's own end was not far off. He was captured by the temporarily victorious Lancastrians and executed. According to Warkworth,[37] he was arrested and arraigned before John de Vere, Earl of Oxford—the son and heir of the Earl he had himself condemned to death—and thereafter beheaded on Tower Hill. The chronicler adds: "so the erle of Worcestre was judged by such law as he did to other menne." Vespasiano da Bisticci (we may suspect that he here relied upon imagination, but we can hardly be sure) gives some detail about the popular response when Tiptoft was arrested. All of the people, he said, cried out for Tiptoft's death "because he had made a law which was against the people, which he had brought from Italy . . . called the law of Padua."[38]

What may seem to emerge as probable from all of this is that Tiptoft, a man of cosmopolitan culture, favored Continental criminal procedure; that during his first tenure of the Constableship, he enlarged the functions of the Constabular court, claiming jurisdiction to dispose of any case of high treason, and proceeded for the purpose upon bases alien to the Common Law;[39] that the Common Lawyers themselves were sensitive to what he was doing, their discontent resulting—once he was away in Ireland—in the experiment of joining a tame serjeant-at-law with his successor for the conduct of at least one inquiry. What, on the other hand, remains obstinately in the realm of merest conjecture is just how far his innovations went. All that can be said is that the impression he left behind makes him—and so the Yorkist administration—a natural object of suspicion in the matter of responsibility for instituting torture at the Tower. Nor if we assume that the reference to the "rake" in the Towneley play was originally topical, do we have much of an obstacle to supposing that such responsibility lay with Tiptoft rather than lying with, or solely with, Henry Holland. It would be impossible not to see these straws blowing in the wind of history. It would also be foolish to grasp at them. Even if we knew recourse to torture to have started in Constabular proceedings, that information could point instead to introduction under Richard II; we know that in the latter's reign, there was extended use of the Constabular court,[40] and English Civilians well before Tiptoft's time probably had some awareness of Continental torture praxis; the *Black Book of the Admiralty* contains[41] a Civilian essay on the *ordo judiciorum* or *praxis*, which Sir Travers Twiss was evidently inclined to ascribe to the first two decades of the fifteenth century, [42] and which recognizes that, for want of other means of reaching a judgment, torture for confession may in grave criminal cases be employed. It declares:[43]

> Sometimes in criminal causes—in fact, where capital and atrocious of-
> fences cannot otherwise be explored, or the truth otherwise investigated[44]—
> torture ought to be used upon the person of the accused . . . Although
> a confession made under torture is not valid unless the deponent perseveres
> in it.[45]

*   *   *   *

I am aware of no alleged cases of the interrogatory use of torture
under Edward IV, later than that of Hawkins; for the short reign of
Richard III, I have found only one allegation of such use: in a letter[46]
written at some time in the second half of the 1530s, Sir Thomas Wyatt
described to his son how splendid character and the grace of God had
preserved his own father, Sir Henry Wyatt, when in prison, "from the
hands of the tyrant that could find in his heart to see him racked."

There is a tradition that Sir Henry's suffering was not on a stretching
rack. In the first half of the eighteenth century, one of the Wyatt family
prepared a collection of their papers; part, after the lapse of more than
a hundred years, was examined by John Bruce.[47] He found them to
show that Sir Henry was "subjected to torture, which was inflicted by
an instrument called the barnacles, which is placed by farriers on the
upper lip of a horse in order to terrify him and keep him quiet under
the operation of bleeding;" he added that "the memory of this fact is
heraldically preserved in an addition to the arms borne by this branch
of the Wyatts, namely a pair of barnacles argent, the ring which unites
them or."[48]

As far as concerns Richard's reign, however, brief reference may be
appended to Polydore Vergil's description of how the Duke of Buckingham came to his end, in 1483.

The Duke engaged in a rebellion against Richard, but Welsh levies
failed him, confederates deserted him, and in the end, he was betrayed
to the King's agents. He was then taken to Salisbury, where the King
had established headquarters. The story of what ensued, as provided by
Edward Halle[49] and adopted by Hollinshed,[50] is as follows:

> The Duke being of certain of the King's Counsell diligently upon inter-
> rogatories examined what things he knew preiudiciall to the King's person,
> opened and delivered frankly and freely all the coniuration . . . trusting
> because he had truely and playnely reueled and confessed all things that
> were of hym required, that he should have lycence to speake to the King

which (whether it were to sue for pardon and grace, or whether he brought
to his presence would have sticked him with a dagger as men then judged)
he sore desyred and required. But when he had confessed the whole fact
and conspiracy vpon Alsouen day without arreignment or judgment, he
was . . . behedded. . . .

It has been supposed[51] that the last part of this story refers to the non-
employment of Common Law process, and that in fact sentence of death
was passed upon the Duke by Sir Ralph Ashton, who was appointed
Constable when the rebellion occurred. If Halle is right, the Duke was
required to answer a list of questions prepared in advance, and no doubt
in that case, his answers were written down. In other words, there was
conformity to a long-established Civilian-Canonical model; however,
we shall in due course encounter such conformity in Conciliar practice;
its occurrance would not necessarily indicate here of an exercise of
Constabular jurisdiction.

Polydore Vergil's account[52] resembles Halle's. Interestingly, on the
other hand, he observed in the course of it that the Duke answered
questions ''without torture.'' This observation suggests willingness, on
someone's part, to torture the distinguished prisoner[53] should he be
obstinate. Yet it may very well be no more than an anachronistic lending
of color or a reflection of the author's own acquaintance with, and
admiration for, the Civil Law.

II. THE FIRST TUDORS

Regarding use of interrogatory torture, the evidence is fainter—if that
is possible—for the reign of Henry VII than for the reign preceding.

All I have found is a curious passage in an Italian *Relation of the
Island of England*,[54] attributed to about the end of the fifteenth century.[55]
It observes that in England criminal cases are tried by jury, and it outlines
contemporary procedure by way of indictment. It interjects an observation that anyone can accuse anyone else of crime, and that this is true
even of weighty matters and open offenses: an observation that may
reflect only the fact that anyone could lay a bill of indictment before a
jury of presentment, but may instead indicate that anyone could lay an
information with the Council or with royal representatives—including,
locally, justices of the peace—and thereby, if it was credited, procure
a bill, the acceptance of which by the presenting jury would be a matter

of form. (The presenting jury, the "grand jury" of more modern terminology, seems generally to be ignored in narratives of sixteenth-century trials, nor do we hear anything of it in the earlier cases of Cook and Hawkins.[56]) Then the *Relation* adds that following such accusation by anyone of anyone of any crime, the accused might be *tormentato* although he did not withhold the truth.[57] If *tormentato* signifies only "discomforted"—say, by imprisonment to await trial—its use here is almost perverse. Surely, what the author of the *Relation* means is that the English had recourse to the interrogatory torture of accused persons, in disregard even of such safeguards and restraints as were admitted by Continental doctrine.[58] If so, and if he is right, we may suppose that what he discloses to us was unvarnished Executive violence, for had a practice of torture been developing under Constabular aegis, increasingly exact observance of Continental doctrine would surely have occurred, rather than its disregard. It may seem incredible that Common Law justices, whose behavior might be viewed critically by the juries from which verdicts had to proceed, and many of whom must have begun the study of law about the time when the *De laudibus* was written, adopted a practice of subjecting accused persons to interrogatory torture; and that, even as a matter of course, without regard to whether or not those persons appeared to be lying. Nor am I aware of any evidence from later reigns that in their judicial role Common Law justices resorted to coercion by torture except for the purpose of exacting a plea, one way or the other, guilty or not guilty, where a prisoner wilfully stood mute.[59]

From the reign of Henry VIII, on the other hand, a considerable amount of material is relevant to our purpose.

At this period of English history, it becomes possible: (1) to use the evidence of documents forming part of the *res gestae*, the transactions in which torture was employed or threatened or otherwise contemplated; (2) to have in most instances a firm view regarding the context.

Let us consider first evidence that points to actual or proposed Executive use of interrogatory torture under Henry and then see whether there is reason to suppose that such torture occurred during his time having any relevance to judicial process. Whether or not by simple coincidence, the earliest indications of Executive recourse to torture come from the 1530s as the rift with the Papacy opened.

So in 1533, the year of Henry's *Act of Appeals*,[60] Stephen Vaughan—writing from Antwerp on 3 August to Thomas Cromwell—remarked that torture would be helpful in the examination of certain friars: ''if the fryers, which were takyn in London before my coming hether, were brought to the brake, theyr counsayle shulde shortly be bewrayed.''[61]

Then according to the Spanish *Chronicle of Henry VIII*, on Mayday, 1536, Cromwell invited Mark Smeaton home to dinner and, after they had entered his house, put to him a suggestion that he had received suspiciously large sums of money from Queen Anne Boleyn. Further, Smeaton's answers seeming evasive, Cromwell resorted to torture:

> He called two stout young fellows of his, and asked for a rope and a cudgel, and ordered them to put the rope, which was full of knots, round Mark's head, and twisted it with the cudgel until Mark cried out, ''Sir Secretary, no more, I will tell the truth,'' and then he said, ''The Queen gave me the money.'' ''Ah, Mark,'' said Cromwell, ''I know the Queen gave you a hundred nobles, but what you have bought cost over a thousand, and that is a great gift even from a Queen to a servant of low degree such as you. If you do not tell me all the truth I swear by the life of the King I will torture you till you do.'' Mark replied, ''Sir, I tell you truly that she gave it to me.'' Then Cromwell ordered him a few more twists of the cord, and poor Mark, overcome by the torment, cried out, ''No more, Sir, I will tell you everything that has happened.'' And he confessed all . . . [62]

Whilst elsewhere the same *Chronicle* asserts that Margaret, Lady Wingfield, was tortured in the same matter of the Queen's adultery and thereafter burnt to death:[63] assertions not buttressed with circumstantial matter or recommended by what we read of the Queen's trial—to which, surprisingly, the *Chronicle* does not itself refer.

In September, 1536, two Worcestershire justices, Sir Gilbert Talbot and John Russell, were informed that James Pratt, a local clergyman, had spoken against the suppression of Studley Priory. They communicated this information to Cromwell who, having consulted the King, sent with the latter's approval directions that Pratt should be subjected to interrogation, under warning of the consequences if he failed to cooperate, and, indeed, with torture. Later, Talbot and Russell reported that, in accordance with Cromwell's letters, they had in their examination resorted to ''pinching with pain,'' but that they had extorted nothing of much significance.[64]

In June, 1537, Robert Dalyvell, of Royston, Hertfordshire, who had travelled in Scotland, was reported to have told of supernatural prophecies that had come to his knowledge there, broadly to the effect that Henry, if he did not change his policies, would lose his realm. This was reported to Cromwell, who, presumably suspecting Dalyvell of being a Papal or Scots agent, had him consigned to the Tower, drew up interrogatories to be put to him,[65] and directed—at the very least—that he should be threatened with the rack. The Lieutenant of the Tower, Sir Edmund Walsingham, wrote to Cromwell[66] that in accordance with the latter's instructions, he had brought Dalyvell "to the rack and there strained him"—which at first sight appears a statement that the rack was used, but the report continues in a way perhaps indicating that it was merely displayed, as a threat. Thus more fully, we have, "I brought him to the rack and there strained him, using such circumstances as my poor wit would extend to; but more I cannot get of him . . . yesternight I proved him at his first coming, and about eight of the clock again, and in the morning after again, by fair means and also by threatenings."

Then torture was mentioned in a letter written on the 14th of April, 1538, by Lord Lawarr to Cromwell.[67] Lawarr referred to certain persons against whom a suspicion of theft could not well be proved, but who he thought would certainly confess major robberies, were they constrained thereto "by a raik or otherwise". Here, for the first time in documents associating Cromwell with torture, the offenses contemplated seem not to have had a primarily political aspect, but whether any precedent existed for use of the rack in the absence of such an aspect, or any serious expectation on Lewarr's part that Cromwell would authorize torture to exact confession of robberies, seems impossible to say.

With a letter written, on the 4th of August, 1538, by the Duke of Norfolk and Sir Roger Townshend,[68] we are back in politics. The letter announced that a hermit had, upon his own confession, been convicted at Norwich of high treason and asked whether the King and Cromwell wanted him brought to the Tower to be tortured. The indicated tendency to localization of torture—at the Tower—may suggest a tendency also towards its institutionalization. The fact that the prisoner had already been convicted, and that the decision whether or not to torture him was treated as one for Cromwell, in consultation with the King, shows that the context was one of Executive Government.[69]

The suggested interest of the King himself will also be noticed. Cromwell probably did, when possible, consult the King—or, at least, keep him informed—when questions of high treason arose. On the 17th of March, 1539, we thus find him writing to the King that satisfactory disclosure had not yet been obtained from an Irish monk who had fallen into English hands after being overtaken by a storm at sea, and that therefore he intended to have the man put to torture, in his own presence, at the Tower. "We cannot, as yet, gett the pyth of his credence, whereby I am advised to morowe ones to go to the Towre, and see hym sett in the brakes, and, by tourment, compelled to confesse the truthe."[70]

Cromwell's *remembrances* for March, 1540, include a note[71] that one Gendon is to be sent to the Tower to be racked, and that persons called Lee, Peters, and Bellesy are to go there to help the Lieutenant in Gendon's examination. Lee and Peters were doctors of Civil Law, the former probably being William Peter, who after sitting in the Court of Requests had become a Master in Chancery, and from 1535 to 1540 probably presided in Cromwell's Vice-Gerential court for ecclesiastical causes.[72] In April, 1537, he and Lee had been directed to join the Lieutenant for another interrogation, where the use of torture is not indicated.[73] Yet in Dalyvell's case, we do not hear of interrogators other than the Lieutenant himself. Probably, specialists were brought in where questions of theology or of Canon Law had to be explored, so that the answers of the examinate might be properly appreciated, any need for improvisation duly met; and perhaps also to instill into the examinate a sense of the solemnity and respectability of the proceedings. The Lieutenant had the Tower and the prisoners in his charge. That was certainly a reason for leaving torture at the Tower under his direct control, and it may have seemed a reason for at least regarding him as included among those responsible for interrogations at the Tower, where use of torture was not proposed.

After Cromwell's fall, political tensions and recourse to torture both continued; for us, records of the latter become available in the Council register, then newly instituted.

Thus entries for the 13th and 16th of November, 1540, [74] show that one Thomas Thwaites, having confessed before the Council that he had spoken words classed by the Council as "traitorous", was ordered to be removed from the Porter's Ward, where he was imprisoned, to the Tower, in order that he might be constrained, if necessary by the rack, to reveal from whom he himself had heard the matter that he had confessed to having spoken.

Thwaites was a servant to a page of the Wardrobe of Robes and was accused by others of his own station. Anxiety arose, no doubt, from apprehension that his master, or someone close to the King, might be disaffected. The order for his torture proceeded from the Council, which may suggest a shift towards corporate responsibility. It was addressed to the Lieutenant alone: Thwaites did not need doctors of Civil Law among his examiners. The Lieutenant was commanded, if Thwaites proved obstinate, to give him a "stretch or two . . . upon the brake." Although evidently the intention was not that extreme severity should be used, the amount of torture was expressly left to the Lieutenant's discretion. Thwaites evidently did not maintain his resistance: whether he was tortured, or threatened with torture, we do not know. He was kept in the Tower until the 25th of May, 1541, when he was again brought before the Council, to be severely reprimanded for his indiscretion and set at liberty.[75] It may seem unlikely that his prosecution at Common Law was ever contemplated. Nor does the record of the 25th of May suggest that the Council itself proceeded with him in a distinctly judicial mood. Nor was the personal confession that could have been felt to justify his summary punishment wanting, before he was sent to the Tower. Nor, on the other hand, is that confession represented as a prerequisite of his torture, a quasi-juridical basis for it.

In a letter[76] dated the 15th of October, 1541, from members of the Council who were looking after business in London to those (more important) members who were in attendance upon the King,[77] the writers reported that they had committed to the Tower certain thieves arrested when attempting to burgle Windsor Castle and had examined them "threatening them with torture". It appears that the councillors in London all went to examine the burglars, who were in the Tower. We cannot tell whether they would have carried out the threat to use torture or, if not, what would have been their reason to abstain. The case appears to have been political only in that it involved an interference with royal property.

Letters written in 1543 show that torture was still being used outside London, but they refer to the remote and untranquil area supervised by the Council in the North (which I shall name in full as such).

A letter[78] of the 14th of March, 1543, from the Council to the Duke of Suffolk, Lord Lieutenant of the Marches, is in Wriothesley's hand. It stated that the King had considered information so far obtained about an alleged plot to incriminate falsely the Porter of Berwick, one Lionel Gray, and ordered the Duke and the Council in the North to investigate with or without torture: "by good means or otherwise by tortures, at your discretions, to get out the very truth."

Later in the same year, the Duke and Cuthbert Tunstall, Bishop of

Durham—a doctor of laws of Padua and former Master of the Rolls, who in 1537 had been appointed President of the Council in the North—wrote[79] to the Council about dealings with a laborer called William Brewer, who had been said by one Roland Wall to have suggested that a local rising was imminent. Suffolk had sent for Brewer, who had at first denied Wall's report. The letter continued:

> For the convicting of his bolde and styff denyall . . . Roland his accuser was brought before him face to face, and ther avouchyd the tale that he had deposyd. Neverthelesse, the said Bruar defyed him and styfflye denyed his sainge, sainge he dyd accuse hym of malice, albeit before in the begynnynge of his examynacion, when he was asked whedr the said Rolande Walle did beare him any malice, or he did beare any malice to the said Rolande, he had affermed constantly ther was no malice betwix theim. Wherupon, bicause the mater was grevous and requyryd to be quickelye handelyd, I the Duke of Suff. commaunded the said Bruar to be put to the torture for tryinge out of the truthe more briefflye, bicause the mater requyryd not to be protractyd. Which Bruar aftre him was put in the stockes, with a payre of newe shooes full of greyse, against a hote fyer, whan at laste he felte paine, he desired to be releysed of his paine, and he wolde tell all to me the Duke of Suff. . . .

The consummation does not concern us.

The King emerges again as interested, in what is to follow about the alleged plot to incriminate Gray. In the letter about Brewer, Tunstall's Civil Law training may be discerned, for the use of torture is justified partly by Brewer's variation from his earlier statement that there was no bad blood between himself and Wall. On the latter use, the style is apologetic, and indeed is repetitively so, in a way that suggests some anxiety on the part of the writers: "bicause the mater was grevous and requyryed to be quickelye handelyd" . . . "bicause the mater requyryd not to be protractyd."

Regarding the general attitude of the Administration to the use of torture, something may perhaps be gathered from a diplomatic incident in 1544.

A prisoner of the Queen of Hungary, Regent of the Low Countries, under torture accused one Octavian Bos, a Milanese resident in Antwerp, of spying for the French. At the time, Bos was on a journey to Calais. In response to the Regent's demands, he was there arrested. Subsequently, he was brought to England, but the King refused to place him in severe imprisonment and intimated that he could not for long be held at all, unless some evidence against him was forthcoming other than such report as had already been supplied.[80] The Regent thereupon wrote[81] to Chapuys, the Imperial Ambassador in England, suggesting the case was one that would probably require torture to exact a confession; and that if the Council did not feel they had enough evidence to allow the submission of Bos to torture, they might be prepared to send him to her so that he might be confronted with his accuser. Subsequently, Chapuys wrote to her that Bos had confessed at the Tower[82] and then that the English had resolved to examine him carefully, by torture if it was needed.[83] However, no judicial proceedings were taken against Bos in England, and it was only after considerable delay that the Regent secured his delivery into her custody. At Brussels, he maintained that he had not confessed to the English.[84] Of course, it does not follow that he escaped torture at the Tower. Probably he was subjected to it, and resisted it, *at Brussels*: for the Regent, when she got him, declared that he would receive his deserts,[85] but in the end he was released. Yet following his release, he obtained from the Council in England a letter to the Deputy and Council of Calais, requiring them to help in recovering property that had been taken from him when he was arrested and explaining that he was detained only because the "lady regent" had so requested.[86] This certainly suggests that in England he may well throughout have retained some measure of favor; hence, it is an argument against his having been tortured or terrorized *in England*. However, if we suppose after all that he was not so treated, we have a choice of explanations. He may have been valuable to the English: as a merchant, even if a French spy; or as a spy, even if a double agent. On the other hand, the Regent's surmise, although probably prompted by acquaintance with Continental criminal praxis, was perhaps broadly correct: the Council may have been restrained from torturing or terrorizing Bos by sentiment that justification was lacking, as long as no significant evidence appeared against him of enmity towards the English Crown.

The last case to be mentioned, before considering possible relationship of torture to judicial process, occurred in 1546. It was remarkable, if only on account of the people involved.

The examinate was a woman: there does not appear to be another reported instance in which one was tortured for information. Anne Askew was the daughter of a Lincolnshire knight who had found her way to Court. She held strongly Protestant views, which led to her arrest. She was, however, in favor with various highly placed women, and the Council was eager to know whether any of them shared her kind of Protestantism. So she was examined at the Tower, but what is here striking is that if we credit an account attributed to her by Bishop Bale,[87] whilst the Lieutenant certainly was present, the examination was conducted by the Lord Chancellor Wriothesley himself and Richard Rich: the Common Lawyer who succeeded Wriothesley in the Chancellorship during the following year. According to the same account, this distinguished pair even went so far as themselves to rack their unfortunate female victim.[88]

> They did put me on the rack, because I confessed no ladies or gentlemen to be of my opinion, and thereon they kept me a long time; and because I lay still, and did not cry, my lord Chancellor and Master Rich took pains to rack me with their own hands, till I was nigh dead.

But the account continues, interestingly: "then the Lieutenant caused me to be loosed from the rack." The date seems to have been Tuesday, the 29th of June, 1546.[89] John Foxe (who was already thirty years old at the time of these events, and may have had information about them from among his acquaintance) adds, in his *Acts and Monuments*,[90] certain details. According to him, after a theological dispute with their victim, those two lawyers set out by road to see the King. The Lieutenant was alarmed, for although he had allowed Anne to be tortured, he had opposed the increasing severity used upon her and in the end had prevented the Lord Chancellor's continuing. Therefore he took a boat, reached the King by river before the others had arrived, and gave his own version of what had transpired. He was lucky. The King, who "seemed not very well to like of their so extreme handling of the Woman," pardoned him for resisting them. It seems likely that the King had been privy to an intention of using the rack: if Foxe is right, he certainly behaved as though the Lord Chancellor and Rich had royal authority to require its use. Whether the matter had been considered by other members of the Council, attendant upon the King, we do not know. Still, a quasi-juridical position seems at least imminent: others might, as representatives of the Crown carry out interrogations under torture at the Tower, but the torture itself, in its physical aspect, was controlled by the Lieutenant. It was for him to interpret any instructions he might receive in that regard.

Anne, it will be noticed, is represented as having done nothing to conceal her own religious beliefs; she is said to have been tortured to inculpate others. Foxe further added[91] that she had already been condemned, without being required to plead or being allowed a jury, at the Guildhall.

From the latter statement, it may be inferred that her condemnation was by the Bishop of London, with the Lord Mayor and aldermen in attendance, and was for heresy. If so, Wriothesley probably had a special official involvement, through subsequent receipt of a *significavit* for a writ *de haeretica comburenda*: through notification, by the Bishop, that a royal order was required, to have Anne burnt. Had she yielded in the theological debate said to have followed her interrogation under torture, presumably no such order would have been issued. Be that as it may, the wretched fact is that she was burnt indeed.

Of course, the catalogue of instances of torture revealed by the material above considered is very unlikely to be complete;[92] how closely it approaches being so can scarcely be judged.

*   *   *   *

In any case, two broad questions may now at last be put regarding this period, although they will be hard to answer: (1) whether the outcome of torture in an immediately Executive context, under pretended authority of the Crown, could influence the subsequent course of justice at Common Law; and (2) whether torture was ever moved out of an immediately Executive context into direct association with Judicature.

The only response that can be made to the first question seems to be by way of generalization and speculation. The results of torture may have influenced the course of Common Law justice in either or both of two ways: first, by determining whether the examinate was put on trial; second, by constituting material to procure his own or another's conviction. Each of these possibilities deserves brief comment.

The statute 33 H.VIII, c.23, in 1541, provided for the trial of those who had been examined by the Council upon suspicion of treason, misprision of treason, petty treason, or murder. Its terms, as far as they concern us, were as follows:

> Forasmuch as divers and sundry persons upon great grounds of vehement suspicions as well of high treason, petty treasons, misprisions of treason,

as of murders, be many times sent for from divers shires and places of
the realm . . . to be examined before the King's Highness's Council upon
their offences, to the intent that convictions or declarations of such persons
should speedily ensue, as the merits of their cases should require; and
albeit that after great travail taken in the examination of such persons it
appear to the said Council by confession witness or vehement suspect
that such persons be rather guilty of such offences whereof they be
examined than otherwise; yet nonetheless such offenders so examined
must be indicted within the shires and places where they committed their
offences . . . if any person or persons being examined before the King's
Council or three of them upon any manner of treasons, misprisions of
treasons or murders do confess any such offences, or . . . the said Council
or three of them upon such examination shall think any person so examined
to be vehemently suspected of any treason, misprisions of treasons or
murder . . . then in every way such case by the King's commandment,
his Majesty's commission of oyer and terminer . . . shall be made . . .
into such shires . . . as shall be named and appointed by the King's
Highness for the speedy trial, conviction or deliverance of such offenders.
. . .

Comparison with Bracton is intriguing. The *De legibus*, f. 143 offers, in
effect, a proposition that a presentment of treason or felony should not
be accepted, before the commissioner has ensured that the verdict of
the presenting jury establishes what would, according to Continental
doctrine, have been in Judicature amply sufficient to authorize procedure
by inquisition ex officio and to constitute an indication for torture. The
Henrician statute, ignoring the jury of presentment, supposed in effect
that the Crown, if it intervened to examine a suspect, would send him
on for trial only if it was satisfied that, by Conciliar examination or
otherwise, it had acquired at least such proof as would under Continental
doctrine have sufficed to support torture, if not condemnation. We thus
confront hypotheses. *If* this supposition was correct, and *if* torture was
sometimes used in support of Conciliar examination, to procure an extra-
judicial confession that would, accordingly, allow the suspect to be sent
for trial, the equivalence of Common Law jury trial to Continental trial
with torture was of lessened import. On the other hand, torture being
de facto available, strong encouragement to its use may have been
afforded by any administrative practice that required the Council to
obtain a confession from a suspect before it could send him for trial.
We shall see that, in later reigns, the Continental doctrine concerned

may seem sometimes faintly to have been invoked by the language in which Conciliar torture warrants presented their own justification.[93]

As to whether confessions obtained by the Crown through use of torture were presented evidentially to trial juries, all that can be said is that—again, as we shall see—in later reigns, statements obtained by the Council do appear sometimes to have been read at trials.

Let us now turn to the question whether, under the second Tudor King, torture for confession or inculpation was ever *directly* associated with judicature.

Regarding ecclesiastical process, only one recorded case seems to require scrutiny. On a December morning in 1514, Richard Hun was found hanged in the Lollard's Tower of St. Paul's Cathedral.[94] He had been held prisoner there by the Bishop of London. According to an anonymous pamphlet, which appeared about twenty-five years after the event under the title "The Enquirie and Verdite of the Quest Panneld of the Death of Richard Hune, wiche was founde hanged in Lolar's Tower," and was reproduced in Halle's *Chronicle* and Foxe's *Acts and Monuments*, a waxchandler named Alan Cresswell told the inquest on Hun's death that on the night before the body was discovered, Hun had been set in the stocks by his jailer and had been heard after release from them to say that he would kill himself with the latter's knife rather than suffer like treatment again.[95] The account in the pamphlet seems quite likely to be authentic.[96] If, however, we suppose it to be so, and Cresswell to have been accurate, still we can only guess at the context of the tragedy to which it relates. That the jailer, when he put Hun into the stocks, was merely indulging sadism or vindictiveness is possible, but we may incline against that explanation on the balance of probability. A venal motive might seem more likely: cupidity is more common than perversion or even resentment. However, it is surprising if either the jailer misjudged badly the means available to his prisoner, or Hun, having the means to buy relief, killed himself rather than use them.[97] Moreover, a little weight may attach to the fact that Hun was said to have spoken of using the jailer's knife to kill himself, not to kill the jailer. On balance, we may incline to the idea that the jailer was acting upon instructions, specific or otherwise, from the Bishop. Unhappily, even this will only launch us upon a further sea of speculation. We do not know whether any judicial steps had been taken, or were to be taken, with Hun. If he was being tortured coercively by the Bishop's orders, we do not know whether it was for confession of heresy, so that he might be convicted, for inculpation of others, so that they might be brought to trial or at least themselves be subjected to investigation, or for submission, so that he need not be brought to trial or, if he had already been tried, so that he might be treated with relative clemency.

On Civilian procedure in Admiralty, the Statute 28 H.VIII, c.15 deserves attention.

At any rate, until the mid-fifteenth century, a usual mode of Admiralty trial in criminal cases was by jury:[98] in the old sense (which, arguably, has never ceased to have some relevance) that whether or not evidence was adduced, the essential proof was the verdict itself. From the statute, however, it appears that by 1536 all criminal causes in Admiralty were the subject of witness trial in the sense that the court reached judgment upon its own appraisal—whether or not governed or guided by doctrine—of testimony. The statute provided that in the future, crimes within the Admiralty jurisdiction should be tried by Common Law procedure under a special commission; it explained that Civilian procedure had been used and had failed to produce convictions because thereunder: "before any judgment of death can be given against the offenders, either they must plainly confess their offences (which they will never do without torture or pains), or else their offences be so plainly and directly proved by witnesses indifferent, such as saw their offences committed, which cannot be gotten but by chance at few times." It would be difficult to find a clearer acknowledgment of the relevance—to which Adhémar Esmein drew attention[99]—of rigidity in the requirements for proof, to the employment of judicial torture. More to the immediate purpose, the statute seems (although a contrary inference has been drawn from it[100]) clearly to imply that whilst Civilian procedure had, down to its enactment, been used in Admiralty criminal trials, torture had not been incorporated. Whether in 1536 such incorporation was contemplated and rejected, or was not even envisaged, we cannot tell, but the draftsman did not feel that arguments against it were needed.

In Chancery, Civilian Procedure had been adopted, and it was employed in the Court of Requests, which, like Chancery, modified by attempted Equity some results of the Common Law, and which during Henry's reign became an established tribunal, seated at Whitehall. There is, however, no hint that respondents or witnesses were tortured for proof by either the Chancery or the Court of Requests. It is, on the other hand, possible that torture for revelation of assets occurred, by the Chancellor's authority or under his presidency, in some cases of debt.

In 1526 the creditors of one George Maynard—held, presumably under Common Law process, in Ludgate prison—petitioned the Chancellor, Cardinal Wolsey, to have him put to torture. He was, they said, concealing goods of large value, so that they would suffer grievous loss unless he "be causid by paynes done to him . . . as hayth bene of late sene in other countryes,[101] to confesse where all thes goodes be." Accordingly, they prayed that he might, indeed, be examined "upon a payne."[102]

Whether this petition was granted, we do not know. However, we ought also to notice the terms of Henry's bankruptcy act of 1542.[103] The latter statute recited that: "divers and sundry persons craftily obtaining into their hands great substance of other men's goods, do suddenly flee to parts unknown, or keep their houses, not minding to pay or restore to any of their creditors, their debts and duties, but . . . consume the substance obtained by credit of other men, for their own pleasure and delicate living, against all reason, equity and good conscience." Thereupon, it provided that the Lord Chancellor and others—members of the Council, and of the Common Law benches—should, upon written complaint, "take by their wisdoms and discretions, such orders and directions, as well with the bodies of such offenders as aforesaid, wheresoever they may be had . . . as with their property." The property was to be realized, or otherwise administered, for the benefit of the creditors. It seems usually to be assumed that the "orders and directions" to be taken "with the bodies" of the debtors concerned would consist of imprisonment such as might have been obtained, following judgment, at Common Law. Probably, this is right; yet possibly, torture was in view.[104] Although there seems no evidence of its actually having been employed under the statute, or later under 13 Eliz., c.7, there is no reason why if it was so employed, we should expect evidence of the fact to be extant.

The Council itself acted judicially, both upon the complaint of individuals and upon official information, and both in private session and at public Star Chamber sessions.[105] The procedure adopted was, again, on a Civilian pattern.[106] As far as concerned public Star Chamber Judicature, evolution during the sixteenth century, although not clearly apparent until later than Henry's reign, was towards the emergence (at least, de facto) of a distinct, judicial institution, with membership extending to the Common Law judges and (at any rate until near the close of Elizabeth's reign) peers other than those who would attend Executive meetings of the Council, and with the practice of imposing upon defendants an oath under which they were required to answer extensive interrogatories.[107] Nonetheless, Coke later concluded[108] that, juridically, the Court of Star Chamber had never been distinct from the Council. This conclusion, which much nearer to our own time was echoed by A.V. Dicey, [109] may have helped to induce F. W. Maitland[110] and William Holdsworth[111] to assert that torture was a Star Chamber device. Whereas in fact there seems no evidence that torture was used as an instrument of Star Chamber Judicature, whether already under Henry's father, or under Henry himself, or at any later time.[112]

Concerning judicial action of the Council in private session, the facts may have been complicated. There seems, once again, in regard to such action, no evidence of intimately related torture for proof; on the other hand, it is possible that the Council in such session sometimes moved, almost imperceptibly, from a phase of Executive action involving interrogatory torture into one of summary Judicature, or vice versa. Robert Dalyvell, after he had been examined in the Tower upon interrogatories drawn up by Cromwell himself, and at very least had been confronted with the rack, was sent back to his own neighborhood for summary punishment by local justices.[113] Had he been of higher rank, or had his conduct been of less distinctly local impact, the Council itself might have proceeded to impose some penalty upon him. Yet it cannot be assumed that at the time of his examination the decision had already been made that he was fit only for summary punishment, or—on the other hand—that the primary aim of his examination was to discover the extent of his own guilt.

The Council in the North does not seem to have received any purported authorization or official encouragement to use torture at its own discretion in any context.[114] Thus as has been noticed, the letter written in 1543 by the Duke of Suffolk and the Bishop of Durham about the torture of William Brewer was apologetic in tone.

On the other hand, as will be seen in the next chapter, from 1553 onwards royal instructions purportedly authorized recourse by the Council in the Welsh Marches[115] to torture of those it suspected of felony or of misdemeanor against the administration of justice or the peace; it may be that this merely recognized a practice already established under Henry. Even if so, however, the Council in the Marches is unlikely to have made torture an integral part of judicial process[116]. It seems usually to have confined its judicial activities, except at Common Law upon commission of oyer and terminer, to mere misdemeanors, although of a public sort, whilst in Cromwell's time it appears to have been reluctant to proceed, even regarding the latter, if they were at all serious, otherwise than by way of jury trial.[117]

By and large, therefore, our response to the question earlier propounded, whether under the second Tudor king torture for confession or inculpation was ever directly associated with Judicature, must be that there seems no evidence to favor an affirmative answer.

chapter 4

FROM EDWARD VI TO THE BULL *REGNANS IN EXCELSIS*

PART I
PARTICULAR WARRANTS

The first Conciliar record[1] for the reign of Edward VI to mention torture is dated the 15th of August, 1550. Recorded a week earlier is a letter written by the Council to Sir John Robsart and Sir William Fermour, informing them that one William Haldesworth, who had been executed at York, had "opened upon his death a privy concealment of plate, money and other treasure" made with one James or John Fowlkes, who lived near to Norwich, and instructing them to search for the hoard he had described.[2] Evidently, they were unsuccessful. The letter of 15th August directed them to persevere and to examine Fowlkes, putting him "in fear of torment."

It is not clear whether this meant that they were to threaten to use torture themselves or to tell Fowlkes that if he did not answer satisfactorily he would be sent to the Council, which might torture him. Not long afterwards, the sending of a suspect to the Council for torture was predicted, although only contingently—instructions are recorded for the 5th of March, 1551, that Sir Anthony Hungerford should proceed at Common Law against one Reed, for robbery—unless he thought that a jury might decline to convict upon the existing evidence, in which case he was to inform the Council, and it would have Reed sent to it for torture.

On the 5th of November, 1551, we encounter direct provision for the use of torture. A letter[3] recorded for that date ordered the Constable of the Tower and "all others that from time to time shall have the ordering of the Tower and the prisoners there" to assist "certain Commissioners newly allotted to the examination" of those prisoners in "putting the prisoners or any of them to such tortures as they shall think expedient." The prisoners concerned were presumably those committed to the Tower upon suspicion of being involved in the alleged treason of the Protector, the Duke of Somerset.

According to Edward VI's *Chronicle*, or *Journal*, in October, 1551, a plot by the Duke of Somerset to take over the government by force of arms, having—as was said—been revealed to the Duke of Northumberland by one of the latter's partisans, Sir Thomas Palmer, Somerset, and others including Palmer himself and one Lawrence Hammond, were arrested. These prisoners, except for Palmer and two others, were sent to the Tower, as subsequently were the Duchess of Somerset, with one William Crane and his wife. According to the *Acts of the Privy Council* (for the 18th of October, 1551), a man called Brend also was sent to the Tower with Crane. The *Chronicle* relates that under examination, Palmer confirmed much of what he was said to have told Northumberland about the plot and that Crane made a corresponding confession, filled in some detail, and inculpated the Earl of Arundel and Sir Michael Stanhope, whilst confessions were also forthcoming from Brend, Hammond, and Lord Strange. The *Chronicle* records Crane's confession for the 26th of October, 1551; for the preceding day, the *Acts of the Privy Council* record a letter to the Lieutenant of the Tower, instructing him to admit persons appointed for the examination of Crane, his wife, Brend, and another man called Bannister. The *Chronicle* further informs us that in November, 1551, Arundel and two of his supporters—Sir Thomas Stradling and St. Albin—were committed to the Tower because "Crane did more and more confess of him"; and that, half a year later, Crane and Bannister were released because of the "large confession" of the former and because little had been proved against the latter. At Somerset's trial, Crane's confession was read, but—unlike Lord Strange—he was not produced. It is said that he was tortured.[4]

For the 15th of October, 1552, we have a record in the *Acts of the Privy Council* that one Thomas Thurland suspected of sedition,[5] and sent to London accordingly by the Earl of Rutland, had been committed to the Tower. A letter recorded for the 30th of October required the Lieutenant to receive also, as prisoner, one Thomas Holland and to keep him from communication with others, especially Thurland. Another, recorded for the following day, directed the Comptroller and two more gentlemen to examine both prisoners upon such interrogatories as they thought fit. Then a letter to the Lieutenant, recorded for the 16th November, required him to examine Holland—putting the man to torture—upon matters to which Thurland had deposed.[6]

A warrant[7] recorded for the 7th of January, 1553, directed the Lieutenant of the Tower to put to torture, upon their being brought to him for the purpose, one Willson and one Warren, suspected of a shocking murder.

Then for the 3rd of June, 1553, we may notice in the *Acts of the Privy Council* an entry, not of, yet that may seem to predict, a torture warrant in defense at once of property and of royal status. Instructions are recorded that Robert Man and James Gardner, suspected of stealing hawks (an act that was a felony by Statute 37 E.III, c.19) from Princess Mary's land, should be sent to the Council, so they might be further examined to admit their guilt and, if they refused, be put to torture "to the example of others." The entry may seem to mean that the suspects would upon denial be ordered to torture by the Council, so that others might understand how little chance would be allowed of escaping punishment for such a crime committed against such a person.

In the reign of Mary, herself, we come first upon a warrant[8] recorded for the 27th of January, 1555, which was addressed to the Mayor of Bristol and referred to counterfeiters of coin who were under arrest in that city. It directed him to put them to the rack, if he thought fit, to discover from them their accomplices and especially the engraver of their plates.

For the 9th of June, in the same year, an entry occurs of a letter[9] to Lord North and other commissioners and of another letter[10] to the Lieutenant of the Tower. The commissioners, with the Lieutenant's assistance, were to "bring such obstinate persons as will not otherwise confess to the tortures, and there to order them according to their discretions."[11]

For the 4th of December, still in the same year, we have the record of a letter[12] written by order of the Council to the Lieutenant of the Tower, directing him to bring Richard Mulcaster, servant to Dr. Caius and vehemently suspected of robbing his master, to the rack and to put him in fear of the torture if he would not confess. The Dr. Caius of this record was probably the founder of Caius College, Cambridge, who, at the date concerned, was physician to the Queen.

Another record[13] is dated a few days after the last—the 11th of

December, 1555—and also refers to robbery. The warrant recorded was addressed to the Lieutenant of the Tower, Serjeant Dyer (afterwards Chief Justice of the Court of Common Pleas), and the Solicitor-General and ordered them to examine a person "vehemently suspected" of robbing a Mr. Keleaway. They were to put to the examinate such interrogatories as the victim might supply, and if they saw cause, they were to "bring him to the rack, and put him to some pain" if he would not confess; whilst, for the same day, another letter[14] is recorded, to the same persons, telling them to proceed in the same way with one Hugh of Warwick, suspected of horse stealing.[15]

For the 16th of February, 1556, a warrant[16] is recorded that was addressed to the Lieutenant of the Tower. It required him to join with Sir John Baker in examining two men and "to put them upon the torture, and pain them according to their discretions" if they would not confess their (unspecified) offenses.[17] For the 21st of June following a warrant[18] is recorded, addressed to Sir Robert Peckham, the Lieutenant of the Tower and "one of the Masters of Requests," and ordered them to put "to the tortures" Richard Gill, who was charged with having committed a murder in Dorsetshire.

Then a record shows that on the 29th of July in the same year, Sir Roger Cholmely and Dr. Marten were required to examine Silvester Taverner and to put him to such tortures as they thought convenient. According to the warrant,[19] Taverner was inculpated by two persons of embezzlement of plate and goods, partly belonging to the Queen, but he maintained his ignorance of the affair. Seemingly a chief aim of the Council was to recover the goods.

A letter[20] recorded for the 19th of July, 1557, directed the Constable of the Tower and other persons to "examine such as Sir Edward Warner inform them of, and to put them to the torture, if they shall think so good." From other entries in the *Acts of the Privy Council*—for the 22nd and 23rd of July and the 27th of August, 1557—it appears that a robbery was committed upon Warner and one Barclay, and that eventually some prisoners were handed over from the Tower to the Sheriff of London, so that they might stand trial for the offense at the Guildhall. It may be assumed that Warner's information, referred to in the letter of 19th July, 1557, accused some persons of the robbery. It is likely that those tried for it at least included those whom he had accused. Whether torture was in fact used, or threatened, we do not know.

A letter[21] recorded for 23rd July, 1557, is interesting in that it authorized torture, but more particularly in that it did so concerning a matter of a mixed, public and private, nature, such as the Council had at its date long been prepared to remedy[22] and had come by then to form an area of Star Chamber judicial activity,[23] while remaining capable of being dealt with at Common Law.

A number of persons having joined in appropriating hay and other goods, the property of a widow called Jane Stourton, and some of the offenders having been arrested by Lord St. John, the Council ordered him to examine them for the purpose of discovering who else was guilty and to use—if they did not answer plainly—"some torture for the better trying out of the truth." He was also instructed to restore to the widow hay and corn that were taken from her and not to allow the offenders bail, but to commit them to secure prison, in irons, until the coming Michaelmas term. He was to proceed with their indictment before that term and when it began, to "signify the same with the examinations" taken of them into Star Chamber. "The same" seems to mean the indictment, which, however, since it was to be proceeded with before approach to Star Chamber, was evidently to be indictment proper: indictment at Common Law; the Star Chamber function was to be supervisory.[24]

Next a warrant[25] is recorded for the 18th October, 1557. Its addressees included the Master of the Horse and the Master of the Ordnance, Sir Richard Southwell. They were to summon before them and examine one Newport and his servant—both held in Newgate—and one Cowley, who was in the King's Bench prison. All three were to be interrogated by them concerning counterfeit crowns discovered in Newport's possession and were to be put to torture at their discretion. But a letter followed, recorded[26] for the 30th of the same month, to the same addressees except for the Lord Chief Justice, plus Sir John Mason and Sir Robert Peckham. They were directed to examine Newport and his servant, who were (it is interesting to notice, still) in Newgate, on suspicion of coining, to bring the servant (only) to the torture, and at their discretion to "put him thereon."

The addressees of another warrant,[27] recorded for the 13th May, 1558, included the Constable of the Tower, the Recorder of London, and Marten. They were instructed to examine a Tower prisoner called French and to terrorize him with a sight of the means of torture: indeed, at their discretion, thereafter to have him tortured.[28]

The earliest Conciliar record of a torture warrant issued under Elizabeth I occurs for a date only about four months after her accession;[29] a letter[30] was sent to the Lieutenant of the Tower on the 15th March,

1559, requiring him to summon the Knight Marshal to assist him in examining two men, named Pitt and Nicholls, accused of robbing a widow in London and, if they refused to confess, to cause them "to be brought to the rack, and to feel the smart thereof" as the examiners might judge "good for the better boulting out of the truth" of the matter. *Boulting*, in the language of the day, meant "sifting".

For the 22nd June, 1565, a warrant[31] is recorded to Lord Scrope, directing him to "proceed somewhat sharply" to make one Nicholas Heath explain fully why he wandered abroad and if he resisted, to put him to "some kind of torture without any grete bodily hurte."

A warrant[32] is next recorded for the 28th December, 1566. It was addressed to Walsh J., the Attorney-General, and others; it required them to examine one Clement Fisher, prisoner in the Tower, for further information about his "lewdness" and for discovery of others guilty with him. Further, it directed them, in both regards, to threaten him with torture: indeed, for the discovery of other offenders, it allowed that he might be made actually "to feel some touch of the rack." This examinate was probably a man who, under the name of "Fisher", had in the preceding October been reported guilty, with accomplices, of the murder at Keswick of one Leonard Stulz: himself probably a German engineer or workman, engaged in the copper-mining enterprise to which the Government attached much importance.[33]

Finally, for the 18th January, 1567, a warrant[34] is recorded that was addressed to the Lieutenant of the Tower and others and required the interrogation under torture of one Rice, upon suspicion of housebreaking committed four years earlier against an official.

PART II
FURTHER INFORMATION AND
INTERPRETATION

I. THE WYATT REBELLION AND THE DUDLEY CONSPIRACY

Seemingly, it was during the 1560s that Sir Thomas Smith, no stranger to public affairs,[35] wrote the following celebrated passage:

Torment or question, which is used by the order of the civile law and
custome of other countries, to put a malefactor to excessive paine to
make him confesse of himselfe, or of his fellowes or complices, is not
used in England. It is taken for servile. For how can he serve the commonwealth after as a free man who hath his bodie so haled or tormented?
And if hee bee not found guilty, what amends can be made him? And
if he must dye, what crueltie is it so to torment him before! The nature
of Englishmen is to neglect death, to abide no torment; and therefore hee
will confesse rather to have done anything,—yea, to have killed his owne
father, than to suffer torment. For death our nation doth not so much
esteeme as a meere torment; in no place shall you see malefactors goe
more constantly, more assuredly, and with less lamentation to their death
than in England. The nature of our nation is free, stout, haulty, prodigall
of life and blood; but contumely, beating, servitude, and servile torment
and punishment, it will not abide.[36]

To say the least, the intimations of the Concilliar records noticed in the
preceding part (of this chapter) make Smith's observations surprising.
Explanations present themselves, but remain speculative. Was he
bewitched by the distinction between judicial practice and precedent
Executive action? Was he, under cover of patriotic complacency, attempting a criticism: may the passage be satirical? May he, after all, have
been unaware that under the Queen's two predecessors torture instructions had sometimes issued, and that since the Queen's accession they
had continued to do so? Or did they so rarely require to be carried out
that the actual practice of torture would seem negligible, even to one
well informed?

On the last question we have to look for evidence outside the *Acts
of the Privy Council*. Within the latter only the record of the Holland
warrant, for the 16 of November, 1552, seems unconditionally to command the infliction of acute torture: that for the 7th of January, 1553,
of the Willson and Warren warrant, does not inform us of the terms in
which examiners or others were instructed—or indeed, whether anyone
ever was instructed—to take the two men to the Lieutenant for execution
of the torture.

Yet even of outside evidence one way or the other, not much exists.
Two plots, or rather their aftermaths, in any case require attention.

In January, 1554, the failure of Sir Thomas Wyatt's rebellion was
followed by interrogations of him and other prisoners.

The Lord Chancellor, Bishop Stephen Gardiner, with several irons

in the fire, wrote[37] on the 11th of February, 1554, to the Principal
Secretary, Sir William Petre:

> Tomorrow, at your going to the Tower, it shall be good ye be earnest
> with one little Wyatt there prisoner, who by all likelihood can tell all.
> He is but a bastard, and hath no substance; and it might stand well with
> the Queen's Highness's pleasure there were no great account to be made
> whether ye pressed him to say truth by sharp punishment or promise of
> life.

The prospective examinate was presumably the "Edward Wyatt" named
in Hollinshed's *Chronicles*[38] as among the captives and by Nicholas
Throgmorton at his trial[39] as one who "knew something." The passage
has two interesting features, the significance of which depends upon
whether, when it was written, Edward Wyatt's examination was already
provided for by a regal or Conciliar torture warrant. To explain the
advice it tenders, it points out the examinate's humble status, and it
tenders that advice without invoking any new regal or Conciliar authority. Now, if a relevant torture warrant had already been issued,
Gardiner may well have meant that, because the Crown would stand to
gain nothing (by way of forfeiture of lands or of goods) from the
examinate's conviction at Common Law, it would be reasonable to
tempt him with an offer of pardon, if to do so seemed the more promising
way, instead of putting him to torture as already authorized. On the
other hand, if such a warrant had not been issued, it would seem that
Gardiner suggested torture, as one alternative expedient; that he mentioned the examinate's social insignificance to encourage recourse to
that alternative—exclusively, or at least as much as to encourage recourse to the other;[40] and that he assumed torture to be available—at
any rate, in the case of a landless bastard—without warrant of the Queen
or Council. In the end, the latter hypothesis may be preferred, since
there seems no evidence that a regal or Conciliar torture warrant ever
issued in the aftermath of the rebellion.

No more does cogent evidence emerge that torture was ever used in
the affair against any examinate.

On the following day, the 12th of February, 1554, Renard reported
to the Emperor that Thomas Wyatt himself had accused Courtenay, Sir
William Pickering and Sir Nicholas Points "without being tortured at
all,"[41] which might imply that this more widely known—and respon-

sible—member of the family had been tortured in some other behalf. However, the way in which Wyatt was handled at his trial[42] suggests that the pressure used upon him consisted rather in hints of possible clemency; Nicholas Throgmorton understood[43] that such was the temptation to which he had in some measure yielded.

*   *   *   *

A little more than two years later—in March, 1556—the Government was apprised of complex plotting, to carry off royal treasure and to levy war against the Crown.[44] The leader, from abroad, was Sir Henry Dudley. Strong suspicion was asserted to exist against a number of noblemen and gentlemen; commissioners were appointed[45] to interrogate suspects who had not escaped the realm.[46]

Acute torture seems not to have been used by them in the case of John Danyell—a dependant of Lord Grey[47] and no doubt a gentleman, although a minor one. Instead, however, he was subjected to the chronic torture of inhuman and degrading imprisonment: being removed, seemingly on the 23rd of April, 1556, to a dismal cell, infested with spiders and newts, and denied the use of a privy. He claimed to have a kidney or bladder disorder, which acerbated his consequent suffering.[48]

A report[49] of a conversation between one of the conspirators William Hinnes (who eventually escaped indictment, perhaps because he was very cooperative) and a "servant" of Christopher Chudleigh may in part reflect the inferior social status of the latter: probably one William Bury, who—like Edward Wyatt[50]—was rated a yeoman, not a gentleman.[51] According to the report, which appears to have been written about the end of March, 1556, he asked Hinnes whether Danyell had confessed anything; Hinnes replied that Danyell had confessed everything known to him, and therefore he—the "servant"—if he wished for clemency had better do the same; he thereupon observed that he had already denied such knowledge as he in fact possessed, but Hinnes said that he would lose nothing on that account, if he changed his tale and made a full confession, as long as it was not drawn from him by torture: "saith Hinnes, it makes no matter so long as ye are not compelled by torment to declare it."[52] So he thanked Hinnes for this advice and said he would act upon it. Of course, we cannot say whether torture of the "servant" was actually contemplated, or even if not, whether Hinnes was speaking in terms of what he himself, from information reaching him of what was going on in regard to other examinates or from threats he had received, regarded as a probable course of events.

Anyway, in the case of William Staunton, we encounter the prospective racking of a gentleman. Staunton's circumstances, it is true, were probably quite modest. Moreover, he was one of those who had sought to find a living, or improve their fortunes, by military service: Henry Machin describes him as a "captain", a "some-time captain."[53] His martial background may have affected the way in which he was treated, as may the fact that he had been involved in Wyatt's rebellion and had only by betrayal of others obtained pardon for his part in it.[54] But whether or not such circumstances were influential, paper from April, 1556, lists "Notes for the Queenes Ma'ties Counsell for Stanton" and, inter alia, "Hints for his conduct when on the rack."[55]

Moreover, it looks likely that the principal among the plotters, in England, John Throgmorton, was racked, and he was a man of good family and personal reputation.[56] Under questioning, apparently in the second half of April, 1556, he made statements inculpating three other conspirators.[57] Possibly, he knew that their situation was already hopeless; very possibly, he was having to contend with torture. The evidence that he was racked is in one[58] of two declarations made by another of the conspirators, Henry Peckham, probably on the 9th of May, 1556. It relates a conversation that had occurred between Throgmorton (who was condemned on the 21st of April and executed on the 28th of April)[59] and a Tower prisoner—or seeming prisoner—who went under the name of Walpole ("Walpull"). According to Peckham, this conversation went as follows:

> *Throgmorton*: Tell me, I pray you, Mr. Walpull, if the Council may rack me, or put me to torment, after the time I am condemned or no?
> *Walpole*: They may if it shall please them.
> *Throgmorton*: Then I fear I shall be put to it again, and I will assure you, it is terrible pain.[60]

Here, "rack me, or" looks an awkward interpolation, but Peckham's account may itself have been hesitant; it is hardly to be supposed that he remembered all that had been said, word for word.

Of course, if Throgmorton indeed was racked, still other gentlemen prisoners, besides Staunton, may have been so as well, although the extensive extant records[61] of the commissioners' "travails" do not reveal that they met with much determined reluctance to talk.[62]

II. CONCILIAR PRACTICE: PLACES AND INTERROGATORS

If there was recourse to acute torture regarding Wyatt's rebellion or the Dudley conspiracy, the indications are that it was inflicted at the Tower.

Again, an instance of terrorization there, under Elizabeth, is revealed by a document among the State Papers.[63] It is a report, made on the 28th of November, 1569, by Henry Knolles and others, of their examination at the Tower of a priest, Thomas Wood, concerning words spoken by him and one William Fenner. It indicates that he was threatened with the rack.

Evidently it was there, also, that the majority of Conciliar warrants of which for the present period we have a record, directing interrogatory torture or terrorization, were to be executed. In some cases, this appears only from the naming of the Constable or Lieutenant for the time being— by his office, or personally—as addressee.

Among addressees of torture warrants, the Lieutenant for the time being figures—sometimes alone,[64] sometimes joined with others[65]— more often than anyone else. It seems probable that where execution was to be at the Tower, the Lieutenant was always an addressee, unless the Constable was named, or there had been previous Conciliar instructions for interrogation, without torture, which was now made available to the original addressees, or there were some other very special circumstances; and that normally, if neither the Constable nor the Lieutenant was addressee of a warrant issued for interrogation under torture at the Tower, the warrant would be supported by instructions to the Lieutenant to lend his assistance.[66]

Conciliar warrants for interrogatory torture in London, yet apparently not at the Tower, were the following: that recorded for the 29th of July, 1556,[67] the place apparently contemplated being Westminster Convict Prison, the subject of inquiry, the location of stolen plate belonging to the Queen and others; those recorded for the 18th and 30th of October, 1557,[68] the place apparently contemplated being in each case Newgate, and the subject of inquiry, the origin of counterfeit coins. In none of those warrants was a means of torture named, but the language in the record for the 30th of October, 1557—"to bring the said servant to the torture and to put him thereon"—suggests that use was in view of a horizontal stretching rack; significance may thus attach to the inclusion as an addressee of the warrant concerned, of the Master of the Ordnance, an officer who may have been responsible for the custody and maintenance of instruments of torture normally kept at the Tower.[69]

Other addressees of warrants for interrogation under torture in London occasionally included Common Lawyers: judges, Law Officers, the Recorder of London, counsel.

Recorded Conciliar torture warrants addressed out of London form a modest minority. The most remarkable was that of the 27th of January, 1555. It concerned coining, a grave crime of direct importance to the Crown; yet it was sent to a municipal magistrate, for execution in his own town.[70] Moreover, it employed the expression: "to put the parties to the rack," which may seem more likely to have contemplated a stretching rack than torture in general;[71] while the design and construction of such an instrument was conceivably a matter of common knowledge— so the Mayor of Bristol could readily have had one made—a probable inference is that at Bristol one already existed. The explanation may be that in 1555 the town (by legal status, a county of a city) was still within the full jurisdiction of the Council in Wales and the Marches (of which more is to be said in part V), although it was a jurisdiction to which the inhabitants were hostile, and which (at any rate, as far as concerned police powers) was excluded in 1562. A rack may have been kept to serve the provincial council's purposes, in the first place; on the other hand, by 1555 the Council (of the Realm), recognizing that the provincial council was unpopular within the town, may already have begun to usurp its police function there, whilst seeking to maintain some element of local devolution.[72]

III. FURTHER, REGARDING SECULAR CHRONIC TORTURE

We have seen that commissioners investigating the Dudley conspiracy put pressure upon John Danyell by consigning him to a cell, at the Tower, which—along with the deprival of amenities that accompanied his incarceration in it—he professed to find hard to support.

Use by the Council of such chronic torture, at the Tower, is revealed by a record in the Council Book for the 3rd of May, 1555. This states that one Stephen Happes was "for his lewde behaviour and obstinacy" committed "to the Towre, to remayne in Little Ease for two or three dayes till he maye be further examyned." Two weeks later, the Lieutenant having reported that Happes was mad, the Council directed the

Lord Treasurer to look into the matter, and if the man seemed really
to be deprived of his senses, to commit him for the time being to
Bedlam.[73] About the nature and location within the Tower of "Little
Ease", there is doubt.[74] The name may have been given to different
places, at different times or even concurrently. However, it suffices to
suggest that the Council subjected Happes to discomfort beyond what
imprisonment in the Tower need entail; the fact that its action was
explained as occasioned partly by his obstinacy seems to show that its
purpose was to promote the further interrogation it had in view.

It is interesting to compare Cecil's "Memorial for the Northern Rebels".

At the end of 1569, following the collapse of the Northern Earls'
rebellion, the Government reacted by putting to death, under pretense
of Martial Law, hundreds of rebels, especially of the poorer sort. This
savage repression was first undertaken, dutifully—although not without
complaints that he was failing in zeal[75]—by Sir George Bowes,[76] whom
Sussex had appointed Provost Marshal,[77] and who was made a member
of the Council in the North.[78] Cecil himself would have liked more
discrimination, with the winkling out of those who had shown themselves
to be potential local leaders of conservative resistance through, if they
had lands worth their forfeiture, Common Law prosecution for treason.
As revealed in the Memorial, which he penned on the last day of 1569,
his immediate concerns at that time were that a full list should be
established of those who had been involved in the rebellion and that
those among them who might lead future uprisings should be rendered
harmless. To obtain the necessary information, he proposed that from
place to place, samples, each of some six or ten rebels, should be taken
and made amenable to interrogation by severe imprisonment, terrorization, and—if necessary—deprivation of food:

> Some persons being apprehended, of sondry parts and hundreds, wold
> be committed to strayte prison, and, being putt in some feare, and thereto,
> also, as nede shold, being pynched with some lack of food, and with
> payne of imprisonment, they wold be examyned at sondry times. . . .[79]

IV. ECCLESIASTICAL CASES

In Elizabeth's reign the view seems to have been widely held that at
St. Paul's, under Mary, Dr. John Story—being Chancellor to Bonner,

then Bishop of London—had, with the latter's authority and support, maintained a system of interrogation involving use of chronic torture.[80]

In aid of this view, John Foxe offers persuasively circumstantial material, particularly with regard to the case of one Thomas Green.

On the other hand, although some Protestants believed that, moreover, Bonner was capable of recourse to extempore modes of acute interrogatory torture, it is possible that under his regime, the use of acute torture was not undertaken at St. Paul's, but depended upon transfer of the examinate to the Tower and the use of authority other than the Bishop might himself assume. The case that here requires notice—and one about which, also, material reaches us through Foxe—is that of Cuthbert Simpson.

Both Green's case and Simpson's case belong to the end of Mary's reign, after the issue by the Crown, in 1557, of a commission[81] for repressing heresy and, particularly, the printing and circulation of heretical books (with such acts of sedition as might consist in or be associated with such printing and circulation) as well as, in London, for dealing with breaches of the peace. In the background, moreover, Statute 1 and 2 Philip and Mary, c.9, made it high treason to speak against the reconciliation with Rome and, of course, Canon Law was ready to deal with obstinate or relapsed heretics, while the secular arm was willing to oblige with writs *de haeretico comburendo* for their destruction. The Commission included, among others, Bonner, the Bishop of Ely, the Master of the Rolls, Sir Roger Cholmeley, Story, and some well-tried royal officeholders, who had been among those appointed to investigate the Dudley conspiracy. Summary powers of punishment were conferred upon those appointed, or any three of them, but they were required to refer obstinate heretics, for trial and sentence, to the Ordinary, who would, of course, commonly be Bonner himself. The terms of their appointment did not expressly authorize them to use torture.

Foxe offered[82] what purports to be an account by Thomas Green of his own experiences. According to this account, he was employed by one John Wayland, a printer, who discovered him to have a Protestant book, called *Antichrist*, and informed against him before Story. What it relates as his consequent treatment comprised the following successive steps:

1. Interrogation by Story and advice by him that the matter of the book was not heresy, but treason, for which the punishment was to be hanged, drawn, and quartered;

2. Close solitary imprisonment at St. Paul's, with stocking and harsh cross-fettering;
3. Release from some of the severity of the stocking, by the keeper who had inflicted it, now expressing sympathy;
4. Continuance, nonetheless, of solitary confinement and stocking;
5. A summons to the presence of Story and a promise by him of release to be obtained by cooperation: by informing against others;
6. Further solitary confinement and stocking;
7. A second summons to the presence of Story and threats by him of hanging up by the hands, cutting out of the tongue, cutting off of the ears;
8. A further, much longer, period of solitary confinement, most of the time in stocks, but for one spell in irons, without bedding;
9. A summons to the presence of Story and of the other commissioners, outside St. Paul's, with a warning imparted on the way by the escorting keeper that racking in the Tower might follow;
10. A surprisingly casual interview with the commissioners, followed by a return to close solitary confinement at St. Paul's;
11. A summons before a Mr. Hussey, who pretended to be sympathetic, where Story had been menacing;
12. A further summons before Mr. Hussey, who revealed knowledge of matters included among those that Green had suffered rather than divulge.

According to the same account, the last stage finished Green. He informed against one other person, pathetically relying upon an assurance that no harm would befall as a result, and was eventually dismissed with a birching, summarily ordered.[83]

It will be noticed that at an early stage, the possibility was mentioned of proceedings for high treason, and that the threat of racking referred to the Tower.

Simpson was deacon to a London Protestant congregation, which used Edward VI's English service. Foxe's first edition, of 1563,[84] affords us the text of what purported to be a letter written by Simpson himself on the 13th of December, 1557, describing his suffering until that date. It recorded that he had been interrogated in the Warehouse at the Tower by the Constable and Cholmeley, who was Recorder of London; that they had asked him to name those whom he had invited to the English service, but that he had declined: whereupon he was "set in a rack of iron"[85] for he thought three hours and released from it only after he had again refused the information demanded; that on a later day, he had been brought back to the Warehouse and interrogated there by the Lieutenant and the Recorder, and since he still refused to name members of the congregation had been tortured as follows: first, they had caused his forefingers to be tied together, and a short arrow to be grated between them with such force that blood flowed and the arrow broke, then he was twice "racked"; that he had remained obdurate; that ten days later the Lieutenant had asked him whether he would not at last answer, but he had refused; and that thereupon he was sent "unto the high priest" (evidently, to Bonner and the consistory jurisdiction), where he had been "greatly assaulted" and had received "the Pope's curse". He was executed by fire on the 28th of March, 1558. In later editions of Foxe, the text of a "Note for Cuthbert Sympson's Pacience" was added,[86] asserting that: Bonner, having condemned Simpson, later remarked that he had been "thrice racked upon one day in the Tower," besides which "in my house he hath felt some sorrowe"; according to the opinion of some, the torture with the arrow was inflicted in Bonner's house. However, the use of an arrow suggests military practice, which would have been more likely, it may seem, to have been encountered at the Tower. Moreover, the reference, in the text of the letter, to Simpson's having been "greatly assaulted" may mean that he was subjected to physical assault, but may alternatively describe doctrinal attacks by Roman Catholic divines. Whilst, if Bonner did acknowledge that Simpson had by his authority experienced "sorrow", he may have had in mind such severe chronic maltreatment as is said to have been practiced upon Green.

The broad lines of the story, in any case, suggest that proceedings started with the 1557 commissioners: that if Simpson had cooperated by informing against other Protestants, they would have regarded it as sufficient sign of repentance to justify dealing with him summarily, but that since he would not inform, they felt obliged to obey their instructions and transmit him to the Ordinary, Bonner, by whom he was condemned after efforts to convert him had proved unsuccessful. This leaves unanswerable the question whether, if so, the terms of the commission were treated as sufficient to support the committal of Simpson to the Tower, and his torture there, or whether Conciliar authority was obtained ad hoc.

V. STANDING TORTURE WARRANTS

The possibility having been noticed[87] that the 1557 heresy commission was regarded as by implication empowering the commissioners to command the use of acute torture in support of their interrogations, we may look for instances in which standing authority to employ interrogatory torture was expressly accorded, not confined to a particular case.

In March, 1555, a commission[88] issued to—among others—Lord North, the Lord Chief Justice of England, the Master of the Rolls, the Recorder of London, and Anthony Bourne (one of the Principal Secretaries) required them to examine those who in London or its environs were imprisoned upon suspicion of felony; additionally within the same area to search for any further felony suspects, commit them to prison, and cause them to be proceeded against according to law. In the light of this fact, the letter recorded for the 9th of June, 1555,[89] by which the Council directed Lord North and "the rest of the commissioners for the examination of prisoners" to bring those obstinately refusing confession to "the tortures" (perhaps, the instruments of torture at the Tower), there to deal with them at discretion, and which the Council backed with instructions[90] to the Lieutenant of the Tower, seems likely to have referred to the investigation of felonies in the metropolitan area[91] and to have shared the standing character of the March commission.

Nothing seems to show that the instructions of the 9th June, 1555, were imitated after Mary's reign. On the other hand, the purported royal authorization of torture to be inflicted by the Council in Wales and in the Marches continued from 1553 through the period covered by this chapter and beyond, into the reigns of the earlier Stuarts. As far as concerns the Tudors, it would be tedious repeatedly to mention the matter, which had better be disposed of here.

The purported authorization was contained in instructions issued, for the conduct of the provincial council, first in 1553,[92] then in 1560,[93] and then at irregular intervals during the remainder of Elizabeth's reign.[94] These instructions purported to confer authority to subject to interrogatory torture those suspected of treason or of any felony: murder was distinctly mentioned. There is a complication. They also purported to confer authority to try persons charged with any felony—murder, rape, and burglary being distinctly mentioned—or any of a long list of offenses of a kind regarding which jurisdiction was exercised in Star Chamber, and to do so, if more convenient, in the "prerogative", Star Chamber

manner, instead of by jury verdict. Hence suggestions[95] may be right
that the provincial council used interrogatory torture as a judicial instrument. However, that council does not appear to have been hostile
by its own tradition to jury trial;[96] to have dispensed with such trial
before a capital sentence would have been a revolutionary step, one
upon which the Council (of the Realm) did not venture. Allowance, it
is true, must be made for the special statutory background that might
be claimed for instructions to the provincial council. At any rate, by
1584 (as is revealed by one of the charges then drawn up by Archbishop
Whitgift against Robert Beale)[97] even the torture instruction was justified, by those who favored it, as implementing and supported by the
final "Act of Union", enacted for Wales in 1543.[98] The latter enactment
provided[99] for the continued existence of the provincial council and of
the office of its president and laid down that the president and council
should have "power and authority to hear and determine by their wisdoms and discretions" such causes and matters as were or thereafter
might be "assigned to them by the King's Majesty as heretofore hath
been accustomed and used." There may seem to have been room for
doubt whether "as heretofore hath been accustomed and used" merely
excused the provisions it terminated or qualified them, and if the latter,
whether it referred only to the mode of assignment or extended to the
subject matter. Yet even one who believed that the provincial council,
were it to try a man for felony without a jury and incorporate torture
for confession into its judicial process, would have indirect statutory
backing might have felt that such a course would be an unwise exercise
of discretion. The fact that the torture instruction extended to treason
cases, but the judical authority of the provincial council under its commission stopped short at felony, suggests that the instruction itself was
framed in contemplation of Executive torture (after the manner of the
Council of the Realm), not of recourse to torture in the judicial context.

VI. TORTURE AND SUBSEQUENT COMMON LAW PROOF

By this time, the shift of emphasis regarding the function of trial
juries had become marked. Receiving evidence, the jury had emerged
as more obviously a tribunal. Indeed, its aspect as such was pointed
out by Nicholas Throgmorton, when himself on trial.[100] Rules of evi-

dence, however, were still few. It appears that a written official account of an extra-judicial confession could, if read at the trial of whomever was said to have confessed, be treated as proof of some value against him.[101] No hint is given that the confession related in such an account must have been "voluntary", unless without two witnesses to prove treason.

Indeed, some of the material reviewed in this chapter indicates that actual, acute torture of a suspect might be undertaken with a view of obtaining a confession for use against him at Common Law. This object (although sometimes a tacit collateral purpose may have been to reassure those responsible for prosecutions that suspects were really guilty[102] before they were thrown upon the mercy of a jury) seems to emerge from the records noticed in part I above for the 5th March, 1551, the 3rd June, 1553, the 7th January, the 9th June, and the 11th December, 1555, the 16th February, 1556, the 15th March, 1599, and the 18th January, 1567.

According to Coke, *Rolston's Case,* to be noticed here for having ensued (1571) upon the Northern Earls' rebellion, established by interpretation of Statute 5 and 6 E.VI, c.11, s.9, that treason might even where two sufficient witnesses (as ordinarily by statute required) were not produced, be proved by a *voluntary* extra-forensic confession; judicial argument turned upon observation that confessions *under torture* did occur before trial (the prospective trial judge not being present), but never in court.[103]

chapter 5

THE 1570s

PART I
PARTICULAR WARRANTS

In 1568 Mary Stuart fled into England, where her presence heightened existing political tensions.[1]

The first treason to ensue was the rebellion of the Northern Earls, brought on with fine tactical judgment by Elizabeth and Cecil, at a time when it was unlikely to receive support from the English South.[2] After its swift defeat, discontent among the southern aristocracy remained a threat to the regime, the special weakness of which was its dependence upon the person of the Queen herself. Moreover, the publication of Pius V's Bull *Regnans in excelsis*, which—dated the 27th of April, 1570—declared her a heretic and purported to deprive her of political authority, acerbated the domestic situations, both in the short and long term.

In the short term, it created among the Queen's advisors a sense of crisis by inducing on their part a mistaken belief that France and Spain must be about to take military action against the realm.[3] Further, although the Government was at first disposed to maintain religious doctrinal freedom in spite of it, it encouraged Puritan militancy, which found an outlet in the Commons during the parliament of 1571.[4] That parliament provided a first legislative riposte, in the Statutes 13 Elizabeth, c.1 and c.2.[5] The former enactment, having confirmed existing law regarding treason by compassing the Queen's death, added, inter alia, that it should be treason to publish, or even hold, an opinion that Elizabeth was not or ought not to be Queen. The latter statute provided that liability for treason should be incurred by obtaining, publishing, or otherwise using any Papal instrument that purported to authorize or approve disobedience to Elizabeth or by purporting, upon the strength of any such instrument, to authorize or approve such disobedience.

The first recorded Conciliar warrants[6] mentioning torture, after the Bull, preceded the above legislation and do not appear to have had any religious or political connection. They were dated the 20th of June, 1570, and perhaps intended to be complementary. Both concerned one Andrews, "vehemently" suspected of a murder in Somerset. Examination was by one warrant confided to a Common Law judge; Executive action was by the other required of the Lieutenant of the Tower: although, whether through a slip or a change of plan, the record of this warrant indicates that the examiners were to be persons appointed by a different judge. Probably the Council meant the examinate in view to be attached to the rack, and so terrorized, but not to be physically stretched.

The next recorded warrant[7] requiring attention also preceded the legislation of 1571, but was squarely on the subject of the Bull. John Felton (Fenton) who had audaciously placarded a copy of that instrument against the Bishop of London's palace, was charged therewith and also that he had conspired with the Spanish Ambassador. Commissioners "appointed for the examination of the Bull" were ordered by the Council to deliver him to the Lieutenant of the Tower: to "be brought to the place of torture, and put in fear thereof". If he did not succumb to such terrorization, they were "to spare not to lay him upon it" so that he might feel "such smart and pain thereof" as they thought "convenient."[8]

In the following year, 1571, the Ridolfi Plot came under investigation. Much requiring our attention about the proceedings taken with the plotters comes to us from some other source than a torture warrant or matter closely related to such a warrant; therefore, I have made this topic one for later review.[9] However, we must here notice that there remains extant the draft,[10] in Burghley's handwriting, of a warrant under the Queen's Signet, directing Sir Thomas Smith and one of the Masters of Requests, Dr. Wilson, to examine two servants of the Duke of Norfolk, Barker and Bannister: the addressees being instructed to have these examinates, if they were reticent on any point, brought to the rack, and should they remain obstinate, to have them put to it, "to find the taste thereof" until they should "deal more plainly." Further, we may notice that such a warrant doubtless was issued, for there are also two letters, published in William Murdin's collection of Cecil State Papers, to Burghley from Smith at the Tower: the first of which,[11] dated two days after the draft, announces, concerning prisoners there, that:

Tomorrow we do intend to bring a couple of them to the rack, not in
any hope to get anything worthy that pain or fear, but because it is so
earnestly commanded to us;

whilst the second,[12] dated the 20th of September, reports that Smith has
examined Bannister by the rack.

Smith's praise of English law, remarked in part II(I) of the last chapter,
for not admitting torture, although probably written before, was apparently published after this personal experience, which he did not
enjoy.[13]

Three warrants recorded for the 1st of April, 1573, concerned one
George Brown, who was suspected of having murdered a man called
Saunders. Two of the warrants were for his transfer to the Tower, and
of these warrants, one,[14] addressed to the Lieutenant, required him—
among other things—to assist those detailed to examine the prisoner,
by bringing him or putting him on the rack.[15] The remaining warrant[16]
was addressed to the Master of the Rolls and two Common Law judges,
dischargeable by any two of them. As it stands recorded, it provided
that Brown should be examined and might be put to torture, and that
others falling under suspicion of the same crime should be examined:
but not that they might be tortured.

For the 29th November, 1574, a letter[17] is recorded from the Council
to five addressees, including the Lieutenant, the Solicitor-General, and
Thomas Norton. They were required to examine Humphrey Nedeham,
then a prisoner in the Tower, and to terrorize him by bringing him to
the rack, although not to stretch him. The latter restriction deserves to
be well marked, especially as Nedeham's offense appears to have been
one rather for Star Chamber punishment, than for indictment. He had
presented to Matthew Parker—the Archbishop of Canterbury and first
among the addressees of the 1559 ecclesiastical commission—forged
papers purporting to be correspondence of the Puritan divine, Thomas
Cartwright, who had fled abroad when a warrant was issued for his
arrest in the autumn of 1573.[18] Using this material in support of a pretense
that he could catch Cartwright, he had fraudulently obtained from Parker
a sum to cover expenses in making the arrest.[19]

For the 6th of February, 1575, the Council Book records an instruction[20]
that Walsingham, the Solicitor-General and the Master of the Posts,
should examine "Cicking"—Henry Cockyn—a bookbinder of St. Paul's;
and an instruction[21] that the Lieutenant of the Tower, to which Cockyn

had been committed, should send him when required to Walsingham's house for examination and should prepare the way by putting him in fear of the rack.

Both the background and the sequel to the issue of these instructions were complicated.[22]

In 1574 information was received from Scotland that Mary Stuart was sending messages to sympathizers through a chain of communication in which Alexander Hamilton, tutor to the Earl of Shrewsbury's children, was an important link. Hamilton was twice examined by Walsingham, but denied any involvement. In January, 1575, however, Walsingham acquired further evidence, in a directive given by the Bishop of Ross to one of his own servants; he reported to the Queen, who seemingly consulted Burghley. In the light of the available facts, Burghley decided that Cockyn, an established suspect who had earlier been examined three times, although without any duress other than imprisonment, ought to be dealt with again.[23] Seemingly, he was now ready to have the man threatened with torture, although still not to have him tortured indeed. The arrest followed, and examination was entrusted to those who afterwards received the above warrant. Walsingham, on the 2nd of February, 1575, wrote to Burghley regarding Cockyn: "without torture, I know we shall not prevail."[24] On the 5th of February, Cockyn was interrogated, but would inculpate neither himself nor others. The next step, according to Burghley's view, would be to threaten torture. Walsingham remained pessimistic and wrote to Burghley: "I think the show of torture (the fellow being so resolute as he is) will little prevail, but rather make him more obstinate."[25] Nonetheless, the instructions for terrorization were, as we see, issued through the Council. Walsingham's pessimism proved well founded. He came to suspect that Cockyn was in receipt of an income from Mary, and that a desire to preserve it was one of the motives of his resistance; in the end, when he took matters into his own hands, he made allowance for that possibility. Cockyn next faced a choice: either he would without torture provide the information required of him, in which case he would receive from the Queen a pardon, material compensation, and protection by concealment of the fact that he had become an informer; or he would suffer torture, with nothing to look for except release from the immediate agony.[26] This worked. Cockyn confessed his own part in the transmission of messages and inculpated a number of other persons. Later, the Queen ratified the promise to him of her favor.[27]

The next Conciliar record requiring attention brings into view the Statute 13 Elizabeth, c.1. Thomas Sherwood, a Roman Catholic layman, having been committed by the Ecclesiastical Commissioners for attending Mass, confessed an opinion that offended against the statute. The Council on the 17th of November, 1577, directed his prosecution at Common Law and his examination meanwhile by the Attorney-General. He was to be interrogated to discover the names of other disaffected persons and to learn from whom he had acquired arguments that had appeared in his confession: orders were given to the Lieutenant of the Tower to consign him, if he were obstinate, to the "dungeon among the rats".[28]

Seemingly, however, such pressure as was brought to bear in pursuance of this instruction was followed upon Sherwood's part only by a tendency to retract the confession he had already made. So for the 4th of December, 1577, we find recorded a Conciliar warrant authorizing the Lieutenant, the Attorney-General, the Solicitor-General, and the Recorder of London to "assay him at the rack," although still simply to discover other offenders, not to obtain renewed self-inculpation.[29]

In the year immediately following, by a warrant[30] recorded for the 4th of November, 1578, which recited that a person named Harding could not by gentler methods be brought to confess, the Lieutenant of the Tower and the Recorder were ordered to bring him to the rack, "thereby to prove whether he will discover any further matter." "Thereby" probably means, "by the rack": not just "by bringing him to the rack", "by terrorization".

Also, by the same warrant, the addressees were to put John Sanford to the rack, to discover the truth concerning activities of John Prescott, to which he was strongly suspected to have been privy, but which nothing had so far persuaded him to reveal.[31]

Sanford had been committed to the Tower for "lewd speeches against the Queen's Majesty."[32] Proceedings were probably contemplated against Prescott and him for treason under one of the statutes of 13 Elizabeth. The concern of the same warrant with Harding may suggest that he was in like case.

Finally, for the present period, we should notice a record for the 11th of June, 1579, of a letter[33] concerning one Robert Wintershall, one Harvey Mellersh, and others, suspected of murdering in Surrey one Richard Mellersh and one Thomas Mellersh, the same Richard's son. The letter was addressed to four persons, including the Lieutenant of the Tower and a Common Law judge. It informed them that the justices of the peace in Surrey had failed to obtain from the suspects concerned admissions sufficient to procure a conviction, and that the consequent delay was causing public dismay; it required them, accordingly, to examine the suspects and if admissions so sufficient could not be extracted from them by other means, to commit them to "the dungeons and like places of obscurities in the Tower", keeping them there on short rations. Further, it required the Lieutenant to cause them to be terrified, if necessary and as he and the other addressees thought convenient, by showing them the rack or otherwise. (Compare, among broadly contemporary warrants, those recorded for the 20th of June, 1570,[34] and for the 1st of April, 1573:[35] of which the earlier probably did not allow actual racking.)

PART II
FURTHER INFORMATION AND
INTERPRETATION

I. FURTHER, CONCERNING THE RIDOLFI PLOT

Roberto Ridolfi was a Florentine banker, in business in London. It struck him to promote a plan for a rising,[36] to be headed by the Duke of Norfolk (to a marriage of whom, with Mary Stuart, some looked who were hoping for the latter's accession to the throne), and supported by an invasion from the Low Countries. The Pope was interested; the Spaniards seem to have thought the proposals absurd; Mary, as ever, was ready for anything that might serve her ambition. Her agent, who when in England pretended to the status of Ambassador, was the Bishop of Ross; he, in turn, was served in this matter by one Charles Bailly— often in official documents described simply as "Charles", "Carlos"— who at a later time was said[37] to have been Mary's paramour, after the murder of Darnley.

Bailly, arriving in England in April, 1571, did not hide the fact that he was in the Bishop's service. He and his baggage were subjected to search, and he was found to have with him not only letters capable of arousing suspicion that the Bishop was involved in some nefarious activity, but prohibited books. Treachery, close to home, prevented the letters' reaching Burghley, but he was informed of the discovery of the books. Bailly was committed to the Marshalsea, and there he came under the surveillance of one William Herle, a gentleman who had been involved in the Northern Earls' rebellion and now very willingly undertook to act as Burghley's spy. Between the 11th and 24th of April, he submitted four reports[38] on Bailly who, on the 25th and 26th of April, was examined by Burghley and Leicester.

The Bishop himself, as I have mentioned further below, had been placed under a measure of restraint, but evidently he was still able to discharge his pretended Ambassadorial role. Bailly wrote to tell the Bishop about his examinations.[39] Burghley, Bailly said, had warned him that, if he did not gain favor from the Government, he would either be executed for treason or (presumably, for sedition) would lose his ears. When he still would not respond in the way desired, Burghley had ordered him to be taken back to prison and to be loaded with irons heavier than previously he had borne.

On the 27th of April, Herle informed Burghley that Bailly had said he knew certain ciphers by rote.[40] Apparently, letters between Bailly and the Bishop had meanwhile been intercepted that were in a cipher, and it had not been penetrated:[41] so this information was à propos. Bailly was transferred to the Tower.

On the 28th of April, an anonymous correspondent in the Marshalsea wrote to the Bishop that the purpose of the move was to separate Bailly, rather than any ''extremity''.[42] However, on the 29th of April, Bailly— according to a letter[43] written by him to the Bishop at the end of that day—was at five o'clock in the morning removed from the Tower and taken before Burghley who, before sending him back to the Tower, threatened him with the rack. As to what happened when he got back, this letter may, at least at first sight, appear self-contradictory. It relates that when he appeared before Burghley, the latter demanded of him the key to the relevant cipher and, upon his claiming not to know it, told him that in the event of obstinacy on his part, one of the secretaries would be sent to the Tower with him, bearing an order to the Lieutenant to put him *on* the torture, to force him to betray the cipher and to make him confess what messages he had carried between the Bishop and the Countess of Northumberland. It adds: he ''threatens me that he will make me tell whether I am induced thereto by force or by friendship.'' So far, its tale is one only of menaces, but then it concludes: ''therefore,

I beg you to write to me, and send me your advice, and do everything you can to secure my release, or at least that I am not put *on* the torture any more: otherwise, I am for ever lost.''

It seems that there were immediate rumors that Bailly had been racked, but the Bishop apparently inferred that he had only been terrorized, although on the rack; Bailly's general style suggests that, had he been racked, he would have complained more specifically and at more length, so the Bishop's inference probably corresponded to the truth. A letter[44] written by the Bishop to Bailly on the 1st of May, which is not entirely easy to understand, appears, on the whole, to convey that according to the Government, the coercion of Bailly had stopped short of actual racking, yet not of placing him on the rack. The Bishop wrote:

> I have . . . [made] . . . great Exclamations, that it is a cruell and terrible
> Practiz to take Embassadors Servants, and to lay them on the Rack to
> confess their Masters' Secrets, and to decipher their Letters. . . . Where-
> upon the Earl of Leicester and my Lord Burghley sent to the Embassadeur,
> and me, to shew that ye have not been so rigorously handled as is reported,
> but only put in Fear; and that allthowgh they have Occasion to do it,
> nevertheless they will cause Moderation to be used hereafter; and all-
> thowgh they will make you afrayd, yet yow shall not be racked any more.

"Yow shall not be racked any more" must either mean "you shall on no future occasion actually be racked" or "you shall not again be brought to the rack". The latter interpretation requires us to suppose that the Bishop used "racked" in a loose way, but it harmonizes with the preceding material and allows to "any more" what may seem its natural sense.

On 2 May, Bailly wrote again to the Bishop,[45] this time complaining that he was confined in a "rheumatic and unwholesome cave." His morale was evidently collapsing. On the same day, he sent to Burghley a letter[46] containing various inculpatory information and an offer, if he was released, to spy on the Bishop. On the 5th of May, he wrote again to Burghley,[47] providing more information of the same kind and representing himself quite convincingly as in a state of complete surrender. However, in neither of these letters to Burghley did he complain of being racked; therefore, when Guerau de Spes reported[48] on the 9th May to the King of Spain that Bailly had been put on the rack, although lightly as yet, he was perhaps only striking a mean between divergent accounts, to be heard in London, concerning what had happened earlier in the month, or else placing his own construction upon the sort of statement, in that regard, that the Bishop had received from Leicester and Burghley.

As the year passed, further information was obtained by the Queen and her advisers, from abroad, and some hard evidence came into their hands against the Duke of Norfolk. The following account is credited by Conyers Read.[49]

One of the Duke's secretaries, Robert Higford, entrusted to a draper, who intended to visit Shrewsbury, a fastened bag for delivery to Lawrence Bannister, the Duke's land agent, in Shropshire. He told the draper that the bag contained fifty pounds in silver, but it weighed more than might in that case have been expected. The draper, becoming suspicious, opened it and found it to contain instead six hundred pounds in gold and letters, of which some were in cipher. The draper reported this discovery to the authorities, and the report reached Burghley. He had Higford arrested and obtained from him a confession that the Duke was privy to the dispatch of the gold.

The picture that at this stage presented itself to Burghley was of a plot to procure rebellion and an invasion of the realm, in pursuit of which the Duke had tried to send a large sum into the Midlands, probably with the intention of its being posted further north[50] by Bannister. From the 2nd of September, 1571, Charles Bailly, Higford, and another secretary of the Duke, William Barker, came under examination at the Tower. Their usual interrogators were at first Sir Thomas Smith and Dr. Thomas Wilson, then a Master of Requests. On the 6th of September, Bannister was arrested;[51] he, also, was sent for examination to the Tower and was dealt with at first mainly by the same two examiners. The Duke himself, having by the Queen's order been placed under restraint in his own house on the 4th of September,[52] was on the 7th of September escorted to the Tower, without ceremony, by Sir Ralph Sadler, Smith, and Wilson.[53]

On the 14th of September, Smith and Wilson took what they seem to have regarded as the largest confession to be obtained from Higford and Barker;[54] they had little from Bannister; probably by that time they had put some questions to Bailly, but although his mood seemingly remained compliant,[55] it is doubtful whether he had much more that he could tell.

As far as concerned Barker and Bannister, at any rate, the Queen and Burghley were not satisfied. According to a conclusion later reached by Smith,[56] Barker had been the most deeply involved in pursuit of the plot. Bannister, it seems, really knew little about the plot itself; this accorded with the impression formed by Smith who, however, found him obstinate. Seemingly, on the 15th of September, Smith and Wilson received, under the signet, the warrant, a draft[57] of which was noticed in part I of this chapter. The warrant advanced, as its own justification, that the examinates had given untrue answers to interrogatories presented without torture and that the matter touched the Queen's safety. In this, it may seem to have hinted of Civilian influence,[58] but if Romanistic allusions were intentionally present, they may have been introduced only because both of the addressees were learned in the Civil Law. On the 16th of September, Burghley wrote to Smith that the confession of Barker and Higford had been shown to the Queen, but that she was not content and looked for an answer to her letter "authorizing you to proceed with Barker and Hygford by torture sent yesterday by Mr. Tremayn."[59] The reference to Higford was perhaps (compare the draft) a slip on Burghley's part, and it may have embarrassed Smith.

At 6 o'clock on the evening of the 17th of September, Smith wrote to Burghley a letter, also noticed above, that appears to have been a reply. He enclosed the results of further examinations, expressed his distaste for the whole business, said that he believed he and Wilson had learnt as much as was possible, but indicated that nonetheless on the following day, they would obediently try terrorization or torture on two of the examinates.[60] Perhaps he avoided naming Barker and Bannister, because Burghley had mentioned Barker and Higford. Anyway, it was with Barker and Bannister that he and Wilson proceeded. In his letter,[61] likewise mentioned above, of the 20th of September to Burghley, he wrote:

> We have good hope at last, that we may com Hom; we thynk surely that we have done all that at this Tyme may be done. Of Banistre with the Rack; of Barker with the extreme Feare of it; we suppose to have gotten all.

It appears that Smith himself was thereafter allowed to withdraw from the business, and there is no hint in State Papers of further recourse to torture or the threat of it against any of the four examinates to whom I have referred. Nonetheless, examinations continued.

In the course of them, on the 29th of September, Bannister made a declaration[62] that was received by Wilson. It was partly an apology, partly a formal deposition. We may notice that, at the outset, Bannister recognized that he had been "charged and commanded" to utter his full knowledge touching the plot, but that notwithstanding:

> neyther upon my Examynacion, had before the Righte Honerable the Earle of Leycestre, and the Righte Honerable Syr Thomas Smythe, Secretarie to the Quene's Majestie, and your Wourshipe, wolde [I] confesse anie Parte of my knowledge towching the premisses befor such Tyme as I was threatened to the Rack and tastid the smart thereof. . . .

He was still under examination at the end of October.[63]

According to the *State Trials*, during the hearing of Norfolk's case, one argument presented by the prosecution was that the Duke had conspired to marry Mary Stuart, but that he had not admired her and, therefore, that he had been moved by treasonable ambition. In this regard, a deposition said to have been obtained from Bannister in October was read out, to which the Duke responded: "Bannister was shrewdly cramped when he told that tale."[64] However, even if we assume that the *State Trials* account is here accurate, the Duke's remark, whilst it looks like an allegation that the deposition concerned had itself been obtained under torture, can hardly be regarded as substantial additional evidence on the treatment that Bannister actually received.

In conclusion, let us briefly return to the Bishop of Ross, who—as noticed above—was after Charles Bailly's arrest placed under a measure of restraint. At Norfolk's trial, depositions obtained from the Bishop were the most powerful evidence available to the prosecution, and according to the *State Trials*, counsel affirmed that the Bishop had been "examined freely, without any compulsion."[65] Assuming that it was made, the latter statement is of a sort that readily smacks of prevarication. However, it may well have been induced only by general discomfort about the known or suspected torture of Bannister. The view has been expressed[66] that the Bishop was indeed himself (expressly) threatened with torture. It may be so, but I have failed to locate the proof. As has been mentioned, the Bishop was placed under a measure of restraint after the arrest of Charles Bailly. On the 19th of October, 1571, he was taken into close custody at the Lord Mayor of London's house, where on the 24th of October, he was examined by members of the Council. His first reaction was to claim the privileges of an Ambassador, but the Crown was ready for this, having obtained the opinion of a number of Civilians[67] that an Ambassador who procured an insurrection, or gave

aid or comfort to any traitor, against the Prince to whom he was ac-
credited, "ought not *jure gentium or civili Romanorum* to enjoy the
privileges otherwise due to an ambassador";[68] the Bishop was warned
accordingly. He himself, in a letter written to Mary on the 8th of
November,[69] said he had been told that he "might be used as a private
man and a subject"—a loose expression, which if actually addressed
to him may have led him to suppose, rightly or wrongly, that he was
being threatened with interrogatory torture. He was then transferred to
the Tower, but such a move was capable of ambiguity: of indicating
willingness to use torture or only willingness to prosecute and punish.
Further examined, when at the Tower, the Bishop quickly surrendered.[70]
Clearly, however, this in itself does not establish that he was, or believed
himself to be, under threat of torture: without more the fear of death
is, for most of us, potent constraint.

II. TORTURE AT BERWICK

From Berwick, on the 3rd of July, 1572, Henry Carey, Lord Hunsden,
wrote to Burghley as follows:

> Yesterday I gate one that came yntoo thys towne as a Scotchman disyrous
> too pass yntoo England whome yn talkyng untoo hym I found too be an
> Inglysheman, whereupon I examind hym further, and the more quystyons
> I askt of hym the further he was too seke and examinyng of him if he
> had any letters he denyed the havying of any, whereupon I made hym
> presently to be serchyd when I fownde about hym . . . a number of
> letters, beedes, agnus deis, friars gyrdils for women in labor and such
> other palterys. . . . I have occupyde this nyght yn perusying of his letters.
> . . . I am now goynge to examin hym further bycawse yette I want that
> I looke for, and therfor I pray your lordship that yf I fynd cause why
> that I may eyther bryng hym or putt hym too the rack a lyttell for he ys
> able to say much. . . . [71]

It is interesting that Carey, in the Eastern Marches, felt the need, at
least in principle, of specific authorization for recourse to torture against
the man concerned: although we may suspect, from the sense of urgency
his letter conveys, that he did not, once it was dispatched, intend to
await a reply before proceeding. Also interesting is the fact that he had
a rack: presumably, a stretching rack.[72] We may conclude that possibly
a significant number of torture warrants were sent to Berwick, and we

may surmise, since none is revealed by a Conciliar record, that if so they issued under the Signet.

III. AN IMPERFECT CONCILIAR RECORD

For the 25th of October, 1576, the *Acts of the Privy Council* contain a record that, evidently, either is itself imperfect or is of an imperfect warrant.

The warrant concerned was sent, in the matter of one Thomas Wells, to the Lieutenant of the Tower and the Recorder of London. It described Wells, who had been found in possession of part of goods of which the Knight Marshall had been robbed, when on a journey to London, as "vehemently suspected" of the crime, but it explained that he denied his guilt. The addressees were to examine him and, if he would not confess and name his accomplices, were—according to the record—to "bring him in fear thereof." Whatever went wrong here, probably the intention was that they should "bring him to the place of torture and put him in fear thereof"—compare the Felton (Fenton) warrant of 1570.[73]

IV. INVOLVEMENT OF COMMON LAWYERS

Conciliar records of torture warrants issued during the 1570s indicate the continued need, if torture was to be employed at the Tower, for specific instructions in that behalf to the Lieutenant.

A striking feature is the frequent inclusion of Common Lawyers among the addressees of torture warrants.

In 1566 a puisne judge had been appointed to examine Fisher for confession, probably of murder, with the use if needed of some measure of duress. There, the evidence suggesting that the offense was murder also suggests that it had peculiar direct importance for the Government. In the present period, murders not so important produced like appointment. We have the appointment of Southcote J. by one of the warrants concerning Andrews recorded for the 20th of June, 1570: although there it appears the Council entertained also another plan, that of leaving interrogation to those to whom Weston J. might delegate the task, and it is not clear which course was in the end taken; also, we have the appointment of Southcote and Manwood JJ. (as well as of the Master of the Rolls) by the warrants recorded for the 1st of April, 1573, in the case of George Brown, and the appointment of Southcote J. by the warrant recorded for the 11th of June, 1579, in the case of Robert Wintershall, Harvey Mellersh, and others.

As far as their circumstances may be discerned, it appears that all of the other warrants, contemplating torture and recorded for the present period, were issued in cases of a political character. Among them, the warrant concerning Felton entrusted his interrogation to commissioners already appointed in the matter of the Bull.[74] Otherwise, we find in each the appointment either of one of the (Common) Law officers or of the Recorder of London.

Thus by and large, it appears that the Council much more consistently relied in this matter upon Common Lawyers than had been its earlier practice. That they did not have to be omitted, even when actual use of the rack was in contemplation, is ideologically interesting. Moreover, their employment clearly suggests the examinations were regarded as capable of relevance to proceedings that might subsequently be taken at Common Law.

V. TORTURE AND SUBSEQUENT COMMON LAW PROOF

Where interrogation was aimed to secure self-incrimination, by the examinate, of a crime punishable at Common Law, the subsequent procedure where the outcome was successful would presumably be to transmit the examinate's confession, so that it might be read out when he was on trial.

The warrant concerning Robert Wintershall, Harvey Mellersh, and others, as recorded for the 11th of June, 1579, clearly indicates that the Council did not consider duress to vitiate an extra-judicial confession as a means of securing a verdict of guilt. On the other hand, that warrant did not extend to actual use of the rack, and the question has to be considered whether, by the present period, juries—although they would probably not be disturbed by allegations of any lesser ill treatment— were likely to be offended by belief that the accused had been racked for confession. Sir Thomas Smith assures us that the English loathed torture,[75] and we may suppose that an accused who had made under torture or threat a confession read to the jury trying him would be likely—unless he had come to pin his hopes on clemency to be shown after he was condemned—to complain of the way in which the confession had been obtained.

The warrants concerning Andrews, recorded for the 20th of June, 1570, permitted only terrorization in what appears to have been a similar case. However, those recorded for the 1st of April, 1573, concerning Brown, although they also were issued in a matter of murder, allowed the rack to be used. The explanation here may simply have been the evident anxiety to gratify the deceased's kinsmen and friends: the examiners' warrant directed that all questioning should be accordant with any instructions received from kinsmen and friends of the murder victim and, even, that such persons should be allowed to attend and themselves to administer interrogatories. (The records show one partial precedent: a 1555 robbery case induced instructions, noticed in chapter 4, part I, for torture in support of interrogatories to be supplied by the victim,[76] but nothing of the sort otherwise appears in the records of torture warrants issued regarding non-political crime, whether murder or robbery, although in some further cases of the latter offense,[77] it is likely that the torture warrant was issued out of special favor—whether grounded in respect or in compassion—towards the victim.) Yet near the close of the preceding period, the warrant recorded concerning torture of Rice for confession of housebreaking and theft had likewise allowed actual infliction of acute torture;[78] so in the present period did that recorded concerning Felton for 25th June, 1570: according to its own terms, primarily aimed to secure a confession of the statutory treason for which, afterwards, the examinate was tried and butchered.

Moreover, for the present period, evidence exists of like difference of treatment between people who were (as appears or at any rate seems likely) examined more for what in matters of treason they might reveal against others than for self-incrimination. Thus whilst the warrants recorded for the 19th of November, 1574, and the 6th of February, 1575, concerning respectively Nedeham and Cockyn, extended only to terrorization, that recorded for the 4th of December, 1577, concerning Sherwood, allowed recourse to the rack. But here matters assume a different complexion. Cockyn, we gather,[79] was promised that his informing against others would be kept secret, and there is no reason to suppose that the promise was insincere. Further, whilst—according to Sir Thomas Smith[80]—juries at ordinary trials would generally refuse to credit a witness's deposition, unless he was produced to testify, it is clear from the State Trials that in political cases written depositions might well be relied upon by the prosecution when it had no intention to call the witnesses concerned: in which case, although the use of torture might have been suggested by the accused as an explanation, he might well not have been able to make the suggestion weigh. Further, some suspects, once induced by torture to inculpate other persons, might have become ready to testify, truthfully or falsely, against them. Therefore, the fact that terrorization, but not actual torture, was authorized when some were questioned against others may well have possessed another underlying cause than concern about jury attitudes; this must militate against a view that such concern accounted for like moderation in certain cases of suspects examined to incriminate themselves.

chapter 6

FROM 1580 TO THE ACCESSION OF JAMES I

PART I
PARTICULAR WARRANTS

With the 1580s, Elizabethan England moved into crisis. The threat of foreign invasion became pressing. If it was realized, an associated domestic rebellion might result; also in association, or independently, an attempt to assassinate the Queen might occur. The sense of insecurity was inevitably heightened as a result of infiltration by English agents, trained abroad, of the Counter Reformation. In July, 1579, a Jesuit mission led by Nicholas Sanders had been established in Ireland; military rebellion, which ensued, was not put down until the end of 1580. By that time, the number of missionary priests, including Jesuits, in England itself reached about 110. In this context, the longer term effect became manifest of the Bull *Regnans in excelsis*. To those whose loyalty lay with the regime, and whose lives indeed depended upon its preservation, the preaching of Roman Catholicism—even if without express political reference—naturally seemed dangerous. Moreover, the Bull served to show that it was pregnant with treason.[1] Nor in this respect was the situation modified by an instruction of Gregory XIII just given to Jesuit missionaries, that the Bull would bind Roman Catholics only when its execution became possible.[2]

In these circumstances, it is not surprising that the Crown made use of all of those instruments that, de facto, were at its disposal for the discovery of its subjects who might attack or subvert it and of their strategies. Those instruments, as is seen from material reviewed in earlier chapters, included torture, and we have reached what, to judge from the relatively large quantity of evidence, was its English heyday. However, political or politico-religious suspects did not at this stage become its only target.

There is no firm evidence of use, during this period, of torture instructions under the Signet. In this part of chapter 6, we shall have to notice only Conciliar activity.

The first Conciliar record requiring mention here is of a warrant,[3] dated the 9th of December, 1580, that concerned a boy called Humfrey, belonging to the household of Sir Drew Drury and thought to have been privy to a theft from the latter's mansion. The warrant ordered that Humfrey, who had refused to name others involved, should be brought to do so by "some slight kinde of torture, such as may not touch the losse of any lymbe, as by whipping."

We confront the politico-religious situation with the record, for the 24th of December, 1580, of a warrant[4] to the Lieutenant of the Tower and the (Common) Law Officers. Three men—Harte, Bosgrave, and Pascall—were to be taken to the Tower and there examined: if necessary, terrorized by confrontation with the means of torture. Bosgrave was a Jesuit, Harte a priest, Pascall a Roman Catholic layman of good family.[5] The warrant indicated that they were subversive missionaries from Rome or elsewhere abroad. The matters for investigation against them were, however, intimated to its addressees in a separate document.

The next warrant[6] recorded—for the 3rd of May, 1581—informed the Lieutenant, Dr. John Hammond, and Thomas Norton of the arrest of Alexander Briant, whom it described as a "seminarie priest, or Jesuit", with treasonable documents upon him. It further instructed them to examine him about those documents. If he would not confess, they were first to seek to terrorize him with a sight of the means of torture at the Tower and then if he remained obstinate, to put him to torture.[7]

For the 22nd of June, 1581, another warrant, for the interrogation of a young person, is recorded.[8] This time, whipping was prescribed. On the other hand, the examinate was a girl,[9] and the case did have politico-religious reference. The Bishop of Chester was directed to have a "young mayden" who had published accounts of visions—evidently, somehow favorable to the Papal cause—secretly whipped to make her reveal her principals. If the warrant was received and executed, the prescribed secrecy may have spared her embarrassment; it may have avoided some risk of a riot in her favor; but it must, in any case, have been desirable from the Government's standpoint to prevent any whom she inculpated being forewarned that they would be pursued.

For the 30th of July, 1581, two warrants are recorded. One,[10] concerned Thomas Myagh, who had been brought from Ireland upon suspicion of complicity in rebellion there. It advised its addressees, the Lieutenant and Norton, that the Secretary for Ireland, Geoffrey Fenton, had been ordered to turn to them for the examination of this prisoner, to whose guilt witnesses had now been found in Ireland, although he himself had not confessed; it instructed them, if he persisted in denial, to put him, as far as they saw reason, to the rack.[11] The other[12] concerned the Jesuit, Thomas Campion. It instructed its addressees, who were the Lieutenant, Norton, and Robert Beale, that if he did not answer satisfactorily interrogatories accompanying it, he was to be put to the rack, and that two other priests, if they did not answer as required of them, were to be threatened with torture.

A warrant[13] recorded, for the 14th of August, 1581, as addressed to the Lieutenant, Hammond, and Beale, or any two of them, required terrorization, if necessary, of Campion; further, it contained a like requirement in respect of two priests—Forde and Peters—and it directed that John Payne, another priest, should be put to torture, since "vehement presumptions" existed against him.

For the 29th of October, 1581, a warrant is recorded[14] to put to the rack Campion, Forde, and other (in the record, unnamed) Tower prisoners. The addressees were the Lieutenant, the (Common) Law Officers, Hammond, Norton, and Thomas Wilkes.

A warrant[15] recorded for the 29th of April, 1582, ordered the examination of Thomas Alfield, a seminary priest, for discovery of the proceedings of missionaries within the realm, and—if in that behalf necessary—his torture by the rack. The addressees included the Lieutenant, Hammond, and Thomas Owen.

*   *   *   *

The Council records from June, 1582, to February, 1586, are lost. However, from this period, at least one Conciliar torture warrant is extant.[16] Dated the 8th of August, 1583, it is addressed to Doctors Aubrey, Jones, and J[ulius] Caesar, as Deputy Judges in Admiralty; its signatories are Burghley, Walsingham, F. Knollys, C. Hatton, and the Bishop of Lincoln, and it is in the following terms:

After our hartie commendacions. There hath today [been] delivered unto us by Edmonde Tirrey in the behalf of himself and others, the complaints and prooues herin enclosed, of some late pirracies comitted uppon the plaintiffs, by Clinton Atkinson and Pursar.[17] We praie yow uppon sight of the matters therin contained among other matters produced against the pirats, dilligentlie to examine them what are become of the goods by them taken from said plaintiffs, where and to what persones they have bestowed them, that therby the parties spoiled (undon by those pirracies) maie be in some sorte releiued, being earnestlie recomended unto us by the L. Generall of Monnster in the Realme of Irelande. And if the pirats shall refuse to discouer, how they haue employed the said goodes, yow maie trauell with them by the terror and torture of the rack in the Tower to draw them to confesse according to the direction of our late letters: wherin we praie yow that the case of these poore men maie be especiallie recomended unto yow. And so we bidd yow hartilie farewell.

Clearly, a complementary warrant to the Lieutenant of the Tower is likely to have been dispatched or the dispatch of such a warrant at least to have been in contemplation.

The interest of the warrant to the Admiralty deputies seems, in any case, considerable.

Although the Statute 28 H.VIII, c.15[18] may well not have induced any alteration of the character—when it was enacted, Civilian—borne by the preliminary investigations of piracy cases[19] (although, in other words, a slot may have remained into which judicial or quasi-judicial torture could have been fitted) had the Admiralty in Elizabeth's reign been treated as having inherent power to torture suspected pirates, we may imagine the Council encouraging use of that power, but not—in ordinary circumstances—feeling a need to authorize the deputies to have recourse to torture at the Tower.

To reconcile the hypothesis that the Admiralty was treated as having such power, with the existence of the present warrant is not, of course, impossible—but sufficient effort is required, at least, to encourage more caution than has sometimes been displayed in this area.

Two reconciliatory explanations occur to me; neither arouses my enthusiasm. First, it is possible that the pirates here in question had already been removed to the Tower and so were under the protection of the Lieutenant. However, the arrangement might have been awkward, since the Admiralty deputies evidently needed to be able to deal with them concerning civil claims; nor do we have any evidence of such a removal. Second, the Admiralty may have assumed power to torture for confession of piracy, but not for the discovery of goods piratically stolen, which is the main concern revealed by the warrant. However, torture for such discovery presumably could have been encapsuled within an inquiry after accomplices, which Continental doctrine certainly would have allowed to be pursued by judicial torture.[20]

The possibility may also be considered that whatever the position regarding preliminary criminal investigation of piracy cases, the Admiralty under Elizabeth employed torture, within limits commonly allowed by Continental doctrine, in examining those against whom pecuniary claims were based on delict.[21] Here again, the present warrant presents a contrary argument, and here again, the above explanations might be adduced in response.

*   *   *   *

For the 10th of April, 1586, a warrant is recorded[22] from the Council to the Lieutenant of the Tower, Richard Young, and one other person, ordering the reexamination of a Matthew Beaumont, concerning a robbery committed against a lady of title and concerning other robberies of which he was supposed to have knowledge. If he proved obstinate, he was to be tortured "in some reasonable manner" on the rack. There follows the record, for the 17th of April, of a warrant[23] to the same addressees, for torture on the rack of a William Wakeman, alias Oavys, to make him confess "misdemeanoures and robberies" charged against him and inculpate any others of whose offenses he was aware. Then for the 13th of May, a warrant[24] is recorded requiring the Lieutenant to transfer from the Tower to Newgate, where they were to await trial, three notorious felons, Beaumont, Wakeman, and another man called Pinder or Pudsey. The warrant explained that they had been sent to the Tower for torture to discover what felonies they had committed and with what accomplices. So a torture warrant presumably had issued also in respect of Pinder, although in his case, no record of such a thing appears.

With the next record, we return to political crime. It is of a warrant[25] dated the 23rd of December, 1586, which was addressed to the Lieutenant and several others, including the (Common) Law Officers, and directed the examination of various persons (whose names, listed in a schedule, show the proceedings to have arisen out of the Babington

Plot:[26] to which I return in part II (III) of this chapter) upon charges of treason, ordering that they were to be put to the rack as seemed to the addressees convenient.

For the 24th of April, 1587, the record is found of a letter[27] addressed to the Lieutenant, Young, and others. It advised them that an "Andreas Van Metter" was charged with a matter affecting the Queen's person and the State, but refused to confess; it instructed them that if he remained obstinate, they should put him to the "accustomed" torture of the rack as often as they thought necessary to obtain a full revelation of his knowledge in the matter.[28]

Next, a warrant is recorded[29] for the 7th of January, 1588, also including among its addressees the Lieutenant and Young. It required the examination of persons, especially one John Staughton and one Humphrey Fulwood, who were going to be charged with "disobedience, misbehaviour, and practices against the state and present government," and if they were obstinate, their transfer to the Tower to be put to "the racke and torture."

For the 14th of January, 1588, a warrant[30] is recorded the addressees of which were the Lieutenant and others—including Young, Owen and William Wade. It required them to examine, with "the Rack and torture," one Roger Asheton, who was believed an associate of Sir William Stanley: Stanley was a captain who had changed sides in the Low Countries, where Elizabeth's Government was supporting the Northern Provinces in their war of independence against Spain. This warrant explained that Asheton was refusing with obstinacy to "utter anie thinge concerning her Majestie or the State."

For the 16th of February, following, a warrant[31] is recorded addressed to the Lieutenant and to others including Young, Owen, and Wade. It ordered them to interrogate, if necessary by the rack, one George Stoker: it explained that he had been caught after being with the enemy in the Low Countries and then entering England; that he was known to have received money from the King of Spain; and that there seemed a likelihood of his having entered the realm bent upon some political mischief.

Then for the 8th of September, 1588—that is, after the defeat of the Armada—a warrant[32] is recorded to addressees including the Lieutenant, Young, and Richard Topcliffe. It was for the transfer to the Tower and the examination there, with torture at the addressees' pleasure, of a man called Tristram Winslade, who had been taken in Pedro de Valdez's galleon, the *Capitana*: the first casualty among the Spanish squadrons.

It is revealed by a letter[33] of the Council recorded for the 24th of February, 1590, that Winslade was indeed put to the rack, but was found to have been with the Spaniards against his will.

The next Conciliar record requiring notice here is of a warrant issued on the 24th of June, 1589, to Richard Young, who had arrested a goldsmith upon suspicion of complicity in a theft of plate from a lady of title. The suspicion was described in the warrant as founded upon the goldsmith's bad character, as shown by his past behavior and upon "present great assumptions." The Council directed his removal to Bridewell and his subjection there to "the torture of the House" in "such sort and measure" as Young thought fit.

For the 24th of August, 1589, a warrant[34] is recorded that was addressed to the Master of the Wardrobe, the Master of St. Katherine's, and the Recorder of London: although if the first-named was not in London, the others were directed to co-opt Young. It was for the interrogation at Bridewell of a printer and two of his assistants, who had all three been arrested near Manchester by the Earl of Derby for printing the Marprelate Tracts,[35] and had so far resisted questioning. If they remained obstinate, they were to be put to torture and would be removed to the Tower: the intended sense probably was that they would be removed to the Tower and were there to be tortured, although such is hardly the natural construction of the record.

Next we must notice two drafts[36] for Conciliar warrants. A record in the *Acts of the Privy Council*, for the 1st of February, 1590, is of a letter directing the (Common) Law Officers to receive from Topcliffe information against "two or three Jesuits or seminars," to consider it, and then to consult about it the Lord Chief Justice and other justices of the Queen's Bench, proceeding to a prosecution if there appeared grounds therefor. Probably, it concerned the same matter. Both of the drafts refer to a seminary priest, Christopher Bayles; his brother John, who was a tailor; Henry Goorney, who was an haberdasher; and two yeomen, Anthony Kaye and John Coxed. The first draft is of a warrant to the Keeper of Bridewell, requiring him to receive all of them into his custody and to allow none to visit them except Topcliffe and Young, who had been appointed to examine them. The other draft is of a warrant to Topcliffe and Young—Topcliffe is named first—directing them:

> to examyne the sayd persons . . . from tyme to tyme, and if they see furder occacyon to remytte them or any of them unto such torture upon

the wawle as is usualle for the better understanding of the trowthe of
matters against her Majesty and the stayte.

The date of these drafts cannot be precisely fixed, but in the *Calendar
of State Papers, Domestic*, they are tentatively assigned to the 1st of
February, 1590. If Bayles, in fact, was one of the priests mentioned in
the Council's letter that is recorded for the latter date, evidently the
Law Officers must have reported that against him and his lay associates,
the existing evidence would not suffice. Anyway, it appears[37] that Bayles
was among priests who, with various of their associates, were condemned before a commission of jail delivery at Newgate, on the 22nd
or 23rd of February, 1590, and that he was one of four among them
who on the latter date were respited: whether or not, for further interrogation. At the time, Roman Catholics believed that Bayles had been
cruelly tortured, by suspension: Robert Southwell, in his report of March,
1590,[38] said that the unfortunate man had been hung up by the hands
for twenty-four hours, with only the tips of his toes touching the ground.

For the 18th of April, 1590, a warrant[39] is recorded that was addressed
to Young. It recognized the care with which he had examined four men,
whom he had committed to Newgate upon suspicion of a robbery that
had occurred in Kent; on the ground that although they would not confess
the offense, the "proofs" were "manifest and evident against them."
it authorized and directed their transfer to Bridewell and directed Young
to obtain the assistance of some of the justices in reexamining them
and, if they would not name their accomplices and confess the whole
truth of the offense, to cause them to be put to the "rack and torture
of the manacles". A postscript required special attention, in the use of
torture, to be paid to one of the men, a butcher called William Brown.

Then a warrant[40] is recorded for the 10th of January, 1591, as having
been addressed to the Lieutenant and, among others, Topcliffe, Beale,
and Dr. Fletcher. They, or no less than three of them, were to examine
a seminary priest, George Beesley (or Passelaw), and one Robert Humberson, who had been his companion, as well as any who came under
suspicion of having assisted either of them. The examination of the two
named prisoners was to be based, first, upon information to be supplied
by Topcliffe; if any of those examined proved obstinate, they were to
be consigned to Little Ease[41] or some other dungeon incarceration in
which was commonly used to aid interrogation of prisoners.

For the 20th of July, 1591, we find recorded a Conciliar warrant[42] addressed to Owen and Young. It concerned the Protestant madman William Hacket, whose blasphemous and seditious ranting and gesticulating were squeezed by the Common Lawyers within the bounds of treason, and whom the Council at this time committed to Bridewell.[43] Owen and Young were directed to go there and, with a view of discovering fully what had been Hacket's purpose and who had aided and abetted him or had been accessories before his misconduct, to examine him with the assistance of such Queen's counsel or others as they chose, putting him at their discretion to the manacles[44] or other torture.

Next a warrant[45] is recorded for the 25th of October, 1591, which was addressed to, among others, Topcliffe and Fletcher. It ordered the very strict examination of Eustace White, a seminary priest, and of one Brian Lassey (Lacey), who it said was a distributor of letters to Papists and similar ill-disposed subjects;[46] and further, that if they refused to answer, they should be put to "the manacles and soche other tortures as are used in Bridewell."

For the 27th of October—two days later—a warrant[47] is recorded that was addressed to the (Common) Law Officers, who were to examine Thomas Clynton, a prisoner in the Fleet, and if he did not satisfactorily respond, were to remove him to Bridewell: to be put to "the manacles and soche torture as ys there used."[48]

Then for the 4th of June, 1592, a warrant[49] is recorded that directed the removal of an Irishman, Owen Edmondes, from the Marshalsea Prison to Bridewell. It declared that "good proof" existed against him on grave political charges, but that he had so far refused to confess; it ordered his further examination at Bridewell, with his submission, in the event of continued obstinacy, to the "torture accustomed in suche cases."

Recorded for the 8th of February, 1593, is a warrant[50] by which three men, called Urmstone, Bagshawe, and Ashe, were ordered to be transferred from the Gatehouse and Newgate to Bridewell and there, in case of need, to be subjected to the torture. The addressees, one of whom was Young, were to act regarding them in accordance with such instructions as might be received from the (Common) Law Officers. Bagshawe and Ashe had been acting as couriers to missionary priests and had a little earlier been arrested in Derbyshire, whilst Urmstone was a Lancashire recusant, thought able to supply intelligence important to State security.[51]

Next we have a record concerning a matter very different, although still of a political nature. A warrant[52] dated the 16th of April, 1593, was addressed to the Lord Mayor of London, whom it ordered to examine an apprentice he had arrested upon suspicion of having written a placard. According to the warrant, the placard concerned had been posted in London and had announced that the apprentices would attempt violence against the foreigners within the City. The Lord Mayor was directed, if he found strong proof of the apprentice's guilt, yet could not obtain his confession, to employ in that behalf the "torture used in like cases."

The issue of another warrant,[53] recorded for the 11th of May, 1593, evidently was occasioned by unrest comprising the offense laid at the door of the Lord Mayor's young prisoner. It mentioned that "divers lewd and notorious libells" had been posted in the City, the worst of them being one that had appeared on the wall of the Dutch churchyard; it directed that persons open to suspicion of responsibility in those matters should be sought, apprehended, and examined: moreover that, if they seemed guilty, yet would not otherwise confess, they should be put to the torture in Bridewell, as often as seemed fit. The addressees included Sir Richard Martin (an alderman who was Warden of the Mint, and Master of the Mint) and Anthony Ashley. The record suggests, but does not make clear, that the reference was to a specific Bridewell form of torture.

A break in the extant Council records occurs from the 26th of August, 1593, to the 1st of October, 1595. Thereafter, for the 12th of November, 1595, a warrant[54] is recorded that was addressed to the Solicitor-General and Wade. It recited that one Gabriel Coleford—who carried into the realm seditious books and messages from the refugees overseas—had recently been arrested along with one Thomas Fawlkes (Foulkes), a Fleet Street tailor with whom Coleford had lodged, that neither of them had divulged such information as he possessed affecting State security; it ordered that they should be put to the torture of the manacles, in Bridewell. A further record, for the 5th of July, 1596, is of a warrant[55] directing Coleford's release upon terms and reciting that he had been put to torture, but he still had not confessed.

For the 25th of January, 1596, a warrant[56] is recorded sent to Sir Thomas Wilkes and Wade, concerning a young Frenchman called John Hardie, who was in Bridewell. Various documents had been found sewn in his doublet. Their purport, apparently, was not clear; as a result, he had fallen under suspicion of some hostile political purpose. The warrant announced the Queen's pleasure therefore to be that he should be further examined and directed that if suspicions formed against him about matter regarding which he failed to tell the truth, he should "by authoritie hereof" be put to the "ordinarie torture" in Bridewell.

Then for the last day of February, 1596, a letter[57] is recorded that was addressed to Sir Richard Martin. It thanked him for having arrested and interrogated one Humphrey Hodges who had not yet revealed what happened to one hundred pounds, which had been buried, and it authorized him to put Hodges to the manacles and so obtain a full disclosure. Seemingly, Hodges's arrest had been for theft from a gentleman on Crown service.[58]

A warrant recorded for the 21st of November, 1596, had among its addressees the Recorder of London and Topcliffe. It authorized torture by the manacles, in Bridewell, of some—who had been brought to London—out of about eighty gypsies arrested in Northamptonshire.[59]

Next is the case of Richard Bradshaw and Robert Burton, which played a considerable part in founding the Common Law doctrine that treason may be committed, constructively, by tumult aimed at a public and general result,[60] but we are concerned with an earlier stage in the proceedings. In Oxfordshire an unlawful assembly had occurred of persons intending to destroy enclosures,[61] and Bradshaw and Burton and two other ringleaders had been sent to London, where they had been lodged in different prisons. For the 19th of December, 1596, a warrant[62] is recorded as issued concerning the four to the (Common) Law Officers—Coke was Attorney-General—to Francis Bacon and to the Recorder of London. The addressees were to examine them and, if they saw cause, have them transferred to Bridewell, there to be put to the manacles.

Then for the 2nd of February, 1597, a warrant[63] is recorded as having been issued to the (Common) Law Officers—Coke, of course, remained Attorney-General—to Francis Bacon and to Wade, directing them to put to the manacles or torture of the rack one William Tomson, "charged to have a purpose to burnne Her Majestie's shipps, or to do some notable villanye," in order to make him reveal his aims and accomplices. Also for that date, the issue is recorded of a warrant[64] addressed to the Lieutenant of the Tower to receive Tompson into close custody.

For the 13th of April, 1597, a warrant is recorded[65] explaining that "Gerratt" (John Gerard), a Jesuit, had been committed to the Tower by the Queen, and directing that he should be examined carefully about letters from the Low Countries and other matters affecting State security and should, if unwilling to reveal the truth—as, the warrant asserted, his allegiance required—be put to the manacles and "suche other torture as is used" at the Tower.

Next a warrant[66] is recorded for the 1st of December, 1597, that authorized its seven addressees—among whom were the Recorder of London and Topcliffe—or any two of them to put to the torture of the manacles, if he would not otherwise confess, one Thomas Travers, whom witnesses had indicated to be guilty of stealing an inkstand belonging to the Queen. The warrant mentioned that he was held in Bridewell.

A warrant[67] recorded for the 17th of the same month referred to scandalous suspicions. The corpse of Richard Aunger, a senior member of Gray's Inn, had been found floating in the Thames. He had disappeared some weeks earlier. Examination of the corpse by surgeons had left a possibility that he had been strangled, or otherwise murdered, and the corpse thereafter thrown into the river. Witnesses had been sought, and a protracted investigation had taken place. In the end, it had been felt that Aunger might well have been murdered by one of his sons with a porter of Gray's Inn; yet not enough evidence seemed available to allow their prosecution. The recorded warrant was addressed to the Recorder of London, Topcliffe, and others. It directed that the suspects should be examined and, if they could not otherwise be brought to confess, should either or both of them be put to the manacles in Bridewell.

For the 17th of April, 1598, a warrant[68] is recorded that was addressed to the Solicitor-General, Serjeant Fleming, Wade, and Francis Bacon. It concerned one Valentine Thomas, who had entered the realm from Scotland and was charged with political offenses. The Council was dissatisfied with his answer to questioning and now directed that he should be further interrogated concerning his own guilt and his accomplices and should be subjected, if necessary, to torture by the manacles in Bridewell. Subsequently, an announcement was made by royal proclamation[69] that he had "without torture, menace or persuasion" declared that he had intended—in pursuance of a plan made with King James—to assassinate the Queen.

Then recorded for the 4th of January, 1599, is a warrant[70] that was addressed to the Lieutenant and Topcliffe, requiring them to cause the committal to Bridewell of men named Richard Denton and Peter Cooper, who—following secret intelligence—were believed privy to some plot against the person of the Queen and the State. They were to be strictly examined and, as far as necessary to make them specific in confession, subjected to torture by the manacles.

Finally, we find recorded for the 21st of April, 1601, a warrant[71] addressed to Wade and another person concerning a scrivener's youthful employee, called Howson, who had written and distributed seditious libels and was in Bridewell for his pains. The Council wanted to know who had been his principals and with whom otherwise he had dealt in the matter, but so far, he had resisted interrogation. The warrant directed that he should be further examined and, if necessary, put to the manacles.

PART II
FURTHER INFORMATION AND
INTERPRETATION

I. FROM 1580 TO MAY, 1582

For the period from the beginning of 1580 to May, 1582, indications from the *Acts of the Privy Council* may be supplemented by entries from an unofficial source, although one, in places, of uncertain reliability: the Diary, of events concerning Roman Catholic priests and some Roman Catholic laymen at the Tower, which is attributed to Edward Rishton,[72] and was appended to Nicholas Sanders's *De origine ac progressu schismatis Anglicani* when that work appeared under Rishton's editorship.[73]

The Diary records various instances of ill-treatment, some of an acute, others of a chronic, nature. Acute physical oppression of which it informs us would seem to have had an interrogatory purpose. Most instances it gives of chronic ill-treatment appear, or appear probably, to have been coercive. On the other hand, whether where that character emerges the aim was to promote interrogation or to induce doctrinal submission cannot always well be judged.

Regarding acute torture, apart from proceedings with Briant, Campion, and Payne,[74] which were expressly contemplated by Conciliar warrants of which we have a record, the Diary notes—

1. for the 10th of December, 1580, that two priests, Thomas Cotam

and Luke Kirby, were subjected for more than an hour to the "Scavenger's Daughter";[75]

2. for later in the same month, that another priest, Ralph Sherwin, was twice racked;[76]

3. for the third of January, 1581, that a priest called Christopher Thompson was twice racked on the day of his arrival at the Tower;

4. for the 27th of March, 1581, that Briant[77] was interrogated, sharp needles being thrust under his finger nails;

5. for the 5th of March, 1582, that a zealously Roman Catholic layman, called Anthony Fugatius Lusitan, had died, and that when already dying he had (a few days earlier) been released from the Tower after two years' imprisonment there, during which he had supported very severe passages on the rack.

Torture by needles under the nails was a method at the time attributed to the Turks.[78]

The spectrum regarding chronic ill-treatment may be partly illustrated by citing entries regarding Briant, one of which embodies also the reference above noticed to acute torture with needles, whilst another also reports his having been racked. We find the following:

27th of March, 1581: Alexander Briant, a priest, is thrown into the Tower from another prison, where he had been almost killed by thirst, and for two days is loaded with the heaviest ankle-irons. Then the sharpest needles were thrust under his finger-nails, to make him confess where he had seen Father Parsons: to admit which, however, he refused with the greatest determination.[79] 6th of April, 1581:[80] The said Briant is thrown into the Tank,[81] and after eight days he was brought thereout to the rack, which he suffered worst of all—once that day, and twice the day following . . .[82]

21st of November, 1581: . . . After his condemnation, they shackled for two days with ankle-irons Alexander Briant, because he secretly shaved his crown . . . and made himself a wooden cross. . . .[83]

A contemporary tract,*The Declaration of the Favourable Dealing* . . .[84] refers to Briant's having been starved, although it asserts that the motive was not to aid his interrogation, but to obtain a sample of his handwriting, which (contrary, as it declares, to his duty) he had refused. He was told that he would receive no food until he wrote to his keeper, requesting some.

*   *   *   *

The Diary is not concerned with prisoners such as Thomas Myagh. However, regarding his treatment before the issue of the warrant, for his torture, which as we have seen is recorded for the 30th of July, 1581, we have presently relevant evidence from other sources.

It appears that upon Walsingham's instructions, he suffered a torture regarded as less severe than the rack; no indication can be found that the Council lent its authority for the proceeding: if not, whether the Secretary, proceeding informally, took the matter entirely upon himself, or whether he first consulted with the Queen, or even the Signet was used, we do not know.

The evidence is as follows: On the 10th of March, 1581, the Lieutenant of the Tower and Hammond wrote to Walsingham. In their letter[85] they relate:

> We have made twoo severall examinations of Thomas Myaghe, wherein we finde nothing but an improbable tale full of suspicion, not mutche encreased by reporte of further matter than heretofore he hathe declared to Your Honour, as by the examinations whiche we sende herewith maie appeare. We have forborne to putt hym in Skeuington's Yrons,[86] for that we received chardge from yow to examine hym with secrecie, whiche in that sorte we could not do, that maner of dealinge requiringe the presence and ayde of one of the jaylors all the tyme that he shall be in those yrons, and in this examination; and besides, we finde the man so resolute, as in our opinions little will be wroonge out of hym but by some sharper torture.

They continued, however, with an assurance that they were ready to do anything the Secretary might wish, and it seems that he insisted upon use of "Skevington's Irons", for we have another letter,[87] written to him by the Lieutenant and Hammond on the 17th of March, containing the following passage:

> We have agayne made twoo severall examinations of Thomas Myaghe, and notwithstandinge that we have made triall of hym by the torture of Skevington's Yrons, and with so mutche sharpenes as was in our judgement for the man and his cause convenient, yet can we gett from hym no farther matter then we have sent herewith in writinge. Of the man we thincke as we dyd before, that he can hardlie be innocent . . .

Moreover, an inscription[88] in the Tower of London harmonizes—except that it suggests a claim to innocence—with the latter passage:

Thomas Miagh, which liethe here alone, That fayne wold from hens
begon; By torture straunge mi trouth was tryed, Yet of my libertie denied.
1581.   THOMAS MYAGH.

II. FROM MAY, 1582, TO MARCH, 1586

For the period of the gap, already mentioned, in the Council records,
we must notice State Papers referring to what is called the "Throgmorton
Plot" and—some with the same, some with other, reference—more
entries in Rishton's Diary.

In the early 1580s, the Duke of Guise entertained the project of
invading Scotland. He received encouragement mainly from Spain and
the Papacy. Walsingham learned through his agents of signs that something of the sort was afoot, but he wrongly supposed France to be the
European power primarily involved. In the first half of 1583, events in
Scotland compelled a revision of the Duke's plan, which was extended
to envisage concurrent invasions of Scotland and England. After this,
Francis Throgmorton was recruited to promote the revised plan as far
as it concerned the southern realm. Fortunately for Elizabeth's regime,
he had some dealings with the French Ambassador, whom (not the
Spanish Ambassador, Mendoza, who was the true diplomatic agent of
the plot) Walsingham was having watched;[89] so he came to be placed
under surveillance. In November, 1583, he was arrested.[90]

Apparently, he was found to have in his possession a list of the
principal ports in England and particulars of the more important Roman
Catholics living in or near to each. His first reaction was to claim that
this matter had been planted on him.[91] He managed to send to Mendoza,
on a playing card (in those days, a sizable object), a cipher message
declaring that he would endure anything rather than inform against
others.[92] Moreover, he tried to make good that undertaking. The story
of his eventual failure, and how it was procured, is usually derived from
a treatise in justification of the proceedings taken with him—evidently,
an intended official account—that exists among the State Papers[93] and
from a letter, which also they include[94] and which was written, on the
18th of November, 1583, by Walsingham to Thomas Wilkes (a Clerk of
the Council). The result of these two sources may be summarized as
follows:

After his arrest, Throgmorton was interrogated. When he would reveal
nothing, he was shown the rack and told that he had a choice between

torture and, by answering satisfactorily without it, obtaining a pardon. He vacillated. The situation was referred to the Queen, who agreed that the Council should, if necessary, put him to torture. Again, he was offered a pardon as the reward for full disclosure and again, he refused. So he was put to the rack, but on the first occasion, he did not submit. Walsingham was undismayed. In his letter to Wilkes, he said that he had seen men as resolute as Throgmorton eventually overcome, and that when the torture was repeated, it would probably work without any need to go to extremes: accordingly, he directed Wilkes to bring Thomas Norton to the Tower, early on the 19th of November, when the torture would resume. His prediction proved correct. Throgmorton was again put on the rack, but before any great severity had been displayed— "before he was strained to any purpose"—he yielded.[95]

What he had to say revealed in detail the most dangerous part of a highly dangerous plot, the full nature of which had not previously been suspected.[96]

Complete reliance obviously cannot be placed upon the official account of what transpired, but having regard to Walsingham's letter, it is likely that Throgmorton was racked on the 19th of November, although of course there may have been a postponement. Rishton's Diary refers to the treatment of Throgmorton, yet gives other dates. On the other hand, Rishton, himself a prisoner and dependent for information upon warders or other prisoners, did not necessarily get everything right. The Diary's account is that Throgmorton was taken to the Tower on the 13th of November, 1583, and was at first kept in Little Ease;[97] that on the 23rd of November, he was twice very severely racked; and that on the 2nd of December, he was twice racked again.

What Throgmorton had disclosed, and perhaps the fact that he had disclosed it only after torture, sealed his own fate. In December, 1583, he was condemned and executed. However, he had by his confession inculpated others: indeed, anyone on his list of Roman Catholics with residences in or near ports was bound to fall under some suspicion. The plot, at the time of Throgmorton's arrest, had contemplated a landing at Arundel. The Earl of Northumberland was one of those listed as having a residence in the vicinity of that port; by the 12th of February, 1584, he was imprisoned in the Tower. Walsingham seems to have been interested in exploring this opportunity to destroy him,[98] and a memorandum of the above date,[99] partly in Walsingham's hand, addressed to commissioners appointed by the Council to investigate the plot, inter alia contemplates the racking of two Roman Catholic gentlemen, William Shelley and Jervais Pierpoint: of whom the former was, like the Earl, in Throgmorton's list as having a residence near Arundel, whilst a marriage of the latter's daughter to the Earl's son seemingly had been urged by one of the plotters, Charles Arundel,[100] who had fled the realm upon Throgmorton's arrest. Walsingham suggested that Shelley could probably provide evidence against the Earl. Pierpoint had been, at any rate since 1582, a prisoner in the Marshalsea; he was evidently an enthusiastic Roman Catholic, who had been well able from that prison to maintain fraternal communications with the outside and even with prisoners in the Tower.[101] However, no evidence suggests that either of these two suspects was in fact tortured.

The Duke of Guise's plot was not the only one brought to light in 1583. Also during that year, a hot-headed young Roman Catholic, John Somerville, left Warwickshire with the intention of assassinating the Queen. He had received encouragement from his father-in-law and mother-in-law (a local squire, Edward Arden, and his wife, Marie) and from a priest, Hugh Hall. He was apprehended, and he and the others, brought to London for examination by the Council, were condemned of high treason at the Guildhall on the 16th of December 1583. On the 19th of December, Arden was taken from the Tower to Newgate, to await execution. It was reported that Somerville had been taken there as well, for the same purpose, but two hours after his arrival had been found to have strangled himself. On the 20th of December, Arden was executed.[102] Hall avoided this fate.[103] It is supposed that he bought his life by supplying information.[104] According to Rishton's Diary, when Throgmorton was racked on—the Diary has it—the 23rd of November, 1583, Arden also was tortured—on the same day and the same rack— whilst Hall was put to the rack on the following day. If Hall indeed was racked, it may be conjectured that he did not submit and seemed unlikely to do so, since otherwise his supposed bargain for his life would not have had much substance. The Diary does not mention torture of Somerville.

Of the other entries in the Diary that here require attention, two concern acute torture. The first, taking us further back in time, records that in September, 1582, John Getter, a young layman who had been captured when returning from France, was tortured in the Scavenger's Daughter and thereafter, having rested in the Tank, was killed by the rack; the second relates that in February, 1584, a priest called Robert Nutter twice suffered in the Scavenger's Daughter.

According to the Diary, Nutter was thus tortured towards the end of passing forty-seven days in the Tank: later in the year, he was sent there for another spell, this time of two months and fourteen days. It mentions further instances in which prisoners went there; some, in which prisoners were shackled. It indicates that the one treatment might follow the other,[105] and it reports that in 1584 three suffered both treatments at once,[106] as well as that, in the same year, Thomas Stevenson, a priest, being shackled, was for much of the time in addition deprived of bedding. However, the most remarkable case of chronic duress that it alleges was in the case of another priest, Stephen Rausam, who, according to an entry for the 14th of August, 1582, ''is locked up in Little Ease: where he remained for eighteen months and thirteen days.''[107] The change of tense would convey that Rausam's consignment to Little Ease began in August, 1582, the entry having been completed after his release. If so, he must have been in the place concerned when, according to the Diary, Throgmorton was sent there; since the Diary in a preface describes the place as a very small cell or hole, one would prefer to believe that two people were not kept in it at once, although such a thing may of course have happened.[108]

III. THE "BABINGTON" PLOT

The Conciliar warrant[109] for torture of ten suspects, which (as noticed in part I of this chapter) was recorded for the 23rd of December, 1586, may be taken to represent activity that was an aftermath of the so-called ''Babington'' plot and was guided by depositions obtained from its principals, especially Anthony Babington himself. How had those principals fared at the hands of the Government?

The true, main architect of the plot was John Ballard.[110] The plan he sought to promote had emerged from meetings at Rheims, in 1585, between persons including William Gifford, the Archbishop of that place, Gilbert Gifford—secretly, an instrument of Walsingham—and one John Savage. Part of the intent was to assassinate the Queen, and Savage came to England to perform that deed. Also in England, Ballard won over Babington, who recruited a small following of young Roman Catholics. However, both Ballard and Babington came under Walsingham's surveillance. Further, Walsingham was successfully intercepting Mary Stuart's confidential mail, and this eventually included a letter by her to Babington, his reply, and—as the Government claimed—another letter by her in response. This last letter formed the principal evidence against Mary, when she was brought to trial under Statute 27 Eliz.I, c.1. Ballard was arrested in London on the 4th of August, 1586. Babington, the following day, gave some of Walsingham's servants the slip and fled to St. John's Wood, where he and a number of confederates hid until hunger forced them to seek help from the Roman Catholic household of Mrs. Catherine Bellamy, at Harrow. There, on the 14th of August, not only Babington and his companions, but Mrs. Bellamy and her two sons were arrested, and afterwards various suspects were taken, individually, in various places. A priest, Anthony Tyrell, who was among them, informed against all and sundry;[111] an explanation of this, entertained in his favor by contemporary Roman Catholic society,[112] was that he had been overcome by the sight of Ballard, crippled by torture, being carried in a chair to fresh examination. Again, according to a story accepted by the Jesuit William Weston,[113] one of Mrs. Bellamy's sons, Thomas, died on the rack, although the authorities afterwards represented that he had hanged himself. Evidently, what such stories offer regarding the treatment of Ballard and Thomas Bellamy can be neither trusted nor ignored. The warrant recorded for the 23rd of December, 1586, is sufficient encouragement to believe that the Council had tortured any of the principal plotters who had fallen into its hands and whom it thought to be withholding information. On the other hand, that warrant authorized recourse to torture only if "the truth might not by convenient means be gotten," and Babington[114] and Savage,[115] at any rate, had willingly confessed everything they knew.

Weston himself, although arrested on the 3rd of August, 1586, and evidently suspected on general grounds of some privity to the plot (but probably not inculpated by any other suspect), was not tortured.[116]

IV. GERARD: THE EXECUTION OF THE WARRANT

Gerard's experiences consequent upon the warrant recorded for the 13th of April, 1597,[117] are described in what is called hereafter the (Gerard) "autobiography": a Latin account of Gerard's life, purporting to be (and quite probably being, at any rate in the main) his own work, which is supposed to have been written in or about 1609. The text, as it stands in one eighteenth-century manuscript, is readily available in English translation.[118] We gather from it that examination in pursuance of the warrant was at the Lieutenant's Lodging and, on the first occasion, by the addressees with the assistance of Coke, then Attorney-General.

Gerard previously had been examined by Wade, who now assumed the role of *Procurateur de la Reine*, while Coke discharged that of *greffier*.[119] The first examination culminated with questions about the whereabouts of the principal Jesuit, Garnet. When Gerard refused to answer them, the warrant was produced—the autobiography explains that, at the Tower, no one might be tortured without an express warrant in that behalf— and thereupon he was taken to a torture chamber, where he was suspended in the manacles. When it was clear that he was determined to resist, his questioners left, although Wade returned once, to demand unsuccessfully his submission. At long last, he was taken back to his chamber for the night. On the following day, he was conducted once more to the Lodging, but on this occasion he confronted only Wade, who renewed the questioning about Garnet. Once more, he refused to answer, and Wade put him in the charge of the Master of the Ordnance, sending him for torture that was to be repeated twice daily until he answered. But already, on this second day, the effects of suspension were so severe that it was thought he was dying, and the Lieutenant was summoned and took charge. Although he would not submit, he was not tortured on any later day.[120]

V. SOUTHWELL, ROBERT FAWKES, AND LOPEZ

Two State letters require attention. The first,[121] written by Topcliffe to the Queen on the 22nd of June, 1592, proposes torture of Robert Southwell, the Jesuit, who had himself by that time been taken. What we have to here concern us is as follows:

Most gracious Sovreiynn havinge . . . Robert Southwell . . . in my stronge chamber in Westminster church yarde I have maede him assured for startinge, or hurtinge of hym self, By puttinge upon his armes a pair of hande gyves: & there, & so can keepe hym eather from view or conference with any, But Nicolas ye underkeeper of the Gaethouse & my boys. . . . It is good foorthwith to enforce him to answer trewlye, & directlye, & so to prove his answers trewe in hart, to the Ende that, such as bee deeply concirned in his treacheries have not tyme to start, or mayke shifte—To use any meanes in comon prisons eather to stande upon or against the wawle (whiche above all thinges exceedeth & hurteth not) will gyve warninge. But if your highness pleasure be to knowe any thinge in his hartte, To stande against the wawle, his feett standinge upon the grounde, & his handes But as highe as he can wratche against ye wawle.

Lyk a Tryck at Trenchmoare, will inforce hym to tell all, & the trewthe
proved by the seqwelle. . . . [122]

It thus appears that the Queen at first interested herself directly in
Southwell's case, bypassing the Council. Seemingly, according to contemporary Jesuit intelligence,[123] Topcliffe in his own house tortured
Southwell—not merely against a wall, but by suspending him in the
manacles (hand gyves)—but obtained no success, whereupon the Queen
ordered the Council to take the matter in hand, and they sent Wade
who, on the 27th or 28th of June, 1592, took matters under his own
control, having Southwell removed next door, to the Gatehouse Prison.
Assuming so much, it is likely that when the Council intervened, it
issued a warrant to Wade and Topcliffe, for the latter was reported[124]
to have said, at Southwell's trial, that he had the Council's letter to
prove that he had been authorized to torture the prisoner, short of death
or maim. Anyway, there is matter for consideration if Southwell indeed
was, for further interrogation, removed from Topcliffe's house to the
Gatehouse, not straight to the Tower: where he was imprisoned before
his trial.[125]

The second letter[126] was written by Richard Young to the Lord Keeper,
Puckering, on the 23rd of December, 1592. The following extracts will
suffice for our purpose:

Mr. Bowyer and I have taken paynes in the Examininge of Ric. Webster
and Robert Vaukes, and did first seeke by all meanes to drawe from them
quickly and curteously what could bee done for her Maiesties service
without Torture. and the said Webster confessed that hee was maried in
the marshalsea about three or four yeares past by George Bisley the
prieste. . . .

The said Fawkes confesseth that about three or four yeares paste before
hee was committed to prison hee gave to one Forreste a priest a gray
nagge with saddle and bridle. . . . And the said Webster and Faukes
being examined concerninge the speeches and matters obiected against
them by Ric. Stone they doe both flatly denye them, whereupon wee did
putt Fawkes to the torture for awhile but could not by any meanes draw
any further matter from him, and as for Webster wee thought good to
acquainte Mr. Attorney with his voluntary confession before wee would
putt him to the torture, and Mr. Attorney is of opynion that he hath
confessed yneughe to touche his life, and gathereth by presumpcions that
he is giltie of the accusacions againste him, and so the matter resteth. . . .

The writers assumed their primary object, "for her Maiesties service," to have been the eliciting of confessions sufficient to procure condemnation of the examinates at Common Law. The fact that they addressed their letter to the Lord Keeper may hint that, once again, the Queen's direct authority had been employed, and the Council bypassed.

A little more than a year later, we gather that in another case, torture was not used or even threatened: in the light of Young's above noticed letter to Puckering about Webster and Fawkes, the probable inference is that it was not needed. A letter[127] was written, on the 28th of February, 1594, by Thomas Cecil to Thomas Windebank. Its subject was Dr. Robert Lopez, who had been indicted of planning—with two associates, and in pursuance of a plot hatched with the King of Spain—to poison the Queen. According to Cecil, Lopez, who had been tried on that day, at first admitted—in accordance with confessions he had made before his trial—that he had talked with the King about the possibility of carrying out so fell a design, but claimed that he had entertained no serious intention of doing any such thing: then (this may seem to be the sense of the letter) when it was pointed out that such an explanation was incompatible with his previous confessions, he claimed that he had only made those confessions to save himself from racking. This explanation, Cecil affirmed, was entirely without substance. The letter expresses satisfaction that Lopez was found guilty and by a "substantial" jury. On the 14th of March, Lopez's associates went the same way, being *convicted on their former confessions*.[128]

VI. HENRY WALPOLE AND EDWARD SQUIRE

To complete this survey, it must be noticed that, according to Roman Catholic sources, a number of instances of torture occurred during this period that are unreflected, or less clearly reflected, in extant official records and correspondence. The Gerard autobiography, for example, has it[129] that Richard Fulwood, Gerard's servant, and Nicholas Owen, who had been captured with Gerard, were subjected—seemingly, in Bridewell—during 1594 to the torture of the manacles. A topic more discussed, however, is the treatment at the Tower, during the same year, of Henry Walpole.

Walpole—like Southwell and Gerard, a Jesuit missionary—was arrested at York, with his younger brother and one Lingen. The younger Walpole and Lingen appear earlier to have been involved under arms

on the side of the Counter Reformation,[130] and Lingen was said to be
in command of three ships, standing off the coast and maintaining
themselves by piracy. The Lingen was examined by the President of the
Council of the North, two of its members, and Topcliffe:[131] doubtless,
the same happened to the two Walpoles. On the 25th of January, 1594,
Topcliffe wrote[132] to the Lord Keeper, Puckering, that Henry Walpole
and Lingen had information that could not be extracted without more
authority than the President of the Council possessed; the two men, he
said, must be dealt with sharply, and the necessary authority in that
behalf must be secured out of the Queen's power. We can hardly suppose
otherwise than that this was an oblique reference to torture; Topcliffe's
letter interestingly confirms that no standing authority to employ that
device had been vested in the Council in the North. It is also interesting
that his letter was to the Lord Keeper, and that it was the Queen's
power—not that of the Council under her—he wanted to invoke.

Henry Walpole, taken to London, was lodged in the
Tower.[133]Afterwards, according to the Gerard autobiography,[134] Roman
Catholics entertained a story that while there he had been tortured in
his own prison chamber as many as fourteen times. More recent Roman
Catholic authority does not go as far, but may be more specific. Augustus
Jessop said[135] that Walpole was tortured during examination, on the 3rd
of May, 1594, by Topcliffe and a Common Lawyer, Serjeant Drewe.
If he was tortured in his own chamber, we might expect to find that
for the purpose Topcliffe, if he did not improvise, employed the manacles; they were portable and could be used anywhere indoors, if a
strong metal peg could securely be driven into a wall or pillar.[136] Part
of the evidence, however, suggests that—supposing torture was used
at all and was by a method more elaborate than hanging up the examinate
with cords, by his thumbs[137]—some kind of stretching rack was employed:[138] this distasteful fact[139] is mentioned not for its own sake, but
for any relevance it may possess to the question whether torture indeed
occurred. On the other hand, in the same aspect, consideration must be
given to what extant State Papers reveal about his examinations: that
in June, 1594, he made what may appear to have been a total doctrinal
submission;[140] and that in the following month he supplied much information about other Roman Catholics in the realm.[141]

So we come to the affair of Edward Squire. As the "Throgmorton"
Plot belonged to the Duke of Guise, so the "Squire" Plot, if ever there
was one, belonged to the Spanish Crown,[142] acting through Richard

Walpole, the Rector of the English College at Seville—or, possibly, to Richard Walpole acting independently. However, its alleged nature was so bizarre that it is a ready object of suspicion and even of derision. Some are confident that it was a fiction:[143] a tool, they generally assert, forged for its own use by a cynical government. Anyone determined not to believe in it, but otherwise willing to give Elizabeth's statesmen the benefit of doubt, might consider the hypothesis that it was invented, under whatever pressure, by a man called Stanley[144]—to whom we shall return—and that unfortunate credulity of the regime was fed by the results of unfortunate recourse to torture.

Any reconstruction of the events must be speculative, but the following account seems at least not to contradict the evidence and admits reservations to protect most active prejudices.

In 1597 Squire and Richard Rolls, who had been in prison in Spain, but had been released and had spent a time at liberty in Seville, sailed to England.[145] The man called Stanley, another English prisoner, may have been released about the same time, but he did not come to England until the autumn of 1598.[146] In the spring of that year, some information was received in London of a plot to assassinate Elizabeth and Essex.[147] When Stanley arrived, he presented himself to the authorities as one who had tricked the Spanish into allowing him to get away with valuable information.[148] However, he was suspected of being himself an intended assassin—or else the Government saw some point in pretending such suspicion—and he was committed to the Tower.[149] Under examination, he maintained—truthfully or untruthfully, and if untruthfully with or without instigation by the authorities—that an assassination had been intended, but the intended assassin had been Squire: perhaps also, that Rolls was in the plot.[150]

Squire was arrested, the task of interrogating him being assigned to Wade and one or more others. At this early stage, no authority to torture issued. Squire may have been presented with a fairly elaborate accusation. At any rate, he told a fairly elaborate story, somewhat as follows: when he was in Seville, Walpole talked to him and seemed to want him to undertake an assassination in England; to get away from Spain, he was ready to humor Walpole by pretending willingness. The Earl of Essex was suggested as a target, but then Walpole observed that whilst to kill Essex would be a meritorious act, it was the death of the Queen herself that was primarily desirable; so it was agreed that Squire should poison both! He asked for a substance with which to carry out this large project, but Walpole said that if he were taken when carrying such a thing, he might fail to destroy or dispose of it. Instead, he advised Squire upon arrival in England to get into touch with Dr. Bagshaw, one of the Roman Catholic prisoners at Wisbech, when all of his needs would be met. So Squire set sail, but he never had intended to carry out any promise he had made to Walpole, and since his arrival in England, he had in fact taken no step that could have promoted the assassination plan.

On the 7th of October, 1598, Wade reported all of this to Essex and Sir Robert Cecil, concluding—ominously—"we can proceed no further until we have warrant to authorize us; then we will not fail of our best endeavours."[151]

From the standpoint of any honest police agent, such as Wade, the obvious immediate need was to investigate Bagshaw's ability to organize, from his prison, treasonable activity outside, and steps in this behalf were taken.[152] Then on the 19th of October, the interrogation of Squire was resumed, at the Tower.

The examiners were Peyton (the Lieutenant of the Tower), Coke (then Attorney-General), Fleming (now Solicitor-General), Francis Bacon, and Wade. They may have been commissioned earlier to investigate the whole matter, and all or most of them had been concerned in the examination of Squire before Wade's report of the 7th of October. Squire now stated that Walpole, in advising him to contact Bagshaw, had said that the latter was well acquainted with the current Jesuit organization in England, and that Walpole had given him written instructions, under his own hand, and a letter for Bagshaw, but that he had thrown them into the sea. By itself, this would have been in harmony with Squire's earlier assertion that he had never intended to carry out the assassination plan. However, he now inculpated himself. He conveyed that Walpole's instructions had referred to the constituents of a suitable poison and its application; that he had remembered them; and that after arriving in England, he had at certain places purchased various of the constituents required.[153]

On the 23rd of October, he was again examined, and—except that Bacon was absent—by the same persons. On this occasion, he said that he had actually attempted to poison both the Queen and Essex: the former, by applying poison to her saddle; the latter, by taking ship with him and, when at sea, applying poison to his chair.[154] Thus whatever might have been thought of the mere purchase of constituents for a poison, he had now confessed to what had to be regarded as an overt act of treason. Still, it was a strange tale, that Walpole had refused to give him poison, but entrusted him with a written prescription for it. On the 24th of October, he was examined still again, although this time by Coke alone; he then acknowledged that, in truth, he had been given by Walpole the poison that he had used unsuccessfully, and he did not know its constituents.[155]

On the 3rd of November, Peyton, Coke, Fleming, and Francis Bacon—Wade was absent—questioned Rolls and a man called William Mundy, who had been in Madrid after Squire and Rolls left Spain.[156]

Mundy deposed that the two men were believed at Madrid to have betrayed the King of Spain by not carrying out the assassination plan and by instead informing against a number of priests. According to him, the understanding at Madrid was that Walpole was concerned in the business, that Squire had undertaken to apply poison to the Queen's saddle, and that Rolls had also promised to kill the Queen.

Rolls acknowledged that Squire and he had sailed together for England, and that before leaving they had together received Communion from Walpole (matter of suspicion, since it would have been a way of sealing a vow). However, he maintained that although Walpole had sought to enlist him in the service of the King of Spain, he had refused.[157]

According to a letter[158] written on the 22nd of November by John Chamberlain to Dudley Carleton, Squire had by then been tried and executed. The letter sets out Squire's offense in accordance with the admissions we know had been obtained from him, but it also asserts that Walpole had wrongly believed Squire to have deserted the plot and had therefore instructed Stanley[159] to inform against him and that Squire, having confessed, had died penitent.

Having regard to Wade's remark, in his report of the 7th of October, about the need for further authority and to the lapse, beginning on 19th of October, of Squire's protestation of innocence, it is not unlikely that on the latter date, if not also thereafter, Squire was tortured. Official papers do not confirm that he was—we have no torture warrant for him or draft or record of such a warrant. Nor from any official document have we anything to suggest even a likelihood that torture was used upon anyone else concerned. The absence of Wade from the examinations of the 3rd of November suggests that on that day, its use was not even contemplated.[160]

On the other hand, on the 19th of November, in the same year,

Richard Bayley addressed to the renegade Sir William Stanley a report on events in England, which included a statement that Stanley, Squire, and Rolls were all expected to stand trial for intending to poison the Queen and had been "sore racked."[161] Moreover, Roman Catholic information is that Squire was indeed tortured—and for five hours—on the rack on the 19th of October, 1598; and that far from dying penitent, he recanted his confession, saying it had been made only to escape from the torture: even in his last statement, at the gallows, rejecting what he had confessed to as having been a lie.[162]

VII. METROPOLITAN PLACES AND PERSONNEL

Where torture was to be used in London, Conciliar records suggest that at any rate until September, 1588, the place would normally be the Tower, whilst at any rate after June, 1589, it would much more often be Bridewell.[163]

Topcliffe's use of torture at his own house (see section V) breaks the pattern. Of course, it was not in pursuance, as far as we know, of any formal instruction. It happened in Southwell's case so, obviously, it also may have happened in others. If, as appears, Southwell was subsequently tortured at the Gatehouse prison, the proceedings may well have been exceptional and determined by what in his case had gone before.

At the Tower, the physical infliction of torture was the business of the yeoman warders: a statement from the government side to this effect is in the 1583 tract, the *Declaration of the Favourable Dealing . . .* ,[164] and in their letter[165] of the 10th of March, 1581, to Walsingham, the Lieutenant and Hammond observed that use of "Skevington's Yrons" required the "presence and ayde of one of the jaylors all the tyme." The Gerard autobiography relates[166] that Wade, when he handed over Gerard for a second day of torture to the Master of the Ordnance— perhaps the Yeoman of the Ordnance is meant—described the latter as Master of Torture;[167] it adds that Gerard knew such an officer existed, although he was someone other than the Master of the Ordnance. In fact, the officer in charge of ordnance at the Tower may well have been required to maintain—may even sometimes have been asked to invent— the ironmongery of torture;[168] if so, it is perhaps conceivable that he received through some channel a stipend on that account. If anyone had special responsibility concerning the actual infliction of torture, it was presumably the Yeoman Jailor: it is likely that any role he discharged, in such respect, was not without reward. Nonetheless—since, unhappily, we are not dealing with the world of Gilbert and Sullivan operetta—it may be suspected that the official existence of a "Master of Torture" was a prison myth, although perhaps one the authorities encouraged.

The addressees of Conciliar warrants for interrogation under torture at the Tower appear generally in this period to have included the Lieutenant. William Tomson's case, in 1597, was exceptional, in that the Lieutenant was not named as an examiner.[169] Moreover, the Conciliar record of the supporting warrant that was sent to him[170] refers only to the imprisonment of the examinate, not to any demand that might be made for assistance in the matter of torture: but this omission may well have occurred only in the record, which is very brief, not in the warrant itself. On the other hand, it does not appear to have been the Council's practice, when purporting to authorize torture at Bridewell, to include the Keeper as an examiner or to address to him an ancillary warrant.

Torture warrants appear no longer, during this period, to have issued to judges of either Bench. On the other hand, eight recorded Conciliar torture warrants[171] (all concerning political or politico-religious cases) were addressed to one or both of the (Common) Law Officers for the time being, although on the 27th of February, 1591, whilst both were directed by the Council to examine Thomas Clinton, they were also directed to hand over the task, should torture appear necessary.[172] The Recorder of London for the time being was addressee of a recorded Conciliar torture warrant in 1589[173] and of four such warrants between 1596 and 1597.[174] Also, the Council occasionally relied in this matter upon Common Lawyers not in lawyerly office under the Crown. Thomas Norton is an example, but rather a special case. Recorded Conciliar torture warrants also issued for a while to Thomas Owen,[175] later to Francis Bacon,[176] and once[177] to Fleming as Serjeant.

Among Civilians in the recorded Conciliar warrants, Doctor Fletcher figures twice[178] as an addressee, whilst Dr. John Hammond, earlier, was addressee of five such warrants between the 3rd of May, 1581, and the 29th of April, 1582,[179] as well as during March, 1581, in the initial torture interrogation of Myagh.[180] Hammond, besides being a Master in Chancery, was active as an ecclesiastical judge, both in High Commission and in ordinary tribunals, and his employment in politico-religious cases at this time doubtless was due, at least in part, to his experience of doctrinal examinations.[181]

Norton, a Puritan and holder of the City office of Remembrancer, was employed about this business at the same period as Hammond, and both were (among others) entrusted with the torture interrogation of Campion the Jesuit. One outcome of Norton's involvement was that he acquired an unfavorable popular reputation as a tormentor.[182] We have seen that Walsingham indeed turned to him for help in the second day's racking of Francis Throgmorton;[183] it looks as though, even in Government circles, he may have been regarded as possessing a certain relevant expertise.

More interesting still are three figures who emerge upon the present scene a little later, and appear to have participated in torture interrogations as part of a much larger commitment to police activity: Richard Young, William Wade, and Richard Topcliffe.

Young held in the Port of London the office of Customer.[184] He was also a justice of the peace.[185] His earliest concern with torture appears to have arisen, under the aegis of the Council, in connection with efforts by him to ensure the punishment of thieves. It seems to have been in the character of a busy justice that he was later drawn into the pursuit of political and politico-religious offenders and so came to be employed by the Council in their examination under torture. In the Conciliar records of torture warrants, his name appears fifteen times:[186] more often than that of any other individual and much more often than the holders from time to time of any particular office. Four of the cases concerned were of theft.[187] He was also named as an addressee in the draft warrant of 1590[188] concerning the politico-religious case of Christopher Bayles and his associates.

In the latter draft, the other proposed addressee was Topcliffe. It was also to Topcliffe and Young that, in 1591, the Law Officers were directed[189] to leave Thomas Clinton, if torture seemed necessary; as "butchers", the two men were linked in Southwell's letter, of January, 1590, to Aquaviva.[190] According to the Gerard autobiography,[191] after Gerard's arrest, his second examination—without torture—was before the two of them, at Young's house. Their relative roles in the Government's business deserve consideration. The Gerard autobiography seems[192] to regard Young as the key figure in the politico-religious police of the metropolis. He was a justice of the peace, proceeding as such, although with peculiar determination, sometimes upon instructions from the Queen, generally in a special working relationship with the Council. Topcliffe was not a justice of the peace and indeed held no public office. He was, however, fanatically hostile to Roman Catholicism and successful in attaching himself to the highest centers of influence. Sometimes, he received instructions from the Council, and—including the case of Thomas Clinton—the Conciliar records show nine instances of his employment where torture might be used. However, he attained to a special working relationship with the Queen herself and came to occupy in the prosecution of Roman Catholics for politico-religious offenses a position de facto resembling that of a justice of the peace, but without territorial limits being placed upon his authority within the realm, and to command from the Judicature more deference than any ordinary prosecuting justice would have received. Moreover, he found the funds to organize a considerable force of agents.[193] He may be regarded, to this extent, as a primeval common ancestor of Pinkerton's and the FBI.

Wade emerges as of better calibre. He was one of the Clerks of the Council. He is named as addressee in the records of eight Conciliar torture warrants.[194] The occasional inclusion among addressees of such warrants of other Council Clerks—Thomas Wilkes,[195] Robert Beale,[196] Anthony Ashley[197]—need not mean more than that they were good at drawing interrogatories.[198] Wade's involvement seems to have been different. Near the end of the reign, he was said to have taken Topcliffe's place as the man most feared by English Roman Catholics.[199] Besides holding Conciliar office, he appears to have been a justice of the peace.[200] A Conciliar record peculiarly suggestive concerning his talents is that for the 25th of January, 1596,[201] regarding John Hardie the Frenchman. It was issued only to the senior Clerk, Wilkes, and to Wade; since the former could have been relied upon to make a due note of the examination, it seems probable that Wade himself was included, as might have been Young or Topcliffe, in the role of hunter. In retrospect, one cannot love such a character, but it is right to say that he appears to have been a man of scruple.[202]

VIII. USES AND CONDITIONS

Among the Conciliar torture warrants recorded for this period, only one[203]—that having Topcliffe among its addressees—concerned murder; seven[204] concerned offenses of theft: in one instance[205]—that where, again, Topcliffe was an addressee—the theft had been from the Queen. We know of one warrant that issued concerning piracy.[206] However, by and large, our evidence suggests that torture was purportedly authorized, by the Queen herself or by the Council, at least four times as often in politico-religious or simply political cases as in others.

Regarding the conditions that induced recourse to torture, and regarding its immediate purposes, politico-religious cases of the early 1580s obtained a semi-official explanation, to which I have already made some reference, and we must now return.

On the 27th of March, 1582, when Thomas Norton—after a spell in the Tower for too radical religious utterance—was suffering the modified sanction of house arrest at the Guildhall,[207] he wrote to Walsingham a letter[208] in which he complained of the evil popular repute into which he had fallen for his supposed part in the examination of Roman Catholic suspects, especially Campion and Briant. He asserted, inter alia, that in the cases concerned:

1. "None was put to the rack that was not first by manifest evidence known to the Council to be guilty of treason";

2. "None was tormented to know whether he was guilty or no: but for the Queen's safety, to know the manner of the treason and the accomplices."

The tract of which the full title is *The Declaration of the Favourable Dealing of Her Majesty's Commissioners appointed for the Examination of Certain Traitors: and of Tortures, unjustly reported to have been done upon them for Matter of Religion,*[209] may be supposed either to have been written by Norton or to have been founded by someone else (possibly, Burghley[210]) upon material at least partly supplied by him. Its argument strikingly resembles that of Norton's letter, although it is more elaborate and here perhaps more circumspect. The letter seems to convey that in using torture, the purpose was never, in the least degree, to obtain evidence for judicial use against the examinate. The tract does not seem to go quite so far. It declares:

> none . . . have been put to the rack or torture, no not for matters of treason . . . but where it was first known and evidently probable by former detection, confessions, and otherwise, that the party so racked, or tortured, was guilty, and did know, and could deliver the truth of the things wherewith he was charged . . . and the rack was never used to wring out confessions at adventure upon uncertainties. . . .

The letter and the tract are sufficient evidence of public anxiety about the torture of Campion and other missionaries. That suspicion of the use of such methods was capable of discouraging a "guilty" verdict is suggested by a remark the Attorney-General, Popham, is reported to have made during the trial in 1589 of the Earl of Arundel. The Earl having alleged that several witnesses were unworthy of credit, Popham's response included an assertion that: "they were never tortured, but confessed all this willingly."[211] It may thus be supposed that the authorities, if they had it in mind to acquire through interrogation evidence for use at a subsequent Common Law trial, whether of the examinate or of someone else, would not use torture unnecessarily.

On the other hand, even as far as concerned political or politico-religious cases, Robert Cecil's letter of the 28th of February, 1594, about Lopez, suggests that extra-judicial confessions might be crucial evidence against those who made them; as we have noticed, Lopez's associates were said to have been convicted upon their confessions.[212] Moreover, Young's letter of the 23rd of December, 1592, to Puckering, about Webster and Fawkes, strongly suggests that need for a confession as evidence could supply a motive to torture.[213] Then in non-political cases, the records of torture warrants sometimes show fairly clearly that the aim was to secure evidence, against the examinates themselves as well as any accomplices,[214] although it is true that the record on the 18th of April, 1590, of a warrant to Young for the interrogatory torture of suspected robbers strikes just the same note as passages above quoted from Norton's letter.[215]

The dealings are interesting that occurred during April, 1586, with Beaumont, Wakeman, and Pinder, the suspected thieves.[216] The Council clearly wanted larger depositions from them than would have been essential to promise the conviction of each on a capital charge. On the other hand, the impression may be gathered that such an essential minimum was itself being sought.

What may be true is that torture was not used, for whatever result, in an entirely cynical mood: that it was not used without a fairly strong sense that the examinate had brought it upon himself by withholding the truth. Before the present period, several relevant Conciliar records in political or politico-religious cases,[217] and one in a case of ordinary crime,[218] refer to obstinacy of the examinate. During the present period, there are seven more instances,[219] although in only one [220] does the record contemplate an ordinary crime. Of course, such references might have been humbug, but we may recall the case of William Weston who, as above noticed, escaped torture, although there is no reason to suppose that without it he liberally supplied the authorities with means of destroying other Roman Catholics.

It should also be observed that even if a frequent purpose of Conciliar torture at this time was to acquire proofs for prospective use at Common Law, the Council evidently adhered in the matter to the Civilian-Canonistical style, adopted for Star Chamber Proceedings by Elizabeth's reign,[221] with prepared lists of questions. Thus a number of torture warrants are recorded as having required the addressees first to frame interrogatories,[222] or as having required them to employ interrogatories supplied to them, or to employ interrogatories supplied to them and to frame additional interrogatories themselves.[223]

Finally, here, a few words perhaps should be added with reference to proof of high treason. As we have seen, *Rolston's Case*, in 1571, appears (according to Coke's subsequent account) to have settled pro tempore that by necessary intendment of Statute 5 and 6 E.VI, c.11, s.9, a conviction of the latter offense might in law be based solely upon a pre-forensic confession: but only provided such confession had been *voluntary*. If so, the Government still could not by recourse to torture make up for a lack of legally-required witnesses. Of course, where an accused pleaded guilty upon arraignment, no witnesses would be required. However, I have not perceived any evidence that the Government at this period used torture upon a calculation that if a suspect were overcome by it extra-judicially, his resistance would suffer such a collapse as to cause him to plead guilty when put on trial.

PART III
JURISPRUDENCE

Among the charges drawn up by Whitgift against Robert Beale, in 1584,[224] two are of present interest:

> He condemneth (without exception of any cause) racking of grievous offenders, as being cruel, barbarous, contrary to law, and unto the liberty of English suspects.

> He . . . giveth a *caveat* to those in the Marches of Wales, that execute torture by virtue of instructions from her Majesty's hand, according to a statute, to look unto it, that their doings be well warranted.

Analytically, the merits of founding upon Statute 34 and 35 H.VIII, c.26, s.3, the regal torture instructions of a standing kind issued to the Council in the Welsh Marches may seem nil, unless that council actually incorporated torture in its judicial process; in which case, the merits of so doing have already been considered.[225]

For the use of torture upon specific instructions from the Queen or from the Council of the Realm, there was no possibility of invoking statutory support. Yet the first of the above charges against Beale assumed that, at any rate in some cases, such use was not "contrary to law," and an impression to like effect must have been encouraged by the participation, in interrogations where torture was used or contemplated, of lawyers and, remarkably of Law Officers, of the Recorder of London, of those without office who had accepted the degree of serjeant. Moreover, Coke—as Attorney-General—is reported to have in Southwell's case and in that of Essex and Southampton used language implying assumption of the lawfulness of torture, under royal authority, in cases that threatened the State. To Southwell, we are told,[226] he said:

> Mr. Topcliffe has no need to go about to excuse his proceedings in the manner of his torturings. For think you that you will not be tortured? Yea! we will tear the heart out of a hundred of your bodies.

Whilst, at the trial of the Earls, we are told[227] that he recommended the evidence thus, referring first to the Queen's interest:

> I think that her overmuch clemency to some, turneth to overmuch cruelty for herself: for, though the rebellious attempts were so exceedingly heinous, yet out of her princely mercy, no man was racked, tortured, or pressed to speak anything farther, than of their own accord, and willing minds, for the discharge of their consciences they uttered. . . .

Nonetheless, it would be reckless to infer that those, whatever their status, who acquiesced in torture had usually addressed themselves to the question of its legality, or even that Coke, if he seemed on occasion to argue in terms of such legality, was expressing thereby the result of any reasoned juridical scrutiny.[228] The other way, when speculating about mental attitudes in the present respect, allowance ought to be made for: (a) the likely influence of pride, which Fortescue had encouraged those who followed him at Common Law to take, in the exclusion of torture from their own judicial process;[229] (b) the invitation to laziness or inert discretion, which must have lain in the fact that the legality of Executive torture could hardly, from a practical standpoint, be expected to require judicial ascertainment.

Certainly, in the records of torture warrants themselves, what we find are not juridical justifications presented firmly as such, but some seeming juridical allusions and some moral posturing.

   *   *   *   *

Seeming juridical allusions occur preponderately in cases of ordinary crime and are to Continental doctrine concerning the proofs required to allow torture of an accused. Thus the warrant recorded for the 14th of August, 1581,[230] which refers to terrorization of Campion and torture of Paine, justifies severity regarding the latter by asserting against him the existence of "vehement presumptions"; comparable expressions will be discovered in the records of warrants for the 24th of June, 1589,[231] and the 17th of December, 1587.[232] Their use was not new: it had occurred in the Statute 33 H.VIII, c.23,[233] and in two torture warrants recorded for 1555,[234] one recorded for 1570.[235] If their resemblance to those occurring in Continental sources[236] is a mere coincidence, it is a remarkable one.[237]

So in the warrant recorded for the 21st of April, 1601, concerning Thomas Hewson, one of the explanations advanced, for contemplating recourse to torture—that "his later examinations are contrary to his former confession"—recalls the Continental torture indication that the suspect has vacillated.[238]

Echoes of Canonical and Civilian doctrine may, moreover, perhaps be discerned in the record for the 9th of December, 1580, of the warrant regarding the suspect boy from Sir Drew Drury's household. The instruction given, to avoid maim, smacks of Canonical influence;[239] the suggestion of light whipping for a young examinate can be found in Justinian's Digest:[240] although, as different from his subjection to questioning by torments—a *quaestio* (*per tormenta*)—so where the Council prescribed "some slight kinde of torture . . . as by whipping," a Civilian with the relevant Digest fragment in mind might have preferred not to use the word *torture* at all.[241]

Even assuming that torture was not used in Admiralty at this period, if preliminary investigation there of capital causes continued to be conducted on a Civilian pattern, a result may have been some importation into actual practice of Continental doctrine on proofs. Also, it appears possible that torture was used by the English in the course of military justice on campaign;[242] if so, some English Civilians must for that reason have had a motive to consult Continental doctrine on the subject. However, whilst Dr. Matthew Sutcliffe stated, in his *Practice, Proceedings and Lawes of Armes*,[243] which was published in 1595, that the proper way to find out offenders is "where the presumptions are sufficient, and the matter heinous; by racke or other paine," the statement does not suggest more than a superficial acquaintance with Continental sources: according to which soldiers were exempt from torture except in respect of specific categories of offense.[244]

* * * *

Morally reinforcing observations occur in some records of warrants issued in political or politico-religious cases. They are (a) that the interest is involved of the Queen and State;[245] (b) that what is being directed will rest upon the authority of the Queen, whether exercised directly,[246] or vicariously, through a decision of the Council;[247] (c) faintly, that it will have the backing of established practice.[248]

On the other hand, whatever moral explanations or reinforcements may have been advanced in particular instances, one feature that during this period begins and emerges strongly, so as to become almost general, in Conciliar torture instructions is an express claim to relevant authority—whether legal or supra-legal is unclear.

Before this development, such express assumption of Conciliar right occurs in the records with reference to the delivery and receipt of prisoners: a sometimes related, but in itself relatively prosaic, matter that—if the distinction were envisaged between legal and (absolute) prerogative power—seems likely to have been supposed to be governed by the former. Thus the Sherwood instruction,[249] recorded for the 17th of November, 1577, and within the present period, the letter[250] about Wakeman, Beaumont, and Pinder, recorded for the 13th of May, 1586, each declared itself a "sufficient warrant" for change of prison.

Subsequently, however, that expression was used concerning torture in the matters of the following: Hacket (20th of July, 1591); the London placarders (11th of May, 1593); and Valentine Thomas (17th of April, 1598). Torture instructions are recorded as having been issued, as to be implemented "by authority hereof" (an expression also used in the

record concerning the London placarders) or "by virtue hereof," in
regard to the following: Beesley (Passelaw) and his companion (10th
of January, 1591: "Little Ease"[251]); Coleford and Fawlkes (12th of
November, 1595); John Hardie (25th of January, 1596); William Tomson (2nd of February, 1597); Gerard (13 of April, 1597): and Thomas
Howson (21st of April, 1601), whilst the instruction[252] recorded regarding Bradshaw, Burton, and others (19th of December, 1596) declared to its addressees: "these shall be to authoryze you. . . . "

                    *   *   *   *

Gerard's statement, to which I have referred,[253] that torture was at
the Tower used only by (written, specific) warrant suggests a degree
of administrative institutionalization that might itself have proved juridically potent. Yet although the Council's general procedure may have
ensured that no instructions could be attributed to the Council itself,
which had not gone out in writing in its name, Topcliffe may—as we
have seen[254]—under his own roof at first have tortured Southwell in
pursuance of informal regal licence; again, perhaps whilst the dignity
of the Lieutenant of the Tower was sufficient to protect his prisoners
from violence without Conciliar warrant or warrant under the Signet,
at Bridewell royal favor allowed Topcliffe for a time to torture politico-
religious prisoners without securing such formal support, if he thought
fit.[255]

In conclusion, we may notice outside the Conciliar records one hint—
again, there is nothing developed to the level of juridical argument—
of justification by positive international custom. In the *Declaration of
the Favourable Dealing*, [256] an apologetic point is made that in the case
of Campion and his associates, the suspicion had been of grave treason,
whereas "by the more general lawes of nations," torture "hath bene
and is judged to be used in lesser cases." Here, what we have may
seem no more than a benign comparison;[257] the tract cannot well be read
as arguing that the Crown would be justified in using torture on a wider
scale, and so, a fortiori, is so in cases of treason. However, in what
may have been an incomplete echo of the tract, Popham CJ is said,
when Southwell at his trial complained of having been grievously tortured, to have answered: "such things are done among all nations."[258]
If this remark really did fall from the learned Chief Justice, his tone
unfortunately is not preserved to us: it may have indicated that he was

improvising what he sensed to be an inadequate excuse, or that he was confidently advancing what seemed to him a sufficient justification.[259] Even supposing that he felt satisfied with his own remark, he had not cast his argument in juridical terms or disposed of the difficulty—to which a Common Lawyer might have been sensitive—that the European practice of which he spoke was intimately associated with the judicial procedure of the "Civil Law".[260] Still, had occasion arisen, such further steps might have been attempted.

chapter *7*

ACCESSION OF JAMES I TO 1640

PART I
PARTICULAR WARRANTS

A long gap in the Council records begins after 1601. However, two Conciliar warrants are extant for the period between King James's accession and his arrival in London. Both concern Philip May, and they are dated the 19th and 20th of April, 1603.

The first warrant[1] is addressed to Popham, the Lord Chief Justice; Coke, the Attorney-General; the Solicitor-General; the Lieutenant of the Tower; or any two or three of them. Its terms are as follows:

> After our hartie commendations to Your Lordship. Whereas we have geven order for the committing to the Tower of one Phillip May for some matters wherewith he is charged concerning the State which are particularly knowne unto Your Lordship, about the which we think it fitt he should be further examyned to discover the further intents of the said practice. These are therefore to pray Your Lordship and the rest, to take some convenient tyme to examyne the said Phillip Maye uppon such poyntes as you shall think meete to charge him; and as you shall find occasion you maie putt him to the torture of the racke, the better to drawe from him a confession of the trewthe if otherwise he will not be induced to confesse playnely the matters of the said practise. And so we bydd you hartilie farewell.

The addressees of the second warrant[2] again include the (Common) Law Officers and the Lieutenant, but the Lord Chief Justice is omitted

148

and Wade brought in. It may be executed by any three of them. The terms are as follows.

> After our hearty commendations. Whereas one Phillip Maye hathe been accused for uttering moste lewde and disloyale speeches, and being committed to the Tower and there examyned, thoughe he doth not acknowledge those words that most bewray his corrupt and trayterous disposition, yet he doth confesse all the other matter and circumstances informed against him, and so fayntly doth deny the same as there is lyttle doubte of the truth of the accusation. These trayterous speeches concerning the person of our dread Sovereign the King's Most Excellent Majestie, wee in all dutie to His Highness do thinke it meete that he be dealt with with all severity, not only to confesse playnely those haynous speeches he used, but to make a true and playne declaration of the cause that moved him to utter the same; of whom he hath heard any such speeches, with whom he hath had any conference touching such matters, and such like questions as you shall thinke meete to be mynistered unto him. Wee doe therefore requyre you to repayre agayne to the Tower, and to examyne him of the said matters, and if he shall not deale playnly and truly to discover the depth of his knowledge, mynde, and conference in all these matters, then you shall by virtue hereof put him to the Manacles, or such other torture as is used in the Tower, that he may be inforced to reveale the uttermost of his knowledge in any practise, purpose, or intent against His Highness. For your better proceeding herein accordingly these shall be your warrant; so fare you hartely well.

The first warrant was perhaps never issued. At any rate, nothing indicates that it was executed by use of torture. Apparently, on the day of its issue, Popham labored hard in examining the prisoner—who was in the service of the Lord Chamberlain, Lord Hunsdon—but without obtaining any significant admission.[3] However, a report in Coke's handwriting, dated the 20th of April, signed by Coke himself and the other addressees of the second warrant—the warrant of that day—reveals that the prisoner made to them a partial admission and then, "upon better consideration", a full confession.[4] This submission by stages is in the circumstances highly suggestive regarding the methods by which it was obtained.

Next, with reference to the Gunpowder Plot[5], instructions[6] dated the 6th of November, 1605 are extant. They are in King James's hand, and prescribe interrogatories for Guy Fawkes, who at the date in question was still known by his assumed name of "Johnson". They direct that, if he cannot otherwise be brought to confess, "the gentler tortures as to be first used unto him, *et sic per gradus ad ima tenditur*" ("and so it is steered stage by stage towards extremes").

In his *History of England*, Samuel R. Gardiner said[7] that Fawkes was: (a) on the 7th of November, 1605, probably subjected to one of whatever measures were regarded as forming the King's category of "gentler tortures"; (b) on the 9th of November, 1605, "undoubtedly subject to torture of no common severity". He called attention to a letter[8] from Sir E. Hoby to Sir T. Edmonds, dated the 9th of November, but containing a passage that—he thought—was evidently written on the evening of the 7th or morning of the 8th of November, and that stated that "since Johnson's being in the Tower, he beginneth to speak English, and yet he was never upon the rack, but only by the arms upright."

However, Gardiner, in another book, *What the Gunpowder Plot was*, suggests[9] that: (a) it was the mere sight of the rack that induced Fawkes to make, on the 8th of November, 1605, a statement that was full except that it omitted the names of his accomplices; (b) probably, the manacles were used on the 9th of November, but the rack was not actually brought into use at all. He observes that in *The King's Book*,[10] Fawkes is said to have been shown the rack, yet never to have been racked, and that Wade in a letter to Salisbury on the 7th of November[11] indicated that, so far, Fawkes had merely been threatened with torture.

Further consideration of Gardiner's sources may suggest that subjection of Fawkes to torture in the manacles began on the evening of the 7th or morning of the 8th of November, and that, probably, it was continued on the 9th of November; that the rack, although not used, probably was threatened at some stage. Certainly, the often-mentioned fact that Fawke's signature to the examination taken from him on the 9th of November was shaky does not necessarily point to use of the rack.[12]

*   *   *   *

Following the gap in the Conciliar records, a warrant is entered for the 18th of January, 1615,[13] that was addressed to Sir Ralph Winwood (Secretary of State), Sir Julius Caesar (Master of the Rolls), the Lieutenant of the Tower, the (Common) Law Officers, two serjeants-at-law, and one of the clerks of the Council, concerning a clergyman, Edmund Peacham. Moreover, a copy of this warrant is extant.[14] It recites that Peacham stands charged with a book or pamphlet containing what is conceived to be treasonable matter, and that he has declined to answer truthfully—as would have become "an honeste and loyale subject"— interrogation thereon. Accordingly, it requires all of the addressees to go to the Tower and there examine him upon such interrogatories as they think fit.

Also extant, is the text of a report by the addressees of the above warrant.[15] It sets out first the interrogatories upon which (pursuant to the warrant) Peacham was examined, then mentions use of torture and confesses lack of success:

1. Who procured you, moved you, or advised you, to put in writing these traiterous slanders which you have set down against his majesty's person and government, or any of them?

2. Who gave you any advertisement or intelligence touching those particulars which are contained in your writings; as touching the sale of crown lands, the deceit of the king's officers, the greatness of the king's gifts, his keeping divided courts, and the rest; and who hath conferred with you, or discoursed with you, concerning those points?

3. Whom have you made privy and acquainted with the said writings, or any part of them? and who hath been your helpers or confederates therein?

4. What use meant you to make of the said writings? was it by preaching them in sermon, or by publishing them in treatise? if in sermon, at what time and in what place meant you to have preached them? if by treatise, to whom did you intend to dedicate, or exhibit, or deliver such treatise?

5. What was the reason, and to what end did you first set down in scattered papers, and after knit up, in form of a treatise or sermon, such a mass of treasonable slanders against the king, his posterity, and the whole state?

6. What moved you to write, the king might be stricken with death on the sudden, or within eight days, as Ananias or Nabal; do you know of any conspiracy or danger to his person or have you heard of any such attempt?

7. You have confessed that these things were applied to the king; and that, after the example of preachers and chronicles, kings infirmities are to be laid open: this sheweth plainly your use must be to publish them, shew to whom and in what manner.

8. What was the true time when you wrote the said writings, or any part of them? and what was the last time you looked upon them, or perused them before they were found or taken?

9. What moved you to make doubt whether the people will rise against the king for taxes and oppressions? Do you know, or have you heard, of any likelihood or purpose of any tumults or commotion?

10. What moved you to write, that getting of the crown-land again would cost blood, and bring men to say, This is the heir, let us kill him? Do you know, or have you heard of any conspiracy or danger to the prince, for doubt of calling back the crown land?

11. What moved you to prove, that all the king's officers ought to be put to the sword? Do you know, or have you heard if any petition is intended to be made against the king's council and officers, or any rising of people against them?

12. What moved you to say in your writing, that our king, before his coming to the kingdom, promised mercy and judgment, but we find neither? What promise do you mean of, and wherein hath the king broke the same promise?

Upon these Interrogatories, Peacham this day was examined before torture, in torture, between torture, and after torture; notwithstanding, nothing could be drawn from him, he still persisting in his obstinate and insensible denials, and former answers. Raphe Winwood, Jul. Caesar, Fr. Bacon, H. Mountague, Gervase Helwysse, Ran. Crewe, Henry Yelverton, Fr. Cottington. Jan. the 19th 1614.

Legally, the problem presented by Peacham's case (since the Crown displayed a disinclination to treat him lightly) was that the only evidence found against him concerned what he had composed, but left, unpublished, in his own study. Might private commission to writing supply an "open deed", as required by construction of the *Statute of Treasons*, 1351 (25 E.III, st.5, c.2)? Plainly, the Crown would have liked to establish that a conspiracy was in the background, that publication had taken place, or at least that an intent to publish had been entertained. Discovery of a conspiracy would, of course, have been valuable from a general standpoint of security, but from a Common Law standpoint, a positive result on either of the other heads would have been useful against Peacham if charged with treason. When such better material was not forthcoming, the King—through the agency, especially of Francis Bacon, who was by this time Attorney-General—took the extraordinary step of consulting judges individually on the question whether the prisoner could be convicted of that offense. Of course, such an approach promised the advantages that judges consulted were less likely to show courage, in resisting what the King regarded as his interest, individually than collectively, and that taken individually, the rest would escape the influence of Coke, who since his elevation to the Bench had turned into something of a liberal. Coke, himself, was in the event resistive.[16] However, Peacham was convicted of treason indeed, although he was not executed, and the legal merits of the conviction remain unsettled.[17]

For the 19th of February, 1620, another torture warrant[18] is recorded. Its signatories included Bacon (who had become Lord Chancellor) and Coke; its immediate addressee was the Lieutenant of the Tower. It recited that Samuel Peacock, a prisoner in the Marshalsea, was "upon vehement suspicion of highe treason against His Majesties sacred person" to be removed to the Tower, and to be examined by the Lord Chief Justice— Sir Henry Montague, who as serjeant-at-law had been one of the addressees of the Peacham warrant—the Solicitor-General, and the Lieutenant. It directed the Lieutenant to take Peacock to the Tower and declared that it authorized him with both or either of the other two named examiners to interrogate the prisoner from time to time and "to put him, as there shall be cause for the better manifestation of the truth, to the torture either of the manacles or of the rack".

Bacon had written to the King: "if we cannot get to the bottom otherwise, it is fit Peacock be put to the torture; he deserveth it as well as Peacham did".[19] Seemingly, from a letter by Chamberlain to Carlton,[20] he was put to it.

Next a warrant[21] is recorded for the 9th of January, 1622, instructing the Attorney-General and a serjeant-at-law to examine in the Tower, for "causes knowen unto them", one James Crasfield. If they found reason, they were to terrorize him with the manacles and the rack and, at their discretion, to torture him by those means.

I have not discovered evidence of the nature of Crasfield's supposed offense, although the choice of examiners indicates that Common Law prosecution—presumably, at least of Crasfield himself—was contemplated.

Locke, in a letter[22] dated the 12th of January, 1623, to Carlton, reported, inter alia, that a servant of Bing, "the counsellor" (that is, counsellor-at-law), had been questioned on the rack and was likely to suffer execution for prophesying a rebellion.[23] Crasfield may have been the unfortunate man here mentioned, but the identification would be more probable if the letter had been written three days, instead of a year and three days, after the warrant. Other contents of the letter indicate that its dating is correct, and nothing suggests that the dating of the Conciliar record is wrong.

*   *   *   *

Between the accession of Charles I and the outbreak of civil war, on two occasions—with an interval of some fourteen years between them—evidence shows that torture was authorized and used.

First, for the 30th of April, 1626, a Conciliar warrant[24] is recorded, the addressees of which included the Lieutenant of the Tower and a serjeant-at-law. It concerned one William Monk, a prisoner at the Tower, and directed his examination upon interrogatories to be indicated by the Lord Chief Justice, with his torture by the manacles if the addressees saw fit. What happened to him, seemingly, was even worse: so a further warrant may have issued, of which we have not a record. According to a Conciliar instruction[25] recorded for the 27th of February, 1628, Monk was accused by one John Blackborne and the latter's wife of high treason and was put (there is no mention of the manacles) to the rack, whereby he was gravely disabled; then it became apparent that the accusation was malicious, so he was released.

The second occasion concerned John Archer, a glover arrested for participating in a tumultuous attack upon Lambeth Palace, the seat of Archbishop Laud. An instruction[26] from the King is extant, dated the 21st of May, 1640, to the Lieutenant, that he and two serjeants-at-law (one of them Heath, a former Attorney-General) shall examine Archer upon questions the serjeants are to propound. The sense seems further to be that Archer is at the outset to be terrorized by sight of the rack: certainly such terrorization is authorized, and the authority given extends to actual use of the rack, if it seems necessary. Yet the warrant contemplates his eventual release from "close custody": probably, therefore, his non-prosecution. According to Rossingham's Newsletter, he was "a very simple fellow, and racked in the Tower to make him confess his companions."[27]

PART II
FURTHER INFORMATION AND
INTERPRETATION

I. PARTICULAR WARRANTS: FACTUAL EXEGESIS

Regarding particular warrants of which we have knowledge during the present period, the following observations are possible.

1. All were for torture at the Tower.

2. It is clear that at least until the early part of Charles I's reign, the rack and the manacles both were contemplated as available means of torture, and that the rack—at any rate—was available in 1640.

3. Unless Crasfield's case was an exception, all of the cases were political.

4. Except in Archer's case, it is in every instance clear or at least probable that one purpose was to obtain the examinate's personal confession. However, with Archer the aim according to Rossingham was to discover accomplices. Also, some of the interrogatories administered to Peacham were apt to realize that aim; Peacock's case, as we have seen, was likened by Bacon to that of Peacham.

5. One or more Common Lawyers—and especially, Law Officers— were generally included among the addressees. As far as concerns involvement of the Common Law Bench: although in May's case, Popham LCJ, included among the addressees of the first warrant we have, was not among those of the second (on which torture probably was in fact used or threatened), Montague LCJ was among those appointed to examine Peacock by a torture warrant that appears to have been executed. However, all this evidently does not suffice to show endorsement of torture by Common Lawyers generally or indeed by Common Law judges generally, even under James I.

6. Sir Julius Caesar (a member of the Council, Master of the Rolls, and a former Master of Requests) seems to have been the only addressee who was distinguished as a Civilian, and his name occurs only in the Peacham case.

II. FURTHER, REGARDING THE GUNPOWDER PLOT PROCEEDINGS

It is evidently possible that others, besides Fawkes, were terrorized or tortured in the aftermath of the Gunpowder Plot.[28]

The King's instructions[29] regarding torture of Fawkes himself suggest that the commissioners had no blanket authority to resort to physical methods whenever and with whomever they thought expedient. Possibly a statement by Robert Abbot in his *Antilogia*[30] contains a contrary implication. There, with the business of the Plot very much in view, he states—I translate his Latin—that special commissioners, appointed to investigate crimes before charges go to a grand jury:

either elicit confessions . . . from the suspects by interrogations, or overwhelm them with substantial proofs and witnesses, or—where necessary—force out confessions with torture.

However, if such an implication is indeed to be discerned in what he said, the King's intervention concerning Fawkes provides reason for treating it cautiously. If other cases of torture, or of terrorization existed in connection with the Plot, other specific warrants, to provide for them, may have existed also.

That Thomas Winter was tortured has been inferred from a letter, dated the 21st of November, 1605, in which Wade—by now Lieutenant of the Tower—informed Salisbury that Winter "doth find his hand so strong, as after dinner he will settle himself to write that he hath verbally declared to your Lordship."[31] Plainly, the inference is insecure, but it may have been torture that affected Winter's ability to write.

Somewhat later, the Jesuit lay-brother, Nicholas Owen—who had been Henry Garnet's attendant—died under arrest in the Tower. Subsequently, it was asserted among Roman Catholics that he had died on the rack, his stomach having been entirely ruptured by the torture. Abbot, again in his *Antilogia*,[32] observes that the verdict of the Coroner's jury was one of suicide. This in itself need not carry much conviction. However, Abbot did not deny that torture was used: a fact that may suggest he was not conveying a tale created by way of Government propaganda; nor did he deny that Winter's stomach had been opened up. He nonetheless disposes, as an anatomical absurdity, of the suggestion that racking caused Owen's injury. His own narrative of events concerned is—translating his Latin—as follows:

Owen, having been caught and shut up in prison—in fact, at the Tower of London—being questioned about Garnet would hardly make any answer: whereupon, to promote his further interrogation, he was hung up for a little while on a [?] vertical support-beam, his thumbs having been tied together.[33] Afterwards, nothing having been vouchsafed on his part, nor, certainly, anything done to him to prevent his soon being able to use both thumbs, but being afraid lest he should be taken to the strings and rack,[34] though he had not yet been threatened with that torture he formed to forestall the torturers a plan full of desperate madness and lunacy. Accordingly, the next day, when he was lying (having previously pretended ill-health) upon his cot, and his dinner was taken to him there by his keeper, who placed in his hand a knife with (as is usual in prisons) the point blunted, to cut up his food, he complained that the sauce was cold and asked the keeper to take it away for heating at a fire; and, while that was being done, he cut open his stomach with the knife, inflicting indeed more than one horrible wound. . . . The keeper having returned, and, discovering what had happened, having obtained the assistance of the Lieutenant and various guests whom the Lieutenant was entertaining to dinner, Owen said . . . that he had feared worse torture, whereby something might be won from him to the prejudice of his Catholic friends.

Clearly, what Abbot meant here to convey was that Owen was hung up by the cord securing his thumbs together; and that subsequently, he pretended to be ill so that food and the knife would be brought to him in his cell, whereas normally he would have eaten in the place where there was a fire. My own inclination is to credit Abbot's account, except his assertion that Owen had not even been threatened with the rack. It would be surprising to learn that torture was used at all at the Tower without a warrant. The vagueness of James's instructions regarding the modes of torture to be practiced upon Fawkes is not generally reflected in other known instructions, or records of instructions, for torture at the Tower in the later sixteenth or seventeenth century: perhaps the nearest thing to it is the phrase "the manacles or such other torture as is used in that place", which occurs in the record of the Gerard warrant. Therefore, if Abbott was accurate here in other respects, and if there was no* some blanket authority covering these cases, speculation seems plausible that a warrant had issued regarding Owen similar in scope to that issued in Crasfield's case, in 1622; and that the examiners, having failed to impress him sufficiently with a sight of the rack and the manacles, instead of proceeding forthwith to actual use of the latter, had felt justified (a fortiori) in trying first the less damaging method of hanging him up by both of his thumbs. Indeed, if the rendering "vertical support-beam" in the above translation is right, we may be reminded of Gerard's description—to which I refer in chapter 9, section VI—of the Tower torture chamber; but then had I not been acquainted with the latter description, that rendering perhaps would not have occurred to me.[35]

Garnet himself, during the period of about six weeks before his trial, was examined more than twenty times by Conciliar commissioners.[36] However, it appears that he was not tortured. There was at the outset of the investigation against him a want of proof, but at his trial, evidence was given of a damaging conversation that, secretly overheard, he had been allowed to conduct.[37] Abbot, in effusive courtly style, says that such artifice was required because the King, in this matter inordinately merciful did not, despite strong motives for suspicion, want torture to be used. So we have here a further suggestion, and from Abbot himself, that in proceedings consequent upon the Plot, examiners did not have carte blanche to use torture whenever they themselves saw a need.[38]

III. THE COUNCIL IN THE WELSH MARCHES

A summary of grievances[39] expressed against the Council in the Welsh Marches during the presidency of the Earl of Bridgwater—that is, from 1631 to 1642—includes an allegation that it "tortured the bodies of the Kinges subjectes for bare suspicion of felonye." So we may gather that the general commissions of the Council were still, during the present period, being executed in a Tudor mood.

IV. MILITARY PROCEDURE

The only express documentary suggestion, of which I am aware, that torture was used in the course of military justice under the earlier Stuarts, occurs in the *Acts of the Privy Council* for the 6th of March, 1629.[40] The entry concerned reveals that during Buckingham's operation in the Ile de Ré, in 1627, a court of war sentenced a Captain Turney to pay one Lancelot Barrowe eighty pounds "for having without warrant put him to the Torture to make him confesse the robbing of him of the like summe." The question arises from whom a warrant would have been considered sufficient, and the answer may be that within an army, the General had torture at his disposal.

Also of interest in this connection, although not expressly mentioning torture, is the first of the Articles of War promulgated by Charles I in 1639. This referred to the trial of persons other than soldiers and (speaking of Civilian influence) provided that inquiry should be made by the oaths of as many as was thought convenient and by the use of "all means of examination and trial of persons delated, suspected, or defamed."[41]

PART III
JURISPRUDENCE

The warrant[42] concerning Philip May, dated the 20th of April, 1603, directs torture "by virtue hereof" and declares, "this shall be your warrant". The Peacham warrant[43] declares that it shall be to each and every of its addressees a "sufficient warrant". The abridged records of the warrants issued in the cases of Crasfield[44] and of Monk[45] do not indicate the use of comparable expressions, but they may nonetheless have been employed. The Archer warrant[46] does declare that it shall be its addressees' "sufficient warrant and discharge".

But was there by the end of the present period an established juridical key to such assumption of authority?

An English lawyer wishing, under the earlier Stuarts, to assert a doctrine regarding torture would have had to consider whether power in the Crown to use it existed under ordinary law, and whether such power existed to use it by virtue of an overriding prerogative. In the way in which these questions were answered, much variety would have been possible. At one extreme would have been the conclusion that no power was available to use torture at all; at the other extreme, the conclusion would have been that unrestricted power was available to use it under ordinary law. Unless the latter conclusion was reached, the broader question would have had to be answered: whether prerogative overriding law existed at all, in any connection;[47] there, an affirmative answer would have led to the murkier question: whether, nonetheless, the law defined the occasions upon which it might be overridden.

To support the existence of some ordinary power to torture, it might have been pretended that the Common Law naturally recognized established administrative practices and supplemented them when necessary by adaptation of Civilian juridical doctrine. Scotland, during the seventeenth century, experienced juridical acceptance, occasionally blended with references to Continental doctrine, of Conciliar torture practice, although doubts arose about its proper scope.[48]

In England, it cannot be said that in this matter anyone had by 1610 firmly and openly grasped all the nettles.

In 1603, at the very beginning of James I's reign, Bacon offered him the advice that: "by the law of England no man is bound to accuse himself. In the highest cases of treason, torture is used for discovery and not for evidence".[49] Probably, the "highest cases of treason" should be taken here as meaning "cases of high treason other than by counterfeiting or impairing coin". The statement that in such cases use was made of torture invited the assumption that within the indicated limits, the practice had some kind of legitimacy, but whether the foundation lay in ordinary law or something more potent, Bacon did not indicate here. What led him to convey that torture had not under Elizabeth been used in lesser cases than of treason, the highest sort of treason, we do not know. It is certainly true that the only known cases, in which he himself had been recipient of a torture warrant, had been political;[50] he may have been influenced by the *Declaration of the Favourable Dealing*.[51]

In 1612, when Coke—as Chief Justice of the Common Bench—was called upon to advise the Council in the *Countess of Shrewsbury's Case*, he propounded a list of privileges of the nobility and included the following item: "for the honour and reverence which the law gives to nobility, their bodies are not subject to torture in *causa criminis laesae majestatis*".[52] It was his way to identify *crimen laesae majestatis* with English high treason.[53] The implication is that commoners *were* liable to torture in, but only in, cases of suspected high treason. This corresponds to the advice given by Bacon to the King, but (1) adds that the basis of the power concerned, to torture, is in the Common Law; (2) does not expressly restrict the purpose for which that power, where it exists, may be employed. I shall call it "Coke's 1612 doctrine".

Some fifteen years later, a letter[54] of the 29th of April, 1627, from the Secretary of Ireland on behalf of the Lord Deputy, announced to Viscount Kilkultagh (Killultagh) in England that a priest, called Glasney O'Cullenan, suspect of exciting to rebellion in the North, was prisoner at Dublin Castle. The letter mentions only one witness against O'Cullenan, but says that the Lord Deputy would not wish, should he refuse to confess, to put him to the rack without warrant from England, for he feared the public opprobrium that would otherwise result to him from the racking of a priest. The letter, then, appears to assume that two witnesses would be required to support a conviction of high treason, unless the accused confessed, but that torture might be a useful mode of inducing a confession in that behalf.[55] Seemingly, it was understood as a request for advice, whether to pay the price of public displeasure. According to a reply,[56] of the 30th May, 1627, the King's view was that the Lord Deputy might, in such cases of "high degree of treason", execute "the uttermost of the law, not only for putting to the rack, but even to take away that man's life." This letter adds that, the matter having been referred to the Conciliar Committee for the Irish business, the latter body had determined that "you ought to rack him if you saw cause, and hang him if you found reason." The blustering is of no present significance, but—the law of England being, no doubt, assumed to prevail in Ireland on the present matter—what was reported as the King's opinion strongly suggests his acceptance of Coke's 1612 doctrine;

what was not indicated at all, however, is whether he considered that there might also be room for torture supra-legally, beyond the limits set by that doctrine.

In the following year, Felton stabbed to death the Duke of Buckingham, who was about to lead abroad a military expedition. According to John Rushworth's account[57] of what ensued:

> Felton was called before the Council, where he confessed much concerning his inducement to the murder. The Council much pressed him to confess who set him on to do such a bloody act, and if the Puritans had a hand therein. He denied they had, and so he did to the last, that no person whatsoever knew anything of his intention or purpose to kill the Duke; that he revealed it to none living. Doctor Laud, bishop of London, being then at the council table, told him if he would not confess he must go to the rack. Felton replied, if it must be so, he could not tell whom he might nominate in the extremity of torture. . . . After this he was asked no more questions, but sent back to prison. The Council then fell into debate, whether by the law of the land they could justify the putting him to the rack. The King, being at the council, said, "Before any such thing be done, let the advice of the Judges be had thereon whether it be legal or no": and afterwards His Majesty, on the 13th of November, 4 Car., propounded the question to Sir Tho. Richardson, Lord Chief Justice of the Common Pleas, to be propounded to all the Justices, viz. "Felton now a prisoner in the Tower, having confessed that he killed the Duke of Buckingham, and said he was induced to this partly for private displeasure, and partly by reason of a Remonstrance in Parliament, having also read some books which he said defended that it was lawful to kill an enemy of the republic; the question therefore is, whether by law he might not be racked, and whether there was any law against it?" "For," said the King, "if it might be done by law, he would not use his prerogative in the point."

So far, it may from Rushworth appear that Felton seemed fit to be tried for murder, not treason; that, accordingly, the King wanted to know whether (as Coke's 1612 doctrine indicated) power to torture existed in law and was not confined (here parting from that doctrine) to cases of treason; that further, he believed himself to possess prerogative power to torture, beyond any limit that might be set to his legal power in that behalf.

Rushworth also indicated that the judicial conference upon the royal inquiry lasted two days. On the 13th of November, 1628, "the Justices of Serjeants' Inn in Chancery Lane did meet and argue that the King may not in this case put the party to the rack.'' This sounds like endorsement of Coke's 1612 doctrine and disregard of the question of prerogative. On the 14th of November, "all the justices being assembled at Serjeants' Inn in Fleet-Street agreed in one, that he ought not by the law to be tortured by the rack, for no such punishment is known or allowed by our law.'' This sounds like a declaration adverse to Coke's 1612 doctrine, as far as the latter admitted torture within the law at all, and avoids the question whether the law recognized its own subjection to absolute prerogative.

However, the middle of November seems late for such an inquiry and conference. Felton was tried on the 27th of the month, and his examination had been under way before the end of September: on the 30th of which Lord Dorchester, writing to the Earl of Carlisle at Venice, said that "there is no more had out of Felton than his first free confession; and no torture hath been used unto him.''[58] David Jardine suggests[59] that probably, no conference of judges was held on torture in this case, and that Rushworth embodied in a spurious report of such an event passages that occurred when the judges indeed were consulted, but not about torture: the question put to them having been, instead, whether Felton's offending hand might be struck off before he was put to death.

As favoring this explanation, Jardine adduces: Lord Dorchester's letter of the 30th of September; one of certain "Notes for the Examination of Felton'' that exist in the handwriting of Heath, at the time Attorney-General;[60] and part of Bulstrode Whitelocke the Elder's account[61] of what transpired concerning Felton.

His argument is striking and incisive. Why was it rejected, and why was Rushworth's version of events accepted without amendment, by Gardiner and, following him, by William Holdsworth?[62]

First, notice the content of the relevant note written by Heath and all that Whitelocke had to say on the matter of judicial opinions given in Felton's case.

According to the note, "upon consideration of the effect of . . . certain . . . examinations,'' the King might, if "such presumptions and *indicia torturae*'' as were fit to justify the course appeared, "give further directions:'' obviously, directions for torture.

Whitelocke's account—the parts of which are separated, seemingly upon a chronological basis, by a reference to proceedings for failure to pay tonnage and poundage—is as follows:

The Council by the King's directions sent to the judges for their opinion, whether he might not be racked by law. They all agreed, that by the law he might not be put to the rack. . . . Felton was tried at the King's Bench, and had judgment of death; he shewed remorse, and offered his hand to be cut off, which the King desired might be done; but the judges said, it could be done by law, and he was hanged in chains.

Of course, "it could be done" does not accord with the preceding "but" or with what follows: Whitelocke must have intended to report that the judges' answer was against the conformity to law of any proposal to cut off the hand.[63]

Jardine argues that Felton's case being one of murder fully confessed, with no evidence or probable inference of the existence of accomplices, Heath's note was apt to conclude the matter: that no occasion to seek further advice could have occurred. From Whitelocke, he uses the passage concerning consultation about the hand, seeming to imply that Whitelocke placed the event before the trial.

So he proceeds to his conclusion regarding what is probable. Yet the following points, some of which may have influenced later historians, oppose his view, or at least favor its modification.

1. The dates supplied by Rushworth, as of judicial discussion regarding the possible torture of Felton, may be surprisingly late, but they are not absurdly so; of course, he might have made a chronological error and yet been right in other respects: for example, what he recounts might all have happened on the 13th and 14th of October.

2. If Heath's talk of *indicia torturae* is assumed to be a serious invocation of Continental doctrine, a difficulty presents itself concerning his meaning: Continental authority allowed torture to reveal accomplices in a range of cases including, not only treason, but assassination;[64] where an accused of either offense had freely confessed his own guilt, one may doubt whether a Continental judge would have felt that, before torturing him to name accomplices, it was necessary to establish a balance of probability in favor of their existence, or any *indicium* comparable with those required regarding guilt itself; whilst, if all Heath meant by *indicia torturae* was practical cause for recourse to torture, then both from Rushworth's account and from Lord Dorchester's letter, above mentioned, to the Earl of Carlisle, we may gather that an inherent probability, or at least risk, was felt that Felton was concealing instigators.

3. Although a declaration that "no such punishment is known or allowed by our law" might seem to have been an awkward, overly general, and unnecessary addition to the preceding sense of the opinion concerned, as Rushworth reported it, still we must allow that: (a) some confusion by English judges of torture with punishment could have resulted from hasty reference to Bracton, *De legibus,* ff. 104a-105a; (b) description of torture as a "punishment" (for the examinate's supposed obstinacy) had occasionally occurred, on the part of the Council, under Elizabeth.[65]

4. Even if the declaration referred to above is in terms that originated with regard to the cutting off of the hand, the King's reported interjection, mentioning his prerogative, is far more likely, if it occurred at all, to have done so with reference to torture for discovery of accomplices, in a matter that touched the State, than with reference to the manner of punishing a felon.

5. Whitelocke in fact agreed with Rushworth that the Council by the King's direction asked for the judges' opinion about use of torture; he placed the judicial conference concerning the cutting off of the hand a week or more later than the dates given by Rushworth for the conference on the former matter.

My own conclusion is that on the balance of probability, the judges in Felton's case expressed a view about the use of torture in relation to the Common Law and in doing so at least denied the existence at Common Law of power to torture other than for cause of high treason.

Coke, at any rate, appears by this time or fairly soon afterwards privately to have gone further. As will be noticed in the next chapter, his Second and Third *Institutes* deny entirely the legality of torture; in this respect, they must presumably be read in the light of their author's earlier assertions that the prerogative itself was subject to law.[66] They may have been completed in or about 1628, the year of publication of the First *Institute: Coke upon Littleton.*[67]

It is, of course, important to distinguish between the question whether torture is criminal, tortious, both, or neither, and the question whether what is obtained by torture ought to be admitted as judicial evidence. Bacon's advice that in treason torture was not used to obtain proof, may partly reflect a view for every offense that if an extra-judicial confession were proved in court, but challenged on the ground that it had been obtained by torture, the jury ought not—unless the allegation were in some way disproved—to be expected to rely upon it. Michael Dalton's

Country Justice, a highly influential work, the first edition of which appeared in 1618, from the 1630 edition onwards imported for witchcraft cases a good deal of demonological material from Richard Bernard's *Guide to Grandjurymen with respect to Witches*, which was published in 1627; during the present period, and later, the courts were advised by the *Country Justice* that juries might properly convict of witchcraft if satisfied that the accused bore upon his person devilish marks, or otherwise that he consorted with devilish familiars. The legal atmosphere was thus, here, favorable to what we readily apprehend as gross and dangerous superstition. Nonetheless, the *Country Justice*, whilst declaring that a confession might be the best evidence possible of witchcraft, laid down that to have probative weight, it must be voluntary.

In conclusion, let us return briefly to the question of Continental influence. So far, in this part, we have noticed two passages that may suggest, at face value, a response to such influence: Heath's reference, concerning Felton, to *indicia torturae* and Coke's talk, earlier, in the *Countess of Shrewsbury's Case*, about torture in *causa criminis laesae majestatis*. A further such suggestion exists in the record of the Peacock warrant,[68] as far as it speaks of "vehement" suspicion. Yet we may feel considerable doubt whether what we have in any of these instances is more than top-dressing.[69]

I have already referred to some difficulty that may be found with Heath's note about torture in the Felton case. Coke, in the *Countess of Shrewsbury's Case*, was presenting a strange distortion of the Continental rule: according to which liability to torture of many commoners existed with reference to all (at any rate, capital) crimes, and privilege of nobility, as far as it was recognized at all, was excluded in case of high treason;[70] whilst the reference to "vehement" suspicion in the Peacock record may really convey no more than a continuing, indigenous Government sentiment that men should not be tortured without strong cause: a sentiment conveyed without any technicality of language in the May warrant of the 20th April, 1603,[71] where the Council is content to say that there is little doubt of the truth of the accusation.

Moreover, any speculation that under Charles I an effort to respect Continental doctrine existed in this matter must confront a well-known passage from *Selden's Table Talk*.

The rack is used nowhere as in England: in other countries 'tis used in Judicature, when there is *Semiplena probatio*, a half-proof against a man;

then to see if they can make it full, they rack him, if he will not confess. But here in England they take a man and rack him, I do not know why, nor when; not in time of Judicature, but when somebody bids.[72]

chapter 8

CIVIL WAR TO REVOLUTION

I. COKE'S POSTHUMOUS CONTRIBUTION

An event for present purposes surely significant, which occurred between Archer's case and the full emergence of civil war, at Edgehill, was the posthumous publication of the later parts of Coke's *Institutes*.

As has already been noticed,[1] the Second[2] and Third[3] *Institutes* declared the illegality of torture. Their content in that regard may be described briefly as follows:

1. In both books, it is asserted that torture offends against Magna Carta, c.39 of 1215, c.29 of 1225. According to the 1215 text:

> No freeman[4] may be taken (and)/(and/or)/(or) imprisoned, or disseised or outlawed, or exiled, or in any way destroyed, unless by a lawful (judgement)/(trial) by peers (and)/(and/or)/(or) by the law of the land.[5]

More specifically, according to the Second *Institute*, a man was, in contravention of the clause, "destroyed" if he was "forejudged of life or limb" or [scil. unless within its exceptions] "disinherited, or put to torture, or death." Here, "disinherited" and "put to . . . death" probably derive from Statute 28 E.III, c.3; interpretation of "destroyed" as extending to maiming is plausible, having regard to the original, medieval context of the clause. Coke, however, does not qualify his view that the word moreover extends to torture: he does not confine the clause's prohibition of torture to such as might cause maiming or death, or was aimed to obtain confession by which sentence to one or the other would be secured more easily. Yet he does not explain this boldness. The most we may perceive, by way of argument, is a dim reflection, in his references to punishment and to torture, of a passage—partly Roman, partly Romanesque[6]—from Bracton,[7] which he actually cites on torture in the Third *Institute*. That passage mentions, as constituting a low grade among punishments, measures resembling the corporal penalties employed in Coke's time by Star Chamber, but it also lists graver punishments, including maiming; it refers to torments as ancillaries to capital execution, which raise such execution to the highest grade of punitive severity and are not to be adopted unless judicial sentence so ordains.

2. In the Third *Institute*, assertions are added that torture—

(a) lacked any positive juridical support;

(b) had been introduced too recently to have been legalized by "prescription";

(c) was declared by Fortescue to be against English law and shown by him to have grave disadvantages.

To judge these assertions as at the time of their publication, we may agree that the first of them, if not entirely conclusive, was cogent.[8] In the second, *prescription* may seem a strange word to have been used by Coke for the establishment by custom of a rule that would have diminished the liberty of—at least—the whole commonalty;[9] the suggestion, arising from its use, that nothing belonged to the Common Law that did not go back to the accession of Richard I,[10] may even in the the seventeenth century have appeared somewhat unrealistic: a plain affirmation might have been more impressive, that the success of Executive authority in pursuing a violent course cannot, even if sustained for a considerable period, render that course lawful.[11] As for the third of the above assertions, it was undoubtedly true: but, of course, anyone who read the *De laudibus* with a critical mind would see that as far as concerned the state of English law, Fortescue's remarks on the non-admission of torture referred to judicial procedure.

Coke did not attempt to dispose expressly of the possible thesis that the Crown could fall back, in support of its use of torture, as of any sort of Executive activity, upon an overriding prerogative or law of *State*. He may have felt such an attempt unnecessary, since the existence of royal power undefined and unrestricted by the Common Law, was denied in his *Reports*.[12]

Anyway, to establish the illegality of torture, his own authority itself contributes much, although doubtless at first it weighed more with Parliamentarian liberals than with Royalist authoritarians. The latter, for the time being, might well continue to believe that torture was an available instrument of royal government, whether assigning the fact simply to existence of absolute prerogative or holding to the view that torture might be used by law in case of treason: and whether or not assuming that if it were used, the aim would be other than to obtain evidence for use at law.[13]

II. THE CIVIL WAR

It is possible that during the Civil War, prisoners in theatres of hostility sometimes were tortured for information. However, regarding events in England, I have seen no reference to such a thing.[14] The only interrogatory torture of which reports are available had nothing to do with the fighting, was of a camouflaged kind, and appears to have depended upon no higher public authority than that of East Anglian justices of the peace.

The context was provided by a brief emergence, upon the English scene, of professional witchfinders. They were a novelty of the mid-1640s,[15] and happily did not endure, although in 1649 to 1650, a Scots "pricker" found employment in Newcastle upon Tyne and County Durham until, at last, one justice of the peace had the courage and good sense to bind him over to appear at Quarter Sessions, whereupon he fled back to Scotland.[16]

No doubt this fellow's victims suffered pain as well as embarrassment at his hands, but although his evidence may have destroyed many of them, there is no reason to suppose that he pricked any of them so mercilessly as to extort a confession. On the other hand, the far more notorious Matthew Hopkins, his helpers, and some imitators proceeded upon theories that provided a cover for what amounted to infliction of very severe duress and is said by its severity to have induced confessions that were allowed to aid the conviction of those who made them.[17]

Hopkins was a lawyer who lived at Manningtree, in Essex. Between 1644 and 1647—in the summer of which year he is believed to have died—he and two companions offered their services—for a fee—as witchfinders in East Anglia. His methods included "swimming" suspects (putting them to a cold water ordeal), "watching" them (forcing them to sit on a stool, for long periods, under close observation), and "walking" them (depriving them of sleep for long periods and further exhausting them by compelling them to walk to and fro). It is not alleged that "swimming" led to confession, although it must have been very distressing and although water tortures have long figured among brutal

supports of interrogation.[18] But Francis Hutchinson plausibly suggested
that subjection to "watching" must in time have become "as painful
as the wooden horse" (the latter being a military punishment, in which
the offender was made to sit astride a wedge, with weights on his legs),[19]
whilst "walking" corresponded to De Marsiliis's torture of deprival of
sleep,[20] in an aggravated form: [21] these are the methods that are said to
have operated in fact as modes of interrogatory torture.

Hopkins's explanations appeared in a well-presented apology, his
Discovery of Witches, in 1647.[22] From that work,[23] we may gather that
the practice of keeping suspects from sleep was condemned by justices
of assize in the second half of 1645 or early in 1646 and was thereafter
abandoned by Hopkins. Clearly, by the time he wrote the *Discovery*,
he had acquired influential critics.[24] In it, he showed full awareness of
what was contained, regarding the proof of witchcraft, in Dalton's
Country Justice: the cardinal propositions there being that (what has
already been noticed[25]) a suspect might be found guilty upon his or her
own confession, yet only provided it had been made without constraint;
and that, otherwise, a conviction might be founded upon any evidence
of association with devilish familiars. Hopkins carefully disclaimed any
interest in enforced confession: "he utterly denies that confession of a
witch to be of any validity, when it is drawn from her by any torture
or violence whatsoever."[26] His interest, he explained, was in evidence
of familiarity with imps; he asserted that if a witch were watched long
enough, her familiars would approach her openly, in view of the watchers, whilst if she were kept from sleep, she would thereby be made
more likely to call those familiars into view.[27]

III. THE LORD PROTECTOR

On 22 February, 1655, the Venetian Secretary in London, Lorenzo
Paulucci, wrote[28] to the Venetian Ambassador in France, Giovanni
Sagredo, that all conspiracies against the Protector were discovered and
that whilst torture was forbidden by law in England, information regarding those conspiracies had been elicited from prisoners by hope of
reward and threat of punishment.

Paulucci's statement regarding the law is valuable; what follows it
naturally and probably conveys (not that the law was being disregarded
to the extent of threatening torture, but) that means of persuasion, which
were being used, included threats of the punishment that would ensue
upon prosecution and conviction.

However, shortly afterwards, a different picture was painted in reports sent home by the Venetian Resident in England, Francesco Giavarina. He told the Doge and Senate—

1. on 22 September, 1656, that some royalists had been arrested to see whether their dealings and understandings with the King (Charles II) could be extracted from them by torture;[29]

2. only on 22 December, 1656, that in London a gentleman had been arrested, along with a low-class woman who had been an intermediary between that gentleman and the King, then at Bruges, that in Scotland a number of leading noblemen had been arrested, and that they were all—apparently, including the two people taken in London—being examined and compelled by torture to disclose their accomplices;[30]

3. on 24 August, 1657, that Thomas Gardiner had been arrested when preparing an attempt to assassinate the Protector and had refused to help in the discovery of his accomplices, although the Government was seeking to extract a confession from him by means of torture;[31]

4. on 31 August, 1657, that three Catholic gentlemen from Shropshire had been arrested (actually, one was from that County, the other two from Staffordshire[32]), that they had confessed, and that it seemed the Government would punish them *and* put them to torture;[33]

5. on 7 June, 1658, that full confessions had been obtained from various persons under arrest, whose mouths had been opened by fear of torture.[34]

It may be felt impossible either to reject or to accept Giavarina's assertions. The situation in the country was prone to encourage Executive violence. At least one rack probably remained at the Tower throughout the Commonwealth:[35] if it did so, there can have been no acute governmental antipathy to the idea of torture. On the other hand, no hint is given that after the Restoration, when—as will be mentioned in later sections—governmental hankerings after use of the rack came to nothing, adverse public opinion was rallied by recollection of such use under Cromwell. Moreover, Giavarina may have been relying unduly upon alarmist rumors within the Royalist underground or deliberately false information fed to him, with a view of influencing foreign opinion, by a Royalist agent. He may have been encouraged to rely upon such rumors or information or even himself to fill out dispatches with references to torture, by having acquaintance with Venetian methods rather than with those of Commonwealth England.[36]

At any rate, this material is all I have found concerning Cromwell's government.[37]

IV. CROWN EXECUTIVE TORTURE AFTER THE RESTORATION

That, after the Restoration, supporters of the new Government were not invariably repelled by the thought of the rack is shown by a letter[38] written on 22 January, 1667, by Colonel J. Long to Arlington's Secretary, Joseph Williamson. In it, Long suggested that one Charles Aland (of Longley Burrell, near Chippenham) would if the rack were shown to him declare all of the chief traitors in the West. Still, the suggestion was moderate: it ran only to terrorization, and we cannot assume that it was seriously intended.

The strongest available evidence of actual movements towards resumed Executive use of the rack relates to two occasions in the 1670s.

In January, 1673, two Dutchmen, whose names were Zas and Arton, disembarked at Harwich. They were arrested and sent to London, where at first they were imprisoned in the Gatehouse. In the preceding month, Zas had been in England and had left upon the orders of the Government.[39] When he returned and was arrested, he immediately wrote,[40] from Harwich, to Arlington, complaining that in returning he had complied with an arrangement made between them, and that his arrest was thus a betrayal. The King, however, believed him to have been sent, with Arton, by Fagell, the Pensioner of Holland, to enter into negotiations bypassing the King himself and his officers of State.[41] On 26 March, 1673, a warrant[42] was issued for the removal of the two prisoners to the Tower, where they were interrogated, a copy of their examination being dispatched on the following day;[43] about this time, a letter from Arlington to the Lieutenant of the Tower announced the King's wish that the rack should be made ready, and the executioner required to attend by ten o'clock the next morning: Lauderdale and Secretary Coventry having been appointed to go to the Tower and to examine "certain prisoners" in the Lieutenant's custody.[44] Subsequent events, to be described in the next section, convey (as it may seem, beyond reasonable doubt): (1) that Zas and Arton were the prisoners concerned; (2) that the King and his officers, whilst not obtaining from them the sort of statements that were desired, did not after all proceed, by an assumption of Executive authority, to put them to the rack; and (3) that what prevented the adoption of such a course was apprehension that it would offend the Common Law.

The second occasion was the murder of Sir Edmund Berry Godfrey.

The latter had been a wood merchant and justice of the peace for Westminster. Seemingly, he had rendered good service during the Plague and the Fire of London and had thereby earned royal appreciation. Nonetheless, he had emerged as a leader of urban Protestant opposition to the beliefs and manners of the Court. Pepys's story,[45] of how Godfrey was imprisoned and came close to being flogged in 1669, is worth noticing, if only for the light it throws upon the King's temper and outlook. Later, it was with Godfrey that Titus Oates deposited his dossier on the "Popish Plot".[46] Thus when Godfrey was found dead—with marks of strangulation and run through with his own sword—the situation was very dangerous, both to Roman Catholics at large and to the Court.

Suspicion of the murder fell upon Miles Prance, a Covent Garden silversmith and himself a Roman Catholic, who before the end of October, 1678, was placed under arrest. We have some notes[47] of an examination to which he was subjected in December of that year. They relate that at one point, the Lord Chancellor, who was among his interrogators, suggested that he should be shown the rack. If this suggestion was indeed made, we must notice that—like the one above noticed, of Colonel Long—it was limited to terrorization. Moreover, although Prance eventually confessed, no evidence exists that the rack was used, even to frighten him.

On the other hand, whatever may have been the truth of the matter, an attempt was made at the time to persuade public opinion that he had been subjected to some kind of physical torment, and that the same experience had befallen another suspect, one Francis Caryll, a coach-man.

Mrs. Elizabeth Cellier was a Roman Catholic who had recently been acquitted of high treason.[48] She boldly published a pamphlet, with references to the treatment of Prance and Caryll, which brought her back to court, this time upon a charge of seditious libel.[49] Her pamphlet, entitled *Malice Defeated*, contained two passages of present relevance.

One of them describes how, on the evening of 9 January, 1679, Mrs. Cellier and some other women heard groans coming, for a considerable time, from a dungeon called the "Condemned Hole", at the entrance to Newgate. Mrs. Cellier and the others were told that the noise was being made by a woman in labor, but they lingered and concluded that the sufferer was a man. In due course, they heard what they thought was the "winding up of some engine." Then an officer came out, in evident distress. He was asked, by one of the other women, whether a man was on the rack and, by Mrs. Cellier herself, whether it was Prance. He answered the first question by saying that what was going on was something like racking; the second, he said that he did not dare to answer. According to the passage, the groans persisted, and when the outer gate of the lodge was locked, Mrs. Cellier, before herself leaving the place, put a woman on watch, to see what she could from the street. This passage continues:

> A prisoner loded with irons was brought into the lodge and examined a long time . . . About four o'clock the next morning, the prisoners that lay in a place above the Hole heard . . . [a] . . . cry . . . about two hours, and on Saturday morning again; and about eight o'clock that morning a person I employed to spy out the truth of the affair, did see the turnkeys carrying a bed into the Hole. She asked what it was for. They told her it was for Prance, who had gone mad, and had tore his bed to pieces. . . .

The other passage states that soon after the above incident, Caryll, who had been suspected of transporting Godfrey's body in his coach and had been arrested, was released from Newgate and that Mrs. Cellier went to see him. She found him crippled by, as he himself asserted, cruel fettering, and he told her of other ill-treatment that he had received: how he had been violently assaulted by a duke, had been kept without food and drink for four days, and had been once "squeezed and hasped into a thing like a trough, in a dungeon underground, which put him to inexpressible torment."

With this second passage must be compared the *Deposition of Francis Caryll*, which was published among the *Fairfax Correspondence* by Robert Bell, and which states that Caryll was arrested by Captain Richardson, the Newgate jailer, who the next day took him to a meeting of a few Privy Councillors. (Apparently, the meeting was treated as one of the Council, for Caryll was examined upon oath.) Those present were Buckingham, Shaftsbury, Winchester, Halifax, and another, whom Caryll did not recognize, and who administered the oath. Caryll suffered a good deal of abuse and various threats of punishment. Buckingham struck him and made passes at his chest with a drawn sword. Then, on whispered instructions from Shaftsbury, he removed Caryll once again to Newgate, where he was "laid in a thing like a trough, in some place in the press-room, and where, with something laid upon him, he was in horrid torment kept for the space of three hours.'' Taken out of the trough, he was once more transported by Richardson to meet the Privy Councillors who had interviewed him, and on this occasion a gentleman of seeming substance was produced as a witness against him, and he was offered every inducement to depose against certain persons. When he declined, he was taken back to Newgate, where, loaded with irons, he was made to fast for four days. Then for a further period of six weeks, he was kept cruelly fettered in a dungeon, without any bedding. There followed another violent interview with his distinguished interrogators, and more than six weeks continued incarceration at Newgate before he was released on bail.

Since Prance, when he confessed, gave evidence leading to the conviction of various alleged accomplices, including an officer of the Queen's chapel and a porter of Somerset House, English Roman Catholics had a strong motive to believe and to assert that his confession and the inculpations it embraced were false: hence, by way of explanation, that he had been tortured. It follows that the weak hearsay used by Mrs. Cellier to link Prance with the groans from the Condemned Hole at Newgate must be regarded with special caution. What Mrs. Cellier recounted of Francis Caryll's story suggests that the generally similar, although more detailed, version in the *Deposition* proceeded from him. Of course, even so, he may not have originated it, but it is a strange tale for anyone to have invented. One deviation is that according to Mrs. Cellier, he said he was squeezed in an underground dungeon; according to the *Deposition*, he suffered that treatment somewhere in the press-room. If the rest is supposed wholly or partly true, it is impossible to say which account is more reliable on this point. Mrs. Cellier may have questioned him tendentiously, to produce what was, or what seemed to her, an answer tending to substantiate her belief about the treatment of Prance: although she does not represent him as having said that the dungeon was close to the entrance to the prison, a fact he might well have remembered. What is certainly interesting, neither account suggests that he was interrogated while he was being squeezed.

On balance, whilst it is impossible to be confident regarding the manner of the treatment of prisoners after Godfrey's death, it is tempting to speculate that recourse was had—against Caryll and some others—

to measures of duress, which at least against Caryll included restricted use of some variant (then employed, at Newgate, upon those who refused to plead to felony indictments, and were sentenced accordingly) of the *peine forte et dure*,[50] but that such duress was made a background to, not an immediate accompaniment of, Privy Council examinations.

V. COURT MARTIAL

In 1673 it seems that only a few days after Arlington's letter to the Lieutenant of the Tower about preparation of the rack,[51] a draft commission for the martial trial of the Dutchmen, Zas and Arton, was submitted to the King by two Civilians—Sir R. Wiseman, who was Advocate General, and Sir W. Walker. The proposed commission was to be directed to eleven military officers and four doctors of Civil Law. It was expressly to authorize interrogatory torture of the accused— though not so as to lame, disjoint, or dismember them—for the purpose not merely of establishing their guilt, but of discovering their entire design. The King's further order was, however, to be required before execution of sentence of death.

On 14 February, the King wrote[52] to the draftsmen, enclosing a copy of their work and declaring his approval. In his letter he set out his justification of the course he intended to be taken, observing:

> In the heate of the warre betwixt Us and the States Generall of the United Provinces, viz. in December last past, the Herr Zas having come over into England in the nature of a Spy and so behaved himself as he might have been proceeded against . . . yet of Our clemency We were pleased at that time to forbeare proceeding against him so that he no more offended in the like kind, and it was Our command intimated unto him that he should depart at his perill within twenty four hours without entertaining discourse with any other than such as was necessary for his returne back to Holland. . . . He upon his returne to Holland . . . communicated what he had gathered up of Our affaires in England to Sieur Fagell the Pensioner of Holland & rendered reasons to him how fitt he was to negociate in the nature of a Spy here in England: and received from the said Sieur Fagell Letters dated the Hague the 9th. of January, 1673 . . . whereby . . . he was to negociate without addressing Us or any of Our Ministers of State, and upon those affaires and therewith he in January last together with one Arton another Hollander or Emissary & Spy came over from

Holland to England and being apprehended stand committed to the Tower of London.

He added that, thereupon, he, the King, had resolved:

upon just cause . . . to have them brought to tryall and judgment as spys.

A commission, conforming to the proposals of Wiseman and Walker, and ready for execution although unsealed, may be seen in the Public Record Office.[53] It is dated 24 February, 1673, and may be supposed an office copy of a commission actually issued on that date: court martial proceedings against the Dutchmen began at the Tower on 1 March,[54] a trial or semblance of a trial getting under way on the following day.[55] On 27 March, however,[56] the commissioners adjourned to 11 April, Zas having first been informed by King's Counsel that he must answer certain questions, including some concerning the source of his instructions, and some concerning the identity of the persons with whom he was to deal in England; that if, after the adjournment, he did not volunteer a clear answer to each of the questions, he was likely to be tortured; and that the commissioners wanted him to reflect and to be ready to make a clean breast when they next convened, so that he might avoid the penalty for intransigence. Yet it seems that when 11 April arrived, the hearing was not resumed.

On 15 April, the King wrote[57] again to Wiseman, reciting the terms we have in the engrossed copy dated 24 February, making the remarkable statement that the commissioners appointed upon those terms were not able to complete their task, because some were otherwise employed upon his business, some upon their own, and directing the preparation of a new commission, which would allow the trial to be continued by other persons. The new commission would resemble the original. However, its provision for torture would advert to a specific juridical base, relate expressly to more than one stage in the process, and be somewhat more specific regarding topics of investigation: the commissioners appointed were to be authorized to inflict upon the accused during the trial or even after sentence tortures such as the law of nations allowed, to compel them to disclose their plans, to name the persons with whom they came to deal, and to reveal how money they had with them was to be expended.

Yet no evidence shows that a renewal of the proceedings ensued, or indeed, that a new commission was ever issued.

In the letter of 14 February, the King's reference to the "heat of the war" may have been intended partly as itself an umbrella justification of martial proceedings, but if so, the intention was misguided: the Common Law doctrine that must have been in view, referring primarily to subjects of the Crown, allowed execution without Common Law arraignment and trial only where Common Law process was rendered impossible by conditions of war;[58] whereas not only were such conditions absent in London in 1673, but had they been present, the use of such a commission as was actually employed would hardly have been congruous. The doctrine was one that after the Restoration—in 1666—Charles had flouted by purporting to make provision, through articles of war—without special statutory authorization—for the military trial of soldiers upon capital charges within the realm. However, in 1672 a retreat had been sounded, through the promulgation of new articles that, in terms, were applicable only abroad.[59] Thus it may be supposed that the time was hardly favorable for attempting to turn the Common Law position by the aid merely of a glaring fiction of strife.[60]

Probably, instead, Charles's reference to the "heat of the war" was meant to be taken in relation to his assertion that Zas had come to England as a spy in the preceding year, although also as qualifying by necessary implication his following assertions about the purposes of the mission upon which Zas and Arton were arrested: in other words, probably the only argument upon which the King relied was that he was entitled to subject the two men to martial trial, with the incidents allowed by European military custom, because they were foreigners who had entered the realm as spies in time of war. Anyway, this was clearly the main argument upon which he took his stand, and it was not a bad choice: whilst the teaching of the "Law of Nations" offered no precise guidance regarding the limits of the category of "spies",[61] Common Law jurisprudence had seemingly failed to incorporate any firm rule about how alien spies, taken outside the theatre of hostilities, but in time of war, might be dealt with in the realm.[62] Thus—although considerable influence may have been operating on Zas's behalf—if indeed even this military avenue was eventually abandoned, as a way of bringing (should it be felt necessary) him and his companion to the rack, the fact suggests a strong sense that the Common Law, however ill-defined in some areas, did condemn interrogatory torture in any context, whether Executive, judicial (although outside its own process), or quasi-judicial.

VI. BARON WESTON'S HISTORICAL REVIEW

In conclusion, we may notice observations reported to have been made by Baron Weston during Mrs. Cellier's trial (1680) for seditious libel.

He is said to have directed that:

> The laws of the land do not admit a torture, and since Queen Elizabeth's time there hath been nothing of the kind ever done. The truth is, indeed, in the twentieth year of her reign Campion was stretched upon the rack, but yet not so but that he could walk; but when she was told it was against the law of the land to have any of her subjects racked (though that was an extraordinary case, a world of seminaries being sent over to contrive her death, and she lived in continual danger) yet it was never done after to anyone, neither in her reign, who reigned twenty-five years after, nor in King James's reign who reigned twenty-two years after, nor in King Charles the first's reign, who reigned twenty-four years after; and God in heaven knows that there have been no such thing offered in this King's reign.[63]

The learned Baron's reported observations are, of course, interesting here for their implication that, at this time, the public was largely ignorant regarding past Government practice and very recent royal ambition. But moreover, a government that, in self-vindicatory proceedings, had been represented judicially as not having used torture, which at the same time judicially was declared to be unacceptable to the laws of the land, would have been ill-placed thereafter to advance an open claim to be entitled to use that expedient, whether under the laws or above them.[64]

chapter 9

ANTIQUARIAN ADDENDA

I. BARNACLES, KNOTTED ROPE, AND BOILING FAT

Interrogatory torture with the barnacles, with a knotted rope, and with boiling fat seem each to be mentioned only once in regard to the history of English Government. On the other hand, each does appear to have been employed on the Continent.

With the story that Sir Henry Wyatt was subjected by Richard III to torture by the barnacles[1] may be compared the following strange description, which Piero Fiorelli[2] points out, in the 1580 edition of Iacopo di Belviso's *Practica criminalis*.[3] Torture, it is there (according to my understanding) said, may be:

> with brakes, with which the lips of ill-disposed horses are stretched, when those horses are being shoed, the wooden parts being placed and drawn tight upon the lips of those to be tortured.[4]

Possibly where I have given "the wooden parts being placed", Belviso intended simply: "placed, fastened", but this is unimportant.[5]

The tightening of a knotted rope around the examinate's head—a method said to have been adopted by Thomas Cromwell with Mark Smeaton[6]—has obtained popular notice by figuring, off-stage, in *Tosca*.[7] On the Continent, it may usually have been extra-judicial, but an *additio antiqua* to Belviso's *Practica*[8] mentions torture by tying small bones (or rather, perhaps, dice)[9] across the examinate's forehead.[10] The torture by heating the examinate's boots, after filling them with fat, which in 1543 was used by Suffolk and Tunstall upon their prisoner Brewer,[11] had on the Continent considerable judicial application. However, as it sometimes caused lasting inability to walk, it was employed only where the offense suspected was grave or in lieu of the strappado where the suspect would, for some special physical reason, have been unable to sustain torture by that means.[12]

II. STRETCHING RACKS

The illustration in Foxe's *Acts and Monuments*[13] of the racking of Cuthbert Simpson, in 1558, and the description of English racking under Elizabeth that, in the latter part of the seventeenth century, was produced by Matthias Tanner[14] agree concerning the design of the instrument employed. They represent it as having been a rectangular wooden frame, with transverse rollers, one near each end, with bearings in its sides, and as having been deep enough for the rollers to be turned when it was standing on the ground. Richard Verstegan offers[15] an illustration of a similar instrument, but with, instead of a complete frame, two stout planks, placed in parallel—and perhaps fixed to a baseboard—with the rollers between them. The Foxe and Verstegan illustrations agree that the instrument was worked, on the ground, by means of levers inserted in sockets in the rollers. Foxe's illustration has one operator at each end, using a long lever with both hands and maintaining pressure on a short lever with one foot; Verstegan's has two operators at each end.[16] Tanner agrees with Verstegan that there were four operators, but does not explain how they turned the rollers. Foxe and Verstegan show the examinate being stretched by four ropes, one attached to each wrist, one to each ankle, and each taken over the nearest roller, to be wrapped round it. Foxe has the ropes to the inside of the levers, Verstegan has them to the outside, at the ends of the rollers, the examinate being shown spread-eagled. Tanner agrees that the examinate might be attached by his wrists and ankles, but says that alternatively, cords might be used, attached severally to his thumbs, fingers, and toes.[17] He supplies the further detail that the rollers turned in iron bearings.

In England the only instrument of apparent antiquity I have seen, broadly conforming to the design of a rack that we may discover from Foxe and Tanner, was bought not long ago in the town of Barnard Castle and given to the museum at Maidstone.[18]

The preface to Edward Rishton's Diary states simply that the rack pulls the examinate's limbs in opposite directions by means of wooden rollers and *certain machines*: levers are not mentioned.

As will be recalled, the letter written on 10 March, 1581, by Hammond and the Lieutenant concerning Myagh,[19] suggests the existence of a severe mode of torture that could be left in operation when the jailers withdrew. Considering the date, it may seem likely that this mode was by racking. Yet none of the sources mentioned above indicate that racks were fitted with ratchet-wheels and pawls or any other means of fixing the rollers after tension had been applied. On the other hand, Isaac Reed, when annotating (in his several reeditions of Shakespeare's plays during the 1790s) the mysterious line from *Measure for Measure*,[20] "Some run from brakes of vice, and answer none," referred to Hollinshed[21] and Blackstone[22] for authority that the "brake" was identical with the "rack", and proceeded:

> A part of this horrid engine still remains in the Tower. . . . It consists of a strong iron frame about six feet long with three rollers of wood within it. The middle one of these which has iron teeth at each end, is governed by two stops of iron, and was, probably, that part of the engine which suspended the powers of the rest, when the unhappy sufferer was sufficiently strained. . . .

Reed moreover supplied a sketch, unfortunately rough, of what he had seen.[23] Viewing it in conjunction with his text, we may gather that the device concerned had the following features, in addition to those he states:

The three rollers were socketed into the frame at a level about halfway between its top and bottom edges and were of a diameter about three times its depth: so what was seen by Reed, if it was used for stretching, must have been raised on trestles or by other convenient means. The sum of the distances of the axes of the outer rollers from their respective ends of the frame was nearly one-sixth of the frame's total length: so the distance between those axes, according to Reed's measurement of the frame, was only fractionally above five feet. The "stops" were pawls set each at one end, and on the inner side, of a metal arm. The two arms, at their other ends, were welded to a rod, which was pivoted across the frame between the inner roller and one of the outer rollers. The pawls worked within ratchet teeth, which were directed towards the axis of the inner roller, being set upon hoops, of about the same circumference as that roller and fixed one at each of its ends. When the device was being driven, they operated by aid of gravity.[24] They could be lifted clear of the ratchets by pulling up either arm.

No means are indicated of directly turning or of otherwise motivating the outer rollers. Evidently, it might have been done from the center.[25]

The explanation of the manner of mounting the ratchet teeth, inwards from the circumference of the inner roller, may be that they were intended to serve also as part of a geared drive, although the driving cog in that case was perhaps specially designed, for they were of the usual ratchet shape, one edge being steep and straight,[26] the other, convex.

The presence of the ratchet and pawl arrangement indicates that the device was meant for stretching; if Reed's measurement of the frame was wrong, the Myagh letter suggests that he saw part of a torture rack such as was in use at the Tower by the early 1580s. Indeed, he may have seen the remains of the kind of apparatus described in the letter attributed to Cuthbert Simpson—published by Foxe in 1563 and referring to events in 1558—simply as a "rack of iron".[27] As is noticed below (in section V), Foxe's illustrator was at least in some measure inaccurate when he dealt with the episode concerned; he may have been totally wrong about it, as well as partly wrong in his illustration of Simpson's being—in the words of the same letter—"later twice racked". It is even possible that by going wrong in the latter respect, he fathered later mistakes regarding what was or had been the English mode of racking, and that the English did not, or did not from the mid-sixteenth century, use a rack that was placed on the ground to be operated, from its ends, by two or four men with levers.

On the other hand, whilst the letter[28] of January, 1673, from Arlington to the Lieutenant of the Tower about Zas and Arton, suggests that after the Restoration, only one rack was at the Tower, and, indeed, only one "rack for torment" is listed in the 1678 Tower Inventory of Stores,[29] yet—as has been noticed—Rishton's Diary records that on 31 October, 1581, John Payne was put to the *same* stretching rack as Campion;[30] the Gerard autobiography (chapter 6, part II, section IV) emphasizes the number and variety of instruments of torture that were in April, 1597, displayed at the Tower to its supposed author.[31] So the Crown may, in the latter part of Elizabeth's reign, have had at its disposal both one or more stretching racks such as that shown in the Foxe illustration and one or more incorporating the kind of part described by Reed.[32]

III. THE WALL AND THE MANACLES

Concerning the character and mode of use of the manacles, fairly detailed information is offered by the Gerard autobiography.[33]

Two wrist-irons were put onto the examinate, each iron having, at right angles to its own aperture, a fixing ring. When the examinate's arms were above his head, a rod—presumably, such as was used with bilboes—was slipped through one of the fixing rings, through a staple projecting from an upright—or, no doubt, from a wall—and through the other ring and then secured by dropping a pin into a hole provided at the end that had been passed through the rings and staple. In the instances described by the autobiography, Gerard was required to mount steps, before his irons were secured to the staple, and the steps were then withdrawn, with the intention of leaving him suspended clear of the ground.[34] According to Jesuit intelligence,[35] Topcliffe on at least one occasion, when Southwell was in the manacles, caused his heels to be strapped to his thighs. This may well have been to deprive him of support, which he otherwise received, from his feet or toes. In fact, alternative methods appear to have been used of total or partial suspension. Southwell, in his report of March, 1590, said[36] that Christopher Bayles had been kept for twenty-four hours hanging by the hands, with the tips of his toes touching the ground.

Among the Council records, the first express reference to the manacles seems to be in that for 18 April, 1590,[37] concerning persons suspected of a robbery. However, their use, having regard to Southwell's account of the way in which Bayles actually was tortured, may be supposed to be contemplated by the draft warrant of February, 1590,[38] concerning Bayles and others, which refers to "such torture upon the wall as is usual." Whilst, upon such supposition, it was probably still earlier contemplated by the warrant recorded for 24 June, 1589,[39] which spoke of the "torture of the house" at Bridewell: where both the Bayles draft warrant and the 1590 recorded warrant, mentioned above, were to be executed. A letter to Verstegan, in 1592, stated that in England the manacles had been used on priests "taken any time these five years."[40]

During the 1590s, however, at least one other similar mode of inflicting pain was used. It sounds less savage. The relation,[41] of his own misfortunes, which is attributed to Thomas Doulton, the young Wisbech convert, states that in Bridewell, at some time during 1595 or early in 1596, he was for ten days made to stand, with his hands stretched above his head, against the wall, in the "standing stocks".[42] From the general content of the narrative, it may be guessed that he was thus treated as a punishment for recalcitrance and to make him more amenable to the prison discipline. Yet the same could plainly have been done as an aid to interrogation; indeed, it was a method advocated for that purpose by Topcliffe, in his letter of 22 June, 1592, about Southwell.[43]

But then, Topcliffe's letter itself creates an uncertainty. It contemplates alternative proceedings—Southwell could be made "either to stand upon or against the wall"—and it adds that the efficacy of making him stand against the wall would be increased if he were placed with "his feet standing upon the ground, and his hands but as high as he can reach against the wall". This, however, leaves the question what Topcliffe meant by *standing upon* the wall. The structure of the sentence strongly suggests that he did not here refer to staying, *hanging*, upon the wall; no doubt a person made to stand up, on top of a stone wall, for a long time would thereby suffer a good deal.

IV. MONSTROUS STOCKS

To causes of chronic suffering that might be encountered in sixteenth-century prisons, Sir Thomas More applied the compendious description, "hard handling". In the twentieth chapter of his *Third Book against Tribulation*, he lists them as follows: "Strayte keping, collering, boltyng, and stocking, with lying on straw or on the cold grounde."[44]

Seemingly, the infliction of irons or stocking might, in the ordinary contexts of imprisonment, reflect fear of the prisoner's escaping; a need to stop his fighting; a purpose of pecuniary extortion; or even mere ill-humor of the jailor.[45]

On the other hand, we find as follows references to them in a context that broadly was one of interrogation.

We have seen that, according to the account preserved by Foxe,[46] in 1558, at St. Paul's, Thomas Green was subjected to fettering and stocking during a protracted process that eventually won some information from him.

Foxe recounts that Green was stocked first in the Bishop's coalhouse; that thereafter he was kept for a period, shackled hand and foot and without bedding, in the salthouse; and that he ended, in stocks, in the Lollard's Tower.[47]

Foxe also reports[48] John Lithall as having complained, in the same year, of Bonner's men, who in the words of Foxe's quotation: "carried me to the Lollard's Tower, and hanged me in a great pair of stocks, in which I lay three days and three nights, till I was so lame that I could neither stir or move."

Further, in 1571, when Story had been executed, the author of a pamphlet[49] recounting his *Life and Death* observed:

He was committed to the Lollardes tower in Powles, where he continued a while, that he might well peruse that place wherein he had most cruelly tormented many a good Christian. But he lacked there one thing, which was the monstrous and huge stockes, that he and Boner, his old faithful friend, had used to turmoyle and persecute the poore and innocent Christians in, hanging some therein by the heles so high, that only their heads laye on the ground; some were stocked in both feet and arms; some also were stocked by both their feet and by both their thombes, and did so hang in the stockes. And some also were stocked by both theyr fete, and chyned by the necks wyth collars of iron made fast behynde theim to a post in the wall. . . . These at his being in the Lollardes tower he myssed. . . . The good bishop Gryndell, late bishop of London, had brent and consumed theym with fire.

Stowe recorded another case of imprisonment in the Lollard's Tower, during the following year.[50] However, no hint appears that under Elizabeth it was used for any kind of interrogatory oppression, although according to one opinion[51] the stocks it had contained at her accession were not promptly destroyed by Grindal, but perished by the fire[52] that destroyed the roof of the cathedral on 4 June, 1561.

Oddly enough, Verstegan nonetheless in the *Theatrum crudelitatum*[53] alleged that—presumably, since the beginning of the Roman Catholic missions to England—the English Protestant authorities had put a certain priest into wooden stocks by which his feet had been pulled up into the air;[54] according to Verstegan, they had kept him so for such a long time that he had been stifled by stench of his own excrement. Possibly, however, some inspiration was here drawn by Verstegan, or his informant, from Foxe.

V. THE TOWER: "LITTLE EASE", "LACUS", AND THE "SCAVENGER'S DAUGHTER"

Room for doubt exists regarding the respective meanings, in connection with the Tower, of the names "Little Ease" and "Scavenger's Daughter" and regarding the location within the Tower of what in Rishton's Diary is called *Lacus*: the "Tank". Here let us begin by cataloging (if at the cost of some repetition of what has been noticed in earlier chapters) available evidence, whether direct or circumstantial and whether tending towards clarification or towards confusion.

1. One fact about the Tower that must be appreciated *in limine* is

the large number and drastic character of the changes that over a long period were made in its fabric, leaving little or no trace, and regarding which little or no documentation is to be found. For example, it is known that among buildings that stood under Elizabeth, but since have been totally or almost totally removed, were the Cold-harbour gateway; the Wardrobe Tower; a large eastward extension of the White Tower;[55] the White Tower forebuilding; the Jewel House; and the Palace buildings: both the older ones, nearer the Wakefield Tower, and the complex further east. Cold-harbour had a prison above the gate;[56] the Wardrobe Tower had probably been a prison.[57] More's "hard handling" by "straight keeping" might have been contrived in basements or closets anywhere. The forebuilding, especially, may have contained a pit.[58]

2. The Conciliar instruction recorded[59] for 16 November, 1552, as addressed to the Lieutenant of the Tower, was "to examine Holland, putting him to the torment in Little Ease." Other recorded warrants concerning torture at the Tower do not seem to have specified a place for its infliction; this one may, by "Little Ease", have meant (not a torture chamber, but) a particular torture instrument: if so, from the way it reads, probably one of acute infliction. On the other hand, the letter recorded for 3 May, 1555, about Stephen Happes, evidently uses "Little Ease" to describe a place or device, at the Tower, imposing chronic discomfort.

3. Regarding the name "Scavenger's Daughter", part of the background is provided by the history of the Skevingtons. Sir William Skevington, who died in 1535, enjoyed the confidence both of the King and of Thomas Cromwell and was rewarded by being made a royal lieutenant in Ireland, where he was Deputy from 1529 to 1532 and 1534 to 1535. He was primarily an artilleryman; before taking up office as Deputy, he was Master of the Ordnance. Indeed, he returned to gunnery during the interval from 1532 to 1534, when he was not in Ireland.[60] His son, Leonard Skevington,[61] became in 1534 Yeoman of the Ordnance at the Tower[62] and continued in that office until his death ten years later:[63] when he was succeeded by a Thomas Skevington, who had been "marshall of the ordnance in the rearward" at the siege of Monstrell[64] and was probably the Thomas Skevington appointed, in 1546, to the post of Keeper of the Ordnance at Nottingham Castle.[65]

4. In 1556 John Danyell complained[66] of being at the Tower among spiders and newts in a dismal dungeon: he said he had not light, all day, to see his hands perfectly.

5. The first edition, published in 1563, of Foxe's *Acts and Monuments*, offers—when illustrating[67] the statement that Cuthbert Simpson was "set in a rack of iron, the space of three hours" and was later twice racked—an inset, with the legend: "The description how Cuthbert Simpson stoode in an engine of iron 3. houres within the Tower, commonly called Scevington's gyves." It shows Simpson standing, in a bent position; he is held by a curious apparatus, the main framework of which consists of a horizontal bar and four converging uprights; the tops of the uprights are hidden, but evidently they hold, or are joined to, a collar around the prisoner's neck; lateral loops on the two outer uprights hold his hands; and the fronts of his feet are thrust forward through loops between the inner uprights and the bar.

Beyond reasonable doubt, this is a misrepresentation of a kind of assembly that will here be called the "tongs". Such an assembly was accurately illustrated at the end of the eighteenth century by Richard Skinner in his *History and Description of London, Westminster and the Borough of Southwark.*[68] Skinner describes it[69] as the "Spanish Cravatt", and lists the "Spanish Cravats" among "spoils of the invincible Armada" that might then be viewed at the Tower. Indeed, visitors to the Tower Armouries may still[70] see such an assembly, and very probably it is that illustrated by Skinner.[71]

The assembly now at the Tower consists at its lower end of a set of bilboes: horseshoe-shaped leg-irons, each terminating in rings at right angles to its own plane, and a locking-rod: a rod, with a knob at one end and with the other end flattened and pierced. A complex addition is made principally out of lengths of iron strip. I once tried to provide an accurate verbal description of this item, and the result could hardly have been comprehended without drawing instruments, paper, and considerable time. Instead, therefore, I hope the following broad account will suffice. The purpose, plainly, was to add constraint of the neck and wrists to that of the ankles, which the bilboes would afford. A hinged collar was used to hold the neck with the ends bent somewhat outwards and continued as straight lengths, to terminate in rings that fit onto the locking rod. Pressure inwards upon these rings would close the collar, at least sufficiently to prevent escape from it. Onto the outside of each of the straight lengths just mentioned is fastened another strip, bent outwards close to the point of attachment to form a semi-circle, then continuing as a straight length and terminating—once again—in a ring that fits onto the locking rod: pressure inwards on this ring, towards the immediately adjacent ring of the main strip, would prevent escape of a wrist from the semi-circle above. The two side strips have not been shaped symmetrically, one to the other; in this respect, we have the work of a tradesman who probably was not a craftsman. The overall length is one yard and eight inches, the weight is eleven pounds and twelve ounces. The present locking-rod has been said by officers of the Armouries to differ in patina from the rest and to seem too long. I would not question the former observation. However, the appropriate length for the locking-rod may depend upon the order in which the various rings were threaded onto it. The tendency is to assume that Foxe's illustrator, however mistaken in detail, was right about the relative positions of the parts. Yet if the leg-irons were placed entirely outside the other parts on the rod, one at each end, the result would approximate that produced by an apparatus, for the hard handling of those in prison, which was known to—or at least imagined by—Ignas (Ignace) Raeth in the mid-seventeenth century.[72]

To be kept in the tongs for any length of time would be for anyone a worse than uncomfortable experience. Moreover, their employment might immediately impose suffering upon a prisoner with a thick neck. According to the Second Report[73] of the Select Committee appointed by the House of Commons on 25 February, 1729, to inquire into the *State of the Gaols,* when, at the Marshalsea, some poor debtors had been caught attempting to escape, the Clerk, who farmed the prison and its profits, called them one by one to the lodge for interrogation: one of them related that to extort from him the names of accomplices in the attempt, he had been tortured in his thumbs, after which "they fixed on his neck and hands an instrument, called a collar, like a pair of tongs: and, he being a large, lusty man, when they screwed the said instrument close, his eyes were ready to start from his head, the blood gushed out of his ears and nose, he foamed at the mouth." Now, the reference to screwing up the instrument obviously may represent a misunderstanding; if it does so, he was perhaps tormented with an example of the tongs, minus the bilboes. The reference to the fixing of the instrument onto his hands, as well as his neck, encourages such conjecture. Nevertheless, the natural purpose of the tongs was the quick and complete trussing of prisoners. Like other fetters, and the stocks, they may have been adapted to purposes of chronic interrogatory torture, but nothing about them suggests that they, in particular, were destined to be used for such purposes.

6. In 1571 Charles Bailly complained of being kept, at the Tower, in a rheumatic and unwholesome cave.[74]

7. The Conciliar warrant recorded for 17 November, 1577, required that Thomas Sherwood, if he refused to confess, should at the Tower be consigned to the "dungeon among the rats".[75]

8. The letters concerning Myagh that were written by the Lieutenant and Hammond on 16 and 17 March, 1581,[76] show that "skevington's Yrons" were a means of acute torture regarded, by the writers, as less severe than some other available mode—presumably, the rack—yet in the use of which they felt some need for moderation and that required for their operation the continuous presence of at least one jailor. An inscription tells us Myagh's torture was "strange".[77]

9. The preface to Rishton's Diary describes: (a) "Little Ease" as aptly named, a very small cell or hollow in which a man could hardly stand erect;[78] (b) *"Lacus"* as a subterranean cavern,[79] twenty feet down, without light; (c) The "Scavenger's Daughter" (so: in the singular) as an iron hoop, with which the hands, feet, and head of the examinate were so encompassed that he formed a ball. It adds the opinion that the name "Scavenger's Daughter" must derive from that of the instrument's inventor. According to entries in the Diary itself, Stephen Rausam remained in "Little Ease" for eighteen months, a period during which Francis Throgmorton was also briefly held in "Little Ease"; Thomas Cottam and Luke Kirby were each, in December, 1580, subjected to the Scavenger's Daughter for more than an hour: an experience that made the former's nose bleed freely.

10. Verstegan's *Theatrum crudelitatum*: (a) describes[80] "Little Ease" as so cramped a place that a man in it could neither stand, nor sit, nor lie; (b) illustrates,[81] as a means of torture used upon Roman Catholics in England, for hours at a time, "an iron instrument, which compresses and rolls up a man like a ball"—the illustration showing a stirrup-shaped device, bolted together at the top, in which a man kneels with his head some little distance above his knees and his hands on his knees.

11. Robert Southwell's *Humble Supplication*, of 1591, complains[82] that some Roman Catholic prisoners "with instruments" (the plural is used) "have been rowle up together like a ball and so crushed that blood spurted out of divers parts of their bodies": but this cannot be assumed a source of information entirely independent of those noticed in (9) and (10) above.

12. Towards the end of the following century, Tanner attempted[83]

to sum up Jesuit intelligence concerning what Rishton called the "Scavenger's Daughter". He wrote:

> The English torture next in importance to the rack is called the Scavenger's Daughter, and (in its operation) is entirely opposite to the latter, since . . . it violently draws together and squeezes the examinate as though into a single ball. When this device is to be used, the body of the examinate is folded into three, shins to thighs, thighs to chest, and in this state is put within two iron arcs, the ends of which are forced together by the labour of the executioners so as to complete a circle, the body of the examinate being meanwhile almost crushed by the horrid pressure . . . some as a result bleed from the extremities of their hands and feet; others, their rib-cages broken, lose much blood from their noses and throats.

We have here an explanation of Southwell's statement that blood spurted from divers parts of the bodies of those subjected to this torture: a notable advance on Rishton's statement that one man was made to bleed from the nose. The description of the device combines what is conveyed by Verstegan's text and what is conveyed by his illustration, although they may seem not entirely consistent. It ignores Rishton's description.

13. The Conciliar warrant recorded for 10 January, 1591,[84] concerning Beesley (Passelaw), directed coercive incarceration, at the Tower, and referred to "prison called Little Ease."

14. According to the *House of Commons Journal*, in May, 1604, the House determined to obtain the release from the Fleet of one of its members. The Warden refused to let him go and was thereupon committed, upon a warrant from the House, to imprisonment in the Tower. He remained intransigent, and the House succeeded in having him consigned, at the Tower, to a place described to a House committee that visited the Tower, as "Little Ease". From that place, he was able to write, on 15 May, to the House. Meanwhile, the committee concerned had reported on 14 May that the "place called Little Ease" was loathsome, and that there was at the Tower "an engine devised by Mr. Skevington, sometime Lieutenant of the Tower, called Skevington's Daughters"—here, once more, we have the plural—"or Little Ease."

15. On 27 May, 1609, Wade wrote to Salisbury[85] that he had clapped a Jesuit into the "dungeon under the White Tower," which he thought "too good a prison for such a varlet."

16. In 1637 a Tower mob threatened to throw a Council messenger into the "Hole".[86]

17. David Jardine, publishing his *Reading* in 1837, supplied[87] a footnote in which: (a) he stated that among instruments said to have been taken from the Armada, which might be seen at the Tower, was "an engine" that "compressed the neck of the sufferer down towards his feet"; (b) he quoted, as explanatory, Tanner's description of the Scavenger's Daughter.

18. In Scotland, in 1596, a confession is said[88] to have been extracted from one Alison Balfour by keeping her for forty-eight hours in an instrument called the "caschielawis"; whilst in 1599, one John Frein complained[89] to the Scots Privy Council that one Patrick Fleming had apprehended him and had put him, although he had committed no offense, "to tortour in ane instrument nameit the caschielawis, and held him thairin the space of two houris, drawing his body, nek, armes and feit togidder within the boundis of ane span," and had "straik wadgeis betwix his schailbanes quhill the blade birsit oute"; in 1607 the Earl of Orkney was said[90] to be the inventor of the "cashelawes" and to have subjected thereto a royal messenger.[91]

19. According to William L.L.F., Baron de Ros's *Memorials of the Tower of London*,[92] in 1866, when that work was published, a mural cell existed in the White Tower, giving onto what is today called the Mortar Room and backing onto the sub-crypt: which cell was called "Little Ease". Seemingly, the place concerned was made by closing the end of the original access to the sub-crypt and disappeared when its back wall was removed to restore means of passing directly into the sub-crypt from the north. In the early 1960s, the Mortar Room end of the passage concerned still showed traces of what may have been used as a prison.[93]

20. In the White Tower, the sub-crypt measures about fifteen feet by forty-seven feet; the whole basement floor is about ten feet above high-water mark, and the basement in all parts is dry.[94] However, in the late seventeenth century, when the intention was to store gunpowder and saltpeter there, dampness was noticed, and to reduce it, the well (in what is now the Cannon Room) was filled in.[95] The basement floor is only slightly below ground level on the north and at ground level on the south. However, access being by descent of the stair in the northeast turret, a mistaken impression might be formed that the floor was many feet below ground level.

21. G. T. Clark, publishing in 1884 his *Mediaeval Military Architecture in England*, stated: (a) that the sub-crypt itself was at the Tower called "Little Ease";[96] (b) that when garderobes north of the Wakefield Tower were in the nineteenth century removed, there was found "a curious hole, about 3 feet diameter and 3 or 4 feet deep, of doubtful use."[97] That at the Tower the sub-crypt was called "Little Ease" was subsequently confirmed by W. H. Dixon.[98] Clark's "curious hole" evidently accorded with Verstegan's description of "Little Ease", but not so well with that supplied by Rishton.

22. It is said[99] that the Bowyer Tower contained a "ghastly hole with a trap-door opening down a flight of steps"; it is also said that the basement of the old Flint Tower was known as "Little Hell".[100] The Bowyer and the Flint Towers were neighbors. Conceivably, the fact here is that under one or the other was a ghastly hole known as "Little Hell".

The difficulties presented by the documentary evidence, and the considerable want of architectural evidence, are great. Broad questions linger that cannot be answered safely: Did some names apply to more than one thing? Are some of the sources inaccurate? Yet brevity is here required. Therefore I propose to advance conclusions that, some of them, go beyond what the evidence could justify and to leave their obvious frailty to call attention to itself, so evoking alternative possibilities. I shall refer to matters in the above list by citing the numbers against which they appear.

The conclusions I venture are as follows:

A. An instrument of acute torture, which will be called the "press", was introduced to the Tower under Henry VIII (3). In the sixteenth century, it went under the names of "Little Ease" (2), (14); "Skevington's Irons" (8)—or perhaps alternatively, "Gyves" (5)—and, later, the "Scavenger's Daughter" (9), (17). For its use, the examinate was fastened, kneeling, hands and feet close together, by means of irons, gyves. Upon his back rested a further part (perhaps an arched and hinged lever, resembling one side of a nutcracker) intended for the exertion of pressure. He might be thus left, in great discomfort. If acute torture was to be used, the efforts of a jailor were required to provide and maintain the pressure. The instrument may have been identical with the Scots Cashielawis; it was certainly similar in its effects (8), (9), (10), (11), (12), (17), (18).

B. The tongs were introduced to the Tower about the same time as the press (3), (5). Whether they also went under the name of "Skevington's Irons"—or "Gyves"—is uncertain, but hardly matters. Whether Cuthbert Simpson, assuming that he was placed in a "rack of iron" at the Tower, was so by being put into the tongs, or under the press, or onto a stretching rack would be interesting to know, but also remains uncertain (5). The tongs could have been called "Little Ease", but no evidence appears of their having received that name.

C. The mural cell described by De Ros (19) existed in the sixteenth century; it was called "Little Ease" (19) and was the place so called by Rishton (9), (13). Access already existed from the east to the sub-crypt, which also was sometimes used as a prison (15) and was sometimes called "Little Ease" (13), (14), (21).[101] The latter nomenclature confused Rishton, who supposed Stephen Rausam to have been shut up in the mural cell, when in fact he was in the sub-crypt. Possibly, prisoners were sometimes crammed into Clark's "curious hole" (21), or some like place and it also acquired the name "Little Ease" (10).

D. Rishton's *Lacus* may have been a pit under the old Flint Tower (22), although even so to suppose leaves further points. Since Rishton does not mention the presence of rats, it is unlikely to have been the dungeon infested with those creatures,[102] to which the Council once referred (7). It may have been identical with Danyell's dark dungeon (4) and even with Charles Bailly's rheumatic prison (6). Whilst, at least if it is *not* supposed to have been under the old Flint Tower,[103] it may have been identical with the "hole" mentioned in 1637 (16).

VI. THE TOWER TORTURE CHAMBER

The Gerard autobiography is believed to have been written, by its subject, about ten years after the experience of torture it relates. Assuming that at least its core is indeed the work of Gerard himself, allowance must be made for that lapse of time and for the nervous tension under which he must have labored during the events leading up to the actual infliction of torture. On the other hand, he was tortured twice: the unfortunate man had in that respect two opportunities for observation. What we are told by the English translations of the Autobiography, aided by a passage that Matthias Tanner cited from a somewhat different Latin account ascribed to Gerard,[104] may be summarized as follows:

1. Gerard on each occasion went to the torture chamber from the Lieutenant's Lodging.

2. Although it was daytime, lights were needed on the way, or at any rate for the last part of it; the passage was underground.

3. The chamber was underground, large, and—especially around the door—dark, it contained a large variety of torture instruments; and its roof was supported by two wooden pillars at least one of which had fixed high upon it a staple for use as with Gerard, of the manacles.

A reference in the autobiography[105] to the treatment of Henry Walpole at the Salt Tower moreover conveys that the ordinary place of torture— presumably, the chamber to which Gerard was taken—was public. We may infer that access to it was usually free to, at any rate, those with official positions in the Tower.

How much of all this, or of what may be distilled from it, ought to be relied upon must be a matter of opinion. I incline to the view that, in 1597, an established torture chamber did exist at the Tower; that access to it was not closely restricted; that it had at least one free-standing wooden roof support; that it could be approached, from the Lieutenant's Lodging, in some way which involved a descent; and that it was not well lit or high above ground level. Having inclined so far, I would venture no assertion about where it was situated.

There is widespread readiness to believe that Gerard was tortured somewhere in the basement of the White Tower,[106] which some have thought was connected to the Lieutenant's Lodging by an underground passage.[107] In favor of the broad hypothesis that Gerard went to the torture chamber, wherever it was, by either an underground or a mural passage, one consideration is that it harmonizes well with the auto-biography—especially, with the Tanner version—and a further consid-eration is that such an arrangement would have prevented examinates on their way to the chamber being seen by members of the general public or prisoners having the liberty of the Tower. Somewhat against the more precise hypothesis, that the underground passage concerned led into the basement of the White Tower, is the fact that it would have had to go through or under the White Tower foundations, and even if it went through them—representing a considerable achievement, since they are twenty-four feet thick—would have been likely to end in an ascent at least fairly marked[108] and such as the autobiography does not mention. However, if no direct route existed and Gerard reached the basement by the northeast stair, candles probably would have had to be lit for the descent, and Gerard might have thought he was being taken underground. In the basement, the west apartment, now the Can-non Room, is large. It was not vaulted, and having regard to its size, its roof may well have been supplied with one or more timber supports. Alan Borg says[109] that such supports existed and were removed in the eighteenth century, when the present brick vaulting was built. I have not myself encountered the evidence of this important fact. (Of course, it is well known that formerly in the White Tower, at both the second and the third stages, eighteen roof props were employed in the west chamber and twelve in the northeast chamber;[110] the usual modern explanation is that they were installed, during the eighteenth century, because openings were made, at each stage, in the wall between the two chambers.[111]) But in any case, such considerable gaps exist in the architectural history of the Tower that I confess on a question of the present sort I would favor reserve.[112]

Nor can the question be answered, for how long whatever arrangements were experienced by Gerard, in 1597, had then existed or for how long they continued thereafter. That in the early 1580s, torture already was most often inflicted, at the Tower, in a place to which a fair number of persons had access is suggested by an entry (for 31 August, 1581) in Rishton's Diary, recording that Campion had been twice *secretly* tortured on the rack. Whilst, for what it is worth, Foxe transmits the statement that at the Tower, under Henry VIII, Anne Askew was "let down into a dungeon where . . . the Lieutenant commanded his jailor to pinch her with the rack."[113] Finally, it is right to recall the Conciliar record,[114] for 16 November, 1552, of instructions to the Lieutenant of the Tower to subject Holland "to the torment in Little Ease:" but I have suggested[115] that, in it, "Little Ease" may be used to describe an instrument of torture, not a dungeon.

VII. BRIDEWELL

Apparently, confinement in Bridewell was experienced as terribly degrading and exhausting by most Roman Catholics who were committed there upon politico-religious grounds in the late sixteenth century.

In the *Theatrum crudelitatum*,[116] Verstegan said that it was: "a vile and abominable prison . . . assigned for the punishment of rogues who, by way of labour, are compelled in it, day in and day out, to turn a certain cornmill"; he added that the authorities "place Catholics, noblemen as well as commoners, among such dregs of humanity, requiring them to grind the mill concerned," and that "these Catholics, not only are subjected to the daily insults of the rogues themselves, but are beaten with the jailors' whips, and driven with great violence to turn the mill, while they hardly receive any sustenance except water and mouldy bread.'' Southwell, writing in January, 1591, to Aquaviva,[117] said: ''the cruelties inflicted are scarcely credible. The tasks imposed are continuous and beyond ordinary strength, and even the sick are driven to them under the lash''; whilst in his *Humble Supplication*, published in the same year, he remarked[118]

> It is not possible to keep any reckoning of the ordinary punishments of Bridewell, now made the common purgatory of priests and Catholics, as grinding in the mill, being beaten like slaves, and other outrageous usages. For to these we are forced at the discretion of such, as being to all others despised underlings, take a felicity in laying their commandments and shewing their authority upon us to whom every warder, porter and jaylor is an unresisted lord.

No doubt this sort of treatment must have damaged the morale of many sixteenth-century gentlemen and so, whether or not the effect was intended or advantage taken of it, have rendered them more vulnerable should they be interrogated.[119] Perhaps, however, humbler people were accorded still worse treatment, yet could sustain it better.

It is interesting to compare the accounts we have of treatment accorded respectively to John Purdye, a Puritan, and Thomas Doulton, a Roman Catholic convert.

Regarding the former, committed by Whitgift in the late 1580s, Henry Barrow said in his *Letter to Mr. Fisher*:

> There likewise died in Bridewell a very godly person, called Jhon Purdie, committed by the archbishop, whom thei there put into their Litle Ease and beate with a great codgel very extreamly because he would not come to their chappel in their house.[120]

Whilst, according to the *Relation* attributed to Doulton,[121] on arrival at Bridewell in 1595, he was sent to work for the first eight months in the hemp-house, where prisoners were required every day to bunch twenty-five pounds of hemp and received no meat unless they completed the task; then, having offended in some way, he was chained for a long period to a block, was thrown into a place that had acquired the name ''Little Ease'', was afterwards locked up in one of the turrets—which he found as bad—and at last was sent to the mill for five weeks; he suffered the punishment, already mentioned, in the "standing stocks", before (as it seems) being either returned to the hemp-house or threatened with return there; and then he in some manner compounded for his liability to enforced labor in that place by receiving twenty lashes "upon the trosse": whereafter he was allowed to join the (other) Catholic laymen.

Neither of these accounts hints that the treatment it describes had an interrogatory purpose. From other sources, however, some information may be obtained about methods of duress used, at Bridewell, deliberately and directly in aid of interrogation.

No evidence suggests that stretching racks were employed there. In the Conciliar warrant recorded for the 18th of April, 1590,[122] the expression "rack and torture of the manacles", used in describing what might be done to promote interrogation of those suspected of a robbery, may be tautologous—"rack" meaning "torture". The "torture of the House", proposed in another robbery case by the warrant recorded for the 24th of June, 1589,[123] was probably a wall torture, at least typically, if not invariably, involving the use of the manacles. However, other Conciliar records concerning torture at Bridewell suggest that the methods adopted there may have displayed considerable variety. As recorded, the Hacket warrant of 1591[124] directed its addressees to employ "the manacles, or such other torture as you shall think good." The White and Lacey warrant, of the same year,[125] is recorded as having directed recourse to "the manacles and such other tortures as are used in Bridewell." Whilst, of the same year also, the warrant recorded concerning Thomas Clynton and referring to Bridewell,[126] spoke of "the manacles and such torture as is there used."

In the *Humble Supplication,*[127] Southwell asserted: (a) that some Roman Catholics were (apparently, to promote their interrogation) subjected naked to excessive whipping; (b) that others were "watched and kept from sleep, till they were past the use of reason, and then examined upon the advantage, when they could scarcely give account of their own name;" (c) that others were tortured in their private parts.

Complaints of recourse to the first of the above methods had been linked with Bridewell in Southwell's report to Aquaviva of the 31st of August, 1588:[128] in which he referred to the whipping—probably, interrogatory—of a female and of a male Roman Catholic and remarked that the latter *also* was whipped in Bridewell. Infliction may well have been, as we are told it was in Doulton's case, "upon the trosse": which may have been a tripod, such as has been used for like abominable purpose in the course of United Kingdom and colonial penal history. On the other hand, according to Thomas Ellwood of Amersham,[129] when he was in Bridewell after the Restoration, sentences of corporal punishment were passed in a justice room and carried out next door, in a room the walls of which were "laid all over from top to bottom in black" and which contained a great whipping post: a room, in fact, with decoration appropriate to a torture chamber;[130] convenient proximity to another room suitably equipped for the psuedo-magisterial interrogation of a suspect; and the facility of a large post that could be used in whipping and, probably, was suitable to hold the manacles.

That such methods were recognized by Continental jurisprudence[131] may seem not to affect one way or the other the probability that allegations of their employment in England were true. Continental sources, if influential at all, may equally well have inspired action by the Government or merely the imagination of its opponents.

VIII. PRECEDENTS IN THE CHRONICLES

We have noticed[132] the story that following the murder of Sir Edmund Berry Godfrey, Francis Caryll was by order of members of the Privy Council squeezed, to induce a confession, into a trough, and the possibility that the method was one being tried at the time, in the case of those under sentence to the *peine forte et dure*.

It is interesting to compare a passage in the (Peterborough) *Anglo-Saxon Chronicle*,[133] which describes how—according to the chronicler—during Stephen's reign, the servants of local potentates tormented defenseless people to extort their valuables. Inter alia, it asserts:

> They put some in a crucet-hus: that is to say, a chest which was short, and narrow, and shallow: and put sharp stones therein, and pressed whomever was therein so that they broke all his limbs.

This passage may be compared with another, in the *Continuatio prima* to Symeon of Durham's *Historia*.[134] In 1141, when the King had been captured at Bristol, David of Scotland pretended to bestow the vacant see of Durham upon his own Chancellor, William Cumin. The latter went to Durham and squatted there after, in 1143, William of St. Barbara, Dean of York, was duly elected Bishop. A siege resulted, and

Cumin held on for some time, having gathered around himself a considerable mercenary force. Meanwhile, according to the *Continuatio*, his soldiers practiced merciless extortion upon the inhabitants. It lists among their cruelties the employment of:

> an exquisite penance, in which the limbs of the sufferer were brought together by being all at the same time compressed into a very small space: a mode of punishment which, in its results, reversed the operation of the old mode, upon the rack; for whereas, in the past, the limbs of the sufferer, extended upon the rack,[135] were lengthened by the punishment he received, the method now described was such that they were subjected to an opposite effect, being forced in upon themselves so that they contracted, and sometimes by compression were broken.

Evidently, what we have here may be use of the crucet-hus, as described in the Anglo-Saxon Chronicle.

Nor is this all, for the *Continuatio* passage supports another comparison: what its author observed about the difference between the crushing torture and racking was closely echoed by Tanner's description of the Scavenger's Daughter.[136]

APPENDIX

KEY TO INITIAL CITATION

Entries in the Appendix are preceded by capital letters to indicate the source or sources from which they have been derived. The key to the lettering is as follows.

D.: *Acts of the Privy Council*, ed. John R. Dasent and others.

H.: Samuel Haynes, *Collection of State Papers*.

J.: D. Jardine, *Reading on the Use of Torture in the Criminal Law of England*.

M.: Original manuscript in the British Library.

N.: *Proceedings and Ordinances of the Privy Council*, ed. Harris Nicolas.

O.: Original manuscript in the Public Record Office.

R.: Thomas Rymer, *Foedera*, 1816–69 edition.

S.: John, Baron Somers, *Tracts*, 1809 ed., Vol. 1.

S. 1: *CONCILIAR RECORDS OF TORTURE WARRANTS AND OF LETTERS MENTIONING ACUTE TORTURE*

[N]   **No. 1**

[13th Nov. 1540.

Thomas Thwaytes servant unto . . . Shyrington page of the Kinges warderobe of robes, was accused by . . . servantes to Richard Cecylle Yoman, to have spoken certain traiterous woordes against the Kinges Majestie; whereupon beyng examined and confessing before the Counsail the woordes layd unto his charge he was committed to the porters ward.]

16th Nov. 1540.

Thomas Thwaytes was sent to the towre of London by captain of the garde with a letter to the Lieutenant declaring his confession and commaundyng him that in case he woold stande stil in denyal to showe of whom he has herd the things he confessed, he shuld gyve him a stretche or twoo at his discrecion uponn the brake.

[25th May, 1541.

Thomas Thwaytes who had bene prisoner in the Towre for speking of certain lewde woordes touching the Kinges Majestie was brought before the Counsail, and having a good lesson gyven him to use his tonge with more discretion hereafter was dismissed and set at liberty.]

[D]   No. 2

15th Aug. 1550.

A Letter to Mr. Robsert and Mr. Fermour to make yet further searche for the money alledged by Haldesworthe to be hidde in Fowlkes house, and to examyne the said Fowlkes eftsones, putting him in feare of torment.

[J] [D]   No. 3

5th Nov. 1551.

A Letter to Sir Arthur Darcie and to all other that from tyme to tyme shall have the ordering of the Tower and the prisoners there. To suffer certain Commissioners newlei allotted to the examination of the prisoners within the sayd Tower, as by a supplement of the same closed in the said lettre (the coppie whereof remayneth in the Counsell chest) may appere, to have accesse to them when and as often as they shall think convenient. And further, to be assisting to the sayd Commissioners for the putting the prisoners or any of them to suche tortours as they shall thinke expedient.

[D]   No. 4

16th Nov. 1552.

A Letter to the Lieutenant of the Tower to examine Holland, putting hym to the torment in Little Ease uppon thexaminacion of Thurland.

[J] [D]   No. 5

7th Jan. 1553.

A Letter to the Lieutenant of the Tower to cause one Willson and Warren, lately taken upon suspition of a haynous murder, to be put to the tortours, when they or any of them shall be brought unto him for that purpose.

[D]   **No. 6**

27th Jan. 1555.

A Letter of thankes gyving to the Maiour of Bristoll, signifieng the receipt of his lettres to the Lords by the Shirief there, together with the countrefeite coynes and other the coyners' instrumentes and toles by him lately apprehended; requyring him for the better tryall and boulting out of suche as be privy with them, and specially the graver of thier yrons, to put the partes to the racke yf he shall so think good by his discreation, and to use all other meanes whereby the trueth and hole circumstances thereof may come to light, and further willing him to proceade with thoffenders justice according to suche Commyssion as is presently sent him downe for that purpose.

[J] [D]   **No. 7**

(a) 9th June, 1555.

A Letter to the Lord North and the reste of the Commissioners for the examination of prisoners to bring suche obstinat personnes as will not otherwise confesse points wherein they are touched to the tortures, and there to order them according to their descretions.

(b) 9th June, 1555.

A Letter to the Lieutenant of the Towre for the same purpose.

[J] [D]   **No. 8**

4th Dec. 1555.

A Letter to Sir Henry Bedingfield to receve the bodie of Richarde Mulcaster, servaunte to Doctor Caius, vehemently suspect of robbing his master, and by the best meanes he can to examin him hereof, and to bring him to the rack and putte him in feare of the torture if he will not confesse.

[J] [D]   **No. 9**

(a) 11th Dec. 1555.

A Letter to Sir Henry Bedingfielde, Sergeaunt Dier, and Mr. Sollicytor to examin substantially one Nicholas Curat, vehemently suspected of robbing Mr. Keleawaie, according to such interrogatories as the said Mr. Keleaway shall deliver unto them for that purpose; and if they shall see cause whie, then to bring him to the racke and to put him to sum pain if he will not confesse otherwise.

(b) 11th Dec. 1555.

A like letter to bring one Hughe of Warwicke, suspected for horse-steling, to the rack, and to do *ut supra*.

[J] [D]   **No. 10**

16th Feb. 1556.

A Letter to Sir Henry Bedingfield to receve from Sir John Baker the boddies of Barton and Thomas Tailor, and to kepe them in safe custodie, and to joyne with the same Mr. Baker in the examyning of them, and to put them upon the torture and paine them according to their descretions if they will not confesse their offences.

[J] [D]   **No. 11**

21st June, 1556.

It was this day ordered by my Lords of the Counsell that Sir Rob. Peckham, Mr. Lieutenant of the Tower and one of the Masters of the Requests, should examin one Richard Guyll, and to put him also to the tortours in case they shall think it so convenient.

[J] [D]   **No. 12**

29th July, 1556.

A Letter to Sir Roger Cholmeley and Dr. Marten, to repaire to the convict prison at Westminster, and there to procede to the further examination of Sillvester Taverner, prisoner there; who, having embeseled certeine plate and other goods, belonging as well to the Quene's Majestie as to sundry other persons besydes, will by no meanes hitherto declare where the same is become, nothwithstanding the matter is alreadie confessed against him by two others. And therefore they are required, for the better atteyning of the truth, to put him to such tortures as by their discretions shall be thought convenient.

[J] [D]   **No. 13**

19th July, 1557.

A Letter to the Constable, &c. to examine such as Sir Edwarde Warner enforme them of, and to put them to the torture, if they shall thinke so good.

[D]   **No. 14**

23rd July, 1557.

A Letter to the Lorde St. John to cause suche as he hathe already apprehended for the ryotte and disorder of late committed upon the goodes and corne of Jane Stourton to be diligently examined who were present besides themselves at the act doing, and if they shall not be plaine therein, then to put them to sum torture for the better trieng out of the truthe, and upon understanding who were the rest he is willed to give order for their apprehencion accordingly, and to committe them all to sure and straight prison in irons, without baile of[1] mainprise, untill Mighelmas Terme next, and in the meanetyme to procede to their enditement, and to signify the same with the examinacions he shall take of them into the Starre Chamber at the beginning of the next Terme, and to restore again to the said Jane Stourton her corne and haye taken from her by the said lewde personnes.

. . .

[D]   **No. 15**

(a) 18th Oct. 1557.

A Letter to the Master of thorsse, the Lorde Chiefe Justice of the Kinges Benche, Sir Richard Southewell and Mr. Nudegate to call before them oone Newporte and his man, remayning presently in Newegate, and oone Cowley, remayning in the Kinges Benche, and to examyne them by the best meanes and waies they can towching certaine counterfeite crownes taken with the saide Newporte, and to put them to the torture if they shall thinke so convenient.

(b) 30th Oct. 1557.

A Letter to the Master of thorsse, Sir Richard Southwell, Sir John Mason, Sir Robert Peckham, Knightes and John Nudygate, esquier, to three or two of them, to examyn oon Newporte and his servant, remayning in Newgate suspect of coyning, by the best waies and meanes they can, and to bring the said servant to the torture and to put him thereon if they shall thinke convenient for the better bulting oute of the truthe hereof.

[J] [D]   **No. 16**

13th May, 1558.

A Letter to Mr. Cunstable of the Tower, Sir Roger Cholmeley, Mr. Recorder of London, Mr. Doctor Marten, and Mr. Vaughan, to procede in the examination of French, presently remayning prisoner in the Tower, and to bring him to the torture and to put him in feare thereof, and also to put him to the payne of the same, if they shall thinke so good.

[J] [D]   No. 17

15th March, 1559.

A Letter to the Lyeutenant of the Tower that where there remayneth in his custody the bodyes of one Pytt and Nycholls, for the robbing of a wydowe called Bate, in St. Ellyns in London, he is requyred to call the Knight Marshall unto him in this matter; and uppon examynation of the parties, if they shall obstynately persist in the denyall of their facte, he is willed to cause them to be brought to the racke, and to feale the smarte thereof as they by theyr discretions shall think good for the better boultinge out of the truth of this matter.

[J] [D]   No. 18

22nd June, 1565.

A Letter to Lord Scrope, in answer of his letters wrytten to Mr. Secretarye, with the examination by him taken of Nycholas Hethe, whom his Lordship is required to procede somewhat sharply withall, to the end he should declare the full truthe why he wandereth abrode. And if he will not be plane, to use some kinde of torture unto him, so it be without any grete bodily hurte.

[D]   No. 19

28th Dec. 1566.

A Letter to Justyce Walshe, the Quenes Attorney Generall and others, &c., where they were heretofore appointed to put Clement Fyssher, now prysoner in the Towre, in sum feare of torture, wherby his lewdeness and suche as he might detect might the better cum to light; they are required, for that the said Fyssher is not mynded to be plaine as thereby the falte of others might be knowen, to cause the said Fyssher according to their discrecions to feale sum touche of the racke, for the better bulting out and openynge of that which is requysite to be knowen in this behalf.

[D]   No. 20

18th January, 1567.

A Letter to the Lieutenant of the Tower and others, &c., whereas one Ryce, a bucklermaker, being lately comitted thyther, was one of those, as it is discoverid, that about iv years past did steal certain plate and money out of the house of Mr. Paine, Keper of the Rolles of the Kinges Bench, they are required when they shall have occasyon, to call the said Ryce next before them to examyne him touching the robbery of the said Mr. Paine. And yf they shall perceve him not willing to confess the same, then to put him in feare of the torture and to let him feele some smarte of the same, whereby he may be the better brought to confess the truthe.

[J] [D]   **No. 21**

(a) 20th June, 1570.

A Letter to Justice Southcoote, to cause one Thomas Androws, presently prysoner in the Marshalsey, to be brought to the Towre, and offered the torture of the racke theare, and examine him of his knowledge touchinge a very heinous murder lately commytted in Somerset shiere, wherof the said Androwes is vehemently suspected and will hitherto confesse nothing, although he hath been divers tymes examined thereupon. And after he shall have taken his confession, the said Mr. Southcote is willed to return him to the Marshalsey againe to be furder procedid withall according to the order of the lawe.

(b) 20th June, 1570.

A Letter to the Lieutenant of the Tower to cause the said Andrewes, when he shalbe brought unto him to be sett to the racke and offerid the torture, and to be examined by suche as shalbe appointed thereunto by Justice Weston. . . .

[J] [D]   **No. 22**

25th June, 1570.

A Letter to Sir Thomas Wroth and others, Her Majestie's Commissioners appointed for the examination of the Bull. Where by their letters it appeareth that John Felton, being charged by William Mellowes both for the having of the printed Bull and speache also with the Spanish Ambassador, he utterlie denieth it, and will in no wise confesse the trouth. For the boulting out of the trothe thereof Their Lordships think it convenient that he be delivered to the Lieutenant of the Towre, wherebye he may be brought to the place of torture, and so put in feare thereof. And yf they shall perceve him to be obstinate and will in no wise confesse that which is to be demaunded of him, that then to spare not to lay him upon it, to the end he may feele such smarte and paines thereof as to their discretions shall be thought convenient.

208

[1st April, 1573.

A Letter to the Knight Marshall to deliver unto the Lieutenant of the Towre George Browne, to be furder ordered as he shall receve from the Lords of the Counsell].

(a) 1st April, 1573.

A Letter to the Lieutenant to receve him and to kepe him in suer custodie, without havinge conference with any, saving the Master of the Rolles, Mr. Justice Sowthcote and Manwoode, or any two of them, whom they have appointed to examine him, willing him to assiste them by bringing or putting him to the racke or otherwise.

(b) 1st April, 1573.

A Letter to the Master of the Rolles, Justice Southcote and Justice Manwood, or any two of them, to examine George Browne and all others suspected to be contrivers of the murdre of Saunders, upon suche instructions as shalbe given them by the brethern and frindes of the said Saunders, to put Browne to tortures if they find cause, to committe such to pryson as they shall finde touched with the facte, and to admitte the brethern and frindes of Saunders to be presente at the examinacion, and to minister interrogatories if they finde cause.

[D]   No. 24

29th Nov. 1574.

A Letter to the Lieutenant of the Tower, Mr. Sollicitour Generall, Thomas Randolph, Henry Knolles, and Thomas Norton, to examyne Humfrey Nedeham, prysoner in the Tower, and for their better procedyng theyr Lordships have written to the Lord Archbishop of Caunterbury to deliver unto them soche letters and writinges as were remayning with him, which the said Nedeham had counterfeited, to thintent thereupon they might examyne him and boult out by all meanes they cold the trouth who set him on: with a *post script* to bring him to the rack without stretching his bodye, to thintent he might discover the trothe.

[D]   No. 25

6th Feb. 1575.

[A Letter to Mr. Secretarie Walsingham, Mr. Solicitour Generall and Mr. Randolph, Master of the Postes, to examine one Cicking, a bookbinder in Powles Churcheyarde, lately committed to the Tower, upon such matter as Mr. Secretary Walsingham was privey of.]

A Letter to the Lieutenant of the Tower to send him to Mr. Secretary Walsingham's howse when he shold be sent for, and to put him in feare of the
racke, thereby to induce him to tell the trothe of soche thinges as he shold be
examined of: yf the said Commissioners shold so thinke convenient.

[J] [D]   No. 26

(a) 17th Nov. 1577.

A Letter to Mr. Atturney Generall, signifying unto him that he shall receve
the examination of one Thomas Sherwood, lately committed by the High Commissioners for hearing of a masse, and since examined by Mr. Recorder of
London; which examination containing matter of High Treason againste her
Majestie's person, Their Lordships have thought good to send unto him and
require him, after he shall have substantiallie considered thereof, to acquaint
the Lord Chief Justice therewith, and particular to give order that the said
Sherwood be this terme arraigned and proceeded against according to the laws
of this realme in that behalfe provided; but before they procede to his arraignment, to take some pains furder to examyn hym bothe uppon the points of his
confession, and also to see if he can discover any others of his knowledge to
be of his opinion; and where, and of whom, he hath gathered the substance of
his arguments contained in his said confession, wherein perchance he may boult
out some other matters or persons worthie to be known.

(b) 17th Nov. 1577.

A Letter to the Lieutenant of the Tower, requiring him to receve into his
hands of Mr. Recorder of London the person of Thomas Sherwood, and to
retaine him close prisoner, and from conference with any person, untill suche
tyme as he shall receive order from Mr. Attorney General, who is appointed
to examyn him upon such matters as he is to be charged withall, and shewing
this Their Lordship's letter to Mr. Recorder, which shall be his sufficient warrant
for the delivery of him.
He is required in a postscript that if the said Sherwood shall not willingly
confesse such things as shall be demanded of him, he is then required to commit
him to the dongeon amongst the ratts.

(c) 4th Dec. 1577.

A Letter to Mr. Lieutenant, Mr. Attorney, Mr. Solicitor, Mr. Recorder, or
one of them, that where Their Lordships by their letters of the 26th of November
do understand the paines they have taken in the examining of Sherwood in the
Tower, for the which Their Lordships doe yield them their ryght hartie thanks;
and where they signify by their said letter that Sherwood doth not onlie stagger
in his first confession, and faine would retracte his wordes, in respect he affirmed

Her Majestie to be an herriticq and usurper, but also will in no case be brought to confesse or answer such other interrogatories as they have propounded unto him, Their Lordships are of opinion that, if he be used thereafter, he can discover other personnes as evil affected towards Her Majestie as himself; they are therefore to assaie him at the racke upon such articles as they shall think meete to minister unto him for the discovering either of the personnes or of furder matter.

[J] [D] **No. 27**

4th Nov. 1578.

A Letter to the Lieutenante of the Tower and the Recorder of London, that forasmuch as Harding can by no milde course of examination be brought to confesse the truthe of those things wherewith he is to be charged, they are required to be brought to the racke,[2] thereby to prove whether he will discover anie furder matter than hitherto hathe been reveyled from him. And where John Sanford, depplie suspected to be privie to the dealings of John Prescott, who by no mylde kinde of proceeding can be induced to discover the truthe; these are likewise required to put him to the racke, and by means thereof to wreste from him the truthe of such things as in that respecte they shall finde he is suspected to be privie unto. And what they shall wring from him they are to certifie to Their Lordships accordingly.

[D] **No. 28**

11th June, 1579.

A Letter to Mr. Justice Southcotte, Sir Owen Hopton and Sir Thomas Browne, knightes, and Robert Levesey, esquire, that where by a letter from Mr. Browne and other Justices of Surrey their Lordships do understande what hathe ben don in the examining of Robert Wintershall, Harvey Mellershe, and others suspected for the murther committed in December last uppon the persons of Richard Mellershe of Dounford in that countie and Thomas his sonne, and where it appearethe by the said letter that uppon their examinacions nothing of moment can be discovered that maie inforce their condemnacion; for which cause (the contry also expecting an ende thereof) their Lordships do require them withe some convenient speede to procead to a new examinacion of the said Wintershall, Mellershe and the reste, severing them as well in places where they may remain assunder, as severallie to examyn them, using the best meanes they can to induce them to confess the troathe. Whereunto (yf by no meanes they shalbe broughte) then are they required to deale with them by shewe of some terror to be offered unto them by committing them to the dungeons and like places of obscurities in the Tower, appointing unto them a shorte portion of diet accordingly. And to that ende their Lordships do require him, Mr. Lieutenante, to receive them into his custodie, and to see them bestowed in places, and severed in places within the Tower, as is aforesaid, and there (yf it shalbe nedeful) to be furder terrified by shewing unto them the Racke or otherwise, as they shall thincke meete, where (joyning together) they are required to continewe their paynes in examining of them from tyme to tyme to bring them to confesse the facte, that thereupon (sufficient matter appearing) they maie be furder proceaded withall, according to law.

[J] [D]   **No. 29**

9th Dec. 1580.

A Letter to Thomas Townsend, Henry Doyly, and William Blennerhasset. That where Their Lordships understande that the house of Sir Drew Drury, Knight, called Catton, hath of late bene robbed by certain rude persons, with the privitie of one Humfrey, a boy dwelling in the house; who, being since committed and examined touching the said robberie, refuseth to discover the reste of his complices; they are therefore required to call the said Humfrey before them, and to use the best means they may to induce him to confesse the robbery; which if he shall obstinately refuse to doe, then are they required by some slight kinde of torture, such as may not touch the losse of any lymbe, as by whipping, wring from him the knowledge of the persons and manner of the robberie; that thereupon order may be taken for their apprehension and punishment according to the lawes, &c.

[J] [D]   **No. 30**

24th Dec. 1580.

A Letter to the Lieutenante of the Tower, Sir George Carye, Knighte, Mr. Atturney and Mr. Solicitor General, signifying that among other persones lately arrested within the realme from Rome and other places beyonde the seas, with intent to pervert and seduce Her Majestie's subjectes, ther are apprehended one Harte and Bosgrave, committed unto the Marshalsea, and one other called Pascall, imprisoned in the Compter of the Poultry, and are to be charged with matters of moment contained in the writings herewith sent unto them, requiring them upon the receipt hereof to cause them all three to be removed from the prisons where they remaine unto the Tower, and there bestowed in several prisons; and after they have substantially considered of the matters, to frame some interrogatories whereupon they may be examined as the rest have been, withe whome by Their Lordships' order they have alreadie proceaded in that place; and if they shall refuse to answere planely and directly unto the interrogatories, they may be brought then unto the torture, and by the terror thereof wring from them the truth of suche matters as they shall finde most necessary to be discovered.

212 APPENDIX

[J] [D]   **No. 31**

3rd May, 1581.

A Letter to the Lieutenant of the Tower, Doctor Hamond, and Thomas Norton, Gentlemen; That whereas there hath bene of laite apprehended among others a certaine seminarie priest, or Jesuit, naming himself Briant, aboute whom there was taken divers bookes and wryghtinges carrying matter of High Treason, and is (as may by good likelyhood be conjectured) hable to disclose matters of good moment for Her Majestie's service. Yt is therefore thought necessarie that he should bee to that purpose substantiallye examyned upon suche interrogatories as may be framed and gathered owt of the said bookes and wrightings, which Their Lordships send them therwith. For the doing wherof especiallie choice was made of them three, and thereby authoritie given unto them to drawe the interrogatories and to examyn the said Bryant accordinglie; and if he shall refuse by perswasion to confesse suche thinges as they shall find him hable to revele unto them, then they shall offer unto him the torture in the Tower; and in case upon the sight thereof he shall obstinatelie refuse to confesse the truthe, then shall they putt him unto the torture, and by the paine and terror of the same wring from him the knowledge of such thinges as shall appertayne.

[J] [D]   **No. 32**

22nd June, 1581.

A Letter to the Bishop of Chester, giving him to understand of the recept of his letter of the second of this present, and the copies of two fayned visions of a young mayden in that countye putt into writing and scattered abroade among the popish and ignorant people of his dyocese. And for that Their Lordships thinke it fytt by all possible meanes to have the inventors thereof founde owte and punished according to their desertes, he is required therein to doe his best endevor to syft and boult oute who be the authors, as well by examyning such as shall be found seised with the copies of the said visions, as by causing the mayden (in case by fayer meanes she shall not confesse the same) to be secretlie whipped and so brought to declare the truthe of this imposture; whereby if he shall not prevaile, then to send her hether to Their Lordships to be further proceaded withall as shall appertayn.

[J] [D]   **No. 33**

30th July, 1581.

A Letter to Mr. Lieutenant of the Tower and Thomas Norton; That whereas Their Lordships have appointed Geoffry Fenton, Her Majestie's Secretarie for the realme of Irelande, to repaire unto them for the examininge of Thomas

Meaghe, heretofore committed to his charge, and to charge him with suche matters as he heretofore hath denied and now are certified from thence to be verified by depositions of witnesses. They are required uppon receipt hereof to call the said Meaghe before them; and in case, being confronted and charged with such matter as the said Fenton shall bringe with him, he shall wilfullie refuse to acknowledge the same, then it is thought meete that they deale with him with the racke in such sorte as they shall see cause. And to advertise Their Lordships of their doings as soon as convenientlie they may.

[J] [D]   **No. 34**

30th July, 1581.

A Letter to Mr. Lieutenant of the Tower, Dr. Hammond, Robert Bele, and Thomas Norton, advertising them how they are further to proceade with Campion in manner as followeth: First, they shall demande of him whether he acknowledge himself to be Her Majestie's subject or no; which if he shall confesse, then shall they minister unto him a corporall othe uppon a Bible of St. Hierome's translation for avoiding losse of time, and also of further cavill to be by him made hereafter, to answer trulie and directlie to such thinges as by them shall be demanded of him, &c. And uppon perusing of his former examinations, and consideration of suche pointes which he denieth to answer, and those which Their Lordships are desirous to have added to his former interrogatories contained in a paper herewith sent unto them, they are required to proceade to his further examination, and in case he continewe willfullie to deny the truthe, then to deale with him by the racke. They are also required to take his answers to such articles as are herewith sent unto them touching one Rochfort, an Irishe man. With the two other priests they are required likewise to proceade in propounding unto them the questions of their allegiance to Her Majestie, and in ministering an othe to them to declare where they have layne, and whether there were a masse said in Mrs. Yate's house or no at their last being there; and if they shall find them to halte, then to put them in feare of the torture, &c. And after this, Mr. Lieutenant is required to sende [them] to the Knight Marshall, to remaine under his charge, for which purpose he shall receave Their Lordships' warrant unto him to receave them. . . .

[J] [D]   **No. 35**

14th August, 1581.

A Letter to the Lieutenante of the Tower, Mr. D. Hammond and Robert Beale, or to anie three or two of them, thanking them for their paines taken in the examinations taken of Campion, and requiring Mr. Lieutenant to receive Philby and Jacob unto the prison of the Marshalsea. They are required to examine

Campion, Peters, and Forde, who refuse to confesse whether they have said anie masses or no, whome they have confessed, and where Parsons and the other priestes be, touching these points, and to put them in feare of the torture if they shall refuse to answere directlie thereto. And touching Keynes, Hildesley, and Cottom, who have confessed the hearinge of a masse at Mr. Yate's, &c., to understand from them what other persons were present there in their companie. Touching Paine sithence there are vehement presumptions that he is guiltie of the fact wherewith he is charged, they are to proceade to the torture with him and to examine him thereuppon. Touching the persones apprehended in Sir Ca. Stoner's house, they are to examine them severallie uppon the interrogatories enclosed. And Mr. Lieutenant is further required to receave into his custodie one Thomas Pounde, whom Their Lordships have thought meete to be sent unto him to be there jointly examined uppon such interrogatories as in Campion's examinations he is charged with.

[J] [D]   **No. 36**

29th Oct. 1581.

A Letter to the Atturney and Solicitor Generall, the Lieutenant of the Tower, Dr. Hammond, Thomas Wilkes, and Thomas Norton, for the examining of Edmund Campion, Thomas Fourd, and others, prisoners in the Tower, uppon certen matters, and to put them unto the racke, &c., according to the minute thereof remaining in the Councell chest.

[J] [D]   **No. 37**

29th April, 1582.

A Letter to Mr. Lieutenant of the Tower, Mr. Thomas Randolph, Mr. Doctor Hammonde, and Mr. Owen of Lincoln's Inne, requiring them to repaire unto the Tower, there to examine one Thomas Alfield, a seminarie prieste, appre-hended and committed thither, who as it is supposed, is hable to discouver many maters touching the practises and proceedings of Jesuites and seminarie priestes within the realme. They shall receave certen interrogatories for the examining of him from Mr. Attourney; and in case he shall not willingly discover such maters as they shall find him hable to declare in this behalf, that then they put him to the racke, and by the torture thereof drawe from him such thinges as he shall be hable to say, &c.

[D]   **No. 38**

10th April, 1586.

A Letter to Sir Owen Hopton, knight, Lieutenant of the Tower, Mr. Mack-williams and Mr. Yong to reexamine Matthew Beaumond concerning the rob-being of the Lady Cheek, and of suche other matters whereof the truth is to be drawen from him, and, finding him obstinate, to trie him in some reasonable manner by torture on the Rack what he can furder disclose of anie robberies by him and others in anie sorte committed. . . .[3]

[J] [D]   **No. 39**

17th April, 1586.

A Letter to Sir Owen Hopton, Mr. Mackwilliam, and Mr. Younge, to put unto the torture of the racke one William Wakeman, alias Oavies, a notoriouse fellon, prisoner in the Tower, and thereby to make him to confesse such mis-demeanoures and robberies as he is to be charged withall and is privie unto of others.[4]

[D]   **No. 40**

13th May, 1586.

A Letter to the Lieutenant of the Tower to cause the persons of Wakeman alias Oavyes, Beaumont alias Browne, Pynder alias Pudsey, committed to the Tower (being notorious fellons, to be there examined by torture for the discovery of certain felonies committed by them and their complices) to be conveyed to the gaol of Newgate, there to remaine till they be furder proceeded with and tried according to the qualities of their offences. And this shall be as well to him as to the keeper of Newgate a sufficient warrant for the delivering and receaveing of the said prisoners.

[J] [D]   **No. 41**

23rd Dec. 1586.

A Letter to Sir Owen Hopton, Knight; Ralfe Rugbie, Master of St. Katherine's; John Popham, Her Majestie's Attorney; Thomas Egerton, Her Majesties Sol-lycitor; Sands, Clerke of the Crowne; and Thomas Owen, to examine these persons whose names are underwrytten uppon such interrogatories as they should think meet for the manyfesting of suche treasons against Her Majestie and the realme as they were charged with or suspected of; and yff the truthe might not by convenient meanes be gotten of them, then to put them to the torture of the rack in suche sorte as to their dyscretions and due considerations should seeme convenient.

Edward Wyndsor, Anthony Tuchenor, Henry Foxwell, Edward Bentley, Thomas Abbington, Thomas Heath, Ralf Ithell, Jerome Payne, Thomas Tipping, Samp-sone Loame

[J] [D]   **No. 42**

24th April, 1587.

A Letter to Sir Owen Hopton, Knight, Thomas Randolph, Henry Killigrew, Richard Yonge, Esquiers; That whereas one Andreas Van Metter, prisoner in the Towre, stoode charged with certain matter concerning Her Majesties state and person, which he did obstinatelie refuse to confesse; Their Lordships required them, if he should still persiste in his said obstinacie, to use the accustomed torture of the racke as oftentimes as they should see cause to force him to confesse what might be had out of him towching the said matters.

[J] [D]   **No. 43**

7th Jan. 1588.

A Letter to Sir Owen Hopton, Mr. Daniell, Mr. Yonge; that whereas of late there were discovered certaine lud persons, who were to be charged with disobedience, misbehaviour, and practices against the state and present government, which allreadie were examined by Richard Yonge, Esquier, but would not be brought by faire meanes and good persuacions to utter their knowledge in divers matters concerning Her Majestie and the State; They are required to call to them the said Mr. Yonge, and to examine such persons as were sent inclosed contained in a schedule, especiallie John Staughton and Humfrey Fullwood, who were deeplier charged than the rest; and if they should shew themselves obstinate and perverse as they have done heretofore, that they should carrie them to the Tower, there to be kept close prisoners, and to be putt to the racke and torture to compell them to utter their uttermost knowledge in all matters they dealt in or are privie unto.

[D]   **No. 44**

14th Jan. 1588.

A Letter to Sir Owen Hopton, Sir Edward Waterhouse, knightes, William Waad, Thomas Owen and Richard Yong, esquiours, that for as much as Roger Asheton, a companion and a man verie inward and greatlie trusted by Sir William Stanley, being examined by them uppon certaine interrogatories whereunto he wilfullie refused to make anie answer, wherby he could not be brought by anie persuasion to utter anie thinge concerning her Majestie or the State, they are by their Lordships aucthorised and willed to put him to the Rack and torture, that he might be compelled to yeild a more true and perfect answer and satisfaction bothe to such interrogatories as had been before demaunded of him, and to such other as they should think convenient to be propounded unto him for the better revealing and manifesting of the truth and his knowledge in anie thing fitte and necessarie to be knowen. . . .

[D]   **No. 45**

16th Feb. 1588.

A Letter to Sir Owen Hopton, knight, William Waad, Thomas Bodley, Thomas Owen, Richarde Younge, esquiers, that whereas George Stoker, presentlie remayning in the Towre, being latelie apprehended not longe before come from the'ennemy out of the Low Countryes, having twise allreadie escaped; forasmuch as he was knowne to have been a pencioner of the King of Spaines, and one evill affected to her Majestie and the present State, it was to be probablie conjectured that his repaire into this Realme was some secrett practise or other notable mischiefe by him to be wrought, they are herebie aucthorised and required forthwith uppon the receipt hereof to conferre with him to declare the truth of the cause of his repaire thither, and likewise to examine him uppon certaine interrogatories by them to be framed for the better discouverie of the truth; whereupon if they should perceave that he should refuse to declare for what cause and to what end he came into this Realme, then it is thought meete that they putt him to the torture of the Racke, therebie the better to withdraw from him the knowledg of his wicked entente and purpose, and likewise secretlie to examine all such suspected personnes as he hathe had conference with since his repaire hither into England, and all such as they could find have been privy to his doinges, and to committ them to prison or salfe custodie according as they should learne from him, that they might receave further direçcion from hence accordinglie.

[D]   **No. 46**

(a) 8th Sept. 1589.

A Letter to Mr. Lievetenant of the Tower, Mr. Younge, Mr. James Dolton and Mr. Topclyffe; whereas one Trystram Winslade remayneth in Newgate, heretofor taken in one of the Spanishe shippes, there Lordships pleasure is that he be conveyed to the Tower under Mr. Lievetenantes charge, and to appointe a tyme of meetinge for thexaminacion of the said Winslade upon the Racke, usinge torture to hime at there pleasure.

(b) 24th Feb. 1590.

A Letter to . . . to sett Tristram Winslade at libertye, for that he hathe not only bene often examined by Sir George Carey, Sir Walter Rauleighe, Sir Richard Grenvile, knightes, Mr. Attorney Generall and Justice Younge and others, as by their handes appeareth, but hath bene also uppon the rack to drawe from him his knowledge of the intended invasyon, and being found by his examinacions and the reportes of other men, taken at the same tyme with him in the shipp of Don Piedro, that he was brought hether against his will; and so taking bondes of him for his appearence at all tymes uppon tenne daies warning to answer any things objected, this shalbe his warrant to discharge him.

[D]   **No. 47**

24th June, 1589.

A Letter to Mr. Richard Younge; whereas we are given to understand that you have apprehended one. . . , a goldsmith, who by the suspicion that is had of him as well for his former bad course of life as also by presente greate assumptions is certainelie thoughte to be acquainted with the robberie committed one our verie good Lord the Lord Willoughby of his plate, but will not through examinacioun confesse the same, we thinke yt therefore meete that you remove him unto Bridewell, and there use towards him the torture of the House in such sorte and measure as you in discrecion shall thinke fitt, to th'end to bring him to the discoverie and manifestacion of the truth in this behalfe.

[D]   **No. 48**

24th Aug. 1589.

A letter to Mr. Fortescue, esquier, Master of the Wardrobe, Mr. Rookesby, Master of St. Katherins, and Mr. Recorder of London, requiring them to examine uppon such interrogatories as they shall thincke meet for that purpose to be sett downe one John Hodgekys, a printer, accompanied by one Valentine Syms and Arthur Thornlyn, the one a setter of letters and the other a worker at the presse, lately apprehended by the Erle of Darby nere unto Manchester in the Countye of Lancaster, where they had begun to printe a very seditious booke penned by him that termeth himself Martyn Marprelate, which together with so muche thereof as they had printed they shall receive herewith. The said Hodgekys, a principall man and by whom the other two were hyered, hathe bene by the said Erle in the countrye examined, and the rest also together with the said Hodgekys have been dealt withall by their Lordships and will confesse nothing. They shall resort to Brydewell, and if they cannot bring them to confesse the truthe, shalbe removed to the Tower. Yf Mr. Fortescue be not at London then may they call unto them for their assistance in this service Richard Younge the Customer.

[D]   **No. 49**

18th April, 1590.

A letter to Mr. Justice Younge. Wee have understoode the paines you have taken in th'examininge of the fower persons lately committed by you unto Newgate upon suspicion of a robbery lately donne at Wickham in Kent, and the discreete meanes you have used to discover the authors of that lewde facte, wherein wee do greatly allowe of the good endevor you have used to bringe forthe the truth of so fowle an acte. But because the proofes are so manifest and evident against them, thoughe they will not be broughte to confesse the same, wee have though yt meete that you shall by virtue hereof remove them to Brydewell, whom upon sight hereof the officers there shall receave, and there you shall with the assistance of some of the Justices see them to be reexamined, and if they will not be brought to confesse the whole truth of that robbery and who were the rest of their complices, then you shall cause them to be put to the racke and torture of the manacles, that they may be compelled to utter all their followers, partakers and abbettors of that robbery, and that which is fitt to be knowne touchinge the perfecte discovery of so lewde a facte. In the meane tyme wee are to warne you that none of them by any meanes may be bailed. *Postscript*:—Amongest others which you are precisely to examine wee require you especially to bolte forth the truth in ministringe the torture to William Browne, a butcher, who knoweth the whole society of theis wicked disposed persons.

[D]   **No. 50**

10th Jan. 1591.

A Letter to the Lieutenante of the Towre, Henrie Killigrew, Robert Beale, Dr. Fletcher, Richard Topclif, or to any fowre or thre of them. Theis shalbe to require at some convenient time by you and Mr. Topclif purposelie set downe that you diligentlie examine George Beesley *alias* Passelaw, a seminarie priest, and one Robart Humberson, his familiar companion and confederate, of such matters as Mr. Topclif the bearer hereof shal enforme you, or as in your discrecion shalbe thought nedeful and expedient for the behoof of her Majesty's service, and likewise you shal examine al such other persons as shalbe suspected or hereafter be apprehended to be any waies believers or favorers of the said Beeseley and Humberson. And if you shal see good cause by their obstinate refusal to declare the truth of such things as shalbe laid to their charge in her Majesty's behalf, then shal you by aucthoritie hereof comit them to prizon called Litle Ease, or to such other ordinarie place of punishment as hath ben accustomed to be used in those cases, and to certify proccedings from tyme to tyme.

[D]   **No. 51**

20th July, 1591

A Letter to Sergeant Owin and Richard Yongue. Whereas it is thought meete that William Hacket, a most pestiferous and seditious person, should be most strictlie and severelie examyned, and that he may be compelled by torture to utter and discover the bottom of his wicked and divelish purpose and the names of those that were auctours, abbetours or anie wise privie to those his leud intentions and doinges, theise shalbe to will and require you to repaire to Bridewell, where at this tyme by our order he remayneth prisoner, there not only to take his examynations with the assistance of soche of her Majesty's Learned Counsel or others as you shall take unto you for that purpose, but to cause him to be put to the manackles and such other tortour as you shal thinke good, therby to enforce him to utter his whole knowledge and that which is mete to be discovered of theise wicked practizes and conspiracies, wherein these shalbe your sufficient warrant. . . .

[J] [D]   **No. 52**

25th Oct. 1591.

A Letter to Doctor Fletcher, Richard Topclyffe, Richard Brantwhayte, and Richard Yonge, Esquiers. Whereas one Eustace Whyte, a semynarye prist, was of late taken and there was also one Brian Lassy, a disperser and distribture of letters to papistes and other evyll affected subjects apprehended in lyke sorte; Theise shall be therefore to will and require you to take the examynations and confessions of both the said persons, and verie straightly to examyn them uppon soche articles as you, Richard Topclyffe, shall administer unto them; and if they shall not declare their knowledges, and answer directly to all soche matters as you shall thynke meet and necessary to be propounded unto them, then shall you be vertue hereof, for the better boultinge forthe of the truthe, cause them to be put to the manacles and soche other tortures as are used in Bridewell, to th'end they may be compelled to utter soche thinges as shall concern Her Majestie and the Estate; and their examynations so taken by you, we pray you to send the same unto us.

[J] [D]   **No. 53**

27th Oct. 1591.

A Letter to Mr. Attorney, Mr. Solycitor. Whereas Thomas Clynton beinge by us comytted close prysoner unto the Fleete, is to be dealt withall and examynyd upon certaine artycles and matters which alreadye have been delivered unto you; Theise shall be to require you strictlye and severelye to take his examynation concerning those matters; wherein if he shall not deale plainelie and truelye in declaringe the truthe of those things which shall be demanded on hym, then you shall send for Mr. Topcliff and Mr. Younge, Esquiers, and cause hym to be by them removed unto Brydewell, and there to be putt to the manacles and soche torture as ys there used, wherebye he maye be compelled to utter the truth as his own knowledge in those matters which are fytt to be known.

[J] [D]   **No. 54**

4th June, 1592.

A Letter to Sir George Cary, Knight, and Mr. Richard Yonge. Whereas Owen

Edmondes, Irishman, standeth at this present chardged verie deeplie with matters concerning the State, and that it seemeth ther is good proof against him for the matters whereof he is so chardged, notwithstanding he obstinately refuseth to confes the same; These shall be therfore to will and require you to remove the said Owen Edmondes from the prison of the Marshalsey, where he presently remaneth, to Bridewell; where, after you shall have examined him agayne touchinge the premises, if he shall still persist in his obstinacye, you shall, by vertue hereof, put him to the torture accustomed in suche cases untill he shall be conformable as [in] your good discretions shall be thought fit. And so praeing you to have care thereof as apperteyneth, we, &c.

[J] [D]   **No. 55**

8th Feb. 1593.

A Letter to Mr. Richard Yonge and Mr. Ellis, to take order that Urmstone and Edward Bagshaw, prisoners in the Gatehouse at Westminster, and Henry Ashe in Newgate, London, be removed to Bridewell, to be proceeded with there as shall be directed from Her Majestie's Attorney and Sollicitor General, and in case of need to pinch them with the torture as in such case is accustomed.

[J] [D]   **No. 56**

16th April, 1593.

A Letter to the Lord Maior of London. Whereas there was a lewde and vyle ticket or placarde set up upon some post in London, purporting some determinacion and intention the Apprentyces should have to attempt some vyolence on the Strangers, and Your Lordship, as we understande, hath by your careful endevour apprehended one that is to be suspected and thought likelie to have written the same. Because oftentymes it doth fall out of such lewd beginnings that further mischefe doth ensue if in time it be not wyselie prevented, Wee have thought good to praie Your Lordship to cause the person by you apprehended and committed upon suspition to have written that libell, to be strictlie and verie carefullie examined of his meanynge and purpose to make that writing, who were any waie privie to the same, and did give him advice or incouragement in what he is hable to discover of that fact. And if there shall be pregnant matter to argue him to be guiltie of the writinge of the said placarde, and yet he will not by faire meanes be brought to utter his knowledge, wee think it convenient he shall by punyshed by torture used in like cases, and so compelled to reveale the same. We trust you are soe carefull in the government of the Citty, as if some lewde persons had such wicked purpose to attempt any thing against Strangers, that by your carefull forsyghte the same shall be prevented. And herein wee praie you to certifie what you shall be prevented. And herein wee praie you to certifie what you shall further understande and learne by the examination of this lewde fellow or by anie other meanes.

[J] [D]   **No. 57**

11th May, 1593.

A Letter to Sir Richard Martin, Anthonie Ashley, Mr. Alderman Buckle, &c. There have bin of late divers lewd and mutinous libells set up within the Citie of London, among the which there is some set uppon the wal of the Dutch Churchyard that doth excead the rest in lewdnes; And for the discoverie of the author and publisher thereof Her Majestie's pleasure is that some extraordinarie paines and care be taken by the Commissioners appointed by the Lord Maior for examining such persons as maie be in this case anie waie suspected. Theis shall be therefore to require and authorize you to make serch and apprehend everie person so to be suspected, and for that purpose to enter into al houses and places where anie such maie be remayning; and upon their aprehension to make like serch in anie the chambers, studies, chestes, or other like places, for al manner of writings or papers that maie give you light of the discoverie of the libellers. And after you shall have examined the persons, if you shall find them dulie to be suspected and they shall refuze to confesse the truth, you shall by authoritie hereof put them to the torture in Bridewel, and by the extremetie thereof, to be used at such times and as often as you shall think fit, draw them to discover their knowledge concerning the said libells. We praie you herein to use your uttermost travel and endevour, to th'end the author of these seditious libels maie be known, and they punyshed according to their deserts. And this shall be your sufficient warrant, &c.

[J] [D]   **No. 58**

(a) 12th Nov. 1595.

A Letter to Her Majestie's Sollicitor General and Mr. William Wade, Esquier. Whereas there is one Gabriel Colford lately apprehended, that brought certain seditious books from beyond the seas into the realm, being a most lewd person, as wee do understand, and one that is emploied for the fugitives beyond the seas in messages hither into the realm: And there is also a tailor dwelling in Fleete street taken in his company called Thomas Foulkes, in whose house this Colford did lodge both now and at other times when he came over hither from the parties beyond the seas; Forasmuch as these parties, having been often examined by the Lord Chief Justice of Her Majestie's Bench, will not by good and fair meanes be brought to reveale those things within their knowledge concerning Her Majestie and the State, These shalbe by vertue hereof to require you to put them to the torture of the manacles in Bridewell, that they may be forced to utter the uttermost of their knowledge in those things that shall concern their dutie and allegeance, and is meet to be by them most trewlie declared. And so wee bid you farewell, &c.

[D]

(b) 5th July, 1596.

A Letter to Mr. Thomas Fleming, her Majesty's Sollicitour, and Mr. William Waad, one of the Clarkes of the Counsell. Whereas one Gabryell Coleford was comitted unto prison upon his repair thither from the partes beyond the seas and bringinge into this realme divers packettes of sedycious bookes, and beinge by you examined and put to the torture he could not be drawne to make other confession but that the bookes were delivered to him packed up by one Verstegh, and he was addressed to leave the same at the house of one Faulkes, a taylor in Fleet Street, where they were founde. Because the freindes of the said Coleford ar knowne to be well affected, and do offer to put in good security for his forthcominge and to use all good meanes to reduce him to conformety, theis shalbe to require you to cause good bondes to be taken to her Majesty's use of some of his friendes for the forthcominge of the said Coleford and not to departe the realme, but to remaine at the house of his mother, the widdowe Coleford, in the county of Essex, and not to goe above five milles from the said house, and upon these bondes so taken he may be sett at liberty.

[J] [D]   **No. 59**

25th Jan. 1596.

A Letter to Sir Thomas Wilkes and Mr. Wade. There hath been of late apprehended and committed to Bridewell one John Hardie, a Frenchman, of the age of xxtie yeares or thereabouts, come into the realme for noe good purposes, as maie be conjectured, for that there have bene found about him secretlie sewed up in his dublett divers letters and memorialls, containing matters of great suspition which he refuseth to disclose; Her Majestie's pleasure therefore is, that forthwith uppon the receipt hereof you peruse the said letters and memorialls, out of which you maie conceave articles and interrogatories to be by you ministered unto him, and soe to examine him verie secretlie thereuppon, and of the causes of his coming hither, and to what persons he hath bene addressed here within the realme; and if he shall refuse to bewray the truth of such thinges and circumstances as you shall probablie see maie be laide to his chardge, then shall you by authoritie hereof trie him by the ordinarie torture there in Bridewell, and by the paine and terror thereof drawe him to confesse and discover his knowledge of the matters committed to his chardge, and his intention here to have bin putt in execution. And this shall be your warrant, &c. &c.

[J] [D]   No. 60

Last day of Feb. 1596.

A Letter to Sir Richard Martin. These are to give you verie hartie thankes for the extraordinarie paines you have taken in the apprehending and examining of Humphrey Hodges, out of whom wee perceave you have gotten much matter fit to be prosecuted and punished according to law, howbeyt that he hath not yet, as appeareth by your letters directed to me, Sir Robert Cecill Knight, discovered his whole knowledge what is become of the hundred poundes hid in the ground; and wee pray and require you therefore presentlie to remove Hodges to Bridewell, and to put him to the manacles, thereby constrayning him to deliver the whole trewth to such questions as you shall in this behalf think fit to administer unto him; whereof we pray you to continue your care and good endeavour.

[J] [D]   No. 61

21st Nov. 1596.

A Letter to the Recorder of London, Mr. Topcliffe, and Mr. Skevington. Whereas there were of late certaine lewde persons, to the number of 80, gathered together, calling themselves Egipcians and wanderers through divers countyes of the realme were stayed in Northamptonshire, whereupon we caused some of the ringleaders of them to be brought up hither and have committed them to prison. Theis shall be to require you by vertue hereof to examine the said lewd persons upon suche artycles and informations as you shall receive from the Lord Chiefe Justice of Her Majestie's Benche; and yf you shall not be hable by faire meanes to bringe them to reveale their lewd behaviour, practyses, and ringleaders, then wee thinke it meet they shall be removed to Brydewell and there be put to the manacles, whereby they may be constrained to utter the truth in those matters concerning their lewd behaviour that shall be fitt to be demanded of them.

[J] [D]   No. 62

19th Dec. 1596.

A Letter to Mr. Attorney and Mr. Sollycitor General, Mr. Francis Bacon, and Mr. Recorder of London, or to anie two of them: You shall understand that there hath been of late a very detestable practize and conspiracye discovered of certaine lewde persons that intended to make a risinge and a commotion in the countie of Oxford, and to drawe more nombers to them out of other counties adjoyninge, as you shall more particularly understand by the examinations that

have been taken of them by our very good lord, the Lord Norreis, and some
other justices of that countie, By whose indevors divers of those seditious persons
are apprehended, and by our directions fower of the ringeleaders are sent upp
hether, whome we have caused to be comytted to sundry prysons, Bartholomew
Starr to Newgate, James Bradshawe to the Compter in Wood-Street, Richard
Bradshawe to the Clynck, and Roger Isbell to the Fleete, and one more of this
crewe that was apprehended here (whose name is Robert Burton) was commytted
to the Gatehouse in Westminster: Because yt is requisite the bottome of thes
wicked practizes should thorrowlie be dyscovered, whereof they had there
begynnynges, what partakers they had, and what further myscheefe they did
intende, These shall be to require and authoryze you to send for these persons
or anie other that maie be touched in the matter; and after you have perused
the former examinations, to procede further to examine them uppon such articles
as you shall think meete to be propounded unto them. And for the better bowltinge
forth of the truthe of there intended plotts and purposes you shall (as you shall
see cause) remove them to Brydewell, and cause them to be put to the manackles
and torture, that they maie be constrayned thereby to utter the whole truthe of
their myschevous devyses and purposes in this wicked and trayterous con-
spyracy. Whereof we praie you to advertize us from tyme to tyme, &c.

[J] [D]   **No. 63**

2nd Feb. 1597.
    A Letter to Mr. Atturney-General, Mr. Sollicitor, Mr. Frauncis Bacon, and
Mr. William Waad: Whereas there is lately apprehended one William Tomson,
a very lewde and daungerous person, that is charged to have a purpose to burne
Her Majestie's shipps, or to doe some notable villanye: These shall be to require
you to examyne the sayde Tomson upon such articles as are delivered to you,
William Waad, towchinge his sayde divellishe purposes and intents, and to
deale earnestly with him by suche perswasions as you shall thinke meete to
declare by whome he hath bin moved thereunto, and who are privye or partakers
in this sayde intended purposes, and what further practises or intent he had or
can discover. Wherein, if by faire meanes and perswasions he shall not be
moved to reveale unto you the whole truth in these matters, then you shall by
vertue heerof cause him to be put to the manacles, or the torture of the racke,
as in like cases hath been used, thereby to force him to declare the truthe, and
circumstances of his whole intent and purposes heerein, and suche further matter
resting in his knowledge concerning Her Majestie or the Estate as shall be fitt
to be drawne from him. And so. &c.

[A Warrant to the Lieutenant of the Tower to receive the sayde William Tomson
to be kept a close prisoner.]

[D]   No. 64

13th April, 1597.

A Letter to Sir Richard Barkley, Lieutenant of the Tower, Mr. Sollicitor, Mr. Bacon and William Waad, esquire. You shall understand that one Gerratt,[5] a Jesuite, by her Majesty's commandment is of late committed to the Tower of London for that yt hath ben discovered to her Majestie he verie latelie did receive a packet of letters out of the Lowe Contryes which are supposed to come out of Spayne, being noted to be a great intellegencer and to holde correspondence with Parsons the Jesuite and other traitors beyond the seas. These shalbe therfore to require you to examyne him strictlie upon such interogatories as shalbe fitt to be ministred unto him and he ought to answere to manyfest the truthe in that behalf and other things that may concern her Majesty and the State, wherein yf you shall finde him obstinate, undutyfull or unwilling to declare and reveale the truthe as he ought to do by his duty and allegeaunce, you shall by vertue hereof cause him to be put to the manacles and suche other torture as is used in that place, that he maie be forced to utter directlie and truly his uttermost knowledg in all these thinges that maie any waie concerne her Majesty and the State and are meet to be knowne.

[J] [D]   No. 65

1st Dec. 1597.

A Letter to Sir Richard Martin, Mr. Recorder of London, Mr. Topcliffe, Mr. Fowler, Mr. Ask, Mr. Vaughan, and Mr. Skevington, or any two of them, requiring them to examine one Thomas Travers, prisoner in Brydewell, being detected for stealing a standyshe of Her Majestie by examination of wytnesses, and yet he still persisteth in obstynate denyal thereof; and yf he shall not declare the truth by your persuasion, then to put him to the torture of the manacles.

[J] [D]   No. 66

17th Dec. 1597.

A Letter to Mr. Recorder of London, Mr. Topcliffe, Nicholas Fuller, Mr. Gerard, and Mr. Altham. Whereas the body of Richard Aunger, a double reader of Graye's Inne, was found on Tuesday last floating on the Thames, he having been myssed almost a moneth. Because upon view of the body by certaine skillful chirurgeons yt is not thought he was drowned in the water but styfled or murthered, and after throwne into the Thames, which by other conjectures is greatlie to be also suspected; and there are great presumptions against one of his sonnes, called Richard Aunger, and Edward Ingram, porter of Graye's Inne, to be the committers of that foule murther. Forasmuch as the facte is so horrible that an auncyent gentleman should be murthered in his chamber, yt is thought meete that the manner of this foule murther should be by all meanes found out. And therefore we have thought good to require you to examyne the porter of Graye's Inne, and Richard Aunger, the sonne, more stryctly upon suche articles as you shall thinke meete, upon former examynations and other circumstances to be propounded unto them. And if by those persuasions and other meanes you shall use, you shall not be able to bringe them to confesse the truthe of this horrible facte, then we require you to put them both or either of them to the manacles in Brydewell, that by compulsory meanes the truthe of this wicked murther may be discovered, and who were complices and privy to this confederacy and fact.

[D]   No. 67

17th April, 1598.

A Letter to Mr. Sarjant Fleminge, her Majesty's Solicitour, Mr. William Waad, esquior, Clarke of her Majesty's Councell, and Mr. Frances Bacon. There hathe bin aprehended of late a leud fellow called Valentin Thomas comming out of Scotlande who ys charged with matters concerninge greatly the Estate, and having bin examined by som of us wee finde he dothe not deale with that truithe and plainnes he ought to do in matters of that waight and moment, for which respect yt ys thought meete he shalbe delt withall with some severity, that the truithe maie be knowne in those thinges he ys charged withall. Theis shalbe therefore to require and authoriz you upon such matter as ys delivered to you, William Waad, to frame suche interrogatories as you shall thincke fitt to be propounded unto him, whereunto if he shall not answer dyrectly, plainly, and to your satisfaccion, then her Majesty's pleasure is you cause him to be put to the manacles in Bridwell and so delt withall that he maie declare his full knowledge, practizes and the truithe of those things he knoweth and hathe bin delt withall and ys anie waye privie unto, for the which purpose you shall by vertue hereof send for him out of the Marshalsea and remove him to the prison of Bridwell. And theis shalbe your sufficient warrant for your proceedings therein. . . .

[J] [D]   No. 68

4th Jan. 1599.

A Letter to Sir John Peyton, Knt., Lieutenant of the Tower, and Richard Topcliffe, Esq. Whereas we understande that in a privye searche made by you the last nighte there were apprehended two persons, namely, Richard Denton and Peter Cooper. (who were lodged in the house of one Egglestone in Finsberry

Fields,) that are supposed to be privie unto some dangerous practise against the person of Her Majestie and the State, as by some secreate intelligence hath bin already somewhat discovered; wee do therefore praie and require you to cause the said Denton and Cooper to be committed to the prison of Bridewell, and to take order for the streight examination of them there by yourselves, using such meanes of torture by the manacles as you shall finde needful to make them particularlie discover and declare the truth of the said practice, and to certifie us of your proceedings herein, which is to be done with dilligence and convenient speed. So wee bidd, &c.

[D]   **No. 69**

21st April, 1601.

A Letter to William Waad, esquier, one of the Clerckes of the Counsell, and Thomas Fowler, esquier, Justices of the Peace in the Countie of Middlesex. Wee have seene the examination that have bin taken of one Thomas Howson, a yonge striplinge that was committed unto Bridewell, beinge servant to a scrivener dwelling in the Strande neare Charinge Crosse, whereby wee perceave his obstinacie to be such as no fayre meanes will induce him to confesse the truth concerninge such rayling and slanderous libelles as have been written and dispersed by him. And because it appeareth that his later examinations are contrary to his former confessions, and there is great likelyhood that hee hath used the advice of some seditious and malicious persons therein and that he hath bin acquainted with the dispersing of divers seditious libells, and there is a leafe torne out of a booke in which he did with his owne hande write twoe most rayling libells, this lewd practise beinge in theis tymes so frequent there would be care used both to discover the authors and dispersers of theis seditious and wicked libells and to see them severely punished. Wee have thought good therefore to requier you againe to examen the said Howson upon such pointes as you shall thincke fitte for the better discovery of the truth therein, and if you cannot perswade him to reveale and lay open unto you those that were privie to this his wicked dealing in such sorte as may give you sufficient satisfaction, then we requier and authorise you by vertue hereof to put the said Howson to the manacles, wherby he may be forced to discover the truth of those particulers that are meete to be knowen and he ought to reveale in this regard. And for your doinges herein theis shalbe your warrant.

[J] [D]   **No. 70**

18th Jan. 1615.

A Letter[6] to Sir Ralph Winwood, Knt., His Majestie's Secretarie of State,

Sir Julius Caesar, Knt., Master of the Rolls, of his Majestie's Privie Councell, Sir Gervaise Helwishe, Knt., Lieutenant of the Tower, Sir Francis Bacon, Knt., His Majestie's Attorny Generall, Sir Henry Montague, Knt., His Majestie's Serjeant at Lawe, Sir Henry Yelverton, Knt., His Majestie's Solicitor Generall, Sir Randall Crewe, Knt., His Majestie's Serjeant at Lawe, and Francis Cottington, Esq., Clerke of his Majestie's Privie Councell, and to every of them; Whereas Edmund Peacham, now prisoner in the Tower, stands charged with the writing of a booke or pamphlett containing matters treasonable (as is conceaved), and being examined thereupon refuseth to declare the truthe in those points whereof he hath beene interrogated. Forasmuch as the same doth concerne His Majestie's sacred person and government, and doth highly concerne his service to have many things yet discovered touching the sayd booke and the author thereof, wherein Peacham dealeth not so clerelie as becometh an honest and loyale subject; These shall be therefore in His Majestie's name to will and require you and every of you to repaire, with what convenient diligence you may, unto the Tower, and there to call before you the sayd Peacham, and to examine him strictly upon such interrogatories concerning the sayd booke as you shall think fitt and necessarie for the manifestation of the truthe. And if you finde him obstinate and perverse, and not otherwise willing or readie to tell the truthe, then to putt him to the manacles as in your discretions you shall see occasion. For which this shall be to you and every of you sufficient warrant.

[J] [D]   **No. 71**

19th Feb. 1620[7]

A Letter to the Lieutenant of the Tower of London. Whereas Samuel Peacock was heretofore committed prisoner to the Marshalsea, and that now it is thought fitt, upon vehement suspicion of highe treason against His Majestie's sacred person, to remove him thence and to committ him to the Tower; This shall be therefore to will and require you to repare to the prison of the Marshalsea, and there to receave from the Keeper of that House the person of the said Samuel Peacock, and him safely to convey under your custodie unto the Tower of London, where you are to kepe him close prisoner until further order. And whereas wee have thought meete to nominate and appointe Sir Henry Montague, Knight, Lord Chiefe Justice of the King's Bench, Sir Thomas Coventrie, Knight, His Majestie's Sollicitor General, and yourself, to examine the said Peacock, for the better discovery of the truth of this treason. This shall be likewise to authorize you, or any two of you, whereof yourself to be one, to examine the said Peacock from time to tyme, and to put him, as there shall be cause for the better manifestation of the truth, to the torture either of the manacles or the racke. For which this shall be your warrante, and soe, &c.

[J] [D]   **No. 72**

9th Jan. 1622.

   A Letter to Mr. Serjeant Crewe and Mr. Attorney General, to repare to the
Tower and to examine one James Crasfield, prisoner there, for causes knowen
into them; and if there shalbe cause, not only to offer him the manacles and
rack, but to use the same as in their discretion they shall find requisite for
discoveringe the trueth of such pointes whereupon hee is examined.

[J] [D]   **No. 73**

30th April, 162ᵕ.

   A Warrant to Sir Allen Apsley, Knight, Lieutenant of the Tower, Mr. Serjeant
/ shley, Mr. Trumbull, and Mr. Mewtas, or any two of them, to take into
ᴠ nination William Monke, close prisoner in the Tower, upon such interrog-
a ies as should be directed by the Lord Chiefe Justice of the King's Bench,
aı. to use the manacles to the said Monke if in their discretion they shall thincke
it fitt. And thereupon to certefie the Board what they finde.

[D]   **No. 74**

27th Feb. 1628.

   Upon consideracion formerly had of the peticion of William Monck com-
playneing as followeth, vizt, that he by the malicious practice and accusacion
tending to high treason of one John Blackborne and his wife was imprisoned
in the Tower of London and ther tortured upon the rack and was therby utterly
disabled to mayntaine himselfe, his wife and nyne children depending upon his
labours; that the same being discovered the petitioner was sett at libertie and a
warrant granted from the Board for apprehending of the said accusers; that the
said accusers out of a conscience of theire owne guiltines were fled and could
not be found; that the said accuser John Blackborne was possessed of lands and
other profitts which he had rented out to one Ellis Wynne and others, out of
which the petitioner humbly sought to be releved; theire Lordships in consideracion of the peticioner's sufferings and distressed estate, and to the end that
the petitioner mought have some meanes and releefe assigned him out of the
said Blackborne's estate, and what rents and profitts were payable to him out
of the same, and thereupon to make certificate to this Board; forasmuch as it
appeares by theire certifficate . . . that there is payable to the said John Blackborne for a house and land 5li *per annum* . . . that there are severall other sums
due to the said Blackborne . . . amounting in the whole to the sum of 37 li
13s. 4d., it was upon consideracion had of the said certificate thought fitt and
ordered that the said justice of the peace or any twoe of them be hereby authorized
and required to take and receave . . . and to pay the same over to the hands
of the said Monck or his assignes. . . .[8]

S.2: *REGAL WARRANTS AND DRAFTS*

[R]   **No. 75**

(a) 15th Dec. 1309.

REX universis & singulis Ministris suis, Custodibus Templariorum. . . . [9]
Mandamus vobis quod Praelatos & Inquisitores, ad inquirendum contra Ordinem Templariorum, & contra Magnum Praeceptorem dicti Ordinis, in Regno Angliae constitutum, & similiter contra singulares Personas & Fratres Ordinis illius nuper per litteras Apostolicas deputatos, de ipsis Templariis & eorum corporibus, quotiens voluerint, ordinare & facere permittatis id quod eis, secundum legem Ecclesiasticam, videbitur faciendum.

Et, ad haec facienda, sitis Praelatis & Inquisitoribus intendentes.

(b) 28th April, 1311.[10]

REX Major & Vicecomitibus Civitatis suae London . . .
Cum nuper, OB REVERENTIAM SEDIS APOSTOLICAE, concesserimus Praelatis & Inquisitoribus, ad inquirendum contra Ordinem Templariorum, quod iidem Praelati, & Inquisitores, de ipsis Templariis & eorum corporibus in quaestionibus, & aliis ad hoc convenientibus ordinent, & faciant, quoties voluerint, id quod eis, secundum legem Ecclesiasticam, videbitur faciendum . . .

Vobis, praefati Vicecomites, mandamus quod illos, quos dicti Praelati & Inquisitores, seu aliquis eorum, cum uno saltem Inquisitore, deputaverint ad supervidendum quod . . . Templariorum . . . custodia bene fiat, id supervidere: & corpora dictorum Templariorum in quaestionibus & aliis, ad hoc convenientibus, ponere. & alia, quae in hac parte, secundum legem Ecclesiasticam, fuerint facienda, facere permittatis. . . .

[Translations:

(a) The King, to all and every one of his officers having charge of the Templars . . . (Whereas) Prelates and Inquisitors (were) recently appointed by Apostolic letters to conduct an inquisition against the Order of the Templars, and against the Grand Preceptor of that Order, holding office in the English realm, and likewise against particular persons and members of the Order: We command you to allow (them) to arrange and do, as often as they please, concerning the Templars themselves and their bodies, what seems to them proper according to Ecclesiastical Law to be done. And you are to render assistance to the Prelates and Inquisitors in that behalf.

(b) The King, to the Mayor and Sheriffs of his City of London . . . Whereas recently, out of reverence for the Holy See, we granted to the Prelates and

Inquisitors who have the conduct of an inquisition against the Templars that they might arrange and do, as often as they pleased, what seemed to them proper according to Ecclesiastical Law to be done. . . . We command you, the Sheriffs aforesaid, to allow those whom the said Prelates and Inquisitors, or any of them including at least one Inquisitor, appoint to ensure that the custody in which the Templars are kept is appropriate, to exercise such supervision, and to allow the said Prelates and Inquisitors, or any of them including at least one Inquisitor to subject the bodies of the said Templars to interrogatory torture and to other measures suitable to the case, and to do other things in this matter which according to Ecclesiastical Law ought to be done. . . .]

[M][11]   **No. 76**

15th Sept. 1571.
[The Queen to Sir Thomas Smith and Doctor Wilson.[12]]

Right trusty and welbeloved we grete you well, and fynding in the trayterous attempts lately discovered that nether Barker nor Bannistar, the Duke of Norfolk's men, have uttred ther knolledg in the undue prudness[13] of ther MS,[14] and of themselves, nother will discover the same withowt torture; forasmuch as the knolledg hereof concerneth our suerty and estate, and that they have untruly allredy answered; We will and by warrant herof authoriss you to procede to the furder examynation of them uppon all poynts that you can thynk by your discretions mete for knolledg of the truth. And if they shall not seme to you to confess playnly ther knolledg, than we warrant yow to cause them both, or ether of them, to be brought to the rack: and first to move them with feare therof to deale playnly in ther answers, and if that shall not move them, than yow shall cause them to be putt to the rack, and to find the tast therof untill they shall deale more playnly, or untill you shall thynk mete. And so we remitt the whole procydying to your furder discretion, requirying yow to use spede herin and to require the assistance of our Lieutenant of the Toure. Gyven under our signet. . . .

[H]   **No. 77**

(a) 1553.
[From Instructions to the Council in Wales and the Marches.]

Hit is the Quene's Hieghnes Pleasure, that the . . . Comyssioners by all their Policies, Wayes and Meanes that they can, shall putt their good and effectual Endevors, Industries and Travailes, to repress all maner of Murthers, Felonyes, Burglaries, Rapes, Riotts, Rowtts, onlawful Assembles, onlawful Reteynors, Peiuries, of what kynde soever they be, and all other onlawfull Mysdemeanors, Offences, Contempts and evil Doeings, whatsoever they be, attempted, doon or comytted by any Person or Persons within the Lymyts of their Comyssion;

and the same to examyne and determyne, aswell by Deposycions of Witnesses, as by all other kynde of Proves by their Discretions. And that the said Comyssioners, or three of them at leaste, uppon sufficient Grounde, Mattier and Cause shall and may putt any Person or Person accused, or vehemently suspected of any Treason, Murther or Felonye to *Tortures*, when they shall thinke mete and convenyent and the cause so requyre, by their Discretions; taking alway good Respecte to the good Order, Peace and Tranquylities of the Shires and Counties appointed within their Authoritie, according as the Quene's Hieghnes hath comytted, and doth comytt her singular Trust in them for the same; and to here and determyne the Premisses and every of them, according to the Lawes and Statutes of England, or otherwise by their Discretions.

[M]¹⁵

(b) 1574.
  [From Instructions to the Council in Wales and the Marches.]

  The Queen's Majesty's pleasure is, that the . . . Lord President, or Vicepresident, and Counsell, by all their pollicies, wayes, and meanes, they can, shall put their good and effectuall endevers to represse all manner of murthers, felons, burglaries, rapes, riotts, rowtes, unlawfull assemblies, unlawful retayners, regrators, forestallers, extortioners, conspiracies, maintenances, periuries, of what kinde soever they be. And also all other unlawfull misdemeanours, offences, contempts, evill doinges, whatsoever they be, attempted, done, or committed, by any person or persons within the lymitts of their commissions, and the same to examine & determine, aswell by depositions of witnesses as by all other kinde of proofes, by theire discretions. And the said L. President & Counsell, or three of them at the least, wherof the Lord President or Vicepresident to be one, upon sufficient grounde, matter and cause, shall and may put any person accused, and knowne, or suspected, or any treason, murther or felonie, to tortures, when they shall thinke convenient, and that the cause shall apparentlie require, by their discretions.

[O]¹⁶   **No. 78**

6th Nov. 1605.
  [*Concerning Guy Fawkes: James I to the Lords Commissioners for the Plot.*]

  This examinate wold nou be maid to ansoure to formal interrogatours,

1 as to quhat he is, for I can never yett heare of any man that knowis him,
2 quhaire he uas borne,
3 quhat uaire his parents names,
4 quhat aage he is of,
5 quhaire he hath lived,
6 hou he hath lived & by quhat trade of lyfe,

7 hou he hath ressaved those woundes in his breste,

8 if he uas ever in service with any other before percie, quhat thay ware & hou long,

9 hou came he in percies service, by quhat meanes, & at quhat tyme,

10 quhat tyme uas this house hyred by his maister,

11 and hou soone after the possessing of it did he beginne to his devillishe preparations,

12 quhen & quhaire lernid he to speake frenche,

13 quhat gentle womans letter it was that was founde upon him,

14 & quhair for doth she give him another name in it than he gives to him self,

15 if he was ever a papiste, & if so quho brocht him up in it,

16 if other wayes, hou was he convertid, quhaire, quhen & by quhom, this course of his lyfe I ame the more desyrouse to know, becaus I have dyvers motives leading me to suspecte that he hath remained long beyond the seas, & ather is a preiste, or hath long servid som preiste or fugitive abroade, for I can yett (as I saide in the beginning heir of) meite with no man that knowis him, the letter found upon him gives him another name, & those that best knowis his maister can never remember to have seene him in his companie. quhair upon it shoulde seeme that he hath bene reccomendit by some personnis to his maisters service only for this use, quhair in only, he hath servid him, & thairfore he wolde also be asked in quhat company, & shipp he went out of englande, & the porte he shipped at, & the lyke questions wold be asked anent the forme of this returne, as for these tromper [ie][17] waires founde upon him, and the signification & use of everie one of thaime wolde be knowin, & quhat I have observid in thaim, the bearare will show you. nou laste, ye remember of the crewallie villanouse pasquill that rayled upon me for the name of brittaine, if I remember right it spake some thing of harvest & prophecied my destruction about that tyme, ye may thinke of this, for it is lyke to be the laboure of such a desperate fellow as this is if he will not other wayes confesse, the gentler tortours are to be first used unto him, & sic per gradus ad ima tenditur, & so god speede youre goode worke.

[O] [J][18]   **No. 79**

21st May,   1640.

[The King to the Lieutenant of the Tower]

Trusty and Welbeloved, we great you well. Our will and pleasure is that tormorrow Morning, by seaven of the Clock, you cause John Archer to be carried to the Rack, and that there youreself, togather with Sir Ralph Whitfield and Sir Robert Heath, Knights, Our sergeants at lawe, shall examine him upon such questions as Our said serjeants shall think fitt to propose to him. And if upon sight of the Rack he shall not make a cleare answer to the said Questions, then Our further pleasure is that you cause him to be racked as in your and theire discretions shall be thought fitt. And when he shall have made a full answer, then the same is to be brought to us, and you are still to deteyne him close Prisoner till you shall receve further Orders. And this shallbe aswell to you as to Our said sergents sufficient warrant and discharge in this behalfe.

[0]   **No. 80**

(a) 26th Jan.   1673.[19]
[Arlington to the Lieutenant of the Tower; initialled by the King.]

I am commanded by his majestie to give you notice that you have the wrack in ye tower made ready and fitt tomorrow morning by 10 of ye clock precisely, and yt the Executioner be ordered to attend at ye same time, his majestie having appointed his Grace the . . . Duke of . . . Lauderdale and Mr. Secretary Coventry to repaire at that houre to ye Tower for the Examining certain prisoners now remaining in your cutody, of which you are not to faile.

(b) 24th Feb.   1673[20]
[Draught Commission to Colonel John Russell and ten other officers, and to Sir Leoline Jenkins and three other doctors of civil law.]

[Authority to try Zas and Arton on charges of espionage; interrogatories being exhibited on certain matters by Sir Robert Wiseman and Sir Walter Walker, authority to obtain answers from Zas and his companion] . . . by such lawfull wayes and meanes as shall appeare to be just and even by paines to be inflicted if otherwise he or they refuse (so as the said paines bee not extended to the lameing, disjoynting, or dismembring of his or theyr bodyes) . . . *[and authority to sentence them, though so that sentence of death shall not be executed without further order of the King.]*

S.3: *TEXT OF THE TRACT, PUBLISHED IN 1583, WHICH WAS CALLED, "A DECLARATION OF THE FAVOURABLE DEALING OF HER MAJESTIES COMMISSIONERS, APPOINTED FOR THE EXAMINATION OF CERTAINE TRAYTOURS, AND OF TORTURES UNJUSTLY REPORTED TO BE DONE UPON THEM FOR MATTER OF RELIGION"*

[S][21]   **No. 81**

TO THE READER

Good reader, although her majesties most milde and gracious government bee sufficient to defende it selfe against those most slaunderous reportes of heathenish and unnatural tyrannie, and cruell tortures, pretended to have bene executed upon certaine traitors, who lately suffered for their treason, and others, aswell spread abroad by runnagate Jesuites, and seminary men, in their seditious bookes, letters, and libels, in forreine countries, and princes courtes; as also insinuated into the hearts of some of our own countriemen and her majesties subjectes: yet for thy better satisfaction, I have conferred with a very honest gentleman, whom I knew to have good and sufficient meanes to deliver the trueth against such forgers of lyes and shameles slaunders in that behalfe, which he and other that do know and have affirmed the same, will at all times justifie. And for thy further assurance and satisfaction herein, he hath set downe to the vewe of all men these notes following.

Touching the racke and torments used to such traitors as pretended themselves to bee Catholiques, upon whom the same have bene exercised, it is affirmed for trueth, and is offered upon due examination so to be proved, to be as followeth:—First, That the formes of torture in their severitie or rigour of execution, have not bene such and in such maner perfourmed, as the sclaunderers and seditious libellers have sclaunderously and maliciously published. And that even the principall offender Campion himselfe, who was sent and came from Rome, and continued here in sundrie corners of the realme, having secretly wandered in the greatest part of the shieres of Englande in a disguised sort, to the intent to make speciall preparation of treasons, and to that end and for furtherance of those his labors, sent over for more helpe and assistance, and cunningly and traiterously at Rome, before he came from thence, procured tolleration for such prepared rebels, to keepe themselves covert under pretence of temporarie and permissive obedience to her majestie, the state standing as it doth, but so soone as there were sufficient force, whereby the bull of her majesties deprivation might bee publikely executed, they shoulde then joine altogether with that force upon peine of curse and damnation. That very Campion, I say, before the conference had with him by learned men in the Tower, wherin he was charitably used, was never so racked, but that he was presently able to walk, and to write, and did presently write and subscribe al his confessions, as by the originales thereof may appear. A horrible matter is also made of starving one Alexander Briant, how he shoulde eate clay out of the walles, gathered water to drinke from the droppings of houses, with such other false ostentations of immanitie; where the truth is this, that whatsoever Briant suffered in want of foode, he suffered the same wilfully, and of extreme impudent obstinacie against the minde and liking of those that dealt with him. For, certaine traiterous writings being founde about him, it was thought convenient by conference of hands, to understand whose writing they were; and thereupon he being in her majesties name commaunded to write, which he coulde very well doe, and being permitted to him to write, what he would himselfe, in these terms, that if he liked not to write one thing, he might write an other, or what he lysted, (which to doe being charged in her majesties name was his duetie, and to refuse was disloyall and undutifull;) yet the man woulde by no meanes be induced to write any thing at all. Then was it commanded to his keeper to give unto him such meate, drinke, and other convenient necessaries as he would write for, and to forbeare to give him any thinge which he would not write. But Briant being thereof advertised and oft moved to write, persisting so in his curst heart by almost two dayes and two nightes, made choise rather to lack foode, then to write for the sustenance which he might readely have had for writing, and which he had indede redely and plentifully, so soone as he wrote. And as it is sayde of these two, so is it to be truely sayde of other, with this, that there was a perpetuall care had, and the queene's servantes the warders, whose office and act it is to handle the racke, were ever by those that attended the examinations specially charged, to use it in as charitable maner as such a thing might be.

Secondly, it is said, and likewise offered to be justified, that never any of these seminaries, or such other pretended Catholiques which at any time in her majesties raigne have been put to the racke, were upon the racke, or in other torture, demanded any question of their supposed conscience, as what they beleeved in any point of doctrine or faith, as the masse, transubstantiation, or such like; but onely with what persons at home or abroad, and touching what plots, practises, and conferences, they had dealt about attempts against her majesties estate or person, or to alter the lawes of the realme for matters of religion, by treason or by force, and howe they were perswaded themselves, and did perswade other touching the Pope's bull and pretense of authority, to depose kings and princes, and namely, for deprivation of her majestie, and to discharge subjectes from their allegiance, expressing herein alway the kingly powers and estates, and the subjectes allegiance civily, without mentioning or meaning therein any right that the queene as in right of the crowne, hath over persons ecclesiasticall being her subjectes. In all which cases, Campion and the rest never answered plainely, but sophistically, deceitfully and traiterously, restraining their confession of allegiance onely to the permissive forme of the Pope's toleration. As for example, if they were asked, Whether they did acknowledge themselves the queene's subjectes, and woulde obey her? they woulde say, yea; for so they had leave for a time to doe. But adding more to the question, and they being asked, if they woulde so acknowledge and obey her any longer than the Pope woulde so permit them? or not withstanding such commandment as the Pope woulde or might give to the contrary, then they eyther refused so to obey, or denyed to answere, or said, that they coulde not answere to those questions without daunger; which very answere without more saying, was a plaine answere to all reasonable understanding, that they woulde no longer be subjectes, nor perswade other to be subjectes, then the Pope gave licence. And at their very arraignement, when they laboured to leave in the minds of the people and standers by, an opinion that they were to dye, not for treason, but for matter of faith and conscience in doctrine, touching the service of God, without any attempt or purpose against her majestie, they cryed out, that they were true subjectes, and did and would obey and serve her majestie. Immediately, to prove whether that hypocriticall and sophistical speech extended to a perpetuitie of their obedience, or to so long time as the Pope so permitted, or no, they were openly in place of judgement asked by the queene's learned counsell, Whether they would so obey, and be true subjectes, if the Pope commanded the contrary? they plainly disclosed themselves in answere, saying by the mouth of Campion, this place (meaning the court of her majesties bench) hath no power to enquire or judge of the holy father's authoritie; and other answere they woulde not make.

Thirdly, that none of them have bene put to the racke or torture, no not for the matters of treason, or partnership of treason, or such like, but where it was first knowen and evidently probable by former detections, confessions, and otherwise, that the partie so racked, or tortured, was guylty, and did knowe, and coulde deliver trueth of the things wherewith he was charged; so as it was first assured, that no innocent was at any time tormented, and the racke was never used to wring out confessions at adventure upon uncertainties, in which doing, it might bee possible that an innocent in that case might have bene racked.

Fourthly, that none of them hath bene racked or tortured, unlesse hee had first said expresly, or amounting to asmuch, that he wil not tell the trueth though the queene commaund him. And if any of them being examined did say he could not tell, or did not remember, if he woulde so affirme in such maner as Christians among Christians are beleeved, such his answere was accepted, if there were not apparent evidence to prove that he wilfully said untruely. But if he said that his answere in delivering trueth, shoulde hurt a Catholike, and so be an offence against charitie, which they said to be none, and that the queene coulde not commande them to sinne, and therefore, howsoever the queene commanded, they would not tell the trueth, which they were knowen to know, or to such effect; they were then put to the torture, or els not.

Fifthly, that the proceeding to torture was alway so slowly, so unwillingly, and with so many preparations of perswasions to spare themselves, and so many meanes to let them know that the trueth was by them to be uttered, both in dutie to her majestie, and in wisdome for themselves, as whosoever was present at those actions, must needes acknowledge in her majesties ministers, a ful purpose to follow the example of her owne most gracious disposition; whome God long preserve.

Thus it appeareth, that albeit by the more general lawes of nations, torture hath bene and is lawfully judged to be used in lesser cases, and in sharper maner for inquisition of trueth in crimes whose conspiracies and the particularities thereof it did so much import and behove to have disclosed, yet even in that necessarie use of such proceeding, enforced by the offenders notorious obstinacie, is neverthelesse to be acknowledged the sweete temperature of her majesties milde and gracious clemencie, and their slaunderous lewdenes to be the more condemned, that have in favour of haynous malefactors, and stubborne traytors, spread untrue rumors and slaunders to make her mercifull government disliked under false pretence, and rumors of sharpenesse and crueltie, to those against whome nothing can be cruel, and yet upon whome nothing hath bene done, but gentle and mercifull.

NOTES

INTRODUCTION

1. *La Torture: son histoire, son abolition, sa réapparition au xxᵉ siecle*, 2nd ed. (Paris: Mame, 1961), p. 12.

2. P. Fiorelli, *La Tortura giudiziaria nel diritto comune* (Rome: Giuffre, 1953, 1954), I, 181–91.

3. The concept of an "administrative practice" seems to have been introduced, by way of a gloss, to produce what was considered moral harmony between aa.24 and 26, although the latter seems to refer only to a.25. Cf. the Judgment, 18 January, 1978, in the proceedings noticed in the main text, para. 159: *British Yearbook of International Law* 49 (1978): 302–3.

4. P. Vidal-Naquet, *Torture: Cancer of Democracy*, trans. B. Richard (Middlesex: Penguin, 1963), p. 25 (M. C. Coste-Floret, Minister for Colonial Territories, in the National Assembly, 22 September, 1948, acknowledging belief that persons accused of rebellion had been subjected to interrogatory violence in Madagascar); and p. 175 (the "Wuillaume Report"—a report regarding the interrogation of suspects in Algeria, submitted on 2 March, 1955, to M. Jacques Soustelle, Governor-General, by M. R. Wuillaume, Civil Inspector-General: describing physical interrogatory violence that could lead to lasting injuries merely as "verging on torture."

5. Judgment, 18 January, 1978, para. 167: *British Yearbook of International Law* 49 (1978): 303.

6. 222 F. 2d. 698.

7. L. Duguit, *Traité de droit constitutionnel*, 3rd ed. (Paris: E. de Boccard, 1927), I, 1-2, remarks that "in all civilised countries there are faculties and teachers of law;" yet "there we have a science . . . regarding neither the object nor the domain of which does agreement exist."

8. "The Path of the Law": *Collected Legal Papers* (London: Constable, 1920), pp. 172-73. Cf. A. V. Dicey, *Law of the Constitution* (1885), "Outline of the Subject": 8th ed. (London: Macmillan, 1931), pp. 23; 30.

9. John Austin, *Province of Jurisprudence Determined* (1832), Lectures I; V: in *The Province of Jurisprudence Determined and the Uses of the Study of Jurisprudence* (London: Weidenfeld and Nicolson, 1954), pp. 11–12; 140–41; cf. 123–26; 137–38; A. V. Dicey, *Law of the Constitution*, 8th ed., pp. 22–24. The judicially enforced sanctions of "law" may be such as to express what Matthew Hale calls its coercive power, or only what he distinguishes as its directive, irritant, power. (*Historia placitorum coronae*, I, 43; 127; *Dialogue of the Common Laws*: in W. Holdsworth, *History of English Law* [London: Methuen, 1924] V, App. III, p. 499). The definition offered in the main text copes, I believe, with this and some other sources of difficulty, but not—unless one is prepared

241

to accept that some rules laid down by the Crown in Parliament fail to qualify as "law"—with the concept, adopted judicially in a few modern cases, of "directory" as distinct from "mandatory" provisions.

10. J. Fitzj. Stephen, *History of the Criminal Law of England* (London: Macmillan, 1883), I, 478–79; *Liberty, Equality, Fraternity*, ed. R. J. White (Cambridge: Cambridge University Press, 1967), pp. 150–55, advanced an aggressive, earthy, almost populistic view of this kind. E. Durkheim, *The Division of Labour in Society* (1893), trans. G. Simpson (1933) (New York: Free Press Paperback, 1964), pp. 97–109, is to broadly similar effect, in a more nervous style. During the present century, the Denunciatory Theory seems to have enjoyed a vogue with the United Kingdom Establishment: cf., for example, Cmnd. 8932 (1953), para. 52. Although it harmonizes with Freudian doctrine, the literature suggests that it received a fillip rather from Hegelianism.

11. An obvious text: Edward Coke, *Commentary upon Littleton*, (1628), f. 11b.

12. *De la République* (1576): London abridged ed., 1756, p. 1.

13. *Enquiry concerning Political Justice and its Influence on Morals and Happiness* (1796), Bk. I, Ch. II (Toronto: University of Toronto Press, 1946), I, 7.

14. Cf. Cmnd. 3165 (1966): on the strange incompleteness of which, see Lord Gardiner, Cmnd. 4901 (1972), Minority Report, para. 6.

15. In each of the Conventions, a.3. is in like terms and concerns "armed conflict not of an international character occurring in the territory of one of the High Contracting Parties." A note supplied to the Compton Committee, and which by official request it included in its Report (Cmnd. 4823 [1971], para. 46), here referred specifically to the *Convention relative to the Treatment of Prisoners of War*. Although terrorist activities in Northern Ireland in 1971 undoubtedly amounted to what R. Trinquier, *Modern Welfare: a French View of Counter-Insurgency*, trans. D. Lee (London: Pall Mall, 1964), pp. 8–9, would (when it is considered with the response of the security forces) class as "warfare", whether the United Kingdom Foreign Office would have agreed that what was going on was "armed conflict" within the 1949 Conventions, quaere?

16. Cmnd. 4823 (1971), para. 46; cf. Cmnd. 4901 (1972), Appendix.

17. Cmnd. 4823 (1971), para. 105; and cf. para. 20.

18. Ibid., paras. 48–51.

19. Ibid., para. 57.

20. Ibid., paras. 46; 48–51.

21. Ibid., para. 105.

22. Cmnd. 4901 (1972), Majority Report, paras. 34–36. The majority moreover proposed that various requirements should be imposed, such as authorization by "a U.K. Minister" who "might be advised by a small and experienced committee whose members are appointed by the Prime Minister after consultation with the Leader of the Opposition." So might the virus have spread to the heart. A remarkable indication offered, is that the practices revealed were never authorized by a Minister of the Crown; indeed, nothing shows that they were known to one. See the Minority Report, para. 8. It may be surmised that at some time a Minister of Defense at least had an opportunity to look at the Joint Directive.

23. Cmnd. 4901 (1972), Minority Report, para. 7(d).

24. Ibid., Minority Report, paras. 8; 10.

25. Cf. *British Yearbook of International Law* 49 (1978): 302.

26. Cmnd. 5847 (1975), paras. 20; 83. Reception, in evidence, of admissions known

to have been made under duress would, in a sense, be more extreme than to hold interrogatory duress itself non-criminal, non-tortious. Nonetheless, where a Northern Ireland trial is upon indictment, in principle the admissibility of a statement made by the accused may depend not on whether it was by Common Law standards "voluntary", but on whether it was obtained without measures contravening conditions stated by borrowing the language of the European Conventions, a.3. Cf. *Northern Ireland (Emergency Provisions) Act*, 1978, s.8; *Hetherington* [1975] N.I. 164. Thus whilst the general question of legality seems here to have been settled, by informed opinion, without help from the European Court, the decision of that tribunal (in the proceedings mentioned above in the main text) may, regarding this particular matter, exert some persuasive influence on United Kingdom courts. If so, it will not necessarily prove benign, for the European Court indicated that its finding of "inhuman or degrading" treatment depended upon the *combination* of methods that had been employed in Northern Ireland: Judgment, para. 167; *British Yearbook of International Law* 49 (1978): 303.

27. Cf. A. Esmein, *History of Continental Criminal Procedure*, trans. J. Simpson (London: John Murray, 1914), Tit. I, Ch. III, and App. B (from work of René Garraud); Fiorelli, *La Tortura giudiziaria*, II, 10–50.

28. French experience may be compared. Cf. the Wuillaume Report (above, n. 4): Vidal-Naquet, *Torture: Cancer of Democracy*, pp. 175–79; Mellor, *La Torture*, pp. 275–84; 299–324; 357–58; 365–66; J.-Ph. Lévy, *"L'Évolution de la preuve des origines à nos jours,"* Recueils de la Société Jean Bodin 17 (1965): 9, at 69. In France, apparently, the illegality of duress by deprivation, during official interrogation, is questionable. Wuillaume regarded the latter method as generally accepted in French society. He also thought that in Algeria torment by electricity and by near-asphyxiation with water ought to be authorized, since the Police considered it necessary, and to turn a blind eye to it was both hypocritical and no longer practicable. J-Ph. Lévy thought—having regard to what he believed the widespread practice of police interrogatory duress—that in the future it might seem better to introduce legal regulation into the matter. It may be supposed, however, that the Quai d'Orsay would, for the time being, see inconvenience in any proposal to make public changes in favor of interrogatory violence.

CHAPTER 1

1. Cf. below Chapter 3 (I).

2. See W. Ullmann, *Medieval Foundations of Renaissance Humanism* (London: Paul Elek, 1977), passim.

3. For outline English-language treatments of all this, see W. Kunkel, *An Introduction to Roman Legal and Constitutional History*, 2nd ed., trans. J. M. Kelly (Oxford: Clarendon Press, 1973), pp. 162–76; 181–83; Barry Nicholas, *Introduction to Roman Law* (Oxford: Clarendon Press, 1962), pp. 38–46.

4. See, for example, John of Salisbury, *Policraticus*, VII, 20; and cf. F. W. Maitland, *Bracton and Azo* (Selden Soc., VIII: 1895), pp. xxviii–xxx.

5. Felix Liebermann, "Magister Vacarius," *English Historical Review* 11 (1896): 305–14; 514; 13 (1898): 297. Francis De Zulueta: in Selden Soc., XLIV (1927), especially pp. xiii–xxiii.

244NOTES

6. John of Salisbury, *Policraticus*, VIII. xxii; Roger Bacon, *Compendium studii*, c. iv: Rolls Ser., p. 420; John Selden, *Ad Fletam dissertatio*, VII. vii.

7. Nicholas, *Introduction*, pp. 46–47; J.A.C. Thomas, *Textbook of Roman Law* (Amsterdam, New York, Oxford: North Holland, 1976), p. 8.

8. D. I.iii.10–13; 17–19; 24–25.

9. Kunkel, *Introduction*, pp. 183–85; Nicholas, *Introduction*, pp. 47–48.

10. F. W. Maitland, *Roman Canon Law in the Church of England* (London: Methuen, 1898), pp. 2-4. The papal legation concerned reflects in various matters acquaintance with the *Corpus Iuris*. It is also the case that the development of Canon Law by and around this Papal contribution seems to have depended upon juridical detachment learnt from the Digest and glossatorial analytical resource that the Canonists and Civilians displayed in common: cf. W. Ullman, *Growth of Papal Government in the Middle Ages* (London: Methuen, 1955), pp. 369–73.

11. Traditionally, in ecclesiastical procedure, an accuser was required (cf. Gratian, C.II, qu. 5, I Pars, Dictum) unless the tribunal was confronted with strong public suspicion of the individual concerned: an exception that appears to have been admittedly originally with regard to offenses of the clergy (Gratian, C.II, qu. 5, II Pars, Dictum; X, 5, 1, 17; 19). (Beware X, 5, 1, 24; 3, 11 in fin.; one must [X, 5, 3, 13; 31; 34, 15] distinguish teaching [in Gratian, C.II, qu. 1, c. 15; X, 5, 1, 9] that an accuser was not required when the crime was "manifest"/"notorious": cf. below, Chapter 2, n. 11.) Where the tribunal did act in the absence of an accuser, the impression might arise that it was itself accusing, as well as judging: a duplication of role that well-founded doctrine would have opposed (see for example Burchard of Worms, *Decretorum*, cc. XIV; XXXI: Jacques Paul Migne, *Patrologia Latina*, CXL, 911; 196; Gratian, C. IV, qu. 4, Dictum; A. Esmein, *History of Continental Criminal Procedure*, trans. J. Simpson [London: John Murray, 1914], p. 80, referring to sources that include Bernard of Pavia's *Summa Decretalium*, written in the 1190s). Traditional ecclesiastical proofs, in grave matters, were by witnesses (see, for example, Hincmar of Rheims, *Capitula Synodica*, XXII: Migne, *Patrologia Latina*, CXXV, 784; Gratian, C.IV, qu. 4, I Pars, Dictum). If proofs, in such matters were wanting, the suspect might be ordered by the tribunal to purge himself of suspicion by his own oath, with or without the support of compurgators (Gratian, C.II, qu. 5, cc. 13; 16 Hincmar, *Capitula*, XXIII: Migne, *Patrologia Latina*, CXXV, 784; X, 5, 1, 19; 34, 5). In effect, this was an ordeal. Success acquitted, but failure (whereas it might have been accounted disobedience, at the most) would serve as proof, or in lieu of proof, to support conviction of the suspected offence (X, 5, 1, 23; Esmein, *History*, pp. 80; 84). Where the tribunal proceeded to trial upon the basis of the suspect's public ill-fame, its examination of witnesses may well have tended to be more thorough than when they were produced by an accuser. On the other hand, doctrine opposing enforced confession (Nicolai Papae I, *Epistolae et Decreta*, XCVII: *Responsum ad consulta Bulgarorum* [866], lxxxvi: Migne, *Patrologia Latina*, CXIX, 1010; Gratian, C. II, qu. 5, c. 20; C.XV, qu. 6) seems to have been against interrogation of the defendant upon his oath in any proceedings. Nonetheless, inquisitorial procedure, approved by Innocent III, admitted such interrogation, as well as interrogation of witnesses. It was adopted in the absence of an accuser; although public suspicion was in principle required, such suspicion did not have to be communicated to the tribunal by public outcry or mass responses: it could be proved by witnesses; cf. X, 5, 1, 21 (1212); Esmein, *History*, pp. 80–85. The latter feature had a secular precedent in procedure introduced for murder cases by Charlemagne, which the Church in his Empire probably borrowed: F. L. Ganshof, *Frankish*

Institutions under Charlemagne, trans. B. & M. Lyon (Providence: Brown University Press, 1968), p. 91. Moreover, although not technically an "inquisition", trial upon a like basis of technically established ill-fame, and by what soon came to be like methods, was now allowed to go forward with the assistance of one who was for practical purposes an accuser, but who presented what technically was deemed less than an "accusation": a "denunciation", exciting the judge to look for relevant ill-fame, but not involving the person who made it in risk, of liability for calumny, run by one who presented an "accusation" (Esmein, *History*, pp. 85–87).

12. W. Ullmann, *Principles of Government and Politics in the Middle Ages* (London: Methuen, 1961), passim; W. Ullmann, *The Carolingian Renaissance and the Idea of Kingship* (London: Methuen, 1969), especially Lectures III and IV; cf. Fritz Kern, *Kingship and Law in the Middle Ages*, trans. S. B. Chrimes (Oxford: Blackwell, 1939), especially pp. 72–73. Of course, in practice the towns and mercantile class formed a third force in the struggle engaging Kings and magnates. Cf. Bruce Lyon, *Studies of West European Medieval Institutions* (London: Variorum Reprints, 1978), VII.

13. According to Inst.I.ii.6 and D.I.iv.1: "What seems right to the Prince has the force of a law: inasmuch as by the regal law, enacted concerning his supreme authority, the people confer upon him all their own supreme authority and power." Cf. Kunkel, *Introduction*, pp. 59, 127, 216, and (on the republican *leges de imperio*) 10n. According to D.I.iii.31: "The Prince is not bound by the laws." This may have originated as a reference only to the operation of particular private law enactments: W. W. Buckland, *Textbook of Roman Law from Augustus to Justinian*, 3rd ed., ed. P. Stein (Cambridge: Cambridge University Press, 1963), p. 15; but its message to the medieval world was not so restricted. That message was, on the other hand, offset by D.XXXII.23[pr.] and C.I.xiv,4, which lay down that since the Prince owes his own authority to the laws, it becomes him voluntarily to observe them. The latter observation was in Italy taken up by Azo (*Summa* [1208–10] : *Summa Institutionum, Proemium*): cf. Maitland, *Bracton and Azo*, ad Bracton, *De legibus*, f.1. In Bracton, ff.5b and 34a, a transmutation may be seen into the view that the Monarch is, after all, bound by the laws.

14. An example of an ordeal, other than battle, that required performance by both parties is the medieval Saxon cruciform ordeal, in which the parties stood with their arms raised and spread, until one allowed his to drop and was thus shown to be in the wrong. See Hermann Nottarp, *Gottesurteilstudien*, 2nd ed. (Munich: Bamberger Abhandungen und Forschungen, 1956), pp. 34; 56; J.-Ph. Lévy, "*L'Évolution de la preuve des origines à nos jours*", *Recueils de la Société Jean Bodin* 17 (1965): 13–15; Lévy describes such competitions as "doubly unilateral".

15. Lévy, "*L'Évolution de la preuve*", p. 23. Cf "Glanvill", *De legibus et consuetudinibus regni Angliae*, XIV.i: " . . . he who is accused must purge himself by judgment of God, that is to say by hot iron or by water, according to his class." Cf. the discussion of purgation in D.XLVIII.i.5, which concerns the conditions in which one who has himself been accused may launch an accusation against another.

16. Cf. "Glanvill", *De legibus*, above, n. 15.

17. H. C. Lea, *Superstition and Force*, 3rd ed., rev. (Philadelphia: H. C. Lea, 1878), pp. 350–51. Nottarp, *Gottesurteilstudien*, p. 57.

18. Psychological value, in some of its forms: Nottarp, *Gottesurteilstudien*, pp. 32–35; cf. 36–37. Conversion into torture? Lea, *Superstition and Force*; cf. Gratian, C.II, qu. 5, c. 20.

19. Lévy, "*L'Évolution de la preuve*", pp. 67–68; Henri Lévy-Bruhl, *La Preuve*

judiciaire (Paris: Marcel Rivière, 1964), pp. 8; 15; 21–22; 40–41; 55–56.

20. Cf. below, n. 48. From its context, the ban by the Fourth Lateran Council, in 1215 (can. 18: X, 3, 50, 9) on participation by the clergy in preparations for ordeals appears to have been due to the association with consequent judgments of life or limb. In Eastern Europe, where the ordeal seems to have continued in use longer than in the West, and to have had upper class support, Canonist objections in the fourteenth century included the unreliability of the process, as well as the fact that it tempted God and the fact that it trespassed upon divine scrutiny of the individual conscience (an objection levelled in Gratian, C.XV, qu. 6, c. 1, to torture): Nottarp, *Gottesurteilstudien*, p. 80. To what extent, if at all, practical mistrust of the ordeal's outcome weighed with the Council in 1215, quaere?

21. Simply under theocratic doctrine, the King had a peculiar concern with criminal justice. Cf. Canute, Proclamation of 1020: H. J. Robertson, ed. and trans., *The Laws of the Kings of England from Edmund to Henry I* (Cambridge: Cambridge University Press, 1925), p. 140. Generally, Ullman, *Principles of Government and Politics*, p. 195; Ullmann, *The Carolingian Renaissance*, pp. 185–86. The theocratic and political absolutist views of kingship would both point to a duty of retribution and repression, since crime would be apprehended as disobedience: the only modern source of which I know, and which regards it in that light, is a Discourse delivered by Pope Pius XII to the Catholic jurists of Italy, 19 November, 1954: *Catholic Documents* (Battersea: Pontifical Court Club, Salesian Press), Pius XII, xvii, at p. 14. On the other hand, in a church-dominated society, the Monarch may with perfect propriety accord to ecclesiastical tribunals a principal role in the repression of offenses: such was the Carolingian solution (Ullmann, *The Carolingian Renaissance*, pp. 32–33).

22. Cf. Esmein, *History*, p. 112, suggesting an early association of revived use of torture with energetic royal repression of crime.

23. Cf. D.XXII.v.3[1] in fin. On the requisite number: D.XXII.v.12; XLVIII.xviii.20. Of private transactions: C.IV.xx.18.

24. Cf. D.XLVIII.xviii.18 [pr.].

25. Cf. D.XLVIII.xviii.22; C.IX.ii.7; iv.1[pr.].

26. Lévy, "*L'Évolution de la preuve*", pp. 38; 57–58; Lévy-Bruhl, *La Preuve judiciaire*, pp. 47–48; Esmein, *History*, Pt. II, Tit. I, Ch. III; and Garraud: appended, in Esmein, *History*, pp. 620–27.

27. D.XLVIII.xviii.1[23].

28. For a condensed survey of the Roman sources, see A. Ehrhardt, s.v. "*tormenta*" (1937), in [August Friedrich von] Paulys, *Real Encyclopädie der classischen Altertumswissenschaft Neue Bearbeitung*, (1893–).

29. D.XLVIII.xviii; C.IX.xli.

30. It appears that after the collapse of the Western Roman Empire, use of torture for proof lingered on in parts of Europe that it had comprised: presumably, this reflected the influence of the Barbarian-Roman Codes, and perhaps the parts of the Theodosian Code and the *Sententiae Pauli*, which had been republished by Alaric, also had some continuing impact. Ecclesiastical councils may even have done something to spread awareness of the method: trial of Jews, not readily accorded an oath, might present an occasion for its use. However, after it had been condemned, in 866, by Pope Nicholas I (*Responsum ad consulta Bulgarorum*, lxxxvi: above, n. 11), absence of evidence suggests that it fell into total desuetude. See Nottarp, *Gottesurteilstudien*, pp. 89–93.

31. Esmein, *History*, pp. 107–8; 112.

32. Text in Fiorelli, *La Tortura giudiziaria*, I, 86.
33. Texts in ibid., II, 43nn.
34. Ibid., II, 85.
35. R. Van Caenegem, *Royal Writs in England from the Conquest to Glanvill* (Selden Soc., LXXVII: 1958–59), pp. 54–85; 174–90.
36. Van Caenegem, *Royal Writs*, p. 376.
37. Maitland, *Roman Canon Law*, p. 4, points out the unusual narrowness of the sense here given to "common". When Fiorelli uses the title "*La Tortura giudiziaria nel diritto comune*", he means "Judicial Torture in the (former) International Jurisprudence of Europe".
38. H. G. Richardson and G. O. Sayles, *The Governance of Medieval England from the Conquest to Magna Carta* (Edinburgh: Edinburgh University Press, 1963), pp. 173–99.
39. The *Ten Articles* of William I, a.6 (Robertson, *The Laws of the Kings of England*, p. 240), gave accused Englishmen the choice of ordeal by iron and battle, the latter alone being prescribed for Normans: twelfth century apocrypha?
40. What accounts we have (cf. below, n. 41) of the Assizes of Clarendon and Northampton refer to ordeal by water. According to "Glanvill", *De legibus*, XIV.i, the ordeal by hot iron was appropriate to freemen; the ordeal by water, to serfs. The Anglo-Saxons appear to have recognized both kinds of ordeal, without distinction regarding the accused's status: III Aethelred, 6. The water ordeal usually indicated by their laws required the accused to lift a weight out of a boiling caldron: II Aethelstan, 7; App. II; III Aethelred, 3(1); 6; II Canute, 22. Ordeal by immersion in cold water (cf. Lévy-Bruhl, *La Preuve judiciaire*, p. 63) is mentioned in II Aethelstan, 23(1); it was used later in parts of Europe: Nottarp, *Gottesurteilstudien*, p. 80.
41. We have a received text (William Stubbs, *Select Charters and other Illustrations of English Constitutional History*, 4th ed. [Oxford: Clarendon Press, 1881], pp. 143–45) of the Assize of Clarendon, and another (Stubbs, *Select Charters*, pp. 150–53) of the Assize of Northampton. According to the Clarendon text, those were to be presented who were "*rettatus vel publicatus*": "(informally) accused or notoriously in the locality suspect." According to the Northampton text, proceedings were to be taken with anyone who "*retatus fuerit coram iustitiariis . . . per sacramentum duodecim* (etc.)": "shall have been accused before the justices . . . by the oath of twelve (etc.)." The Northampton text wavers into narrative style, but Richardson and Sayles, *Governance of Medieval England*, pp. 197–98, vigorously question the authenticity, in various respects, of the Clarendon text.
42. The Northampton text gives a longer list of presentable offenses than does the Clarendon text, but this might simply show the system in course of development. Strangely, however, "Glanvill", *De legibus*, XIV, seems to point to operation of presentment only in the case of high treason: which is listed in neither of the Assize texts; the same source indicates that it did not apply in the case of another appealable offense against the King, concealment of treasure trove.
43. Cf. III Aethelred (Wantage), 3. Richardson and Sayles, *Governance of Medieval England*, pp. 205–6, favor an English origin.
44. Cf. Van Caenegem, *Royal Writs*, pp. 51–54.
45. This conforms to the Clarendon text; the Northampton text makes the jury accusers: above, n. 41. Records of proceedings in the thirteenth century, when a stage of jury trial was superimposed upon one of jury presentment, may encourage inference that here the

Clarendon text is right. Cf. Charles L. Wells, "The Origin of the Petty Jury," *Law Quarterly Review* 27 (1911): 347–61, especially 351; on "Glanvill", below, n. 46.

46. "Glanvill," *De legibus*, XIV.i, tells us that proceedings for high treason may arise either upon an appeal or where public suspicion exists—*"fama"*—which, although it alone, publicly accuses an individual: *"solummodo eum publice accusat;"* and that in respect of concealment of treasure trove, it is not the practice that people should be compelled to purgation on account of such suspicion: *"ob infamiam."* Among the Canonists, later, the doctrine was accepted that in the inquisitorial procedure, the judge was not to be regarded as doubling in the role of accuser, because proof of public ill-fame, suspicion, took the place of the appearance of an accuser: Esmein, *History*, p. 81. On traditional Canonical reference to ill-fame, see above, n. 11. On general ecclesiastical inquisitions, see Esmein, *History*, pp. 83–85. Those concerned were "general" in that they did not necessarily start with suspicion even of any specific offense; however, Bartolus (*Digestum novum commentaria*, ad D.XLVIII.xviii.12) later so described an inquisition concerning such an offense, but which did not begin with proof of suspicion directed against a specific individual.

47. Eadmer, *Historia Novorum in Anglia* (*Rerum Britannicorum Medii Aevi Scriptores*: Rolls Ser.), p. 102, alleges that William Rufus reacted with alarming profanity to the acquittal by ordeal of all of one group of fifty accused: "What is this? God is a just judge? Away with anyone who so believes henceforth! So, by . . . ! my judgment alone will be answered, not that of God."

48. Assize of Clarendon, c.14: Stubbs, *Select Charters*, pp. 144–45. F. W. Maitland, *Select Pleas of the Crown* (Selden Soc., I: 1887), p. 75, points out the apparent uselessness of the ordeal to secure convictions between 1202 and 1219. Of course, for the latter part of that period, an explanation might have been found in the determination of the Fourth Lateran Council (above, n. 20) that the clergy should not participate.

49. Cf. Maitland, *Roman Canon Law*, Ch. IV.

50. Cf. Marc Ancel, *La Défense sociale nouvelle* (Paris: Cujas, 1954), pp. 17–40.

51. Distinguish torment to *plead*—either "guilty" or "not guilty" at the prisoner's choice. This was later adopted in English practice. During the thirteenth century, use of trial juries in felony cases seems to have started (as far as concerned the general issue) where proceedings rested on jury presentment. (Cf. above, n. 45). There was felt—as in parts of France, where proceedings were based only on public suspicion and trial was by "inquest" on some locally developed pattern—a need for acceptance, by the prisoner, of the contemplated mode of trial. Accordingly—as, also, in parts of France (Esmein, *History*, p. 65)—he was placed under constraint thereto by harsh incarceration with restricted diet: cf. Statute of Westminster I (1275), c.12; Y.B. 30–31 E. I.: Rolls Ser., p. 529, at p. 531. For some reason, from Edward I's reign (cf. *Britton*, I.xxiii; xxiv; *Fleta*, I.xxxii), even where an accuser existed—in an appeal—the view usually adopted was that the accused must, subject to such constraint if he refused, expressly choose between battle and jury trial. (The view by then may have somehow come to prevail that no one could be tried, in any mode, without his consent: cf. F. M. Powicke, *King Henry III and the Lord Henry* (Oxford: Clarendon Press, 1947), I, 82, and sources there cited on Hubert de Burgh's case). By the end of the Middle Ages, the mode of constraint employed had become the *peine forte et dure*—a quickly lethal acute torture by pressing; cf. Sir Thomas Smith, *De republica Anglorum*, II, xxiii. Subsequently, its severity was in various ways even further increased, until it was at last abolished (the need to obtain

a plea being removed) by Stat. 12 G.III, c.20. See L. O. Pike, *History of Crime in England illustrating the Changes of the Laws in the Process of Civilization* (London: Smith, Elder, 1873–76), I, 210–11; 387; II, 194–95; 283; 346. On a non-lethal thumb torture, used—at any rate, in London and nearby—during the eighteenth century as a preliminary, see Pike, *History of Crime*, II, 283–85; 638. This bizarre lesser evil may have been an adaptation of a macabre ceremonial used at the later stage, of *allocutus*: which, in turn, may have originated as a counter-witchcraft precaution. (Cf. John Howard, *State of the Prisons* [London: J. M. Dent; New York: E. P. Dutton, Everyman ed., 1929], p. 162, with Francis Hutchinson, *Historical Essay concerning Witchcraft* [1718], p. 64). The difference between the *peine forte et dure* (the same, obviously, would go for the latter-day thumb torture) and interrogatory torture for proof, on the Continental model, was pointed out by Blackstone, *Commentaries*, IV, xxv, and by Lord Ellenborough in *R. v. Thomas Picton*, 30 St.Tr. 225, at 895–96.

52. Fiorelli, *La Tortura giudiziaria*, I, 119. When printed in the sixteenth century, it was attributed to Piacentino; but according to Fiorelli, following Hermann Kantorowicz, the author was I. di Porta Ravegnana.

53. Bk IX, Tit. xxv.

54. I.iii, *De episcopis et clericis* . . . ; IX.vii, *Ad legem Iuliam maiestatis*; IX.viii, *Ad legem Iuliam de adulteriis*. Ambiguity of the Latin may have prevented some medieval readers of the only relevant passage under the last title from recognizing that it concerned torture.

55. De Zulueta: in Selden Soc., XLIV (1927), Ch. VI, pp. lxviii-lxxii.

56. Below, n. 59.

57. I have made general use of De Zulueta's ed.: Selden Soc. XLIV. However, for the title *De quaestionibus*, I have been content with a reproduction of the Bruges Public Library manuscript (375), ff. 136b; 137, which was most obligingly sent to me by the Bruges Assistant City Librarian, Mr. Josef Ghyssaert. De Zulueta himself relied primarily upon the Bruges manuscript for everything after Book IX, Title ix.

58. To take two examples. According to D.XLVIII.xviii.1[pr.-1]: *"In crimininibus eruendis quaestio adhiberi solet. Sed quando vel quatenus id faciendum sit, videamus. Et non esse a tormentis incipiendum et divus Augustus constituit neque adeo fidem quaestioni adhibendam, sed et epistula divi Hadriani ad Sennium Sabinum continetur. Verba rescripti ita se habent . . ."* Vacarius writes: *"In criminibus servandis quaestio adhiberi solet. Sed quando vel quatenus id faciendum sit videamus. Et non esse a tormentis incipiendum et divus Augustus constituit. Verba rescripti ita se habent . . ."* (N.B. the retention of *"et "* before *"divus"*). D.XLVIII.xviii.1[26] begins: *"cum quis latrones tradidit, quibusdam rescriptis continetur non debere fidem haberi eis in eos, qui eos tradiderunt: quibusdam vero, quae sunt pleniora, hoc cavetur, ut neque destricte non habeatur, ut in ceterorum persona solet, sed causa cognita aestimetur habenda fides sit nec ne . . ."* Vacarius repeats this, except that he ends: *"ut neque districte habeatur ut in ceterorum persona debet, sed causa cognita extimetur habenda sit fides nec ne."* His abridgment of the first of the above Digest passages may be taken to reflect the view that one Roman Emperor need not, for medieval juridical purposes, be distinguished from another. In his ending to the second passage, the omission of *"non"* before *"habeatur"* is obviously unintentional; and use of *"debet"* for *"solet"*, although for medieval reading an improvement, is not presently significant.

59. The gloss mentioned above in the main text is to *Liber pauperum*, IV.xvii, *De*

testibus. It imports the matter of Nov.XC, pr. and (in part) 1. For our purposes, the instruction is that wherever respectable persons are available as witnesses, it is they who should be relied upon; whilst, if testimony has to be received from persons of low repute, they may be beaten if necessary to exact the truth. The Novel is primarily concerned with proof of wills. On the same subject, D.XXII.v.21[2] lays down that if any gladiators, or persons of similarly low character, have to be received as witnesses, they shall be subject to *tormenta*—torments—an expression connoting severity beyond beating. However, although Vacarius includes in the main text of the title concerned all the rest of D.XXII.v.21, he omits this sentence. Clearly, it is one rule that those who appear simply as witnesses may be tortured if they vacillate; another that they should be tortured if they are of low character.

60. See further below in the main text.

61. See further below in the main text.

62. Cf. D.XLVIII.xviii.10[pr.]; XXIX.v.1[33].

63. See further below in the main text, and n. 71.

64. I have placed upon this fragment what appears to me the obvious interpretation: that torture of a slave in a pecuniary cause required admissible evidence to have been first introduced in the same desired sense, and that witness evidence was not admissible unless at least two witnesses would testify to the same matter (cf. D.XXII.v.12). The developed medieval doctrine of legal proofs did not allow capital condemnation to be based on testimony unless at least two witnesses were available to all essentials; D.XLVIII.i.20 combined with other fragments to suggest a general rule, regardless of the nature of the cause, that slaves might not be tortured for evidence unless there was prior proof which, if it came from witnesses, must have come from at least two of them; the medieval tendency was to generalize *Corpus Iuris* rules, extending them out of their literal context. Thus an uncomfortable confrontation arose here, between the apparent *Corpus Iuris* restriction and a desire to use torture for confession where to one or another essential only a single witness was available. Azo's interpretation of D.XLVIII.i.20 showed ingenuity equal to the occasion: Fiorelli, *La Tortura giudiziaria*, II, 43. In the same work, I, 119n., it is pointed out that the early *tractatus criminum*, mentioned above in the main text, accepted that the deposition of a single witness was not enough to allow torture.

65. Followed by a sentence that I decipher thus: *"per consequenciam nec iudex debet inquirere an quis meliores testes habuerit."*

66. Cf. D.XLVIII.xviii.1[16].

67. C.IX.xli.1[1] subverts masters' immunity: cf., then, D.XLVIII.xviii.10[4], ascribed to the perhaps two-headed "Arcadius Charisius".

68. Possibly twelfth-century readers would understand by "fraud upon the census"— the Latin is, *"fraudati census accusationes"*—fraudulent evasion of military liabilities? I apprehend that in the Code it refers to fraudulent evasion of the *"annona"*—of taxation, upon the late Imperial model, in kind. The exception to masters' immunity for cases of treason is also recognized in C.IX.viii.6[4]. On the exception for cases of adultery, see D.XLVIII.v.28[6]; [15]; C.IX.ix.3; 31: *Liber pauperum*, IX.viii.

69. Being derived from D.XLVIII.xviii.9[pr.].

70. C.IX.xli.16.

71. *Liber pauperum*, IX.xxv. The latter part reads: *"Maiestatis tantummodo reos quaeve* (C.: *"et quae"*) *nefanda dictu sunt conscios aut molientes ex ordine municipali maneat tam cruenta condicio."* I would in C. understand, *"eorum quae nefanda dictu*

sunt'' and the reference as being to acts of sorcery (cf. C.Th.IX.xvi.6: C.IX.xviii.7).
But if *quae nefanda dictu sunt* are indeed not acts of treason, the drafting is by modern
standards the more awful, for reference is made to principals in one kind of crime, to
accessories in another.

72. C.IX.xli.17.

73. *"Principali . . . honore munitae."*

74. For this and the preceding Code entry, a historical context is provided by other
Roman texts, as follows. Constantine and Constans laid down (C.Th.XI.vii.7: a mere
fragment is preserved in C.X.xxi.2) that provincials should not be beaten with lead-
weighted scourges or imprisoned on account of debts, which should instead be enforced
by taking (real) security. This position was not maintained. Valentinian, Valens, and
Gratian issued the constitution, part of which is retained in C.IX.xli.16: but which
C.Th.IX.xxxv.2 records more fully, showing it to have been concerned with enforcement
of public revenue liabilities and to have laid down that beating with lead-weighted scourges—
as distinct from the tortures of criminal praxis—was permitted in the case of municipal
senators other than those of the top grade, *decemprimi*. (Cf. Lactantius, *De mortibus
persecutorum*, XXI.). The common aim would be to discover, if we are to judge by
C.Th.XI.vii.7, not the existence or extent of default (although this doubtless was sometimes in view: cf. Lactantius, *De mortibus persecutorum*, XXIII), but resources out of
which liability might be satisfied. Subsequently, Gratian, Valentinian, and Theodosius
extended (C.Th.XII.i.80) full protection in this matter to all municipal senators; they
were insistent on the point: all municipal senators were to be immune to beating with
lead-weighted scourges "for whatever fault, or negligence or mistake" (C.Th.XII.i.85:
in C.X.xxxii.33[pr.] entered without the restriction to scourging). Yet six years later,
Valentinian, Theodosius, and Arcadius provided that all ranks of the Order were to be
subjected to beating with lead-weighted scourges, if found to have been fraudulent, or
unreasonably demanding, in respect of the revenue: C.Th.XII.i.117; retained, C.X.xxxii.40.
Then we have the constitution, of Arcadius and Honorius, recorded in C.Th.IX.xxv.6
and in C.IX.xli.17: the *principium* of which, seems to convey that immunity to measures
of physical violence was allowed only to the more important of the Order; but what
follows in which appears to extend to those retiring from the Order, although they have
not been of the higher rank. (The C.Th. entry has *"principalitatis . . . honore munitae"*;
this, even more strongly than the *"principali . . . honore munitae"* of C., suggests
concern only with the more important members: cf., on the *"principales"*, A.H.M. Jones,
The Later Roman Empire. A Social, Economic and Administrative Survey [Oxford: Blackwell, 1964], p. 731). The truncation, by Justinian's compilers in C.IX.xli.16, of
C.Th.IX.xxxv.2, probably would have been understood by a contemporary jurist as
intended, by those responsible for C.IX.xli, to make effective the policy of treating all
members of the Order equally, in accordance with C.X.xxxii.40. (Use of metal-weighted
scourges is shown in a miniature, probably from a Byzantine original, of the Second
Winchester School, which appears in the Psalter of Henri de Blois: MS. Cotton Nero
Civ: monochrome reproduction, O.E. Sanders, *English Illumination* [Florence: Panther;
Paris: Pegasus, 1928], I, pl. 38).

75. D. XLVIII, xviii, 16 [pr.]; 18[1].

76. Fiorelli, *La Tortura giudiziaria,* II, 143–54.

77. N.B. reference to slaves was not irrelevant. The Latin name was "servi", and
although authentic slavery was disappearing: H. G. Richardson and G. O. Sayles, *Law*

and Legislation from Aethelbehrt to Magna Carta (Edinburgh: Edinburgh University Press, 1966), pp. 142-43: "servi" (which had received its proper sense in Domesday Book: see Command ed., III [1816], 497 [Inquisitio Eliensis]) was coming to denote villeins: cf. Rotuli Litterarum Patentium, 1201-16, ed. T. D. Hardy (London: Record Commission, 1835), p. 55 (and, after the middle ages, Edward Coke, Littleton, 116a-17b). Villeins, who no doubt were the unfree obliquely contemplated by Magna Carta, c.39 (John, 1215)/ c.29 (Henry III, 1225), were juridical hybrids. On their forensic situation, see in the thirteenth century Magna Carta c.20/c.14; Bracton, De legibus, f.141a; in the fifteenth Thomas Littleton, Tenures, ss. 180-96. On their lords' limited powers of chastisement, see Holdsworth, History of English Law, III, 503–4; R. B. Pugh, Imprisonment in Medieval England (Cambridge: Cambridge University Press, 1968), pp. 52–55; 217.

78. Fiorelli, La Tortura giudiziaria, I, 103n.

79. On the vigorous study in England of Continental Canonist literature, see Maitland, Roman Canon Law, pp. 8; 97–98; Van Caenegem, Royal Writs, pp. 367–70.

80. Gratian, C.XV, qu.6, c.1, Dictum.

81. Gratian, C.XV, qu.6, c.1: Decretales Psuedo-Isidorianae et Capitula Angilramni, ed. P. Hinschius (Leipzig: B. Tauchnitz, 1863), pp. 95–98.

82. Gratian, C.V, qu.5, c.4: Decretales Psuedo-Isidorianae, ed. P. Hinschius, p. 231.

83. For Rufino's gloss ad C.XV, qu.6, c.1, see Fiorelli, La Tortura giudiziaria, I, 128–29n.

84. Pipe Roll, 34 H.II: Northamptonshire, Ro.10: Pipe Roll Soc., XXXVIII, p. 131; "Petrus Filius Ade reddit compotum de xxxv marcis quia cepit quandam mulierem et eam tormentavit sine licentia regis . . ."

85. History of Crime, I, 16–17; 427.

86. 32 H. II: Northamptonshire, Ro.1: Pipe Roll Soc., XXXVI, p. 8; 33 H.II: Northamptonshire, Ro.8: Pipe Roll Soc., XXXVII, p. 103.

87. Henry I's Charter of Liberties: Stubbs, Select Charters, pp. 100–101; Assize of Northampton: Stubbs, Select Charters, p. 150; Rotuli de dominabus et pueris et puellis: Pipe Roll Soc., XXXV. Two situations were possible: (1) the girl was a royal ward; (2) she was heir presumptive to a tenant in chief. In the former case, she was truly de donatione regis; but in the latter, the King's consent was required for her marriage, or she faced disinherison. See "Glanvill", De legibus, VII.ix; xii.

88. Pipe Roll Soc., XXXVII, p. 100.

89. "Pro uxore quam duxit sine licentia regis cum esset de donatione regis . . ." So with giving such a woman, sine licentia (e.g., Pipe Roll Soc., XXVI [23 H.II], p. 110); and with marrying (off) one's daughter, sine licentia (e.g., Pipe Roll Soc., N.S., V (6 R.I), p. 162.

90. For the character of Plantagenet taxation and mode of its enforcement, see S. K. Mitchell, Taxation in Medieval England, ed. S. Painter (New Haven: Yale University Press, 1951). A fair view of the available accounts (Roger of Wendover, Flores: Rolls Ser., II, 160–66; 171–73; Chronica de Mailros, de anno 1216: ed. J. Stevenson in The Church Historians of England, Pre-Reformation Series, IV, Part I (London: Seeleys, 1853), 122; Matthew Paris, Chronica Maiora: Rolls Ser., II, 640; and Historia Anglorum: Rolls Ser., II 171–72: in both, following Wendover) is, that during John's northern campaign of 1215–16; violent extortion, although tolerated and even encouraged by him, was undertaken by his soldiery on their own behalf and was remote from being an institutionalized fiscal process.

91. Cf. S. Painter, *The Reign of King John* (Baltimore: Johns Hopkins, 1949), pp. 139–40; H. G. Richardson, *English Jewry under the Angevin Kings* (London: Methuen, 1960), Ch. VIII; Pugh, *Imprisonment in Medieval England*, pp. 55–56.

92. Roger of Wendover, *Flores*: Rolls Ser., II, 54–55; following him, Matthew Paris, *Chronica maiora*: Rolls Ser., II, 528; *Historia Anglorum*: Rolls Ser., II, 121. The allegation, accepted by S. Painter, is that Jews of both sexes were severely tormented to make them give up their wealth: I would suppose that they were hiding it. The only instance cited, however, is of a Jew who was told that he would suffer the extraction of one molar per day, until he paid the King ten thousand marks, and who gave in when he had but a single molar left. If this is true, it is strange that he should have delayed so long. Perhaps he felt a point had been reached at which the King would consider worse had to be done than simply complete the treatment.

93. *De legibus*, XIV.i.

94. Ibid., XIV.iii; vi.

95. *Select Pleas of the Crown*, I: Selden Soc., I, pl. 96.

96. Lea, *Superstition and Force*, p. 502n.

97. Nottarp, *Gottesurteilstudien*, p. 93.

98. Hildebertus, Ep. II, 52: Migne, *Patrologia Latina*, CLXXI, 277.

99. Augustine, *De civitate Dei*, XIX.vi, treats the need so to use torture as a sore misfortune of secular magistrates, which goes to show that the Stoics are wrong to maintain that righteous contentment is possible in this life. Mellor comments, *La Torture*, p. 141. that the underlying thought is not abolitionist.

100. In European post-Roman history, the only known praxis that entrusted torture of a freeman, for confession, to his accuser seems to be that adopted by the Visigoths during the dark age in Spain; even they required the proceedings to be under judicial supervision: see P. D. King, *Law and Society in the Visigothic Kingdom* (Cambridge: Cambridge University Press, 1972), pp. 112–13, and sources there cited.

CHAPTER 2

1. Council, Can. 3: X,5,7,13.

2. Secular rulers who, if politically they resisted papal pretensions, did so by theocratic counter-pretensions of their own might display religious intolerance proportionate to their autocratic ambitions: W. Ullman: in H. C. Lea, *The Inquisition of the Middle Ages* (London: Eyre and Spottiswood, 1963), p. 34.

3. About 1223. Bernard Gui, *Practica Inquisitionis Heretice Pravitatis*, cura C. Douais (Paris: Alphonse Picard, 1886), pp. 304–11.

4. Henri Maisonneuve, *Études sur les origines de l'Inquisition* (Paris: Librairie Philosophique J. Vrin, 1960), pp. 248–49; 296.

5. On the bulls, see Fiorelli, *La Tortura giudiziaria*, I, 80; on jurisdiction, see, for example, VI, 5,2,11(2) (Clement IV); 17 (Boniface VIII); 18 (Boniface VIII); the subject is frequently mentioned by Maisonneuve, *Études*; see, for example, pp. 293; 296; 308; 324–25; 329–30.

6. For an interesting geographical interpretation of heresy-hunting and later witch-hunting, see R. H. Trevor-Roper, *The European Witch-Craze of the Sixteenth and Seventeenth Centuries* (Middlesex: Penguin: Pelican Books, 1969), pp. 29–33.

7. S. 25: Latin text, abridged, in Fiorelli, *La Tortura giudiziaria*, I, 80.

8. On methods used by the Inquisition, see Lea, *The Inquisition of the Middle Ages*, pp. 168–77; G. Mollat, *Bernard Gui, Manuel de l'inquisiteur* (Paris: Librairie Ancienne Honoré Champion, 1926), p. xxxvi; Gui's *Practica*, ed. Douais, especially pp. 107; 218–19; 284; Jean Duvernoy, *Le Registre d'inquisition de Jacques Fournier*, 1318–25 (Toulouse: Edouard Privat, 1965), 139b; 144a; 146c (acute torture); 148c; 156c; 163c; 190a; 191c. On the relaxation by Alexander IV, see Lea, *The Inquisition of the Middle Ages*, pp. 175–77; Fiorelli, *La Tortura giudiziaria*, I, 81; Nicholas Eymerich, *Directorium inquisitorum*: French abridgment (Lisbon: 1762), pp. 82–83. According to the latter, before long, inquisitors came to see in the faculty of mutual absolution for irregularity a useful protection in case of such unfortunate accidents as the death of the examinate under torture: Bartolus, *Digestum novum commentaria*, ad D.XLVIII.xviii.7, gravely observes, as a matter of his own experience as a judge, that to kill an examinate now and again is really unavoidable, having regard to concealed cardiac weaknesses and so on.

9. Lea, *The Inquisition of the Middle Ages*, p. 176.

10. Ibid., p. 177. Clement's decree: Clem. 5,3,1(1). Gui later expressed firmly his dissatisfaction with the restraints imposed: *Practica*, ed. Douais, pp. 174; 188.

11. Civilians and Canonists shared in the development of this doctrine; apart from some disagreement (which recurred: below, n. 15) concerning the requirement of ratification (below, in the main text), its main features seem to have been settled by about the middle of the thirteenth century. Cf. Fiorelli, *La Tortura giudiziaria* , I, 86n.; II, 43nn.; 105n.; 107 and n.; 108–9n. It is said (*Recueils de la Société Jean Bodin*, XVII: J.-Ph. Lévy, p. 27; J. Gillisen, pp. 784–85) that the pursuit of confession, and recourse to torture in that behalf, were promoted by special doctrine concerning *notoriousness* of crimes. According to Canon Law (X,5,1,24: Fourth Lateran Council, c.8), a tribunal acting, on the basis of public suspicion, ex officio, by inquisition (so, by trial upon proofs) against a priest, could not impose upon him the full ("capital") penalty of degradation. However, this restriction could be bypassed where the crime was "notorious"; eventually, it was held not to apply if the priest confessed, and his confession was corroborated: Esmein, *History*, p. 83. But did a confessed crime come to rank fictitiously as notorious? By unrefined doctrine, de facto notoriety, might be held to remove the need not merely for an accuser, but for trial itself. By refined doctrine, dispensation with trial depended upon the judge's having himself witnessed the crime and the offender's not denying guilt. Still, if either or both those requirements was unsatisfied, only summary trial was required. Further, judicial confession without torture or ratified after torture made the crime notorious de jure. At this point, however, the chain of explanation becomes fragile. Notoriety de jure was only a rebuttable presumption of notoriety de facto and one that generally arose only for the purpose of subsequent causes, not of the instant cause; therefore, in the latter, confession *as such* induced judgment of guilt. Nonetheless, it also might be conceived to render judgment on that issue technically unnecessary (cf. D.XLII.ii.1). So perhaps *sentence* in the instant cause was sometimes ascribed to notoriety if it arose from judicial confession. Sources include: Gratian, C.II, qu. 1 (cf. C.XXIII, qu. 4, c.19); Frederick Barbarossa, *Constitutio* (*de incendiariis et pacis violatoribus*) *Decet fidelitati*: in *Corpus Iuris Civilis*, ed. Edward Osenbruge (Leipzig: Baumgertner, 1849), III, 881–82; X,5,1,19; 3,13; 31; 34,15; Albertus Gandinus, *De maleficiis*: in Hermann Kantorowicz, *Albertus Gandinus und das Strafrecht der Scholastik* (Berlin and Leipzig: 1926), 5; 94–96; 100–01. Cf. Bracton, *De legibus*, ff. 121a; 126b; and Maisonneuve,

Études, Ch. VI, especially pp. 299–300, on the legislation and doctrine of the Inquisition. In England, under the first three Plantagenet Edwards, reference to notoriety formed one thread in a doctrinal tangle concerning procedure for treason: cf. L. W. Vernon Harcourt, *His Grace the Steward and Trial of Peers* (London, New York: Longmans Green, 1907), pp. 399–400; J. G. Bellamy, *The Law of Treason in England in the Later Middle Ages* (Cambridge: Cambridge University Press, 1970), pp. 19–54; 89–90; and further sources there cited. Regarding the doctrine at the period here under review see further n.54, below. For modern Roman Canon Law on the subjects of notoriousness and confession, see the *Codex Iuris Canonici Pii Papae X auctoritate Benedicti Papae XV promulgatus* (Rome: Typis Polyglottis Vaticani, 1918), can. 1747; 1750; 1751; 2197; R. Naz, *Dictionnaire de droit canonique* (Paris: Librairie Letouzey et Ané, 1949), IV, 1087–8.

12. Cf. Bartolus, *Digestum novum commentaria*, ad D.XLVIII.xviii.10; 22.

13. In general doctrine on proofs, examination of *indicia* was intimately connected with the subject of torture: Fiorelli, *La Tortura giudiziaria*, II, 13.

14. Cf. the *Registre criminel du Châtelet de Paris* (ed. *La Société des Bibliophiles Francais*, 1861–64), I, 208: Florent de Saint Lieu, suspected of thefts upon evidence that was considered very strong, was nonetheless put to torture for confession of those thefts partly upon the ground that *bigamy* had actually been proved against him; he confessed, but only a theft in the act of which he had been taken: a sort of candor popularly supposed to have been revealed, in childhood, by George Washington. This theft alone was held insufficient to support a capital sentence; therefore he was tortured again, brought to confess other thefts, and sent to the gallows: date 1390. It is not clear to me that regarding any theft other than that in which he was taken, there was before the torture what necessarily amounted to proof of the corpus delicti. The court thought that goods found upon him were stolen: they did not know when or from whom.

15. Unless there were grounds, held to be legitimate, for refusal: Fiorelli, *La Tortura giudiziaria*, II, 125–26. Later, the view that ratification was essential was occasionally rejected: H. C. Lea, *Superstition and Force*, 3rd ed., rev. (Philadelphia: H. C. Lea, 1878), p. 485. In France, in the sixteenth and seventeenth centuries, successive editions of J. Imbert, *Institutionum forensium libri—La pratique judiciaire tant civile que criminelle*, Ch. 14, s.7, laid down that a confession under torture, which upon review seemed persuasive, remained a valid basis for condemnation even if, after the torture, it had been revoked. Cf. John H. Langbein, *Prosecuting Crime in the Renaissance* (Cambridge, Mass.: Harvard University Press, 1974), pp. 224; 241. However, not long before the Revolution, Muyart de Vouglans asserted the need for ratification: *Les Lois criminelles dans leur ordre naturel* (1780), pp. 797–98. (He cited the *Constitutio criminalis Carolina*, a.57, which prescribed repetition of torture, in the event of retraction—not justified by special legal grounds—of a confession obtained by it.) In 1757 Serpillon, *Code Criminel*, p. 922, had been constrained to support the assertion, "a confession under torture has always been regarded as equivocal," by tendentious citation of Cicero: whereas Gandinus (Kantorowicz, *Albertus Gandinus*, II, 100) had used D.XLVIII.xviii.1[23]—juridically far more powerful—in explaining to medieval audiences the requirement of ratification by reference to awareness of the tendency of torture to evoke false confession.

16. Pro, in the thirteenth century: Th. de Piperata (Peverata), *De fama*, n. 42: Fiorelli, *La Tortura giudiziaria*, II, 35. Much later, Josse de Damhouder, *Praxis rerum criminalium* (Antwerp ed.: 1554), c.xxxvi, p. 97, declared that public suspicion of guilt generally did not *by itself* authorize torture.

256

17. A fuller narrative is provided by—for example—G. Lizerand, *Clément V et Philippe IV le Bel* (Paris: Hachette, 1910), pp. 85–160; 258–68.

18. Cf. X,5,1,19, and Dictum.

19. Lizerand, *Clément V et Philippe IV le Bel*, p. 81; G. Lizerand, *Le Dossier de l'affaire des Templiers* (Paris: *Les Classiques d'histoire de France au moyen age*: Honoré Champion, 1923), pp. 1-15.

20. Lizerand, *Clément V et Philippe IV le Bel*, pp. 82–83, on Philip's motives. Ambitious to promote royal authority, he may have resented the Order's prosperity within his realm. He also seems to have hoped to appropriate its property there. The great wealth of the Order proceeded not only from gifts, but from international banking operations, in which its competitors were the Italian merchants: Prosper Boissonnade, *Life and Work in Medieval Europe, Fifth to Fifteenth Centuries*, trans. E. Power (London: Kegan Paul Trench Trubner, 1927), pp. 167–68: and from land reclamation—its landed property, throughout Europe, was vast: Boissonnade, *Life and Work*, p. 228.

21. Instructions to royal commissioners: below in the main text.

22. See, for example, the warrant addressed to the Bailiff of Rouen: Lizerand, *Le Dossier*, pp. 16–25.

23. Lizerand, *Le Dossier*, pp. 24–29.

24. Ibid., pp. 180, 181: "*protestantur quod si aliqua dixerunt fratres Templi . . . contra se ipsos et ordinem Templi, non prejudicent ordini predicto, cum notorium sit quod coacti et compulsi aut corrupti . . . dixerunt . . .*" This refers to interrogations, whether by royal or by ecclesiastical commissioners. However, see Lizerand, *Le Dossier*, pp. 188–91, where the reference is clearly to interrogation by the former.

25. Ibid., pp. 62–71

26. Ibid., pp. 70–83. I shall not, in the main text, entirely follow their original order.

27. Cf. the Bull *Faciens misericordiam*: below in the main text.

28. Cf. *Chronicle of Walter of Guisborough* (Camden 3rd Ser.), p. 387; *Registrum Roberti Winchelsey, Cantuariensis Archiepiscopi* (Canterbury and York Ser.), II, 1005–9.

29. Cf. the Bull *Ad omnium*, below in the main text.

30. Cf. *Chronicle of Walter of Guisborough*, p. 392; *Registrum Roberti Winchelsey*, II, p. 1007.

31. Lizerand, *Le Dossier*, pp. 138–45.

32. So much for the delicacy of Innocent IV! On torture, the instruction reads: "*Comminetur eis de tormentis . . . et ostendantur eis, sed non cito ad tormenta ponantur; et si non proficiat comminacio, procedi poterit indiciis precedentibus ad quaestiones et aliqua tormenta, sed primo levia, ad alia, ut racionis fuerit, processuri. Per tortorem clericum idoneum et modo debito et non excessivo procedatur.*" Since the threat of torture is prescribed before the expression *indiciis praecedentibus* is used with reference to torture itself, that expression perhaps refers to indications conceived already to exist when the episcopal inquisition started: the ablative being not absolute, but of the instrument; however, these were early days, and rough: the Bishop may have been advised that terrorization did not require prior indications.

33. The story is reflected in selected depositions presented by Lizerand, *Le Dossier*, pp. 146–95.

34. Cf. ibid., pp. 200, 201: Philip to Clement, 24 August, 1312.

35. On the public image of the Order in England, before Philip's attack, see Thomas

W. Parker, *The Knights Templars in England* (Tucson: University of Arizona, 1963), p. 107.

36. Lizerand, *Clément V et Philippe IV le Bel*, p. 99 and sources there cited.

37. Above, main text (I).

38. Cf. Thomas Rymer, *Foedera*, III, 34–35 (N.B. that citations of Rymer refer to the Record Commission ed.: 1816-69); *Gesta Edwardi de Carnarvon: Chronicles of Edward I and II*: Rolls Ser., II, 32.

39. Before 1310, their lands within the realm were at the disposal of the Wardrobe: S. B. Chrimes, *Administrative History of Medieval Europe* (Oxford: Basil Blackwell, 1952), p. 185; those lands were surrendered to the Hospitallers in 1313: Cal. Pat. Rolls, 1313-17, p. 52; H. M. Chew, *Ecclesiastical Tenants-in-Chief* (London: Oxford University Press, 1932), p. 16.

40. *Chronicle of Walter of Guisborough*, p. 387; *Registrum Roberti Winchelsey*, II, p. 1005; cf. *Archbishop Greenfield's Register*, IV, ed. W. Brown and A. H. Thomas (Surtees Soc., CLII), No. 2281.

41. *Chronicle of Walter of Guisborough*, p. 392; *Registrum Roberti Winchelsey*, II, p. 1007; cf. II, 309. David Wilkins, *Concilia Magnae Britanniae et Hiberniae, a Synodo Verolamiensi A.D. CCCCXLVI ad Londinensem A.D. MDCCXVII* (London: R. Gosling and others, 1737), II, 309.

42. Wilkins, *Concilia*, II, 311; *Archbishop Greenfield's Register*, IV, No. 2272.

43. *"Inquisitores eiusdem pravitatis haereticae"*.

44. Wilkins, *Concilia*, II, 313-14: *"Omnes suffragani praesentes, et praedicti inquisitores, ibant ad dominum regem, et petebant ab eo, quod ipsi et alii locorum ordinarii possent procedere contra Templarios secundum constitutiones ecclesiasticas; et quod praeciperet ministris suis, quod essent ipsis in hac parte intendentes."*

45. Rymer, *Foedera*, III, 195; Calendar of Patent Rolls, E.II, 1307-13, p. 203; below Appendix, No. 74. Here, and in subsequent royal orders, "inquisitors" probably includes, in principle, all members of the papal commission.

46. Wilkins, *Concilia*, II, 349.

47. Pat. 3 E.II, m.3c: Cal. Pat. Rolls, 1307-13, p. 2: *"tam in separatione . . . quam in artacione, in victualibus, carceribus et quaestionibus ipsis Templariis secundum legem ecclesiasticam . . . faciendis, quousque secundum legem ipsam in ipso inquisitionis negotio veritas sciri possit."*

48. Rymer, *Foedera*, III, 202–03.

49. Wilkins, *Concilia*, II, 367; Bodl. MS. 454, ff. 103–16: C. Perkins, "The Trial of the Knights Templars in England," *English Historical Review* 24 (1909): 432, at 436.

50. Cotton MS. Julius B. xii, ff. 83a et seq.; C. Perkins, *English Historical Review* 24: 437.

51. *". . . [in eis] nichil utilis et fidelis efficacie executionis quaestionum reperimus nec volunt procedere ad executionem quaestionum licet per nos et ex parte nostra fuerint legitime et cum magna instancia pluries requisiti."*

52. *"Et nichil fidelis custodiae vel fidelis executionis fieri possit quamdiu dominus Rex teneat Templarios sicut sciunt omnes qui praeterita et presencia facta vident."*

53. Cf. X,5,34.

54. An order to purgation was appropriate where after judicial enquiry, suspicion remained, but proofs required to support a definitive sentence had not emerged. Failure in purgation would open the way to such a sentence: as noted above, Chapter 1, n.11.

(Doctrine which developed regarding torture presents obvious analogies.) It followed that in case of notorious guilt, purgation was inappropriate. Cf. X,5,34,15, and above, n.11.

55. Purgation, obviously, would have been hard to achieve; nonetheless, having regard to the fact that there was no accuser (cf. X,5,1,21), this alternative pointed towards a moderate definitive sentence.

56. Cf. above, Chapter 1, n. 51.

57. *"Sexta via est quam multum amplectuntur omnes praelati, quod mitterentur in Pontivum qui est terra Regis Anglie vel alibi extra Angliam, et quod ibi quaestionarentur . . ."*

58. Perkins, *English Historical Review*, 24: 439; H. C. Lea, *History of the Inquisition of the Middle Ages* (New York: Harbor Press, 1955), III, Ch. V, p. 300. I have not seen this letter: the references given are to Reg. Clem. V, No. 6378. C. G. Addison, *History of the Knights Templars*, 2nd ed. (London: Longman, 1842), p. 507, offering a less precise reference and assigning his source to June, 1310, cites from what nonetheless I would suppose to be, or to repeat, the same message, as follows: *"Inhibuisti ne contra ipsas personas et ordinem per quaestiones ad inquirendum super eisdem criminibus procedatur . . ."*

59. Cf. VI,5,2,18.

60. Rymer, *Foedera*, III, 225; Cal. Close Rolls, 4 E.II, pp. 279–80.

61. Wilkins, *Concilia*, II, 314.

62. Rymer, *Foedera*, II, 227–29.

63. Cal. Close Rolls, 4 E.II, pp. 290–91.

64. Ibid., 4 E.II, pp. 291–92.

65. Perkins, *English Historical Review* 24: 439; Reg. Clem. V, No. 6670.

66. Rymer, *Foedera*, III, 260; Cal. Close Rolls, 4 E.II, p. 308.

67. Below, Appendix, No. 75. The original membrane in the Close Roll bears the date 22 November, 1310, which is accepted in Rymer, *Foedera*, III, 202; however, Cal. Close Rolls, 4 E.II, p. 308n. points out that ample grounds existed for assigning this order to late April, 1311.

68. Wilkins, *Concilia*, II, 383–88; 391. The records of the Inquisition in the Middle Ages rarely stated that a confession was first made under torture, although it is clear that torture, especially in chronic, but also in acute, form, was relied upon: Lea, *The Inquisition of the Middle Ages*, (1963), pp. 175; 177. Perhaps by not recording use of torture, where a confession it had produced was subsequently ratified, the inquisitors closed the door to embarrassing complaint that sufficient juridical grounds for such use had not existed. On the recording of confessions, first obtained under torture, as made *spontaneously*, see, a little later, Bartolus, ad D.XLVIII.xviii.1(27).

69. Cf. Perkins, *English Historical Review* 24: 441.

70. Wilkins, *Concilia*, II, 391.

71. Cf. Perkins, *English Historical Review*, p. 443.

72. Wilkins, *Concilia*, II, 393.

73. Cal. Close Rolls, 5 E.II, p. 523.

74. Alias Gyseburne, Hemingford, Hemingburgh.

75. The relevant part of the *Register* is covered by Surtees Soc., CLII.

76. Perkins, *English Historical Review* 24: 436, referring to Bodl. MS. 454, ff. 126–29; 131–32.

77. *Chronicle of Walter of Guisborough*, p. 386.

78. *Archbishop Greenfield's Register*, IV, 2320.

79. *Chronicle of Walter of Guisborough*, pp. 391–92.

80. On the theological background, see Perkins, *English Historical Review* 24: 445.

81. There was, of course, no Canonical dislike of voluntary confession; if entirely spontaneous, it would earn from the Inquisition a large measure of clemency: Maisonneuve, *Etudes*, p. 297. Moreover, at this early stage doctrine Civilian as well as Canonical would appear to have accepted judicial confession as a complete proof (above, in the main text): Esmein, *History*, pp. 262–63, points out that acceptance by most jurists of D.XLVIII.xviii.1(27), as meaning that even voluntary and judicial confession required to be corroborated, came later, in the sixteenth and seventeenth centuries. Confession (otherwise than of relapse) to the Inquisition after judicial process had begun would save the suspect, as penitent, from the prospect of being, if convicted without it, put to death by fire: Maisonneuve, *Études*, p. 300.

82. *"An sunt supponendi quaestionibus et tormentis licet hoc in regno Anglie nusquam visum fuerit vel auditum?"*

83. *Archbishop Greenfield's Register*, IV, s. 344.

84. *Chronicle of Walter of Guisborough*, p. 392.

85. *Archbishop Greenfield's Register*, IV, 2359.

86. *Chronicle of Walter of Guisborough*, p. 395.

87. Ibid., p. 395.

88. Bracton, *De legibus*, ff. 101b; 105a: the latter embodying a passage from D.XLVIII.xix.8(9), and cited by Coke, 3 Inst. 34.

89. Cf. the 1289 case of the Jailer of Newgate's servant: Pugh, *Imprisonment in Medieval England*, pp. 176; 184.

90. See Bracton, *De legibus*, f. 145a.

91. Fleta, I.xxvi.

92. Writs of trespass *vi et armis* to the person, returnable in the royal courts, were common from the middle of the thirteenth century onwards; such a writ came in time to be included on the Register, for maltreatment of a prisoner by his jailer: Holdsworth, *History of English Law*, III, 317.

93. T. Plucknett, *Concise History of the Common Law*, 2nd ed. (London: Butterworth, 1936), p. 237; cf. Northumberland Assize Roll, 40 H.III (Surtees Soc., LXXXVIII), pp. 163–64.

94. *State Trials of Edward I*, ed. T. F. Tout and H. Johnstone (Camden 3rd Ser.). p. 59; *Thomas Silvester v. Roger of Lincoln*. Later, at any rate, abuse of public office was at Common Law treated as a misdemeanor (*Crowther's Case*, Cr. Eliz 654) and as ground for deprival (Cf. Coke, *Littleton*, f. 223a.)

95. Cf., for example, Northumbrian Assize Rolls, 40 H.III (Surtees, Soc., LXXXVIII), pp. 63; 83; G. L. Turner, *Select Pleas of the Forest* (Selden Soc., XIII: 1899, pub. 1901), pp. 20–21; 44–55. Pace L. Ehrlich, *Proceedings against the Crown*, 1216-1377: *Oxford Studies in Social and Legal History*, ed. P. Vinogradoff, XII, in Vol. VI (Oxford: Clarendon Press, 1921), p. 129. If instead he inflicted pecuniary loss, he might be proceeded against in the Exchequer: cf. Ehrlich, *Proceedings against the Crown*, p. 200.

96. Cf. Ehrlich, *Proceedings against the Crown*, p.129; James C. Davies, *The Baronial Opposition to Edward II* (London, Frank Cass, 1967), pp. 9–10.

97. Stephen, *History of the Criminal Law*, I, 258–61. Pace Faith Thompson, *Magna*

Carta (Minneapolis: University of Minnesota Press, 1948), p. 70.

98. I take this to have been put beyond reasonable doubt by Maitland, *Roman Canon Law*, Chs. I–III.

99. Bracton, *De legibus*, ff.1b; 5b; 55b; 107b; 412a.

100. Cf. Philip to Clement, 2 March, 24 August, 1312: Lizerand, *Le dossier*, pp. 196, 197; 200, 201: *"Sanctissimo patri . . . Clementi . . . divina providentia . . . universalis ecclesie summo pontifici, Philippus eadem gratia Francorum rex."* The end of this greeting conveys the tone of Philip's conduct in 1307.

101. Maitland, *Roman Canon Law*, pp. 53–56.

102. Cf. Rymer, *Foedera*, III, 45; 56; 204–05.

103. A. Esmein, *Cours élémentaire du droit français*, 15th ed. (Paris: R. Génestal, Sirey, 1925), p. 617.

104. F. 60.

105. Later, under Edward III, the Common Law courts began in the area concerned to resist papal pretensions, but even then they did not entirely reject the Bull: account and sources, Maitland, *Roman Canon Law*, Ch. VI.

106. Holdsworth, *History of English Law*, I, 630–31, and sources there cited. In Ireland, during 1324, when Richard Ledrede, a Franciscan who had become Bishop of Ossory, was proceeding by way of general inquisition concerning witchcraft at Kilkenny, he was able to obtain imprisonment of suspects by the secular authorities in the Pale only after he had excommunicated them and the forty days had run (Cf. VI,5,2,8: the date was just before that of the Bull *Super illius speculo*, which in effect allowed the Inquisition to assume the heretical character of witchcraft): for an account of Ledrede's in the end successful, and highly eventful, struggle with the secular arm, see *Proceedings against Dame Alice Kyteler*, ed. Thomas Wright (Camden Old Ser.).

107. Bracton, *De legibus*, ff. 123b–124a.

108. Below in the main text, Chapter 8(I).

109. Ibid.

CHAPTER 3

1. Stephen, *History of the Criminal Law*, I, 221–22, suggests that "the extremely summary character of our early methods of trial, and the excessive severity of the punishments inflicted" had more to do with English non-employment of judicial torture than "the generalities of Magna Carta or any special humanity of feeling." This accepts Fortescue's juridical perception, whilst rejecting his moral judgment. Stephen continues: "people who, with no sort of hesitation, hanged a man . . . simply because twelve of his neighbours , reporting village gossip, said he had stolen a dress worth two shillings, cannot be called scrupulously humane"; he adds: "if their conscience had declined to hang him till they had tortured him for a confession capable of being verified independently, they would perhaps have been a little more humane, though this certainly admits of doubt." It may be thought that Stephen is not entirely just, when he assumes such complete similarity between the functioning of a medieval jury of trial and that of one of presentment, post-Bracton (cf. the *De legibus*, f.143a-b: below in the main text). Nor do I know of a rule, in medieval Continental doctrine, that required that a confession made under torture

should not be used unless capable of being "verified independently" after it was made: Stephen's suggestion of such a requirement possibly stemmed from acquaintance with an (equally mysterious) passage in the *Rhetorica ad Herennium,* II, 7, and may have been influenced by events in cases such as *Warwickshall,* 1 Leach, 263; *Griffin,* Russ. and Ry. 151; and *Gould,* 9 C. and P. 364.

2. Fortescue, *De laudibus,* c.xxii.

3. Fiorelli, *La Tortura giudiziaria,* I, 206–7.

4. Ibid., I, 194–97.

5. Ibid., I, 204: *not* the torture of the wet veil, although Fiorelli there says that it was the characteristic French torture of the fifteenth century.

6. Fortescue, *De laudibus,* c.xxii.

7. *Criminosus:* the sense is somewhat uncertain; it may mean, an accused.

8. The Yorkist grantee of part of Fortescue's land: Cal. Pat. Rolls, 1461–67, p. 183.

9. As is shown below in the main text, the story had an earlier part, that Fortescue might have been expected to know and to mention, if he knew of and thought worthwhile to refer to Cook's misfortune at all. Moreover, from a Lancastrian standpoint, his description of the knight was remarkably favorable, if it was indeed Cook whom he had in view, and his use of *criminosus* was cold, if it was indeed Hawkins whom he had in view.

10. Fiorelli, *La Tortura giudiziaria,* II, 90–92, points out Baldus's view (In *C.VII-XI,* and C.IX.xli. 18, n. 2: I have not seen it) that if an accused or suspect under torture confessed his own guilt and inculpated another person, the inculpation would stand by itself, without ratification, which was required only for the personal confession; but also other opinions, including one that an inculpation under torture did not require ratification unless mixed with personal confession, when the whole required it.

11. *Rerum Britannicorum medii aevi scriptores:* Rolls Ser., II, 789–90.

12. 1577: 1587 ed., II, 670.

13. *"Ibidem comburitur pedibus in tormentis Cornelius ad confitendum multa."* Cf. below in the main text, Chapter 9 (I).

14. *Chronicle* (Camden Old Ser.), p. 9.

15. Ibid., 1811 ed., p. 656.

16. Ibid., 1809 ed., II, 12.

17. *Three Fifteenth Century Chronicles* (Camden New Ser.), pp. 164–85, at p. 182.

18. On which, see further below in the main text, Chapter 9 (II).

19. Cal. Pat. Rolls, H.VI, 1446–52, p. 146.

20. Ibid., H. VI, 1446–52, p. 32.

21. 3 Inst. 35.

22. Vergil, *History of England* (1534), xxiii: 16th Century trans. (Camden Old Ser.), p. 72.

23. That Henry Holland is the Duke here contemplated is assumed by S. B. Chrimes, *Sir John Fortescue* (Cambridge: Cambridge University Press, 1942), p. 166.

24. Cal. Pat. Rolls, H.VI, 1446–52, p. 565.

25. Surtees Soc. ed., p. 218. We have the following lines, in a passage with a more lilting metre than the rest:

Yee, for as modee as he can loke,

He wold have turnyd an othere croke,

Myght he have had the rake.

In fayth, syre, sen ye callyd you a kyng
Ye must prufe a worthy thyng
That falles to the were:
Ye must just in tornamente
But ye sytt fast els ye be shent,
Else downe I shalle you bere.

The Towneley manuscript is described by Hardin Craig, *English Religious Drama* (Oxford: Clarendon Press, 1955), p. 207, as written in a "sound clerkly hand of about 1450". The possibility here entertained is that it was written after 1460, and that the above passage was then a recent addition to the play. The reference to jousting could have been topical at any period: for example, a tournament was held at Smithfield before Edward IV and the King of France in 1467.

26. For a general biography of John Tiptoft, see R. J. Mitchell, *John Tiptoft* (1427–1470) (London: Longmans Green, 1938).

27. Cal. Pat. Rolls, E.IV, 1461–67, p. 74; Vernon Harcourt, *His Grace the Steward and Trial of Peers*, p. 407.

28. *Chronicle* (Camden Old Ser.), p. 5. Cf. Latin Chronicle in *Three Fifteenth Century Chronicles* (Camden New Ser.), pp. 162–63. Also, by pretended right of his office as Constable, and of the office, which he likewise held, of Steward of the Household, Tiptoft meted out—in a way that may have gained him enemies—summary justice within the Household: Cal. Pat. Rolls, E.IV, 1461–67, p. 300.

29. Thomas, Duke of Gloucester, in the *Black Book of the Admiralty*: Rolls Ser., I, 300, at 314. Cf. Coke, *Littleton*, f. 74b; *Rea v. Ramsay* (1631), 7 St.Tr. at 483, 497, per the Earl Marshall.

30. Cal. Pat. Rolls, E.IV, 1467–77, p. 191; Vernon Harcourt, *His Grace the Steward and Trial of Peers*, p. 407.

31. "*Summarie et de plano, sine strepitu et figura judicii*". Cf. Decretal *Saepe*: Clem.5,11,2; Henry IV to the Pope: Nicholas, *Proceedings and Orders of the Privy Council*, I, 116; Vernon Harcourt, *His Grace the Steward and Trial of Peers*, p. 393n; J. G. Bellamy, *The Law of Treason in England in the Later Middle Ages* (Cambridge: Cambridge University Press, 1970), pp. 160-61.

32. 15 May, 1469; Catesby had been made sergeant only on 18 April: see Cal. Pat. Rolls, E.IV, 1467–77, pp. 170; 193.

33. Cal. Pat. Rolls, E.IV, 1467–77, p. 178.

34. Ibid., E.IV, 1467–77, p. 205.

35. *Chronicle*, p. 9.

36. Mitchell, *John Tiptoft*, pp. 131–32, says that it was unusual at the time for captives to be put to death, unless they were nobles, in the course of civil war. This aspect of the matter may have contributed to the general resentment of Tiptoft's conduct.

37. *Chronicle*, p. 13.

38. *Vite di uomini illustri*, I, 324: cit. Mitchell, *John Tiptoft*, p. 80.

39. Henry VI's government had not prevented the hearing by the Constable and Marshall of appeals (which, at least if better proof was wanting, would lead in their court to trial by battle) concerning treason committed within the realm: cf. Nicholas, *Proceedings and Ordinances of the Privy Council*, VI, 57–59; 129.

40. Cf. *Rot. Parl.* iii, pp. 65; 420; Stat. 13 R.II, c.2; 1 H.IV, c.14.

41. Rolls Ser., II, 178.

CHAPTER 3 263

42. Ibid., II, xxxv.
43. Ibid., II, 218.
44. *"Cum capitalia et atrociora crimina aliter explorari non possunt, seu veritas aliter investigari . . ."* Cf. D.XLVIII.xviii.8: *"cum capitalia et atrociora maleficia non aliter explorari et investigari possunt quam per servorum quaestiones . . ."* and Bartolus, ad id.: *"Nota quod ad tormenta pervenitur in subsidium, cum aliter veritas explorari non potest."*
45. Cf. Bartolus, ad D.XLVIII.xviii.1(27).
46. *The Poetical Works of Sir Thomas Wyatt* (London: 1831): *Memoir*, p. xxxv.
47. The *Gentleman's Magazine*, 1850, II, 235 et seq. The Wyatt ms. book was deposited with the British Museum: Loan Collection 15.
48. Bruce pointed out that, according to the ms., Sir Henry himself caused the barnacles to be incorporated conspicuously in the design of certain carpets, one of which was in 1735 in the possession of the then head of the branch of the family, Francis Wyatt, of Quex.
49. *Chronicle*: 1809 ed., p. 395; cf. Grafton, *Chronicle*: 1809 ed., II, 135.
50. *Chronicle*: 1808 ed., III, 418.
51. Vernon Harcourt, *His Grace the Steward and Trial of Peers*, p. 395.
52. Camden trans., p. 201.
53. Fiorelli, La Tortura giudiziaria, I, 300: exception (C.IX.viii.: Gratian, C.VI, qu.1, c.23) to privilege of nobility, in cases of treason; but cf. Coke in the *Countess of Shrewsbury's Case*, 2 St.Tr. at 769, 773: below Chapter 7 (III).
54. Text and trans., Miss C. A. Sneyd (Camden Old Ser.).
55. Miss C. A. Sneyd, Camden trans., p. vii; Hawden Brown in Cal.S.P.Eng.,Venet., I, 269n; Cf. Emma Gurney Salter, *Tudor England through Venetian Eyes* (London: Williams and Norgate, 1930), p. 17.
56. According to doctrine as settled at a somewhat later time, an information might be in some cases presented, at the suit of the King, for trial without any indictment. However, Hawkins, *Pleas of the Crown*, Bk. II, Ch. 26, ss.1 and 3 (7th ed., 1795, by Thos. Leach, IV, 85 and 86), explaining that "it hath been holden, that the King shall put noone to answer for a wrong done principally to another, without an *indictment* or *presentment*, but that he may do it for a wrong done principally to himself," and adding "but I do not find this distinction confirmed by experience," goes on to say: "I do not find it anywhere holden, that such an information will lie for any capital crime, or for misprision of treason."
57. *"Si può accusare alcuno di cose grande e aperti malefitji, che sia tormentato, benchè il insegni apertamente il vero."*
58. The mention of "open offences" recalls the tendency of Continental jurisprudence to ease the way towards conviction of those against whom the suspicion was of clandestine offenses. On the readier justification of torture in such cases, see Baldus, ad C.I.iv.3: per Fiorelli, *La Tortura giudiziaria*, I, 248. The circumstance contemplated, that the accused did *not* withhold the truth, recalls the doctrine of the Continental penal *ancien régime*, that the judge must have grounds for recourse to torture, but that his conviction that the accused could be seen to be lying would suffice: below, Chapter 5, n. 41. Students of Italian literature will be acquainted from Alessandro Manzoni, *La Colonna d'infamia*: trans., sub tit. "The Column of Infamy", by K. Foster (London: Oxford University Press, 1964), in which see especially pp. 133–34: with this area in former Continental

practice; but Manzoni's account may seem more dangerously tendentious than that in Pietro Verri's posthumously published *Osservazioni sulla tortura* (text appended to Alessandro Manzoni, *Opere complete* [Paris: Bandry: Libreria Europea, 1843]); which he set out to refute.

59. Some historians have asserted that Common Law judges had recourse to torture during the fifteenth century: cf. J. E. Baldwin, *The King's Council (in England) during the Middle Ages* (Oxford: Clarendon Press, 1913), p. 298; David Ogg, *Joannis Seldeni ad Fletam dissertatio*, (Cambridge: Cambridge University Press, 1925),p.1ii. I do not know the explanation. Such action by the judges might have seemed least surprising, where they proceeded without a jury under special statutory provisions (cf. W. H. Dunham, Selden Soc., LXXV, p.1iii); on the other hand, since the offenses concerned were all less than capital, to have introduced judicial torture regarding them, when it was not used in capital causes, would have been incongruous.

60. 24 H.VIII, c.12.

61. *State Pap.*, VII, 489; 490.

62. M.A.S. Hume, *Spanish Chronicle of Henry VIII* (London: G. Bell and Sons, 1889), p. 61; on the mode of torture described, see below in the main text, Chapter 9 (I).

63. Pp. 65; 66.

64. *Letters and Papers Foreign and Domestic* (L.P.F.D.), XI, 407; 495; R. B. Merriman, *The Life and Letters of Thomas Cromwell* (Oxford: Clarendon Press, 1902), II, 30; 32.

65. L.P.F.D., XII, II, 74.

66. Ibid., XII, II, 80.

67. Ibid., XIII, I, 759.

68. Ibid., XIII, II, 34; Henry Ellis, *Original Letters illustrative of English History*, 1824–26 (3rd Ser.), I, II, 85–89; G. R. Elton, *Policy and Police* (Cambridge: Cambridge University Press, 1972), p. 342.

69. Cf. the judgment (21 June, 1549) on Jacques de Coucy, for having delivered Boulogne to the English: Francois André Isambert, *Recueil général des anciennes lois françoises, depuis l'an 420 jusqu'à la révolution de 1789* (Paris: Berlin-Le-Prieur and others, 1821–33), XIII, 88; Mellor, *La Torture* p. 88; and concerning the *question préalable*, at a later date, cf. de Vouglans, *Les Lois criminelles,* pp. 59–60. In France, torture after condemnation became part of the judicial sentence; yet in what other sense, if any, it was itself judicial, is not clear to me. Presumably, an inculpation of another person, obtained from the condemned man or woman under torture, was of some evidential value, via the record.

70. *State Pap.*, I and II, 601; L.P.F.D., XIV, 1, 538.

71. L.P.F.D., XV, 438.

72. Elton, *Policy and Police*, p. 248. Earlier, he had in 1518 been appointed to sit in the Court of Requests: per Sir Julius Caesar: I. S. Leadam, *Select Cases in the Court of Requests* (Selden Soc., XII: 1898), p. civ. He was knighted in 1543.

73. L.P.F.D., XII, I, 900; 914 (April, 1537).

74. Appendix, No. 1.

75. Ibid.

76. *State Pap.*, I, 685; L.P.F.D., XVI, 1261.

77. As to the restricted commission of the councillors in London, see L.P.F.D., XVI, 141; as to the separation of the councillors into two groups, one in London, one with the

King, see G. R. Elton, *The Tudor Revolution in Government* (Cambridge: Cambridge University Press, 1953), p. 315; G. R. Elton, *The Tudor Constitution* (Cambridge: Cambridge University Press, 1960), p. 90n.

78. L.P.F.D., XVIII, I, 157. Cf. ibid., 115; 134; 137–38.

79. B.L. Add. MSS., 32651, f. 93.

80. L.P.F.D., XIX, I, 469; 470.

81. Ibid., p. 547.

82. Ibid., p. 550.

83. Ibid., pp. 590; 603.

84. Ibid., p. 897.

85. Ibid., p. 832.

86. L.P.F.D., XIX, I, 240.

87. 1547: *Select Works of Bishop Bale* (Parker Soc.: 1849), pp. 224–26.

88. Bishop Gilbert Burnet, *History of the Reformation of the Church of England* (Dublin: R. Gunne, J. Smith, and W. Bruce, 1730–33), 2nd ed., III, in Vol. I, 342: doubted, but of course was unable to refute, the story that Wriothesley himself operated the rack.

89. L.P.F.D., XXI, I, 1181.

90. 1684 ed., II, 488; Foxe included the account from Bale. (Cf. L.P.F.D., XX, I, 391, of which every explanation that occurs to me is lamentable.)

91. *Acts and Monuments*, 4th ed., rev. (London: Religious Tract Society, 1877), V, 546.

92. Thus scrutiny of signatures appended by George Gisborough, respectively to the reports of two examinations to which he was subjected, after the Walsingham conspiracy in 1537, at Cromwell's house in Stepney, suggested to Elton that on the second occasion he was tortured, although no record of the fact is available: (Elton, *Policy and Police*, p. 144.) Again, regarding possible proceedings in the Welsh Marches, see below in the main text.

93. Below in the main text, Chapter 6 (III); Chapter 7 (III). N.B. also Robert Abbot on the role of Conciliar commissioners: Chapter 7, Part II (II).

94. Below in the main text, Chapter 9 (IV), concerning this prison.

95. Stocking could be exacerbated in various ways: for example, by forcing the ankles far apart, or by raising the stocks so that his feet were far above his head. Below in the main text, Chapter 9 (IV).

96. Arthur Ogle, *The Tragedy of the Lollard's Tower* (Oxford: Pen-in-hand, 1949), p. 14, commenting upon observations by Miss E. Jeffries Davies in English Historical Review 30: 477–79.

97. On exactions by jailers, see Pugh, *Imprisonment in Medieval England*, p. 178 et seq.

98. *Black Book of the Admiralty*: Rolls Ser., pp. 41–47; 245; 255 et seq.; Reginald G. Marsden, *Select Pleas in the Court of Admiralty* (Selden Soc., VI: 1892), I, xvi.

99. *Histoire de la procédure criminelle en France* . . . (Paris: L. Larose et Forcel, 1882), pp. 99–100: Le "*rapport entre la rigueur des preuves et l'emploi de la question sera un cercle vicieux, dans lequel tournera jusqu'à son dernier jour notre ancienne procédure criminelle.*" John Simpson's translation, *History of Continental Criminal Procedure* (London: John Murray, 1914), to which generally I have referred, p. 113, is hardly felicitous.

100. By D. Barrington, *Observations of the More Ancient Statutes,* 4th ed. (1775),

p. 495; John H. Langbein, *Torture and the Law of Proof* (Chicago: University of Chicago Press, 1977), p. 188, moderately holds that this, contrary, inference is "dubious".

101. Fiorelli, *La Tortura giudiziaria*, I, 253, says that on the Continent, outside criminal praxis, torture was particularly common in bankruptcy. However, I do not know what Continental example Maynard's creditors had in view. In Italy, state legislation authorizing the torture of insolvents began—according to Fiorelli—in the fourteenth century; on the other hand, in France bankruptcy provision of any sort began to be made only in the seventeenth century: L. Lacour, *Précis de droit commercial* (Paris: Librairie Dalloz, 1945), p. 432. It is however, possible that in parts of France, torture had been introduced in the *action paulienne*.

102. L.P.F.D., Add., I, I, 515.

103. Stat. 34 and 35 H.VIII, c.4.

104. Cf. Edward II's frequently reiterated declaration that the Inquisitors were to be allowed to execute Ecclesiastical Law on the Templars *and their bodies*: above, Chapter 2; below, Appendix, No. 75.

105. For an admirable, brief, account, see Elton, *The Tudor Constitution*, Ch. 6. Much discussion has centered on Stat. 3 H.VII, c.1; 21 H.VIII, c.20. For contemporary Common Law views cf. *Onslow's Case*, 2 Dyer, 242b; 243a: 73 E.R. 537; *Earl of Leicester v. Sir Christopher Heydon* (argument), 1 Plowden, 384, at 393: 75 E.R. 595; J. Hawarde, *Les Reportes del Cases in Camera Stellata*, ed. W. P. Baildon, (London, 1894), p. 4.

106. Cf. per Sir Julius Caesar: Leadam, *Select Cases in the Court of Requests* (Selden Soc., XII: 1898), p. xxi.

107. Cf. Coke, 4 Inst.: 4th ed., p. 63.

108. Ibid.

109. A. V. Dicey, *The Privy Council* (London: Macmillan, 1887), pp. 101–06.

110. F. W. Maitland, *Constitutional History of England* (Cambridge: Cambridge University Press, 1908), p. 263.

111. Holdsworth, *History of English Law*, I: 5th ed., p. 505; V, 185. See also Glanville Williams, *The Proof of Guilt* (London: Stevens, 1955), p. 38.

112. Elton, *The Tudor Constitution*, p. 170n.

113. See Elton, *Policy and Police*, pp. 384–85: where it is pointed out that local justices of the peace generally regarded Conciliar instructions as sufficient warrant for executing summary justice in respect of indictable misdemeanors: a state of affairs in harmony with the fact that Sir Gilbert Talbot and John Russell put James Pratt to torture upon Cromwell's instructions (above, main text).

114. The Council in the North appears to have originated under Richard III. It was organized by Cromwell, following the Pilgrimage of Grace (1536). It exercised criminal jurisdiction at Common Law under commission of oyer and terminer; moreover, the Crown purported to confer upon it power to deal with various misdemeanors by jury trial or by "prerogative"—Star Chamber style—trial, in the alternative: this special commission of the Council in the North is thought to have been little altered from an early period in its history onwards; north of the Trent, it also had unrestricted police responsibility. (R. R. Reid, *The King's Council in the North* [London: Longmans Green, 1921], pp. 157–59; 281; and [setting out the commission of 1530] 502–03.)

115. Under Henry VII, a council was appointed to act on behalf of Arthur, Prince of Wales. In 1525 it was reconstituted at Princess Mary's Council. Subsequently, Thomas Cromwell remodelled it: on the lines adopted for the Council in the North, and to exercise

in Wales a comparable range of functions. The second "Act of Union", 34 and 35 H.VIII, c.26, provided for its subsequent constitution and confirmed that the King had power to confer judicial authority upon it. After Henry's death, royal instructions required it to try cases of felony and breach of the peace. (Below in the main text, Chapter 4, Part II(V); generally, on this body, P. Williams, *The Council in the Marches of Wales under Elizabeth* [Cardiff: University of Wales Press, 1958].)

116. Although some historians might appear to have made a contrary assumption. Below, loc. cit.

117. Cf. Elton, *Policy and Police*, pp. 384–85.

CHAPTER 4

1. Appendix, No. 2.

2. *Acts of the Privy Council* (A.P.C.), 7 August, 1550. If Haldsworth was to be regarded as having been in possession of the hoard at the time of his conviction, according to Stanford (*Pleas of the Crown*, 188; *Prerogative*, 45) the whole was thereupon forfeit to the Crown.

3. Appendix, No. 3.

4. In the King's *Chronicle*, see for October, 1551, entries 16 and 19; for November, 1551, entries 3 and 8; for June, 1552, entry 13. Wilbur Kitchener Jordan, in his edition, *Chronicle and Collected Papers of King Edward VI* (London: Allen and Unwin, 1966), p. 89, writes: "little is known of William Crane. Under torture he implicated Somerset in the alleged conspiracy, who at the trial demanded that he be permitted to face his accuser." The latter detail comes from the *Chronicle* itself: Jordan's ed., pp. 98–99. If Crane indeed was tortured, and was so only in pursuance of the warrant recorded for 5 November, 1551, the *Chronicle* would suggest that he had by then very little more that he could say against Somerset; but torture under the warrant may have brought him to inculpate Arundel.

5. "For certaine seditious reportes . . ."

6. Appendix, No. 4.

7. Ibid., No. 5.

8. Ibid., No. 6.

9. Ibid., No. 7(a).

10. Ibid., No. 7(b).

11. Below in the main text, Part II (V).

12. Appendix, No. 8.

13. Ibid., No. 9(a).

14. Ibid., No. 9(b).

15. "To bring" him "to the rack, and to do *ut supra.*" One may wonder whether truncation of the record was simply due to a desire for brevity or whether it partly reflected distaste.

16. Appendix, No. 10.

17. D. Jardine, *Reading on the Use of Torture in the Criminal Law of England previously to the Commonwealth* (London: Baldwin and Cradock, 1837), pp. 19–20, notices, with understandable reserve, apparent reference of the incident, by Burnett, *History of the Reformation*, III, 256, to the proclamation "against stage plays". A proclamation of 1 Mary (1553) offered freedom of conscience, but prohibited religious

268   NOTES

controversy and the presentation of unlicensed plays and unlicensed printing. Censorship
of plays was continued by proclamation after Elizabeth I's accession. See P. L. Hughes
and J.F. Larkin, *Tudor Royal Proclamations* (New Haven and London: Yale University
Press, 1964), II, Nos. 390; 458.

18. Appendix, No. 11. An entry for 23 June, 1556, records the authorization of his
dispatch to Dorset, to be there tried for murder.

19. Appendix, No. 12.

20. Ibid., No. 13.

21. Ibid., No. 14.

22. Cf. Stat. 13 H.IV, c.7, s.2; 3 H.VII, c.1.

23. Cf. Elton, *The Tudor Constitution,* No. 87 (1500) and (more especially) No. 88
(temp. H.VIII).

24. Cf. Elton, *The Tudor Constitution,* p. 171.

25. Appendix, No. 15(a).

26. Ibid., No. 15(b).

27. Ibid., No. 16.

28. Jardine, *Reading,* pp. 20–22, after referring to this record, observes correctly that
indications of the use of torture, in the Council Book for Mary's reign, do not discernibly
concern religious persecution.

29. Elizabeth I ascended the throne on 17 November, 1558.

30. Appendix, No. 17.

31. Ibid., No. 18.

32. Ibid., No. 19.

33. Cal.S.P.Dom., Eliz., xxxvi, 25; xxxvii, 30; 34; xl, 81; 83; cf. M. B. Donald,
Elizabethan Copper: The History of the Company of Mines Royal 1568-1605 (London:
Pergamon, 1955), passim; Mary Dewar, *Sir Thomas Smith: A Tudor Intellectual in Office*
(London: Athlone, 1964), pp. 149–50. (The references at the beginning of this note to
the *Calendar of State Papers Domestic* [Cal.S.P.Dom.] make convenient here to explain
some modes of citation. The *Calendar of State Papers Scotland* [Cal.S.P.Scot.] and much
of the *Calendar of State Papers Domestic* and of the *Calendar of State Papers Ireland*
[Cal.S.P.Ireland] were published in volumes internally divided according to a distribution
of the papers concerned, with a series of volumes [of papers] for each reign and numbered
items within them. In this book, where such division occurs in a published volume of
one of the above Calendars, citation relies upon it. The number of an item is given in
Arabic numerals, preceded by the number of the containing volume [of papers], given
in lower-case Roman numerals, and an indication of the reign. The *Calendar of State
Papers Mary Queen of Scots* [Cal.S.P.Mary Qu.Sc.] and the *Calendar of State Papers
Domestic* for the period from the death of Charles I, in 1649, to the Restoration, in 1660,
similarly refer to volumes [of papers] and to items within them, but without indicating
the reign [for the former, that of Queen Elizabeth I, for the latter, according to the post-
Restoration view, that of Charles II]. In this book, once again citation is by reference to
the numbers of volumes [of papers], given in lower-case Roman numerals, and to the
numbers of items, given in Arabic numerals. In citation of the *Calendar of State Papers
Domestic* for the interregnal period, "Interregnum" is inserted before the number of the
volume [of papers].)

34. Appendix, No. 20.

35. Smith had served during the last two years of Somerset's administration as second

Secretary to the King. Arrested after Somerset's fall, he had been restored to public service under Elizabeth. He was Ambassador in France, 1562–66. Dewar, *Sir Thomas Smith*, Chs. III; IV; VII–IX.

36. *De republica Anglorum, a discourse on the commonwealth of England,* ed. L. Alston (Cambridge: Cambridge University Press, 1906), II, Ch. 27. Alston, in his Introduction, says that the work was written between 1562 and 1566, although first published (after some revision) in 1583. It is interesting to compare an observation made considerably earlier—in 1551—by Barbaro, then Venetian Ambassador to the English Court. He explained, in one of his reports (translation: 5 Cal.S.P.Venet., p. 340), the English use of juries, and continued: "this mode of judicature appears to the English perfectly just and safe, as they affirm that torture is a violent and compulsory method, which often induces a man to confess what he has never committed, nor even thought of doing; and injures both the body and life of an innocent person; and they are also of opinion that it is more just to release a guilty person than to condemn one who is innocent." It is, however, evidently possible that the Ambassador was not quoting contemporary English opinion, whether Common Law or Civilian, but relying upon John Fortescue, *De laudibus legum Anglie,* c.xxvii (above, Chapter 3[I], *in limine*). Smith himself probably drew upon a classical education in the above passage. In particular, his statement that the English take torture for servile recalls Suetonius, *Augustus, XXVII: "Q. Gallium praetorem . . . per centuriones et milites raptum e tribunali servilem in modum torsit . . ."*

37. Cal.S.P.Dom., Mary, iii, 22.

38. 1807 ed., IV, p. 21.

39. 1 St.Tr. (1809 ed.), at 870; 879.

40. Under Edward VI, in the matter of the Duke of Somerset's alleged plot, it is an obscure figure, William Crane, who seems most likely to have been tortured. Cf. above, n. 2.

41. 12 Cal.S.P.Span. (Calendar of State Papers Spanish), p. 96.

42. 1 St.Tr., at 861–63.

43. Ibid., at 870, 885.

44. Cal.S.P.Dom., Mary, vii, 23.

45. Robert Swift to the Earl of Shrewsbury: Edmund Lodge *Illustrations of British History* . . . (London: G. Nicol, 1791), 2nd ed. (1838), No. xxii: but dated 22 June, 1566—very late in the story.

46. *The Diary of Henry Machin, 1550–1562,* ed. J. G. Nichols (Camden Old. Ser.), p. 103.

47. D. M. Loades, *Two Tudor Conspiracies* (Cambridge: Cambridge University Press, 1965), p. 208.

48. Letters from Danyell to the Commissioners: Cal.S.P.Dom., Mary, viii, 36; 38. The texts are reproduced, with minor expurgation, by J. A. Froude, *History of England: Reign of Mary Tudor:* (Everyman's Library; London: J. M. Dent, 1913), p. 268. For present purposes, it is fortunately unnecessary to scrutinize the chronological sequence of documents concerning Danyell. A memorandum regarding the treatment of prisoners at the Tower, Cal.S.P.Dom., Mary, viii, 26, which is thought to have been made on or about 23 April—the day on which it would otherwise appear that Danyell was subjected to more severe imprisonment—proposes that he "be gently used and given some freedom" so that he may be brought "as if by accident" into contact with certain among the other prisoners; whereas a further memorandum, Cal.S.P.Dom., Mary, viii, 72, thought to

have been made on or about 13 May—that is, after Danyell had been tried and con-demned—declares that he "being yesterday removed to a worse lodging, begynneth this day to have been more open and playne. . . ."

49. Cal.S.P.Dom., Mary, vii, 43.

50. Loades, *Two Tudor Conspiracies*, p. 109 and n.

51. Ibid., pp. 222; 235.

52. Cf. ibid., pp. 220–21.

53. *Diary*, pp. 105; 106.

54. See further, Loades, *Two Tudor Conspiracies*, p. 207.

55. Cal.S.P.Dom., Mary, viii, 28. The editors of the Cal. attribute this material, tentatively, to 23 April: a date, acceptance of which is encouraged by reference that it contains to Fernando Lygyns, Lygens (cf. Cal.S.P.Dom., Mary, viii, 27; 29); Staunton was under examination earlier: Cal.S.P.Dom., Mary, vii, 64; viii, 4; 5. No record can be found of a confession by him on or after 23 April.

56. Loades, *Two Tudor Conspiracies*, p. 206.

57. Cal.S.P.Dom., Mary, viii, 14.

58. Ibid., viii, 53.

59. Machin, *Diary*, p. 104.

60. Froude, *Reign of Mary Tudor*, p. 267; where, however: the document is described as "Walpole's deposition"; Walpole is identified as one of Throgmorton's examiners (? Waldegrave); in place of the manner of citation doubtless intended by the author ("Mary, vol. viii"), we have "MS. Lodge's *Illustrations*, vol. viii.

61. Cal.S.P.Dom., Mary, vii; viii.

62. Froude, *Reign of Mary Tudor*, p. 267, assumed that Richard Uvedale, the Captain of the Isle of White, was put to the rack. It is not necessarily so, although the poor man certainly did not resist his interrogators. Loades, *Two Tudor Conspiracies*, more generally observed that by the end of March, 1556, the prisoners in the Tower were pouring forth information "either under the inducement of torture or through the more subtle persuasions of alternate hope and fear."

63. Cal.S.P.Dom., Eliz., lix, 43.

64. Appendix, Nos. 4; 8; and perhaps 5 (where the recorded warrant is addressed to him alone, but may be supplementary to another, for interrogation, addressed elsewhere.)

65. Appendix, Nos. 9(a); (b); 10; 12; 13; 16; 17. The Lieutenant himself may have been one of the "others" of Appendix, No. 19. If not, the warrant concerned may have reinforced an earlier one, to the same addressees, that did not provide for torture, but execution of which without it had proved difficult. Cf., on Appendix, No. 7(a), below in the main text, Part II (V).

66. Appendix, Nos. 3 and 7(b).

67. Ibid., No. 12.

68. Ibid., Nos. 15(a); (b).

69. Cf. Chapter 6, Part II (VII).

70. Appendix, No. 6. Treason, to counterfeit the Queen's coin: Stat. 25 E.III, 5, c.2; foreign coin, current by her consent: Stat. 1 Mary, c.6. At Bristol, 4 April, 1555, four men had the punishment of treason, for coining: W. Adams, *Chronicle of Bristol* (Bristol: J. W. Arrowsmith, 1910), p. 103.

71. Cf. Appendix, No. 1, on "the brake" and No. 23 (Chapter 5, Part II [I]). According to Foxe, *Acts and Monuments*, 1st ed., p. 1651, text and illustration, "*a* rack" might

be other than a stretching rack, but "to be racked" readily meant "to be tortured on a stretching rack". Later, see Shakespeare, 1 H.VI, ii.5.3; Lear, v.3.314. On modes of torture, see below in main text, Chapter 9.

72. Williams, *The Council in the Marches*, pp. 48; 197–98.

73. A.P.C., 16 May, 1555.

74. Chapter 9 (V).

75. Sussex to Bowes, 14 January, 1570: Cuthbert Sharp, *Memorials of the Rebellion of 1569* (London: John Bowyer Nichols, 1840), p. 153.

76. Cf. Sussex to Bowes, 10 January, 1570: Sharp, *Memorials*, pp. 143–44 (with facsimile).

77. 15 December, 1569: Sharp, *Memorials*, p. 99.

78. 29 January, 1570: Sharp, *Memorials*, pp. 168–69.

79. Cal.S.P.Dom., Add., Eliz., xv, 138; Sharp, *Memorials*, pp. 126–27n. On the Rebellion, see more broadly, R. R. Reid, "The Rebellion of the Earls, 1569," *Transactions of the Royal Historical Society* (2nd Ser.), 20 (1906): 171–203.

80. After Elizabeth's accession, he appeared entirely unrepentant: John Hayward's *Annals*, ed. J. Bruce (Camden Old Ser.), p. 25. Eventually, he went into exile in Flanders, but he was lured back, tried and executed in 1571: 1 St.Tr. (1809 ed.), at 1087; Somers's *Tracts:* 1809 ed., I, 477.

81. The text is given in Foxe, *Acts and Monuments*, 4th ed., rev., VIII, 301; and cf. Burnet, *History of the Reformation*, II.ii,32. Its terms were largely echoed in Elizabeth's ecclesiastical commission of 1559 (G. W. Prothero, *Select Statutes and other Constitutional Documents*, 4th ed. [Oxford: Clarendon Press, 1913], p. 227 et seq.; abridged, Elton, *The Tudor Constitution*, p. 221–25).

82. *Acts and Monuments:* 1684 ed., III, p. 758 et seq.

83. Ibid., pp. 759–60.

84. P. 1651.

85. Chapter 9 (II); (V).

86. 1576 ed., p. 1925.

87. Above in main text (IV).

88. A.P.C., 17 March, 1555. It may seem that a context for the commission was provided by the contemporary statute, 2 and 3 Philip and Mary, c.10, which—building upon Stat. 1 and 2 Philip and Mary, c.13—imposed upon justices of the peace, in felony cases, the duty to examine suspects and prospective prosecution witnesses, to reduce what they said to writing, and to "certify" the results, in writing under their hand, into the next session of general jail delivery. It had been supposed (Holdsworth, *History of English Law*, IV, 528–29) that Stat. 1 and 2 Philip and Mary, c.13, reflected Continental influence. John H. Langbein, *Prosecuting Crime in the Renaissance* (Cambridge, Mass: Harvard University Press, 1974) adduces (pp. 24–28) cogent arguments against supposition that the draftsman of the statute intended to promote a shift towards Continental procedure, with judgment based on a written dossier, and most plausibly concludes (pp. 119–22) that its result was to seal the fate of the jury of accusation, however, at the trial to validate the jury's role as a trier of fact. Nonetheless, the new emphasis on pre-trial magisterial investigation brought in occasional inquisitorial modes of thought; regarding such investigation, an English judge might, as late as the nineteenth century, speak somewhat as though he had been raised on the French ordinances of 1498 and 1539: Stephen, *History of the Criminal Law of England*, I, 227. (On the French ordinances, see Esmein, *History,*

Pt. I, Ch. III, ss.2 and 3. With a slight omission, aa.139–67 of the 1539 ordinance are translated by Langbein, *Prosecuting Crime in the Renaissance*, pp. 310-13.)

89. Appendix, No. 7(a).

90. Ibid., No. 7(b).

91. Religious persecution and Government attack on dangerous rumor propagation have each been suggested as the context here: Jardine, *Reading*, p. 18.

92. Appendix, No. 77(a).

93. Cf. Historical Manuscript Commission, *De l'Isle and Dudley*, I, 326, with Appendix, No. 77(a).

94. 1570 (cf. Historical Manuscript Commission, *De l'Isle and Dudley*, I, 334, with Appendix, No. 77[b]); 1574 (Appendix, No. 77[b]); 1586; 1601; 1602 (regarding proposals before which, cf. Cal.S.P.Dom., Eliz., cclxxxiv, 66; 67). Further, and for extant unprinted texts, see Williams, *The Council in the Marches*, pp. 56; 362-63.

95. Cf. Williams, *The Council in the Marches*, p. 81; Elton, *The Tudor Constitution*, p. 199.

96. Chapter 3 (II).

97. John Strype, *The Life and Acts of John Whitgift* (Oxford: Clarendon Press, 1822), I, 401–2. See further, Chapter 6, Part III.

98. 34 and 35 H.VIII., c.26.

99. S.3.

100. 1 St.Tr. (1809 ed.), at 870, 881.

101. Cf. Smith, *De republica Anglorum*, II, Ch.23.

102. However fatuous the method may to us appear: cf. Augustine, *De civitate Dei*, xix.6.

103. 3 *Institutes*, 25. The Edwardian statute in terms allowed conviction of treason where the accused, "arraigned", did "willingly, without violence" confess. Cf. Stat. 7 and 8 W. III, c.3, s.2.

CHAPTER 5

1. J. E. Neale, *Elizabeth I and her Parliaments, 1559-1581* (London: Cape, 1953), p. 178.

2. The rebellion was mentioned above in the main text, Chapter 4, Part II (III) and cf. the notes thereto.

3. Conyers Read, *Mr. Secretary Walsingham and the Policy of Queen Elizabeth* (Oxford: Clarendon Press, 1925), I, 81–83.

4. Neale, *Elizabeth I and her Parliaments*, Pt. IV, Ch. 2.

5. Legislative background: ibid., p. 225 et seq.

6. Appendix, Nos. 21(a); (b).

7. Ibid., No. 22.

8. He was later condemned and he was executed before the Bishop's gate with the full rigors of the Common Law sentence for treason: 1 St.Tr. (1809 ed.), at 1085; Cal.S.P.Span., 1568–79, No. 203 (p. 267).

9. See further in the main text, Part II (I).

10. Appendix, No. 76.

11. William Murdin, *Collection of State Papers Relating to the Affairs of Queen*

Elizabeth Left by William Cecil Lord Burghley (London, 1759), pp. 95-96.

12. Ibid., pp. 95-96.

13. Ibid., p. 95. Regarding the composition and publication of Thomas Smith's *De republica Anglorum*, see above, Chapter 4, n. 36. On Smith's involvement in examinations of the Duke of Norfolk and others in the matter of the Ridolfi Plot, see Dewar, *Sir Thomas Smith*, pp. 125–27.

14. Appendix, No. 23(a).

15. The other warrant concerning his removal to the Tower ordered his delivery by the Knight Marshal: Appendix, No. 23, parentheses.

16. Appendix, No. 23(b).

17. Ibid., No. 9(a).

18. Cf. Neale, *Elizabeth I and her Parliaments*, p. 316 and sources there cited.

19. Cal.S.P.Dom., Eliz., xciii, 4.

20. Appendix, No. 25, parentheses.

21. Ibid., No. 25.

22. See Read, *Mr. Secretary Walsingham*, II, 347 et seq.

23. Much of the documentary evidence from this point onwards is listed in Cal.S.P.Mary Qu.Sc., x.

24. Harleian MSS., 6991, No. 57.

25. Ibid., No. 58.

26. Walsingham to the Queen, 22 February, 1578: text printed in Read, *Mr. Secretary Walsingham*, II, 350–51. Cf. Cal.S.P.Mary Qu.Sc., x, 12.

27. 11 March, 1571. Cf. Cal.S.P.Mary Qu.Sc., x, 20.

28. Appendix, Nos. 26(a); (b).

29. Ibid., No. 26(c).

30. Ibid., No. 27.

31. In A.P.C., 10 November, 1578, one Prescall is said to have been examined, as well as Sanford, both having been committed to the Tower.

32. A.P.C., 10 November, 1578.

33. Appendix, No. 28.

34. Ibid., Nos. 21(a); (b).

35. Ibid., Nos. 23(a); (b).

36. For a succinct account of the plot, see Conyers Read, *Lord Burghley and Queen Elizabeth* (London: Cape, 1960), Ch. III.

37. Cf. Anon., Cal.S.P.Scot., Eliz., xlv, 37 (April, 1590).

38. Cf. Cal.S.P.Mary Qu.Sc., vi, 37; 40; 45; 48.

39. Murdin, *Collection of State Papers*, pp. 7–8.

40. Cf. Cal.S.P.Mary Qu.Sc., vi, 51.

41. Burghley's account: quoted by Read, *Lord Burghley*, p. 39, from Public Record Office (S.P. 12) 85, item 11. (In subsequent notes, "Public Record Office" is abbreviated to "P.R.O.")

42. Cf. Cal.S.P.Mary Qu.Sc., vi, 52.

43. Murdin, *Collection of State Papers*, p. 8.

44. Ibid., p. 8.

45. Cal.S.P.Mary Qu.Sc., vi, 55.

46. Murdin, *Collection of State Papers*, pp. 9–10.

47. Ibid., pp. 11–12.

48. Cal.S.P.Span., 1568–79 (p. 251).

49. Ibid., p. 41.

50. Cf. Cal. S.P. Scot., Eliz., xix, 59(II) (4 October, 1570). This entry also serves to illustrate another phenomenon of the time: communications to Elizabeth and her advisers of the results of interrogatory torture in Scotland. On at least one occasion, the Queen took it upon herself to urge torture of an examinate by the Scots: cf. Cal.S.P.Scot., Eliz., xxi, 50; 76; 99: 1583.

51. Murdin, *Collection of State Papers*, p. 130.

52. Ibid., p. 148.

53. Ibid., p. 149.

54. Ibid., pp. 93–94.

55. Cf. Ibid., p. 102 (20 September, 1571); Cal.S.P.Span., 1568–79 (p. 285).

56. Murdin, *Collection of State Papers*, pp. 101–2 (20 September 1571).

57. Appendix, No. 76.

58. Compare, on minor indications, *adminicula*, for torture, as comprising (inter alia) lying, believed by the judge to be apparent: Bartolus, *Digestum novum commentaria*, ad D.XLVIII.xviii.22; Damhouder, *Praxis rerum criminalium*, c.36: Antwerp 1554 ed., p. 97; Farinacius, *Variae quaestiones et communes opiniones* (1588): sub tit. *Praxis et theorica criminalis*, Lyons, 1634-50: Qu.52. Long-standing Civilian practice being to apply *Corpus Iuris* texts by analogy, texts on servile evidence, or on witnesses, might be invoked with reference to the treatment of accused persons; hence compare: concerning torture in case of treason touching the safety of the Prince, C.IX.xli.1(pr.); on torture and lying, two Greek texts, C.IV,.xx13(pr.); 15(1); and on torture and vacillation, D.XLVIII.xviii.15(pr.).

59. British Library (B.L.) MS. Cotton Calig. c.III, 248.

60. Murdin, *Collection of State Papers*, pp. 95–96.

61. Ibid., pp. 101–2; cf. pp. 99–101 (Barker's confession, 19th September, 1571); pp. 132–33 (Bannister's examinations, 18 and 19 September, 1571).

62. Murdin, *Collection of State Papers*, p. 133 et seq.

63. Ibid., p. 122.

64. 1 St.Tr. (1809 ed.), 957, at 992.

65. 1 St.Tr., at 978.

66. Paul Johnson, *Elizabeth: a Study in Power and Intellect* (London: Weidenfeld and Nicholson, 1974), p. 184.

67. Civilian concern with this matter may be referred to the existence of two *Corpus Iuris* titles: D.L.vii and C.X.1xv. Doctrine could find root, especially, in D.L.vii.18.

68. Murdin, *Collection of State Papers*, pp. 18-19.

69. Ibid., p. 54 et seq. This letter is a prime source of information concerning the dealings, down to its own date, of the Council with the Bishop, in the matter of the plot.

70. Cf. ibid., p. 57 (Wilson to Burghley, 8 November, 1571); and Somer's *Tracts:* 1809 ed., I, 187 et seq.

71. Cf. Cal.S.P.Dom., Add., Eliz., xxi, 67.

72. Cf. Chapter 9 (II).

73. Appendix, No. 22.

74. Ibid., No. 22.

75. *De republica Anglorum*, II, Ch. 27: quoted in the main text above, Chapter 4, Part II (I).

76. Appendix, No. 9(a).
77. For example, Appendix, Nos. 8; 17; 29; 38; 46; and cf. the A.P.C. entry for 25 October, 1576, above in the main text (III).
78. Appendix, No. 20: above in the main text, Chapter 4, Part I.
79. Above in the main text, Part I.
80. *De republica Anglorum*, II, Ch. 23.

CHAPTER 6

1. For a statement of the Government's moral position, see Lord Burghley's tract, *Execution of Justice in England* (1583); Raphael Hollinshed, *Chronicles* (1807–8 ed.), IV, 515; John, Baron Somers's *Tracts:* 1809 ed., I, 189. (On this tract: Read, *Lord Burghley*, pp. 215, 566).

2. Cf. R. C. Bald, editing Robert Southwell, *A Humble Supplication to Her Majestie* (Cambridge: Cambridge University Press, 1953), p. xxi.

3. Appendix, No. 29.

4. Ibid., No. 30.

5. Rishton's *Diary* (on which see further below in the main text, Part II) records for 31 December, 1580, that Harte was brought to the rack, and that the same was done with Henry Orton, a Roman Catholic layman of good family. (I think the *Diary* means no more, regarding the treatment it mentions, although it uses an elaborate expression—*ad equulei cruciatum deductus*. For commonly, where it means "racked", it simply says so, using expressions such as *"equuleo subjici," "equuleo torqueri."*

6. Appendix, No. 31.

7. See further below in the main text, Part II (I).

8. Appendix, No. 32.

9. Other females alleged to have been tortured in England during the sixteenth century are Anne Askew (above, Chapter 3[II]) and a woman called Margaret, in 1588 (Southwell to Aquaviva, 31 August, 1588: Catholic Rec. Soc., V, 323).

10. Appendix, No. 33.

11. On Myagh's case, see further below in the main text, Part II (I).

12. Appendix, No. 34.

13. Ibid., No. 35.

14. Ibid., No. 36.

15. Ibid., No. 37.

16. P.R.O. (H.C.A. 14) 22, item 191; cf. Marsden, *Select Pleas in the Court of Admiralty*, II (Selden Soc. XI: 1897), lxxvii, referring to an old P.R.O. location.

17. Clinton Atkinson and Pursar (spelled "Purser") are mentioned, along with one Carter, in a letter (P.R.O. [H.C.A. 14] 22, item 193: cf. Marsden, *Select Pleas in the Court of Admiralty*, II, lxxvii, referring to an old P.R.O. location) to Dr. Jones and Dr. Lewis (as "judges of the Admiralty") from Burghley, dated the 30th of July, 1583. According to the letter, they and other men had recently been apprehended as pirates by a Mr. Burrough. Jones was recommended to attend to petitions, forwarded to Burghley by the French Ambassador, from French subjects in respect of ships and other goods said to have been seized by the prisoners. Regarding their colorful careers in the immediately

preceding period, cf. Cal.S.P.Dom., Eliz., cliv, 74; clvi, 7; Cal.S.P.For. *(Calendar of State Papers Foreign)*, 1583, No. 343 (at p. 380); and below in n. 20.
    18. Above, Chapter 3(II).
    19. Cf. Langbein, *Prosecuting Crime in the Renaissance*, p. 81.
    20. Cf. C.III.xii.8; D.XLVIII.iii.6[1]; Damhouder, *Praxis rerum criminalium*, c.XXXV,9; Fiorelli, *La Tortura giudiziaria*, II, 93–103. A copy exists (cf. Cal.S.P.Dom., Eliz., clxxviii, 23) of a report dated 16 April, 1585, from Julius Caesar and Dr. Val. Dale to Walsingham, that examinations of Tirrey (described as of Cork) and of Atkinson showed that the inhabitants of Lydd had helped the pirates when their ship ran ashore.
    21. Fiorelli, *La Tortura giudiziaria*, I, 253–56.
    22. Appendix, No. 38.
    23. Ibid., No. 39.
    24. Ibid., No. 40.
    25. Ibid., No. 41.
    26. Of those listed, some can be identified. Edward Windsor, brother to Lord Windsor, was inculpated by Babington: J. H. Pollen, *Queen Mary and the Babington Plot* (Scottish Historical Soc., 3rd Ser. 3, 1922), pp. 62; 70; 94: cf. 90. Ralph Ithell, a priest, arrived in England from France in 1585 and was thought to have had contact with the emigrants: Cal.S.P.Dom., Eliz., clxxviii, 72; it seems therefore likely that he was suspected of complicity in the Babington affair; in December, 1586, someone rated him fit to be hanged: Cal.S.P.Dom., Eliz., cxcv, 72; however, he survived, to spend many years as a prisoner at Wisbech before, apparently, becoming compliant: Hist. MSS. Commn., *Salisbury*, VIII, 382. Thomas Abington was a Worcester gentleman with a brother, Richard, who lived in Hertfordshire. Both, and especially Thomas, had earlier been suspected of harbouring priests: Cal.S.P.Dom., Eliz., cli, 10; moreover, from 10 August, 1586, both were away from home—a fact for which Thomas was called upon to account when they had been arrested, early in September, 1586: Cal.S.P.Dom., Eliz., cxciii, 15; it may thus reasonably be supposed that they also were Babington suspects; eventually, although Thomas was still in the Tower in 1588—Cal.S.P.Dom., Eliz., ccxv, 19—they both appear to have been set free: cf. Cal.S.P. Dom., Eliz., ccxxxii, 30 (28 May, 1590). Jerome Payne was servant to Thomas Salisbury, who was tried with Babington: Cal.S.P.Dom., Eliz., cxcii, 43; Pollen, *Queen Mary and the Babington Plot*, pp. 54; 57; 68; 76; 90; 1 St.Tr. (1809 ed.), at 1127: he was held at the Tower, and under interrogation, as late as 25 May, 1588: Cal.S.P.Dom., Eliz., ccx, 30; at the time of the plot, he had accompanied his master to London; doubtless, he came under suspicion of complicity. About the suspected offenses of the others whose names were scheduled to the warrant, I would not even conjecture. Sampson Loame (Loane), who was of Sevenoaks, Kent, appears to have been a Roman Catholic and at least an acquaintance of the redoubtable Gervais Pierpoint, who had been implicated in the Throgmorton Plot: Cal.S.P.Dom., Eliz., clxvii, 17, VII; below in the main text, Part II. Of the rest: Thomas Heath was considered to have committed treason in Staffordshire; in September, 1588, he was with one James Harrison returned there for trial: Cal.S.P.Dom., Eliz., ccxvi, 21; cf. 22. Anthony Tuchenor (Tretchener) was, like Payne, still under interrogation in May, 1588: Cal.S.P.Dom., Eliz., ccx, 30.
    27. Appendix, No. 42.
    28. Cf. Cal.S.P.Dom., Eliz., ccx, 30.
    29. Appendix, No. 43.

30. Ibid., No. 44.

31. Ibid., No. 45.

32. Ibid., No. 46(a).

33. Ibid., No. 46(b).

34. Ibid., No. 48.

35. Cf. A.P.C., 3 July, 1590.

36. Cf. Cal.S.P.Dom., Eliz., ccxxx, 57.

37. A.P.C., 22 and 23 February, 1590 (1589–90, pp. 371; 378).

38. Christopher Devlin, *Life of Robert Southwell* (London: Longmans, Green, 1956), p. 213.

39. Appendix, No. 49.

40. Ibid., No. 50.

41. Some ambiguity may lurk here: see further, Chapter 9(V).

42. Appendix, No. 51.

43. A.P.C., 20 July, 1591. Another associate, Nicholas Fuller, was sent to the Fleet, to be interrogated by Owen and Young. Earlier, orders had been given for the examination of all three men by two members of the Council with the assistance of the Lord Mayor: A.P.C., 16 July, 1591. On Bridewell, see below in the main text, Part II (VII); Chapter 9(VII).

44. See below in the main text, Chapter 9(III).

45. Appendix, No. 52.

46. Under examination in 1584 by Sir William Heydon, who was the Vice-Admiral of Norfolk, and by William Blenerhasset, Richard Lacey of Brockdish, Norfolk (Brian's brother) (Augustus Jessop, *One Generation of a Norfolk House,* 2nd ed. [London: 1879], p. 266) had deposed that Brian was in the service of Sir John Arundell, and that two men had said, if Heydon and John Stubbes could get hold of him, they would rack him *even until the nails should start from his fingers:* Cal.S.P.Dom., Eliz., clxix, 19. This strange tale is hardly evidence that Heydon had received or assumed authority to use torture in pursuit of Roman Catholic missionaries and their supporters in his county.

47. Appendix, No. 53.

48. It is possible that this Thomas Clinton was a man of that name who had been arrested in Ireland when seeking to ruin the former Deputy, John Perrot (cf. Cal.S.P.Ireland, Eliz., clxi,61).

49. Appendix, No. 54.

50. Ibid., No. 55.

51. A.P.C., 7 and 24 January, 1593; 7 February, 1593. A "Mr. Dr. Bagshawe" was among the Wisbech prisoners in 1598 and came under investigation as a result of the Squire affair: Hist. MSS. Commn., *Salisbury,* VIII, 382; below in the text, Part II (VI). I conjecture that he and the present Bagshawe were not identical, but they may of course have been kinsmen. Members of respectable Roman Catholic families acted as guides and aids to the Counter Reformation missionaries, assuming the role of servants when the missionaries' own disguises required it.

52. Appendix, No. 56.

53. Ibid., No. 57.

54. Ibid., No. 58(a).

55. Ibid., No. 58(b).

56. Ibid., No. 59.

57. Ibid., No. 60.

58. Cf. Cal.S.P.Dom., Eliz., cclxii, 91.

59. Appendix, No. 61. For the background, see Stat. 22 H.VIII, c.10; 1 and 2 Phil. and Mary, c.4; 5 Eliz. c.20. Under the last two enactments, if gypsies stayed within the realm for more than one month, they thereby committed felony without benefit of clergy. Thus five were hanged at Durham in 1592: John Sykes, *Local Records or Historical Register*, 2nd ed., by J. Fordyce (Newcastle upon Tyne: J. Fordyce, 1865), I, 81.

60. *Bradshaw* (1597), Poph. 122, 2 And. 66; cf. *Hardie* (1821) 1 St.Tr.(N.S.), at 624. Jardine, *Reading* p. 42.

61. Cf. Cal.S.P.Dom., Eliz., cclxi, 10; 13: the desperate hardship inflicted by enclosures on the peasantry in West Oxfordshire was reported to the Council as explaining the trouble; but punitive repression was the only response.

62. Appendix, No. 62.

63. Ibid., No. 63.

64. Ibid., No. 63, parentheses.

65. Ibid., No. 64.

66. Ibid., No. 65.

67. Ibid., No. 66.

68. Ibid., No. 67.

69. Cf. Cal.S.P.Dom., Eliz., cclxix, 20: 20 December, 1598.

70. Appendix, No. 68.

71. Ibid., No. 69.

72. *"Indiculus seu diarium rerum pro religione Catholica in Turri Londinensi gestarum ab anno Domini 1580 usque 1585* . . ." (Cf. a Latin letter from a priest in the Tower to Roman Catholics in another prison, catalogued Cal.S.P.Dom., Eliz., cxlix, 61.) The *Diary* is translated in C.D. Dodd's *Church History of England chiefly with regard to the Catholics* (originally pub., Brussels, 1737-42, and printed, W. Bowyer, London), Tierney's ed., III, 148. It is there attributed to Rishton.

73. *Doctissimi N. Sanderi De origine ac progressu schismatis Anglicani liber, editus et auctus per E. Rishtonum: Coloniae Agrippinae* (1585): printed by Bartolomeo Bonfadino, Rome, 1586. Bonfadino's work is splendid.

74. Appendix, Nos. 31; 35; 36.

75. Below in the main text, Chapter 9(V).

76. Cf. Appendix, No. 30: 24 December: terrorization of Harte, Bosgrave, and Pascall—mentioned by the Diary in the case of Harte and another prisoner, Orton; but no reference to Sherwin or to actual use of the rack.

77. Below in the main text.

78. Fiorelli, *La Tortura giudiziaria*, I, 205n., citing Bodin *[De la démonomanie des sorciers*, 1580:] *De magorum daemonomania, seu detestando lamiarum et magorum cum Satana commercio* (Frankfort: 1603), IV, 1; and O. Cavalcani, *De brachio regio* (Venice: 1608), III, 57.

79. *"Alexander Briantus presb. ex alio carcere, ubi siti fere enectus fuerat, in Turrim conjicitur, compedibusque grauissimis per duos dies oneratur. Tunc aciculi acutissimi sub vngues ei immisi fuerunt vt confiteretur quo in loco P. Personium vidisset, quod fateritamen constantissime recusauit."*

80. Quaere whether this entry ought to have been for 6 May, 1581: cf. Appendix, No. 31.

81. Below in the main text, Chapter 9(V).

82. *"Idem Briantus in Lacum conjicitur, indeque post octo dies retractus est ad Equuleum, quod passus est omnium graviss. hoc ipso die semel. & die postero bis . . ."*

83. *"Alexandro vero Brianto quod coronam sibi secreto vasisset . . . crucemque ligneam sibi composuisset . . . post condemnationem compedes ferreos ad biduum iniecerunt."* According to the Diary, for the same date, another prisoner was punished with manacles because he was too cheerful under sentence of death.

84. For the text of the *Declaration,* see below, Appendix, No. 81.

85. Cf. Cal.S.P.Ireland, Eliz., lxxxi, 18; Jardine, *Reading,* pp. 29–30.

86. Below in the main text, Chapter 9(V).

87. Cf. Cal.S.P.Ireland, Eliz., lxxxi, 3.

88. To be seen (1978) in the Beauchamp Tower. Mentioned by Jardine, *Reading,* p. 30. John Bayley, *History and Antiquities of the Tower of London* (London: T. Cadell, 1821), I, 134, also noticed it and another inscription (which I have not located) as follows: "By torture straunge my truth was tried yet of my libertie denied there for reson hath me perswaded that paysens must be ymbrasyd thogh hard torture chasyth me with smart yet paysens shall prevayl."

89. Cf. Cal.S.P.Mary Qu.Sc., xii, 61; Cal.S.P.Scot., Eliz., xxxi, 126.

90. Cf. Cal.S.P.Dom., Eliz., clxiii, 65; clxxi, 78. For an account of the plot, of its discovery, and of what ensued, see Read, *Mr. Secretary Walsingham,* especially II, pp. 374 et seq.

91. Cf. Cal.S.P.Span. Eliz., iii, No. 362 (p. 510); No. 364 (p. 512).

92. Cf. ibid., No. 363 (p. 510).

93. Cf. Cal.S.P. Dom., Eliz., clxxi, 86.

94. Cf. ibid., clxiii, 65.

95. The fact seems to have been kept secret by the Council: cf. F.V. to Charles Paget, 20 December, 1583 (Cal.S.P.Dom., Eliz., clxiv, 47).

96. Cf. Read, *Mr. Secretary Walsingham,* II, 385.

97. Below, Chapter 9(V).

98. He died when still a prisoner, in the Tower. The circumstances have remained mysterious.

99. Cf. Cal.S.P.Dom., Eliz., clxviii, 14.

100. Cf. ibid., clxix, 34.

101. Cf. ibid., clv, 27; clvii, 62; clxvii, 17: and N.B. ibid. cxlix, 61; clxviii, 21. A "Mr. Shelley"—probably, William Shelley—was at the time prisoner in the Marshalsea: cf. ibid., clv, 27.

102. For the narrative thus far, see Hollinshed, *Chronicles:* 1807–8 ed., IV, 510; and cf. Cal.S.P.Dom. Eliz., clxiii, 54; 55; Cal.S.P. Span., 1580–86, No. 364 (p. 512).

103. Cf. Burghley's *The Execution of Justice in England* (1583): Hollinshed, *Chronicles:* 1807–8 ed., IV, 523; Somers's *Tracts:* 1809 ed., I, 198.

104. Read, *Mr. Secretary Walsingham,* II, 321.

105. One such case, reported in the *Diary,* was that of John Hart in 1582–83; but cf. above, n. 4.

106. Entries for 4 and 5 March, 1584: James Fenn, Thomas Hemmerford, John Nutter.

107. *"Stephanus Rausamus presbyter in Litilesium compingitur, ubi mansit decem et octo mensibus ac diebus 13."*

108. See further, Chapter 9(V).

109. Appendix, No. 41.

110. An impressive outline, with citation, will be found in Read, *Mr. Secretary Walsingham*, Ch. XII. Useful material is accessible in 1 St.Tr. (1809 ed.), at 1127 et seq.; and Babington's own confessions are in Pollen, *Queen Mary and the Babington Plot*.

111. Cf. Cal.S.P.Mary Qu.Sc., xix, 68.

112. John Morris, "The Fall of Anthony Tyrell": *Troubles of our Catholic Forefathers* (London: Burns and Oates, 1872), II; Devlin, *Life of Robert Southwell*, p. 122.

113. Trans. Philip Caraman, sub tit. *William Weston, the Autobiography of an Elizabethan* (London: Longmans, Green, 1955), p. 104.

114. Cf. Pollen, *Queen Mary and the Babington Plot*, especially pp. 62; 70; 94.

115. 1 St.Tr. (1809 ed.), at 1129 et seq, cf. Cal.S.P.Mary Qu. Sc., xix, 39; 91.

116. Cf. Caraman, *William Weston*, pp. 73–74; 92.

117. Appendix, No. 64.

118. Philip Caraman, *John Gerard, the Autobiography of an Elizabethan* (London: Longmans, Green, 1951). An earlier translation is by John Morris: in *Condition of the Catholics under James I, Father Gerard's narrative of the Gunpowder Plot*, 2nd ed. (London: Longmans, Green, 1872): much of the relevant part of which is reproduced by Jessop, *One Generation*, pp. 144–47. Caraman says that the oldest complete Latin version he has found is an eighteenth-century manuscript at Stonyhurst, and that Morris's translation, although abridged, is "exact": which judgment has, however, to be considered with the fact that the differences between the two translations do not appear to be merely stylistic. Matthias Tanner, *Societas Jesu apostolorum imitatrix* (Prague: Charles-Ferdinand University Press, 1694), especially at p. 677, cites from a Latin account, ascribed to Gerard, of the latter's sufferings at the Tower. The passages cited present a version generally somewhat briefer than that offered by the English translations of the autobiography.

119. Cf. Cal.S.P.Dom., Eliz., cclxii, 123: 14 April, 1597.

120. Cf. Caraman, *John Gerard*, pp. 106 et seq.

121. B.L. Lansdowne MS. 72, f.113: published with modernized spelling by Strype, *Annals:* 1824 ed., IV, 185–86.

122. I apprehend that "To use . . . common prisons" completes the preceding sentence, and that "Eather to stande . . ." begins a new one. Trenchmore was a lively dance.

123. Devlin, *Life of Robert Southwell*, pp. 286–87.

124. MS. "*A Brefe Discourse of the Condemnation and Execution of Mr. Robert Southwell*": Devlin, *Life of Robert Southwell*, p. 310.

125. Cf. Cal.S.P.Dom., Eliz., ccxlviii, 68, 11.

126. Cf. ibid., ccxliii, 93.

127. Cf. ibid., cclxvii, 97.

128. Cf. ibid., ccxlviii, 24. For accounts of the treason alleged against Lopez, cf. ibid., 7 (Wade); 16. Between the cases of Fawkes and Lopez, another had intervened in which it is said that torture was actually used: the statement being, when regard is had to the circumstances, plausible enough, although I have not yet located the evidence on which it is based. The alleged victim was Henry Barrow the Puritan Separatist. In the late 1580s he appears to have been committed to the Gatehouse by High Commission for

refusing to take the ex officio oath, to have spent some six months there, and then to have been moved to the Fleet. While there he was, by order of the Council, examined to discover the author of some writings against royal domination of the Church in matters spiritual and to have acknowledged at least the egalitarian sentiments those writings contained. (For Barrow's own, incomplete, account, from Harleian MSS. 6848, f.28v., see Leland H. Carlson, *The Writings of Henry Barrow, 1587-1590* [London: Sir Halley Stewart Trust, per George Allen and Unwin, 1962], pp. 171-72.) His examinations, around the same time, by High Commission on questions of doctrine may probably here be ignored. Subsequently, on 11 March, 1593, he was examined by Popham LCJ and E. Anderson—no doubt, in pursuance of Conciliar instructions—and whilst admitting his own and John Greenwood's respective responsibility for certain writings, expressed his inability to name their printers. This examination doubtless had in view prosecution, which ensued, of the two men for publishing seditious matter with malicious intent against the Queen, contrary to Stat. 23 Eliz., c.2, s.4. They and others were brought to trial at Common Law under that section on 21 March, 1593, and they were condemned to death. They were subjected to one abortive execution (so the Government may well have thought at this late stage that Barrow might be frightened into conformity), but a little later were hanged indeed. (Stowe, *Annals*, Reg. Eliz., 35; G.B. Harrison, *The Elizabethan Journals* (London: George Routledge, 1938), I, 219; 220; 222). According to L.A. Knafla, *Law and Politics in Jacobean England, The Tracts of Lord Chancellor Ellesmere* (Cambridge: Cambridge University Press, 1977), p. 63, Barrow was racked, Egerton (then Attorney-General) justifying the procedure by citing the *Declaration of the favourable dealing* . . . (Appendix, No. 81). Such citation, if it occurred, was shrewd enough, whether the tract concerned was attributed in Government circles to Burghley or to Thomas Norton; in a manner of speaking, it hoisted the Puritans with their own petard, for Burghley had appeared to favor toleration of them; Norton had himself been one of them. The probable purpose of torturing Barrow would have been to obtain from him, between 11 and 21 March, 1593, an identification of the printers of the books, responsibility for which brought him and Greenwood to trial and subsequent execution. Earlier, the *Protestatyon of Martin Marprelat* (Haseley: R. Waldegrave, September, 1589; Leeds: Scolar Press, 1967, sub tit. *The Marprelate Tracts* [1588-1589]), p. 13, had complained that the Puritans' enemies found no answers to their arguments, except "whorish impudencie, halter, axe, bonds, scourging, and racking".

129. Caraman, *John Gerard*, pp. 57; 72.

130. Cf. Cal.S.P.Dom., Eliz., ccxlvii, 21.

131. Cf. ibid., ccxlvii, 17: 21 January, 1594.

132. Cf. ibid., ccxlvii, 21.

133. Downstairs in the Salt Tower: Caraman, *John Gerard*, p. 105.

134. Ibid., p. 105.

135. Jessop, *One Generation*, pp. 255–56.

136. Caraman, *John Gerard*, pp. 108–9; and Chapter 9(III).

137. Cf. what is alleged regarding the examination of Owen, following the Gunpowder Plot: below, Chapter 7; Jardine, *A Narrative of the Gunpowder Plot* (London: John Murray, 1857), p. 200.

138. Cf. Chapter 9(II).

139. It emerges from comment in the Gerard autobiography (Caraman, *John Gerard*, p. 105) and a remark ascribed to another Jesuit, Holtby (Jessop, *One Generation*, p. 253),

that by the time of his return to York for trial and execution, Walpole's handwriting had vastly deteriorated. Apparently, Gerard thought that he had lost the use of his fingers; Holtby, that the trouble was in his thumbs. The former explanation was consistent with his having been put to the manacles; the latter explanation, was hardly so. Cf. Caraman, *John Gerard*, pp. 114–15; and Chapter 9(II) and (III).

140. Cf. Cal.S.P.Dom., Eliz., ccxlix, 13.

141. Cf. ibid., ccxlix, 44; 45.

142. Cf. ibid., cclxviii, 113 (Mundy's deposition).

143. Cf. Hugh Ross Williamson, *The Gunpowder Plot* (London: Faber and Faber, 1951), pp. 44; 45. He says of the present "plot": "today there is no historian who would take it seriously." I am glad *(quia egomet nescio)* that for present purposes we are not concerned with Squire's actual conduct or intentions, before his arrest.

144. Cf. Cal.S.P.Dom., Eliz., cclxviii, 111; 115.

145. Cf. ibid., cclxviii, 113 (Roll's deposition).

146. Cf. ibid., cclxviii, 111.

147. Cf. ibid., cclxvii, 5.

148. Cf. ibid., cclxviii, 111.

149. Cf. ibid., cclxviii, 111.

150. Cf. ibid., cclxviii, 115.

151. Hist. MSS. Commn., *Salisbury*, VIII, 382.

152. Hist. MSS. Commn., *Salisbury*, VIII, 382.

153. Cf. Cal.S.P.Dom., Eliz., cclxviii, 83; 84; 85. Important passages are reproduced by Williamson, *The Gunpowder Plot*, pp. 44; 45.

154. Cf. Cal.S.P.Dom., Eliz., cclxviii, 89.

155. Cf. ibid., 91.

156. Cf. ibid., 113 (Mundy's deposition).

157. It would have been some sort of safeguard, to send an innocent man with an intended assassin; it is not clear what service Rolls could have rendered, given that the plan was as Squire without torture had described it to Wade.

158. Cf. Cal.S.P.Dom., Eliz., cclxviii, 115.

159. Is it possible that the Stanley here concerned and William Mundy were the same?

160. Cf. below in the text (VII).

161. Cf. Cal.S.P.Dom., Eliz., cclxviii, 111.

162. Cf. Williamson, *The Gunpowder Plot*, pp. 44; 45.

163. This pattern will easily be seen to emerge from the content of the Appendix: the only extant Conciliar records for torture at the Tower in the 1590s being those entered there as Nos. 63 and 64. As noticed above in the text (VI), Roman Catholic information indicates that other cases occurred; they possibly rested on direct regal warrants. At Bridewell torture of course may—under whatever authority—have begun before the earliest relevant extant Conciliar record. Cf. Robert Southwell to Aquaviva, 21 August, 1588: Catholic Rec. Soc., V. There seems nothing substantial regarding provincial torture, except by the Council in the Marches: Chapter 4, Part II(V): and in the anomalous cases of the Drewry houseboy (Appendix, No. 29) and the Chester maiden (Appendix, No. 32). Cf. above, n. 46.

164. Hollinshed's *Chronicles:* 1807–8 ed., IV, 512; Somers's *Tracts:* 1809 ed., I, 209–12; below, Appendix, No. 81.

165. Above, n. 5.

166. Caraman, *John Gerard,* p. 112.

167. Ibid., p. 112: "Master"; Morris's version: "Superintendent".

168. Cf., on the Skevingtons, Chapter 9(V). The translators of the autobiography refer to the man concerned as in charge of the "artillery", but it is reasonable to assume that Gerard himself, using English, would have said in this connection, "ordnance".

169. Appendix, No. 63.

170. Ibid., parentheses.

171. Ibid., Nos. 30; 36; 41; 58; 61; 62; 64; and 67.

172. Ibid., No. 53.

173. Ibid., No. 48.

174. Ibid., nos. 61; 62; 65; and 66.

175. Ibid., Nos. 37; 41; 44; 45; and 51.

176. Ibid., Nos. 62; 63; 64; and 67.

177. Ibid., No. 67. N.B. that the warrant was further addressed not only to Wade, but to the Solicitor-General and Francis Bacon.

178. Appendix, Nos. 50 and 52.

179. Ibid., Nos. 31; 34; 35; 36; and 37.

180. Cf. Cal.S.P.Ireland, Eliz., lxxxi, 18; above, n. 5.

181. Hammond appears to have devilled for Burghley on the excommunication question in the preparation of the tract on the *Execution of Justice in England:* B.L. Add. MSS., 48063, f.6; Read, *Lord Burghley,* p. 566.

182. Cf. Cal.S.P.Dom., Eliz., clii, 72; below in the text (VIII).

183. Cf. Cal.S.P.Dom., Eliz., clxiii, 65.

184. Cf. Appendix, No. 48.

185. Cf. (for example) ibid., No. 49; Cal.S.P.Dom., Eliz., ccxlviii, 14, 1 St.Tr. (1809 ed.), at 1257; Caraman, *John Gerard,* p. 68. Caraman (p. 233n.) suggests that another man, an Essex justice, had the same name: *sed quaere.*

186. Appendix, Nos. 38; 39; 42; 43; 44; 45; 46; 47; 48; 49; 51; 52; 53; 54; and 55.

187. Ibid., Nos. 38; 39; 47; and 49.

188. Cf. Cal.S.P.Dom., Eliz., ccxxx, 57.

189. Appendix, No. 53.

190. Catholic Rec. Soc., V; Devlin, *Life of Robert Southwell,* p. 211.

191. Caraman, *John Gerard,* p. 68.

192. Ibid., p. 68.

193. On Topcliffe, cf. Jessop, *One Generation,* p. 70; and in *Notes and Queries* (5th Ser.), VII, pp. 270–71; Devlin, Life of Robert Southwell, pp. 210–11; and in *The Month,* March, 1951, pp. 151 et seq.

194. Appendix, Nos. 44; 45; 58; 59; 63; 64; 67; and 69.

195. Ibid., Nos. 36 and 59; and cf. Cal.S.P.Dom., Eliz., clxiii, 65 (Francis Throgmorton).

196. Appendix, Nos. 34; 35; and 50.

197. Ibid., No. 57.

198. Although it appears that in addition, Wilkes and Beale had some expertise in the pursuit of interrogatories: cf. Cal.S.P.Dom., Eliz., ccxlviii, 68; Young to Puckering, 14 April, 1594.

199. Cf. Cal.S.P.Dom., Eliz., cclxxxiv, 32(2): John Penkerville to Robert Cecil, 14 June, 1602.

200. Cf. Appendix, No. 69.

201. Ibid.

202. Wade is the subject of a solid article in the *Dictionary of National Biography*. Under James I, his zeal won him appointment to the Lieutenancy of the Tower, although his conscientiousness in due course cost him loss of that office; he was in occupation of it when he participated in examinations following the Gunpowder Plot (below, Chapter 7).

203. Appendix, No. 66.

204. Ibid., Nos. 29; 38; 39; 47; 49; 60; and 65.

205. Ibid., No. 65.

206. Above, in the main text, and n. 16.

207. He had lodgings in the Guildhall, as City Remembrancer (above in the main text [VII]): an office which he was the first to hold, as was called to my attention, following an inquiry I made in 1964, by the Guildhall Librarian, Mr. A. H. Hall.

208. Cf. Cal.S.P.Dom., Eliz., clii, 72.

209. Above, n. 161.

210. Cf. Read, *Lord Burghley*, pp. 251; 566.

211. 1 St.Tr., at 1258; cf. Shakespeare, *Merchant of Venice*, iii.2: "I fear you speak upon the rack, where men enforced do speak anything."

212. Cf. Cal.S.P.Dom., Eliz., ccxlvii, 97, ccxlviii, 24.

213. Cf. ibid., ccxliii, 93; above in the text (V).

214. Appendix, Nos. 38; 39; 47; and 66.

215. Ibid., No. 49: and, on 1 December, 1597 (Appendix, No. 65), the aim may have been only the recovery of the royal plate.

216. Above in the main text, Part I; Appendix, Nos. 38; 39; 40.

217. Appendix, Nos. 7(a); 17; and 22.

218. Ibid., No. 17.

219. Ibid., Nos. 31; 38; 42; 43; 54; 64; 69; and cf. Nos. 33 and 34.

220. Ibid., No. 38.

221. Cf. C.G. Bayne, *Select Cases in the Council of Henry VII*, ed. W.H. Dunham (Selden Soc., LXXV: 1958), pp. xcvi–xcvii.

222. Appendix, Nos. 30 (Common-Law Officers among addressees); 31 (Briant warrant); 41 (Common-Law Officers among addressees); 45 (Common Lawyer among addressees); 52 (Topcliffe, seemingly, to frame the articles); 59; 67 (Solicitor-General and other Common Lawyers among addressees). Cf. Appendix, Nos. 60; 62; 64; 66; 69.

223. Appendix, Nos. 34 (Campion warrant); 37 (Common Lawyer among addressees); 53 (immediate addressees, the Common-Law Officers); 63 (Common-Law Officers and another Common Lawyer, among the addressees); 44 (Common Lawyer among addressees). Cf. earlier, Appendix No. 9(a).

224. Strype, *Whitgift*, I, 401–02.

225. Above, Chapter 4, Part II (IV).

226. The report is in the *Brefe Discourse:* above, n. 121.

227. 1 St.Tr., at 1338.

228. Langbein, *Torture and the Law of Proof*, p. 129, points out that there is no sign of lawyers' having at the time consciously identified power to torture as part of the Prerogative.

229. Some influence broadly adverse to torture may also have been exercised by records

of efforts made by medieval parliaments to curb use of duress by sheriffs and jailors to make prisoners *approve* other persons: cf. Devlin, *Life of Robert Southwell*, p. 212, referring to William Harrison's *Description of England*. Harrison was a collaborator with Raphael Holinshed in the *Chronicles* that ordinarily are attributed to the latter. For his *Description of England*, see those *Chronicles:* 1807-8 ed., I, 221-421.)

230. Appendix, No. 35.

231. Ibid., No. 47.

232. Ibid., No. 66.

233. Above, Chapter 3(II).

234. Appendix, Nos. 8 and 9(a).

235. Ibid., No. 21(a).

236. Use of *présomptions*—"presumptions"—in this context by French jurists is illustrated in Muyart de Vouglans's *Les Lois criminelles*, p. 737. See further Esmein, *History*, pp. 261; 264; 266; 267-70. "Vehement", "vehemently", were favorite terms, again in this context, of Simancas: see his *De Catholicis institutionibus liber* (Rome: 1575), Tit. LXV, pp. 8; 15; 22; 34.

237. Points suggestive of Conciliar contact with Continental praxis emerge in other connections also. The Star Chamber procedure *ore tenus* (Coke, 4 Inst. 63–64; William Lambard, *Archeion or a Commentary upon the High Courts of Justice in England:* completed 1591, pub. 1635: pp. 211–13) may suggest Civilian-Canonical assimilation of judicially confessed crime to notorious crime (above, Chapter 2, n. 11); however, Star Chamber doctrine did not recognize notoriousness-in-fact as an independent basis for procedure *de plano*. According to Lambard, one of the circumstances that would justify it was that the accused had been taken red-handed—in which case, of course, there might sometimes have seemed enough moreover to constitute notoriousness—and confession of the "body and substance of the crime" was here to be made "upon examination, freely and without torture." The Star Chamber practice, developed during the sixteenth century, of examining the defendant and doing so upon his oath (Bayne, *Select Cases in the Council of Henry VII*, pp. xciv–xcvi), in any case itself deserves to be recalled concerning such contact.

238. Cf., for example, Bartolus, *Digestum novum commentaria*, ad D.XLVIII.xviii.22; Damhouder, *Praxis rerum criminalium*, c.xxxvi, p. 97.

239. *"Citra membri deminutionem:"* Bull *Ad extirpanda* (1252), s.25. Cf. above in the main text, Chapter 2(I).

240. D.XXIX.v.1[33]. Cf. De Marsiliis, *Practica causarum criminalium* (Lyons: 1542 ed.), ff.lxvii; cxlvi.

241. Private whipping was prescribed by the warrant, recorded for 22 June, 1581, in respect of the Chester maiden. The record there, however, does not hint of doctrinal influence; also, one must bear in mind the identity of the addressee: it may have been felt that quasi-parental chastisement was the most that could be asked of a diocesan within his diocese.

242. Cf. Cal.S.P.Dom., Eliz., cclxxi, 86.

243. At pp. 339 et seq.

244. Pierino Belli, *De re militari et bello tractatus* (Venice: Franciscus de Portonariis, 1563; *Classics of International Law* Ser. [Oxford: Clarendon Press, 1936] I), VII.iii.31 and 34, confines it to treason and desertion: which, insofar as it does not discriminate between kinds of the latter offense, is blunter than the doctrine set out under the Digest

title *De re militari:* D.XLIX.xvi.5[pr.]; 7; cf. C.IX.viii.4.

245. Appendix, Nos. 31; 41; 42; 43; 44; 45; 50; 52; 58(a); 63; 64; and 68.

246. Ibid., Nos. 59; 67; and cf. No. 64: Gerard "by her Majesty's commandment . . . committed to the Tower . . ."

247. Ibid., Nos. 44; 50; 52; 57; 63; 69: and cf. No. 46: "their Lordships' pleasure." The draft of 1590 concerning Christopher Bayles and others was described as containing the matter of a "warrant": cf. Cal.S.P.Dom., Eliz., ccxxx, 57.

248. Cf. Appendix, Nos. 52; 53; 54; 55; and 59; Cal.S.P.Dom., Eliz., ccxxx, 57.

249. Appendix, No. 26(b).

250. Ibid., No. 40.

251. N.B. that in terms the communication by the Council recorded for 17 November, 1577 (Appendix, No. 26[b]) had merely "required" Sherwood, if uncooperative, to be put in the "dungeon among the rats".

252. Appendix, No. 62.

253. Above in the main text, Part II (VII).

254. Above in the main text, Part II (V).

255. Cf. Southwell to Aquaviva, January, 1590, and Verstegan to Parsons, 3 August, 1592, Catholic Rec. Soc., V. In the former, Southwell said that Topcliffe and Young had "complete license to torture" at Bridewell; but, similarly, in the latter, Verstegan said that Topcliffe had "authority to torture priests in his own house, in such sort as he [should] think good": this seems out of harmony with Topcliffe's letter to the Queen about Southwell, above in the main text, Part II (V).

256. Appendix, No. 81.

257. Southwell may seem to have failed, in the *Humble Supplication* (ed. Bald, p. 33), to meet the awkward pro-Government argument that torture, of which the Jesuits complained, was much used by the Inquisition and by Roman Catholic secular tribunals. "Contrary," he there wrote, "to the course of all Christian lawes, we are by the extreamest tortures forced to reveal our very thoughts." Of course, old Canonical authority existed against enforced confession and asserted that God alone was the proper judge of what men chose to keep in their hearts. (Cf. above, Chapter 1, nn. 11; 81.) However, what the Roman Catholic Church held to be heresy was, in some circumstances, punished by the secular arm; the Inquisition extorted confessions of heretical belief. Perhaps, Southwell felt it morally acceptable, when addressing Queen Elizabeth I, to leave unexpressed a qualification in that behalf. Cf. further below, n. 259.

258. Cf. Simancas, *De Catholicis institutionibus,* Tit. LXV, s.8: Ludovic Vives, in condemning torture, "took sides against the laws and customs of nearly all nations." Popham, as Solicitor-General and, subsequently, as Attorney-General, had been among the addressees of several warrants for terrorization or for torture: cf. Appendix: Nos. 30; 36; 41; 53.

259. However the Lord Chief Justice felt about it, the only response that, according to the *Brefe Discourse* (above, n. 124), Southwell produced was that torture was used in his case with unreasonable severity. In the passage cited above, n. 257, is then the key to the intended argument provided by the word *extreamest?* Cf. Cicero, *Pro A. Cluentio Avito,* LXIII, for a suggestion that torture (of slaves) aids the discovery of truth as long as it is not taken to extremes; and D.XLVIII.xviii.10[3] for advice to the judge to be sensibly moderate in the matter.

260. During the sixteenth century, torture doubtless occurred in Continental countries,

sometimes with a simply executive, not judicial, context. (Cf., for example, Cal.S.P.Venet. [*Calendar of State Papers Venetian*], VI[II], Nos. 793; 797). If so, however, such occurrence probably was not—as must, broadly, have been its judicial use—a matter of common knowledge.

CHAPTER 7

1. Cf. Cal.S.P.Dom., 1603–10, p. 4 (30); Jardine, *Reading,* pp. 103–4.
2. Cf. ibid. (41); Jardine, *Reading,* pp. 104–5.
3. Cf. Cal.S.P.Dom., 1603–10, p. 4 (31).
4. Cf. ibid. (42). Compare Bacon's catalog of modes in which a subject might constructively compass the King's death: 2 St.Tr., at 874.
5. See further in the main text, Part II (II).
6. Appendix, No. 78: 6 November, 1605. Cf. Wade to Salisbury, 7 November: Hist. MSS. Commn., *Salisbury,* XVII, 479: Fawkes "concluded that he knew not what torture might do, but otherwise he was resolved to keep his vow." The letter comes close to declaring the intention to implement the royal torture instruction. Cf., also, Cal.S.P.Dom., 1603–10, p. 247.
7. *History of England from the Accession of James I to the Outbreak of the Civil War, 1603–1642* (London: Longmans Green, 1899–1901), I, 266.
8. Thomas Birch (1705–66), *The Court and Times of James I,* ed. R. F. Williams (London: Henry Colburn, 1848), I, 53.
9. At p. 32.
10. An account published, anonymously, at some time before 26 March, 1606.
11. Cf. Wade to Salisbury, above n. 6.
12. *Pace,* for example, Mrs. M. A. Everett Green, in Cal.S.P.Dom., 1603–10, p. 247.
13. Appendix, No. 70.
14. P.R.O. (S.P.14) 80, item 10; cf. Cal.S.P.Dom., 1611–18 (p. 270).
15. James Spedding, Bacon's *Letters and Life* (London: Longman, Green and Roberts, 1861–62), V, 93–94. 2 St.Tr., at 869–871.
16. 2 St.Tr., at 871–75. (In 3 Inst. 29; 30, he denies the propriety of the Crown's consulting the judges, even as a body, in the anticipation of trial and when the prospective accused is absent.)
17. Cf. the cases of Algernon Sidney (1638), 9 St.Tr., at 818, and of Lord Preston (1691), 12 St.Tr., at 646.
18. Appendix, No. 71.
19. Spedding, *Letters and Life,* V, 93–94; 2 St.Tr., at 869–70.
20. Cal.S.P.Dom., 1619–23, pp. 125–26: 25 February, 1620.
21. A.P.C.: for warrant, see Appendix, No. 72.
22. Cal.S.P.Dom., 1619–23, p. 336.
23. We have to speculate concerning the gravamen of the charge against this man.
24. Appendix, No. 73.
25. Ibid., No. 74.
26. Ibid., No. 79.
27. Rossingham's *Newsletter:* B.L. Add. MSS., No. 1467, f.115b.

28. Although witnesses must have been available to what might easily have been held a sufficient overt act of high treason to sustain the indictment of Fawkes, when the latter was arraigned it was along with others—Robert Winter, Thomas Winter, Grant, Rockwood, Keyes, and Bates—and against all of them the prosecution relied upon their confessions, which, obligingly and without demur, they ratified at the bar. Had they instead asserted their innocence (alleging, for example, that they had confessed only under torture or threat of torture, and had sought to conform to what the authorities required of them), it would, of course, have been a nuisance to the prosecution. The explanation of their submissiveness may have been simply that they were compelled to it by conscience, all which they had said being true; or it may have been that they were broken by their treatment since arrest; or they may have been told, or have calculated, that if they were compliant, they would have a better chance of some leniency in execution of the dreadful sentence to be passed upon them. Cf. Peacham's case where, as the time for trial approached, Bacon told the King that the accused probably intended to deny even such admissions as previously he had made: 2 St.Tr., at 876.

29. Appendix, No. 78.

30. *Antilogia adversus Apologium . . . pro Henrico Garneto Jesuita proditore* (London: *ex officina* Thomas Adams, 1613), p. 6b. Abbot, brother to the Archbishop Abbot of Canterbury, was Regius Professor of Theology at Oxford, Bishop of Salisbury, and then Bishop of Lichfield and Coventry. I was most helpfully allowed to use the copy of his book belonging to the Chapter Library at Durham Cathedral.

31. John Gerard (the later), *What was the Gunpowder Plot?* 2nd ed. (London: Osgood, McIlvaine, 1897), p. 167, citing B.L. Add. MSS., No. 6178, f.84.

32. Where his discussion of this matter will be found at pp. 114–14b.

33. *"Colligatis manuum pollicibus pro quaestione porro facienda paululum ad furcam appensus est"*.

34. *"Veritus ne ad fidiculas et equuleum traheretur."* The *fidiculae* seem from the *Corpus Iuris* to have been one of the prime means of torture in the later Roman Empire. Cf., for example, C.IX.viii.4: Gratian, C.VI, qu.1, c.23. They were presumably ligatures of some kind. The nature of the Roman *equuleus* (cf. Italian, *cavaletto,* Spanish, *cabalette,* French, *chevalet*) has been discussed since the sixteenth century: cf. A. Gallonio, *Trattato degli istrumenti e delle varie maniere di martirizare* (Rome: G. de Guerra, 1591), a translation of which has been made by A. R. Allinson: *Tortures and Torments of the Christian Martyrs* (Paris: Fortune Press, 1930). The sources are numerous and cannot be cited here in full. I believe that, at any rate in the later Empire, this instrument was a kind of rack, with a vertical or near-vertical beam, on which examinates were hoisted into the air and might be stretched and tormented by additional means: references to *suspensiones* concern not hangings by the neck, but use of the *equuleus*. Cf., for example, C.IX,xviii.7; XII.xlix.1; N.Val.I.iii,2; N.Maj.II.i.2; Valerius Maximus, *Factorum et dictorum memorabilium libri,* III.iii.5; Ammianus Marcellinus, *Rerum gestarum libri,* XV.vii.4–5; XXIX.i.23; Eusebius, *Ecclesiastical History,* VIII.x.5; Augustine, *Epistulae,* CXXXIII.2; Jerome, *Epistulae,* I.3. Abbot probably understood by *fidiculae* the strings attaching the examinate to the mechanism of a rack: Cf. F.G.A. Wasserschleben, *De quaestionum per tormenta apud Romanos historia commentatio* (Berlin: 1836), p. 27; he doubtless, like Rishton's Diary, meant by *equuleus* a contemporary English style of rack: cf. Gallonio, *Trattato,* p. 168.

35. *Furca* (above, n. 33) means primarily any two-pronged fork; thus, inter alia, it

may describe a forked wooden upright. Abbot's mention of *fidiculae et equuleus* may, however, indicate some acquaintance with the *Corpus Iuris*, where (D.XLVIII.xix.28[pr.]; 38[1]) the word designates a means of execution: presumably a cross or a fork serving like a cross; thus it is possible he meant that Owen was suspended from a gibbet.

36. 2 St.Tr., at 220–21.

37. Ibid., at 246–47.

38. *"Quia . . . neque . . . Rex in hac causa praeter exemplum clementissimus quicquam ab illo per tormentum extorqueri voluit, verum est rem arte tractatam esse."* Of course, the King's refusal to allow torture may be an invention to help excuse the *tractatio arte.*

39. C.A.J. Skeel, *The Council in the Marches of Wales: A Study in Local Government during the 16th and 17th Centuries* (London: Hughes Rees, 1904), p. 140, citing Bridgewater MSS., Welsh Council Papers, pp. 2; 3.

40. A.P.C. 1628 July-1629 April, No. 1104.

41. C. M. Clode, *The Administration of Justice under Military and Martial Law* (London: J. Murray, 1872), p. 30. Reliance upon Continental models in matters of military discipline is shown by the provision, in the Articles of War of 1629, for punishment of drunkenness on guard by the strappado and for the erection of such an instrument—as well as of a gibbet, which of course it would resemble—in every market: Clode, *Administration of Justice*, p. 74. On the continent, the strappado was much used as a means of torture, but in some places was employed for purposes of corporal punishment: Fiorelli, *La Tortura giudiziaria*, I, 194–97; 225–29; *illustrazione* II.

42. Above in the main text, Part I.

43. Appendix, No. 70.

44. Ibid., No. 72.

45. Ibid., No. 73.

46. Ibid., No. 79.

47. Pro: e.g., Rot. Parl. i, 71 (1292); iii, 65 (1379); Jean Bodin, *De la république* (abridged ed., 1756, p. 266); John Cowell's *Interpreter* (Cambridge: Printer John Legate, 1607), s.v. "King" and "Prerogative"; Charles Howard McIlwain, *Political Works of James I* (Cambridge, Mass.: Harvard University Press, 1918), p. 333; and cf. per Fleming CB, *Case of Impositions*, 2 St.Tr., at 371, 387. Con.: e.g., Bracton, *De legibus*, ff.5b; 34a; 107a; *Case of Prohibitions*, 12 Co. Rep. 63; *Case of Proclamations*, 12 Co. Rep. 74. Cf. (on the Elizabethan Puritans) Faith Thompson, *Magna Carta*, pp. 216–17; for a general review, and the position [pro] of Lord Ellesmere, see Knafla, *Law and Politics*, Chs. II and IX.

48. The Scots Privy Council adopted in the matter a position closer to Judicature than did the English. Cf. 6 St.Tr., at 1207 (*James Mitchell's Case*); 1228–32; and n. at 1217–23; 10 St.Tr., at 725 (*Spreull's and Ferguson's Case*); 751–72; and n. at 751–53. More generally, on the practical domination of the course of justice by the Scots Privy Council, where it was interested, and its inquisitorial methods, see Stair A. Gillon, in *Selected Justiciary Cases, 1624–50* (Stair Soc., XVI: 1953), I, 7–8; 242–43.

49. Spedding, *Letters and Life*, III, 114. Cf. Norton (Chapter 6, Part II[III]).

50. The only known cases in which he himself had been addressee of a torture warrant were political: cf. Appendix, Nos. 62; 63; 64; 67.

51. Above in the main text, Chapter 6, Part II (VIII); Appendix, No. 81.

52. 2 St.Tr., at 769, 773.

53. Cf. *The Gunpowder Case,* 2 St.Tr., at 159, 184.

54. Cf. Cal.S.P.Ireland, 1625–32, p. 227.

55. Cf. above in the main text, Chapter 6, Part II (VIII), regarding Stat. 1 E.VI, c.12, s.22, and 5 and 6 E.VI, c.11, s.9.

56. Cf. Cal.S.P.Ireland, 1625–32 (pp. 238-39).

57. *Historical Collections of Private Passages of State, Weighty Matters in Law, Remarkable Proceedings in Five Parliaments* (London: D. Browne and others, 1721–2), I, 638–9; 3 St.Tr., at 371.

58. Cf. Cal.S.P.Dom., 1628–29, pp. 339–40.

59. Jardine, *Reading,* pp. 10–12; 59–62.

60. Cf. Cal.S.P.Dom., 1628–29, p. 321.

61. *Memorials of English Affairs from the Beginning of the Reign of Charles I to the Happy Restoration of King Charles II,* 1st ed., posthumous, compiled by William Penn (London: E. Curll, E. Sanger and J. Pemberton, 1709; ed. here used: Oxford: Oxford University Press, 1853), I, 32.

62. Gardiner, *History of England,* VI, 359; Holdsworth, *History of English Law,* V, 185–86n: although Langbein, *Torture and the Law of Proof,* p. 211, is confident that Rushworth distorted the event, and judges that Jardine "set the record straight in a brilliant bit of analysis."

63. The 1853 ed. inserts "not" in square brackets, after "it could".

64. Fiorelli, *La Tortura giudiziaria,* I, 299–305.

65. Appendix, Nos. 55 and 56; above in the main text, Chapter 6, Part II (VII). Cf. the Byzantine view that interrogatory torture to disclose fraud might itself serve as a punishment—C.Th.XI.ix.1—and the classification of torture for confession, under the French *Ordonnance* of 1670 (Tit. 23, a.13) as a punishment for a capital offense incompletely proved. Langbein, *Torture and the Law of Proof,* p. 48, reproving "the literature", explains that *Verdachtsstrafe,* punishment for suspicion, really represented an intrusion, into practice regarding grave offenses, of the use of convincing (as distinct from legal) proofs, which use had always prevailed in the summary punishment of minor offenses. This explanation, if not understood as limited geographically, heightens the interest of the fact that under the Ordonnance, French doctrine continued to base recourse to torture upon the thinking of the legal proofs system: Muyart de Vouglans, *Les Lois criminelles,* p. 797. The matter is indeed complicated, for one tendency of the latter system must have been to encourage precipitate moral conviction of the guilt of accused persons.

66. In the *Case of Prohibitions,* 12 Co. Rep. 63, and the *Case of Proclamations,* 12 Co. Rep. 74. For Lord Ellesmere's response to this kind of thing, see Knafla, *Law and Politics,* p. 131 and Ch. XV.

67. Coke died in 1634.

68. Appendix, No. 71.

69. The impression that what hints on the part of English lawyers in the early seventeenth century of Continental learning may be little more than a rhetorical flourish can arise also out of other passages; cf., for example, 2 St.Tr., at 185 (Coke A.-G.) and 219 (Croke Sjt.).

70. Cf. Fiorelli, *La Tortura giudiziaria,* I, 299–305.

71. Above in the main text, Part I.

72. CXLIII: Everyman (compendium of) *Table Talk,* ed. James C. Thornton (London: John Dent; New York: E. P. Dutton, 1934), p. 101. Selden was born in 1584 and died

in 1664. Milward, Selden's amanuensis, who compiled the *Table Talk,* was born in 1609 and died in 1680. The *Table Talk* was not published until after Milward's death. He claimed that it resulted from his listening to Selden's conversation over twenty years. The arrangement of the contents is not chronological in any way. Thus assuming that Selden did so refer to use of torture in England, we cannot at all precisely date the occasion, but the remark that Milward records could have been prompted by Archer's case.

CHAPTER 8

1. Above, Chapter 7, Part III.
2. P. 48.
3. Pp. 34–35.
4. This restriction was dropped in Stat. 28 E.III, c.3 (below, main text).
5. *"Nullus liber homo capiatur vel imprisonetur, aut disseisiatur aut utlagetur, aut exuletur, aut aliquo modo destruatur, nec super eum ibimus nec super eum mittimus, nisi per legale judicium parium vel per legem terrae."* In the discussion that follows in the main text, I have assumed—with Coke—that in the clause *lex terrae* did not extend to any law, although valid within the realm (cf. Coke, *Littleton,* f.11b), which later was distinguished from the Common Law. *Pace* Lord Ellenborough LCJ in *Burdett v. Abbot* (1811), 14 East, 10, at 136. Generally, see J. C. Holt, *Magna Carta* (Cambridge: Cambridge University Press, 1965), pp. 226-29.
6. Cf. D.XLVIII.xix.5[2]–8[3].
7. *De legibus,* f.104b–5a. Cf. ibid., ff.112b; 118b; Fleta, I.xvi; xxi.
8. It would hardly be possible to discover juridical authority for use of interrogatory torture in the *addicio* to Bracton, at f.151b (cf. Britton, I, Ch. 25, s.8) of a quotation of D.XLVIII.xix.3.
9. Cf. Coke, *Littleton,* f.115b.
10. Littleton, *Tenures,* s.170. The use of torture was not regarded by Coke later in the *Institutes* as a new operation of a recognized general head of prerogative: cf. the Case of the *King's Prerogative in Saltpetre,* 12 Coke Rep. 12a.
11. Cf. 19 St.Tr., at 1029, 1066: judgment represented as having been delivered by Lord Camden in *Entick v. Carrington* (1765).
12. 12 Coke Rep. 74: the Case of *Proclamations,* 1610: in his *Law, or a Discourse thereof,* first published (in French) three years later, H. Finch put the position rather mystically, saying that the prerogative "groweth wholly from the reason of the Common Law": 1627 (English) ed., p. 85.
13. Hobbes, *De cive* (1642), c.II, s.19, says that answers forced from a man in torture are not proofs of the fact alleged against him, but only aids to the discovery of the truth; and that, consequently, the examinate is entitled to answer either truthfully or falsely or, if he prefers, to remain silent. To me, it is not clear exactly what is the distinction taken in his expressed premise, or how he reaches his conclusion from it. (Cf. his assertion, *Leviathan,* Chs. XIV; XXVII; XXVIII, that the Social Contract cannot constrain a man to any act tending to his own destruction.)
14. According to Samuel R. Gardiner, *History of the Great Civil War* (London: Longmans, Green, 1901), I, 112, on or after 22 March, 1643, one Colonel Reade, an emissary

of the Irish royalists, was captured and racked by the anti-royalist authorities in Dublin. The Dublin situation was at that time one of apparently extreme military danger.

15. John Gaule, *Select Cases of Conscience touching Witches and Witchcraft* (London: Richard Clutterbuck, 1646), p. 6, says that the profession of witchfinder was "never taken up in England till this."

16. R. Trevor Davies, *Four Centuries of Witch Beliefs, with special reference to the Great Rebellion* (London: Methuen, 1947), p. 152; R. H. Robbins, *Encyclopedia of Witchcraft and Demonology* (London: Nevill, 1959: 1960), s.v. *"pricking"*.

17. Francis Hutchinson (Bishop of Down and Connor), *Historical Essay concerning Witchcraft, with observations tending to confute the vulgar errors on that point* (London: R. Knaplock and D. Midwinter, 1718), Ch. IV. Regarding Hopkins and his activities, see C. l'Estrange Ewen, *Witchcraft and Demonism* (London: Heath Cranton, 1933), pp. 257–301; A. Macfarlane, *Witchcraft in Tudor and Stuart England* (London: Routledge and Kegan Paul, 1970), Ch. 9.

18. Fiorelli, *La Tortura giudiziaria*, I, 204–5; Mellor, *La Torture*, pp. 267–69; Vidal-Naquet, *Torture: Cancer of Democracy*, p. 172 (the Wuillaume Report).

19. Hutchinson, *Historical Essay*, p. 63.

20. De Marsiliis, *Tractatus de quaestionibus* (Lyons: 1542), f.vi; Fiorelli, *La Tortura giudiziaria*, I, 200. This method was recommended for witchcraft cases by some Continental authorities: H. C. Lea, *Materials towards a History of Witchcraft* (Philadelphia: University of Pennsylvania Press, 1939), II, 900.

21. Cf. Hutchinson, *Historical Essay*, p. 64; Gaule, *Select Cases*, pp. 78 and 79; C. l'Estrange Ewen, *Witch-Hunting and Witch Trials, the indictments for witchcraft from 1373 Assizes* . . . (London: Kegan Paul, Trench, Trubner, 1929), App. VI: from B.L. Add. MSS., 27402.

22. London: R. Royston. Republished in *A Collection of Rare and Curious Tracts relating to Witchcraft* . . . *between the Years 1618 and 1664* (London: 1838; Norwich: H. W. Hunt, 1931, facsimile); A.J.-M.A.M. Summers, *The Discovery of Witches. A Study of Master Matthew Hopkins, commonly called Witch Finder General* (London: Cayme Press Pamphlet, 1928).

23. *Query* VIII, *Answer*.

24. Cf. Hutchinson, *Historical Essay*, p. 64.

25. Above, Chapter 7, Part III.

26. *Query* XI, *Answer*.

27. *Queries* VIII and IX, *Answers*. The effect of the methods concerned upon the minds of the watchers and walkers may sometimes have ended with the inducement of hallucinations. In the country hovels of the time, plenty of small creatures were probably available, which the credulous could identify as familiars.

28. Cal.S.P.Venet., XXX, No. 29.

29. Ibid., No. 365: *"per veder con tormenti di triargli dalla bocca le prattiche e le intelligenze del Re Carlo."*

30. Ibid., No. 401.

31. Cal.S.P.Venet., XXXI, No. 79: *"per via di tortura e di ogni altro tormento."* Under examination when he was a prisoner in the Gatehouse on the 6th of August, 1657, Gardiner sought to explain away suspicious circumstances of which there were witnesses against him: John Thurloe, *Collection of State Papers* (London: Mr. Fletcher Gyles's

executor and others, 1742), VI, 447; cf. ibid., 441–2. His answers on that occasion suggest that he was not under torture. Their character, however, was such as to invite his further interrogation.

32. Cal.S.P.Dom., 1657–58, pp. 51 (Interregnum, clvi, 6[2]), 549.

33. Cal.S.P.Venet., XXXI, No. 81.

34. Cal.S.P.Venet., XXXI, No. 182.

35. Below in the main text (IV).

36. Cf. Chapuys's dispatches, a little more than a century earlier, about the treatment of Octavian Bos: L.P.F.D., XIX, Part I, 550; 590; 603: above, Chapter 3 (II): although if anyone misled Chapuys in that matter, it was probably an officer of state, if not the King himself.

37. The article on "Torture" in the *Encyclopedia Britannia*, by J. Williams and G. W. Keeton, states that three Portuguese were tortured at Plymouth during the Commonwealth, and this statement is relied upon by Mellor (*La Torture*, p. 123). However, in 1962, Professor Keeton wrote to me that the statement looked to him "a little legendary" and pointed out that, since the article had been written nearly thirty-five years previously, any notes upon which it was founded had probably been destroyed. On the other hand, he mentioned a possibility that if torture indeed was used at Plymouth during the Commonwealth, the occasion had arisen out of sittings there of the Court of Admiralty. Therefore, I sought the help of Mr. W. Best Harrison, the Plymouth City Archivist, who wrote to tell me: (1) that in all his experience with Admiralty Court records from the seventeenth century, he had noticed no reference to torture; (2) that the only reference he could find to Portuguese during the Commonwealth was in a letter of 5 April, 1654, contained in the City archives (W.361), according to which "Dr. Walker . . . hath promised several Marchants that now hee will sett time apart to Dispatch the Portugall Business": a reference, of course, not necessarily to Portuguese after all. Pepys later, in his *Diary*, mentions: on 23 August, 1660, an Admiralty Judge, "Dr. Walker"; and on 13 April, 1663, two Civilians, "Dr. Walker" and "Dr. Wiseman": whom I suppose to have been Sir William Walker and Sir Robert Wiseman, still later concerned in a royal project of securing the torture of two Dutchmen (below in the main text [V]).

38. Cal.S.P.Dom., 1666–67, pp. 465–466.

39. Ibid., 1672–73, pp. 556–57.

40. Ibid., 1673, p. 439.

41. Ibid., 1672–73, pp. 556–57; 1673, p. 95.

42. Ibid., p. 483.

43. Ibid., p. 483.

44. Appendix, No. 80a.

45. *Diary,* 26 May, 1669: almost the last entry.

46. Cf. William Palmer to Lord Henry Fairfax, 28 October, 1678: the *Fairfax Correspondence, Civil War*, II, 296.

47. Cal.S.P.Dom., 1678, p. 593.

48. 7 St.Tr., at 1043.

49. 7 St.Tr., at 1183.

50. Cf. the Inquisitors' memorandum, of 16 June, 1310, in the matter of the Templars: above in the main text, Chapter 2 (III). See also below in the main text, Chapter 9 (VIII).

51. Appendix, No. 80a; above in the main text (IV).

52. Cal.S.P.Dom., 1672–73, pp. 556–57.

53. Now numbered 54a, in S.P.Dom., Case F (Cal.S.P.Dom., 1672–73, p. 605); Appendix, No. 80b.

54. Cal.S.P.Dom., 1673, p. 95.

55. Ibid., p. 6.

56. Ibid., p. 95.

57. Ibid., p. 144.

58. "Glanvill", *De legibus, Proem,* echoing *Constit. Imperatoriam maiestatem*; cf. Bracton, *De legibus,* f.1; Vernon Harcourt, *His Grace the Steward and Trial of Peers,* p. 327, and sources there cited; Fleta, I.xvi: *"per recordum regium . . ."; Rymer, Feodera,* XVII, 647; 751–52; *Petition of Right,* 1628; Coke, *Littleton,* f.249a-b; 3 Inst. 52; Matthew Hale, *History of the Common Law,* 6th ed. (London: Butterworth, 1820), Ch. II, p. 42.

59. C. M. Clode, *Military Forces of the Crown: Their Administration and Government* (London: Murray, 1869), I, 12; Maitland, *Constitutional History of England,* p. 327; Holdsworth, *History of English Law,* I, (5th ed.), p. 577; Cf. Sir William Coventry to Thynne, 7 July, 1673: *Longleat Papers,* Christie, II, 150.

60. Under James II, after the defeat of Monmouth, execution of military justice upon soldiers belonging to the royal army was forbidden, as having been lawful only during the rebellion: Clode, *Military Forces,* I, 477–78.

61. Cf. Gentilis, *De iure belli,,* II.ix; Grotius, *De iure belli et pacis,* III.iv.18. N.B., later, Vattel, *Le droit des gens ou principes de la loi naturelle:* 1758 ed., III, 155 (where the term is still not confined to those seeking *military* information).

62. Authority specifically regarding alien spies arrested in wartime outside the theatre of hostilities seems to start with Hale, *Historia placitorum Coronae,* pp. 93–94, according to which they could not be indicted at Common Law of treason; Hale cited Coke's report of Calvin's Case (containing assertions regarding the case of Perkin Warbeck: 7 Coke Rep. 1a, at 7a), and as a result, the implication probably was that they were liable instead to trial and punishment by the Constable and Marshal, upon special commission. N.B. that in 1940, when moving the second reading of the *Treachery Bill* in the House of Commons, the Home Secretary said he was advised that the Common Law doctrine of local allegiance, which in some circumstances allowed aliens to be convicted of treason, "could not reasonably be held to apply to aliens who had come to this country in a clandestine way for a hostile purpose, intending, whether by espionage or by committing acts of sabotage, to undermine our system of national defence:" 361 H.C.Deb. 5s, pp. 186–87: whether Zas and Arton, on arrival at Harwich, attempted to conceal their identities, we do not know. They landed openly.

63. 7 St.Tr. 1183, at 1204–5; cf. the *Declaration of the Favourable Dealing:* Appendix, s.3; Blackstone, *Commentaries,* IV, Ch. 25, p. 320.

64. Sir Walter Scott (Somers's *Tracts,* I, 209) said that a prisoner of state was racked in England under William III, but probably he was thinking of Neville Paine, racked in *Scotland* in 1690 (10 St.Tr., at 753–55n). After the Union, when the Westminster Parliament made interrogatory torture illegal in Scotland (7 Anne, c.21, s.5), the implication was clear, that its illegality in England was already established. Thus a big battle had been won with really very few shots fired. This state of affairs was reflected when, in 1804, proceedings being taken against a former (British) Governor of Trinidad for signing a torture warrant there under Spanish law that had been established before conquest of the territory by the British, Counsel for the prosecution observed: "I shall not cite

many authorities to prove that torture is in itself absolutely illegal and that it has ever been held so by the law of this country. Many authorities cannot be required to establish so clear a proposition:'' and contented himself with mention of Fortescue, *De laudibus,* of Coke's Second *Institute,* and of the first book of Blackstone's *Commentaries* (where no more is cited than the Second *Institute*): *Picton,* 30 St.Tr. 225, at 741.

CHAPTER 9

1. Above, Chapter 3 (I).
2. *La Tortura giudiziaria,* I, 205n.
3. 3,7,2.
4. *"Cum braconibus cum quibus labra malorum equorum distringuntur, quando ferrantur, positis lignis et strictis in labiis torquendorum."* Richard Davey, *The Tower of London* (London: Methuen, 1914), p. 118n., suggests that in English sixteenth-century sources, references to the "brake" concern a device for mouth torture; but the language of the Council record for 16 November, 1540 (Appendix, No. 1) indicates that the word *brake* then already meant, in the context of torture, a rack for stretching the whole body. Cf. Thomas More, *Third Book of Comfort against Tribulacion,* bd. with *Utopia* (New York: E.P. Dutton, Everyman ed., 1910), p. 327: "wrenched and wronged and braked in . . . paynfull wise"; and Coke, 3 Inst. 35: explicit, nearly a century later.
5. In context, *ligatis* is the doubtful word.
6. Above, Chapter 3 (II).
7. Act II.
8. Ad 3,7,2, gl. *Vitrum.*
9. *Taxilli.*
10. Fiorelli, *La Tortura giudiziaria,* I, 199n.
11. Above, Chapter 3 (II).
12. Fiorelli, *La Tortura giudiziaria,* I, 200, and sources there cited.
13. *Acts and Monuments:* 1st ed. (1563), p. 1651.
14. *Societas Jesu usque ad sanguinis et vitae profusionem militans* (Prague: Charles-Ferdinand University Press, 1675), p. 12.
15. *Theatrum crudelitatum haereticorum nostri temporis* (1588), p. 73. Cf. Gallonio, *Trattato,* p. 168.
16. This would provide the maximum force and seem the naturally intended mode. However, according to the account attributed to her by Bale (above, in the main text, Chapter 3 (II), Anne Askew was racked by Wriothesley and Riche: the suggestion is that they took over the whole labor. Also, an illustration opposite p. 246 in the crude and nasty *Generall Martyrologie* of S. Clarke (1656) represents the torment of a man, on a rack somewhat similar to that illustrated in Foxe, by only two operators: who use one lever each, where those in the Foxe illustration use two.
17. Cf. the story (above in the main text, Chapter 6, Part II [VI]) that torture of Henry Walpole left him affected specially in his thumbs. There is possible faint relevance in the following exchange, from Shakespeare, *Measure for Measure,* V, 1: (Escalus) "To the rack with him—We'll touze you joint by joint, But we will know this purpose—What! Unjust?" (Duke) "Be not so hot; the duke dare no more stretch this finger of mine than he dare rack his own. . . .''

18. An antique dealer claimed to have found the device concerned and one lever, apparently associated with it, in the course of excavations that he conducted to the rear of what used to be called Blagrove(s) House, in the Bank at Barnard Castle. When the castle there was under siege, in 1569, according to popular tradition an inn was situated somewhere within the present curtilage of Blagrove(s) House: if so, it may have been on the site of the present main building or behind, in the area the antique dealer excavated. Either way, the use of such an inn as rebel headquarters during the siege would not have been unlikely. The antique dealer sold the device and lever to a peer who later (I believe, after some discussion with the Tower Armouries) bestowed them upon the museum, where many years ago I found them lying in the open. (The curator explained to me that the rack was infested.) I judged the rack to be smaller and lighter than that illustrated in Foxe. The distance between the rollers was only about eight feet; they looked modern, but I thought the lever and the wood of the rack frame to be ancient. Moreover, the frame was so crudely constructed, out of odd pieces, that I thought it unlikely to be a fake or any old instrument (such as a linen-stretching rack) that need not have been put together in great haste.

19. Above in the main text, Chapter 6, Part II (I).

20. II, 1.

21. *Chronicles:* 1587 ed., II, 670; above in the main text, Chapter 3 (I).

22. 4 *Comm.,* Ch.XXI, p. 320.

23. Whatever it was seems no longer to be in the Tower. Jardine did not, in 1837, mention having seen it, although he did mention another object there (main text [V]). This recommends caution regarding the statement, in *Treasures of the Tower: Torture and Punishment* (H.M.S.O.: Department of the Environment: 1975), p. 6, that it "was doubtless destroyed when the Storehouse was burnt down in 1841."

24. I here assume that when Reed viewed the object concerned it was upside down.

25. Viscount Dillon, in an article on "The Rack": *Archaeological Journal* 62 (2nd Ser., XII: March, 1905): 48, at 51, having referred to Reed's note and illustration, wrote: "the centre roller would, of course, only require one man to rotate it."

26. Reed's illustration is perhaps somewhat undecided about this, but I presume in favor of the otherwise probable!

27. *Acts and Monuments:* 1st ed., p. 1651.

28. Above in the main text, Chapter 8 (IV); Appendix, No. 80. Cf. Cal.S.P.Dom., 1672–73, p. 483.

29. Treasures of the Tower, p. 6.

30. *"Eiusdem equulei cruciatu vehementissime exagitatus"*: cf. above in the main text, Chapter 6, Part II–(I); and Appendix, No. 35.

31. Caraman, *John Gerard,* p. 108. Below in the main text (VI).

32. Cf. a small reconstruction of the rack, long on show in the White Tower.

33. Caraman, *John Gerard,* Ch. XV.

34. According to the text that has been translated, of the autobiography, the removal of the steps left Gerard's toes on the ground, which was scraped away until they hung clear: no mention of this in Tanner, *Societas Jesu apostolorum imitatrix,* p. 677; nor did Tanner's account refer to the fixing-pin. On the other hand, it states that on the upright, the fixtures from which the rod hung consisted of hooks and rings.

35. Devlin, *Life of Robert Southwell,* p. 288.

36. Ibid., p. 213; cf. Southwell, *Humble Supplication,* p. 34.

37. Appendix, No. 49.

38. Cf. Cal.S.P.Dom., Eliz., cxxx, 57; above in the main text, Chapter 6, Part I.

39. Appendix, No. 47.

40. Dodd's *Church History*, III, 117n. The preface to Rishton's Diary lists—although no mention is made of them in the Diary itself—certain "hand-irons"—*ferae chirothecae*—as included among instruments of oppression used upon Roman Catholics at the Tower in the first half of the 1580s. It says that, by them, "the hands are enveloped, and very severely crushed." Possibly the description is mistaken, the instruments in view being the manacles: suspension in which affected the hands in a way that might have been supposed due to crushing (cf. Caraman, *John Gerard*, pp. 112; 114; 116–17). The manacles appear only later, in the recorded warrants, but torture by suspension at the wrists was not a novel idea among the English, for according to the account of personal sufferings attributed by Foxe (*Acts and Monuments*: 1684 ed., III. 758; above in the main text, Chapter 4, Part II (IV) to Thomas Green, Story in 1558 threatened to hang him up "by his hands with a rope." (Among the mysteries: cf. Palsgrave, *L'Esclaircissement de la langue françoyse* (c. 1530), cit. O.E.D.,—"I manakyll a suspecte person to make him confesse thynges";—"and he will not confesse it, manakyll him, for undoubted he is guilty.")

41. Hist. MSS. Commn., 12th Rpt., App., Pt. IV, pp. 334–36; Caraman, *William Weston*, pp. 242–44; below in the main text (VII).

42. It may seem a plausible conjecture that the "standing stocks" had planks that fitted in the horizontal plane around the ankles or shanks and, either by their construction or by being placed against a wall, excluded the adoption of a sitting posture.

43. Lansdown MS. 72, f.113. Above in the main text, Chapter 6, Part II (V).

44. Everyman ed. (with the *Utopia*), p. 321.

45. Cf. More, *Third Book against Tribulation*, pp. 320; 322; William Smith, *State of the Gaols in London, Westminster and the Borough of Southwark* (London: 1776), p. 40; John Howard, *State of the Prisons* (London: J.M. Dent; New York: E.P. Dutton, Everyman ed., 1929), pp. 5; 12; Pugh, *Imprisonment in Medieval England*, p. 177.

46. *Acts and Monuments*: 1684 ed., III, 758. Above in the main text, Chapter 4, Part II (IV).

47. "Coal"—"cole"—used at this date adjectively to describe a place may (as, with "Coalharbour") indicate that it was cold. The "Lollard's" Tower, "Lollards" Tower, was the southern of a pair of towers that stood, respectively, at the two west corners of Old St. Paul's. It originally may have been a bell-tower. We do not know when it was built or when it became a prison, although a plausible conjecture is that it entered upon the latter role after, in 1416, Archbishop Chichele ordered the Bishop of London regularly to conduct an inquisition after heretics and when he discovered any, to keep them imprisoned until the following convocation: Wilkins, *Concilia*, III, 378. The name "Lollards Tower" seems somehow to have been transmitted to a less ancient edifice, at the west end of the chapel at Lambeth Palace. This is supposed to have been built at the instance of Chichele around 1430, even so the transmission may have occurred only after the destruction of Old St. Paul's in the Great Fire. (See S.R. Maitland, *Essays on Subjects connected with the Reformation in England* [London: Francis and John Rivington, 1849], p. 24, "The Examination of Thomas Green"; H. P. Clunn, *The Face of London* [London: Simkin Marshall, 1932], p. 335.)

48. 1684 ed., III, 736.

49. Somers's *Tracts*: 1809 ed., I, 477; cf. 1 St. Tr., at 1087.

50. *Survey of London* (1603): L. Kingsford's ed. (Oxford: Clarendon Press, 1908), II, 19.

51. Edward Solly, in *Notes and Queries* (5th Ser., X), p. 474.

52. Cf. A. F. Pollard, *Tudor Tracts, 1532–1588* (London: Constable), pp. 401-8.

53. At pp. 76 and 77. Cf. Gallonio, *Trattato* (Latin ed., Antwerp, 1678), pp. 168–69.

54. Verstegan included, in his *Theatrum crudelitatum*, p. 77, an illustration evidently of an imaginative kind.

55. This extension appears in the much-reproduced (see, for example, *History of the King's Works*, ed. H. M. Colvin [H.M.S.O.: Min. of Public Buildings and Works], II, [1963], 145) 1742 engraving of the 1597 bird's-eye view of the Tower Liberties (William Hayward and J. Gascoyne), owned by the Society of Antiquaries. It does not show in the *London Panorama* of Anthony van den Wyngaerde, which was executed temp. Henry VIII (Ashmolean Museum: reproduced by Peter Hammond, *Royal Fortress* [H.M.S.O.: Dept. of the Environment, 1978], p. 29). From a view drawn for Lord Dartmouth, James II's Constable of the Tower (Hammond, *Royal Fortress*, p. 49), it seems during the seventeenth century to have been extended: probably onto the site of and to incorporate any part left standing of, the Wardrobe Tower: which in the 1597 view stands just to its East, although perhaps communicating with it. It may be seen, still standing, in a painting of the Tower by David Roberts R.A. (1796–1864). However, G. T. Clark, *Mediaeval Military Architecture in England* (London: Wyman and Sons, 1884), II, 219, reports that by the period of his investigations, it had been demolished; he adds that it was believed to have been built by Edward III.

56. Above the gateway: *History of the King's Works*, III (I) (1975), 274; V (1976), 380.

57. *History of the King's Works*, II, 729n.: "the round tower next the dungeon."

58. Of earlier forebuildings, that at Newcastle upon Tyne contained a chapel: W. H. Knowles, *Archaeologia Aeliana* (4th Ser.) 2 (1926); Parker Brewis, *Guide to the Royal Castle of Newcastle upon Tyne* (Newcastle upon Tyne: Society of Antiquaries of Newcastle upon Tyne, 1963), p. 9; Barbara Harbottle, *The Castle of Newcastle upon Tyne* (Newcastle upon Tyne: Society of Antiquaries of Newcastle upon Tyne, 1977), pp. 2 and 3. However, that at Castle Rising contained a pit, probably used as a prison, which was entered by a trap-door from the vestibule: Clark, *Mediaeval Military Architecture*, I, 373–74.

59. Appendix, No. 4. Above in the main text, Chapter 4, Part I.

60. *Dictionary of National Biography*, s.v. "*William Skeffington*".

61. Ibid.

62. L.P.F.D., VII, 1681.

63. Ibid., XX, I, g. 621, 10.

64. Ibid.

65. Ibid., XXI, I, 585; 2, 775, f.82; A.P.C., II, p. 74. Quaere, was he the Leicestershire gentleman occasionally employed by the Council, around 1580: A.P.C., XX, 290; Cal.S.P.Dom., Eliz., ccxxxiii, 30?

66. Above in the main text, Chapter 4, Part II (I).

67. At p. 1651. Above, Chapter 4, Part II (IV).

68. Opposite p. 70.

69. At pp. 66–67.

70. 1978.

71. The view formerly held (Dillon, "The Rack," p. 55) and accepted in the *Inventory of the Tower Armouries,* which was published in 1916, was that the present instrument was acquired at the sale in 1826 of a collection belonging to a Mr. Deney, of Craven Street, London. However, Mr. A. N. Kennard pointed out to me that the catalog of the sale concerned contained no such item: it is surprising, if the Tower Armouries somehow disposed of the apparatus illustrated by Skinner and then in 1826 purchased back the same apparatus or bought another of the same kind.

72. The Museo Correr, in Venice, possesses a print (P-*rovenienze* D-*iverse* S-*tampe* 3072) depicting a prison in which men are being subjected to various harsh measures. According to the legend, we see the range and severity of the armoury employed by criminal justice under Julius Caesar. Somewhat apart from the rest of the legend, and in smaller type, the locative *Romae* presumably does not form part of the title, but indicates the place of publication. No publisher is named, and no engraver. However, the identity of the draftsman is revealed by the appearance, within the design, of a roman capital I, followed by a period, then by a roman capital R, then by another period. This is the mark of Ignas (Ignace) Raeth, who was born at Antwerp in 1626, in 1644 became a Jesuit, thereafter for some time worked in Madrid, from 1652 worked for a decade at Bamberg, and then settled again at Antwerp, where he died in 1666. Devices represented in the print include the strappado and a forearm press (cf. Fiorelli, *La tortura giudiziaria,* I: 198, on a similar leg-press), as well as very heavy stocks (cf. below in the main text, (IV)), another contraption, which could well reflect hearsay concerning the tongs, and another, which could well be the artist's attempt to compromise between Foxe's illustration of "Scevington's gyves" and a description, noticed below in the main text, offered in Rishton's diary, of the "Scavenger's Daughter". The depicted contraption which recalls the tongs, comprises a metal collar at one end of a metal rod (which I shall call the "vertical") terminating at the other end with a ring, the plane of which is at right angles to that of the collar. There is a set of bilboes, which slid onto the locking bar first one leg-iron, then the ring of the vertical, then the other leg-iron. To each side of the vertical, nearer to the collar than to the ring, there is a manacle, joined to the vertical by a very short bar parallel to the locking-bar. The prisoner's hands are thus brought quite close together, his ankles being further apart: a disposition which, with the tongs, would have been better achieved by placing the leg-irons at each end of the locking-bar, entirely outside the manacle strips.

73. William Cobbett, *Parliamentary History of England from the Norman Conquest . . . to the Year 1803* (London: R. Bagshaw and others, 1806–1820), VIII, 731 et seq. (The *Parliamentary History* appeared in 36 volumes. From Vol. XIII (pub. 1812) it was not ascribed to Cobbett and its title was simplified. It is classified as "Parliamentary Debates" and normally shelved before the Hansard series.)

74. Above in the main text, Chapter 5, Part II (I).

75. Appendix, No. 26(b). Above in the main text, Chapter 5, Part I.

76. Cf. Cal.S.P.Ireland, Eliz., lxxxi, 18; 33. Above, in the main text, Chapter 6, Part I.

77. Above in the main text, Chapter 6, Part I; and see Chapter 6, n. 8.

78. *"Cubiculum quoddam seu antrum arctissimum vix hominem erectum capiens . . ."*

79. *"Spelunca quaedam subterranea . . ."*

80. 1588 ed., p. 71.

81. Ibid., p. 74.

82. P. 34.

83. *Societas Jesu usque ad sanguinis et vitae profusionem militans*, pp. 18–19.

84. Appendix, No. 50. Above in the main text, Chapter 6, Part I.

85. Cf. Cal.S.P.Dom., Jam. I, xlv, 74.

86. Cf. Cal.S.P.Dom., Ch. I, cccl, 33.

87. At p. 37.

88. Pitcairn, *Criminal Trials*, II, 375.

89. Reg.P.C.Scot., 1st Ser., VI, p. 49.

90. Sc. Acts, IV, 396.

91. Various similarly sounding names—for example, "caspie-claws"—are said to be corruptions: cf. *Scottish National Dictionary;* O.E.D. In the late eighteenth century, the word *caschielawis* was thought to have described an instrument for torturing the arms; in the nineteenth, to have described an iron case in which an examinate's legs were placed, and which was then heated: *Scottish National Dictionary*.

92. P. 29: illustration, opposite p. 133.

93. My attention was directed to them by Mr. Kennard. They included the mark, in the floor, of a staple and ring, suitable for holding a chain attached to a prisoner. Last time I was in the White Tower, I did not discern them. Works had been carried out in the basement, but perhaps I was at fault.

94. Ministry of Works, *Guide Book* (1957); Dillon, "The Rack," p. 49.

95. Hammond, *Royal Fortress*, p. 50.

96. II, 209.

97. II, 224.

98. W. H. Dixon, *Her Majesty's Tower* (London: Hurst and Blackett, 1869–71), I, 103.

99. W. and E. Thornbury, *Old and New London: A Narrative of Its History, Its People, Its Places* (London: Cassell), II, 94.

100. Borg, *Treasures of the Tower: Torture and Punishment*, p. 2. The Flint Tower was, as Borg points out, rebuilt in 1796. Brick was then used, but in the mid-nineteenth century it was again rebuilt, this time of stone: Clark, *Mediaeval Military Architecture*, II, 233.

101. An inscription, supposed to be in its original position, indicates that in 1553 the crypt itself served as a prison for at least one of Sir Thomas Wyatt's Kentish supporters. Another name has been added at the bottom, in greater haste or with less skill. Hammond, *Royal Fortress*, p. 37, conveys that a number of the rebels were kept in the crypt.

102. If it came to guessing the location of the "dungeon among the rats", I would favor either the projection, which existed in the sixteenth century, of the Lanthorn Tower, or the Cradle Tower in its sixteenth-century state. Clark records, *Mediaeval Military Architecture*, II, 233, that the floor of the Well Tower basement was, when he viewed it, scarcely above water level in the ditch, but seemingly it provided the only access to the upper chamber: which might have made inconvenient its use as a prison.

103. The Hayward and Gascoyne bird's-eye view shows a very large building, or a close-packed row of buildings, immediately south, and running from one end to the other, of the bailey north wall, in which the Flint Tower stood. That tower, we may therefore suppose, would have been difficult of access to a mob.

104. Caraman, *John Gerard*, p. 106; Tanner, *Societas Jesu Apostolorum imitatrix*, p. 677.

105. Caraman, *John Gerard*, p. 105.

106. Ibid., p. 108n.; Borg, *Treasures of the Tower: Torture and Punishment*, p. 4. Cf. Williamson, *The Gunpowder Plot*, pp. 188–89; Hammond, *Royal Fortress*, p. 38.

107. Cf. Caraman, *John Gerard*, p. 108n.

108. Clark, *Mediaeval Military Architecture*, II, 209, reported that a tunnel, driven "in modern times" through the foundations of the White Tower in the direction of the quay, was reached, from the southwest corner of what is now the Cannon Room, by a (ten-foot) shaft.

109. In Borg, *Treasures of the Tower: Torture and Punishment*, p. 4.

110. Bayley, *History and Antiquities of the Tower of London*, p. 115, and illustration opposite; cf. Clark, *Mediaeval Military Architecture*, II, 210.

111. Hammond, *Royal Fortress*, p. 8.

112. For example, the case is worth considering, for judging that Gerard's torture chamber was in a still-existing place, the basement of the Wakefield Tower. It is not very big, but neither is it small, and it has deep recesses. It was very dark: cf. Clark, *Mediaeval Military Architecture*, II, 221. Its roof was not supported by two wooden pillars, but it was supported by one: an arrangement restored in 1970. (If in the sixteenth century the sixteen additional posts existed, supporting concentric octagonal frames, which Clark found there [*Mediaeval Military Architecture*, II, 222], and which appear in an illustration provided by William L.L.F., Baron de Ros, *Memorials of the Tower of London* [London: John Murray, 1866], opposite p. 225, then use as a torture chamber must have been much impeded; but they must recall the eighteenth-century props formerly in the White Tower, and may well have been installed considerably after Gerard's time.) Approached by descent from the upper chamber, it might have been thought subterranean. There is said to have been free passage between the Lieutenant's Lodging and the Bloody Tower, which the Wakefield Tower adjoins: cf. Dixon, *Her Majesty's Tower*, I, 103. I have seen what appeared the remains of a mural or juxta-mural passage behind outhouses of the Lodging (now called the "Queen's House"), running east in the direction of the Bloody Tower; but I was unable to determine how far they extended, or, of course, where the passage itself, supposing there was one, had terminated.

113. *Acts and Monuments*, 4th ed., rev., pp. 547–48. The illustration in Foxe's first ed. (p. 1561), of Cuthbert Simpson's suffering, shows the rack as placed near the bottom of a flight of steps.

114. Appendix, No. 4.

115. Above in the main text (V).

116. P. 72.

117. Catholic Rec. Soc., V, 329–30; Devlin, *Life of Robert Southwell*, p. 211.

118. P. 34.

119. Cf. Paul Ignotus, *Political Prisoner* (London: Routledge and Kegan Paul, 1959), pp. 77–78, on the case of Cardinal Mindszenty.

120. Leland H. Carlson, *The Writings of John Barrow, 1587–90* (London: Sir Halley Stewart Trust, per Allen and Unwin, 1962), pp. 254–55. In a note to the same passage, Carlson calls attention to a reference by Martin Marprelate, *Epistle to the Right Puisante and Terrible Priests My Cleargie Masters of the Convocation-House . . .* (East Molesey: R. Waldegrave, October, 1588): *in The Marprelate Tracts* [1588-1589] (Leeds: The Scolar

Press, 1967), p. 28, to "Little Ease at the Counter". Thus "Little Ease", as the description of a cell, was not confined to the Tower, or even to the Tower and Bridewell. Its first use was not necessarily at the Tower: cf. Pugh, *Imprisonment in Medieval England*, p. 177.

121. Above, n. 41.

122. Appendix, No. 49.

123. Ibid., No. 47.

124. Ibid., No. 51.

125. Ibid., No. 52.

126. Ibid., No. 53.

127. P. 34.

128. Catholic Rec. Soc., V, 323–24.

129. Cit. A. J. Copeland, *Bridewell Royal Hospital, Past and Present* (London: Wells Gardner, Denton, 1888), Ch. VI.

130. Cf. Howard, *State of the Prisons,* Everyman ed., pp. 105–6: on the Prison de la Cour, Munich.

131. Deprival of sleep and torture by the testicles: De Marsiliis, *Tractatus de quaestionibus:* ad D.XLVIII.xviii.1(pr.), No. 27(55). Beating with rods: Damhouder, *Praxis rerum criminalium,* c.XXXVII,22: cf. what is shown under the rack, in the *Justicia* of P. Brueghel the Elder. On the first two modes of torture, and whipping, see Fiorelli, *La Tortura giudiziaria,* I, 206 and n.

132. Above in the main text, Chapter 8 (IV).

133. Ed., from MS. Bodley Laud. Misc. 636, C. Clark (London: Oxford University Press, 1958), pp. 55–56.

134. *Symeonis monachi opera omnia:* Rolls Ser., I, 252–54.

135. Cf. Augustine, Epist. CXXXIII.2: Migne, *Patrologia Latina,* XXXIII, 509.

136. Above in the main text (V).

APPENDIX

1. Sic.

2. Sic: doubtless by error, in place of "they are required to bring him to the rack."

3. Cf. below in the main text, No. 40.

4. Cf. below in the main text, No. 40.

5. John Gerard: cf. Cal.S.P.Dom., Eliz., cclxii, 123: examination by Coke, Fleming, Bacon, and Wade, 14 April, 1597.

6. Cf. Cal.S.P.Dom., Jam. I, lxxx, 6.

7. Coke is recorded as present at Council on this date.

8. Cf. further, in the *Acts of the Privy Council,* under the dates of 9 June and 2 July, 1628.

9. Seven copies were distributed of this instruction.

10. Cf. Cal. Close Rolls, 4 E.II, p. 308.

11. MS. Cotton Calig. c.III, f.237 (formerly f.229). With the omission of a brief passage, this warrant was published by Henry Ellis, *Original Letters in Illustration of English History* (1st Ser.: 1824), p. 260.

12. Both surnames have been partly obliterated; yet correspondence between Smith and Burghley (MS. Cotton Calig. c.III, f.248) and other State Papers (cf. William Murdin, *Collection of State Papers relating to the Affairs of Queen Elizabeth from 1571 to 1596 left by William Cecil, Lord Burghley*, pp. 97–101) leave no doubt as to the identity of the addressees in this instance.

13. Quaere, "prudness": the ms. is here frayed.

14. Evidently, Mary Stuart.

15. Lansdowne MS., No. 155, f.222b (formerly f.219b), and f.228 (formerly f.225): published, with some modernization of spelling, by R. H. Clive, *Documents connected with the History of Ludlow* (1841), p. 309, at p. 318.

16. Gunpowder Plot Book, No. 17: Cal.S.P.Dom., 1603–10, p. 241.

17. MS. frayed.

18. Cf. Cal.S.P.Dom., Ch. I, cccliv, 39; a corrected draft is cataloged after the warrant itself.

19. Cf. Cal.S.P.Dom., 1672–73, p. 483.

20. When I copied it, this paper was numbered 54a in Case F, among the Domestic State Papers at the Public Record Office.

21. See also Hollinshed's *Chronicles:* 1807–8 ed., IV, 512.

A SELECTED BIBLIOGRAPHY ON TORTURE

ON INTERROGATORY TORTURE

Books

Piero Fiorelli, *La Tortura giudiziaria nel diritto comune* (Rome: Giuffre, 1953; 1954).

Franz Helbing (David Haek), *Die Tortur, Geschichte der Folter im Kriminalverfahren aller Zeiten und Völker*, 4th ed., ed. Max Bauer (Berlin: P. Langenscheidt, 1926).

David Jardine, *Reading on the Use of Torture in the Criminal Law of England previously to the Commonwealth* (London: Baldwin and Cradock, 1837).

John H. Langbein, *Torture and the Law of Proof: Europe and England in the Ancien Régime* (Chicago; London: University of Chicago Press, 1977).

Alec Mellor, *La Torture: son histoire, son abolition, sa réapparition au xxe siècle*, 2nd ed. (Paris: Mame, 1961).

Rudolf Quanter, *Die Folter in der deutschen Rechtspflege sonst und jetzt: ein Beitrag zur Geschichte des deutschen Strafrechts* (Dresden: H. R. Dohrn, 1900).

Wilhelm H. Wasserschleben, *De quaestionum per tormenta apud Romanos historia commentatio* (Berlin: 1836).

Articles

Francesco Calasso, s.v. *"Tortura,"* in the *Enciclopedia Italiana*.

Alfred P. Dorjahn, "Evidence by Torture in Ancient Athenian Courts," *Studi in onore di Vincenzo Arangio-Ruiz* (Naples: Jovene, 1953): 77.

Arnold Ehrardt, s.v. *Tormenta* (1937) in [August Friederich von] *Paulys Real-Encyclopädie der classischen Altertumswissenschaft, neue Bearbeitung* by Georg Wissowa (Stuttgart: J. B. Metzlerscher, 1893-).

J. W. Headlam, "On the προκλησις εις βασανον in Attic Law," *Classical Review* 7 (1893): 1.

———. "Slave Torture in Athens" (note), *Classical Review* 8 (1894): 136.

A. Lawrence Lowell, "The Judicial Use of Torture," *Harvard Law Review* 11 (1897): 220; 290.

Giuseppe de Luca, *"La Tortura nei rapporti tra processo e pena,"* *Rivista di diritto processuale civile* (Padua) 4 (1949), Parte I: 318.

Pasquale del Prete, *"Quaestio de servis contra dominos,"* *Annali del Seminario Giuridico-Economico dell'Università di Bari* (1933), Parte II: 90.

Theodor Thalheim, s.v. βάσανοι (1897) in *Paulys Real-Encyclopädie der classischen Altertumswissenschaft, neue Bearbeitung.*
Walter Ullman, "Reflections on Medieval Torture," *Juridicial Review* 56 (1944): 123.
Note on "The Third Degree," Harvard Law Review 43: 617.

PRIMARILY ON ORDEALS, BUT INTERESTING ON INTERROGATORY TORTURE

Hermann Nottarp, *Gottesurteilstudien,* 2nd ed. (Munich: Bamberger, 1956).

WIDER STUDIES, REFERRING TO INTERROGATORY TORTURE

Books

Ernest Alabaster, *Notes and Commentaries on Chinese Criminal Law* (London: Luzac, 1899); (chiefly founded on writings of Sir Chaloner Alabaster).
Derek Bodde and Clarence Morris, *Law in Imperial China, exemplified by 190 Ch'ing Dynasty Cases* (Philadelphia: University of Pennsylvania Press, 1973).
Robert J. Bonner, *Evidence in Athenian Courts* (with Hansen C. Harrell, *Public Arbitration in Athenian Law*) (New York: Arno Press, 1979).
Robert J. Bonner and Gertrude Smith, *Administration of Justice from Homer to Aristotle* (Chicago: University of Chicago Press, II (1938).
W. W. Buckland, *The Roman Law of Slavery: the Condition of the Slave in Private Law from Augustus to Justinian* (Cambridge: Cambridge University Press, 1908; reprinted, 1970).
Aristide Calderini, *La Manomissione e la condizione dei liberti in Grecia* (Milan: Ulrico Hoepli, 1908).
André Chastagnol, *La Préfecture urbaine à Rome sous le Bas-Empire* (Paris: Presses Universitaires de France, 1962).
Michel A.E.A. Clerc, *Les Métèques athéniens: étude sur la condition légale, la situation morale et le rôle social et économique des étrangers domiciliés à Athènes* (Paris: Thorm et fils, 1893).
G. R. Elton, *The Tudor Constitution: Documents and Commentary* (Cambridge: Cambridge University Press, 1960).
Adhémar Esmein, *History of Continental Criminal Procedure,* (trans. J. Simpson; Continental Legal History Series; London: John Murray, 1914).
Peter D. Garnsey, *Social Status and Legal Privilege in the Roman Empire* (Oxford: Clarendon Press, 1970).
G. Glotz, *Etudes sociales et juridiques sur l'antiquité grecque* (Paris: Hachette, 1906).
Robert H. Van Gulik, *T'Ang-Yin-Pi-Shih: Parallel Cases from under the Pear Tree,* Sinica Leidensia 10 (Leiden: 1956).
A.R.W. Harrison, cur. D. M. MacDowell, *The Law of Athens: Procedure* (Oxford: Clarendon Press, 1971).
James Heath, *Eighteenth Century Penal Theory* (London: Oxford University Press, 1963).

Sir William Holdsworth, *History of English Law* (London: Methuen, 1924), V.

A.H.M. Jones, cur. J. A. Cook, *Criminal Courts of the Roman Republic and Principate* (Oxford: Basil Blackwell, 1972).

John W. Jones, *Law and Legal Theory of the Greeks, an Introduction* (Oxford, Clarendon Press, 1956).

P. D. King, *Law and Society in the Visigothic Kingdom* (Cambridge: Cambridge University Press, 1972).

Franz Lämmli, *Das attische Prozessverfahren in seiner Wirkung auf die Gesichtsrede* (Paderborn: F. Schöningh, 1939).

John H. Langbein, *Prosecuting Crime in the Renaissance* (Cambridge, Mass.: Harvard University Press, 1974).

Charles H. Lea, *Superstition and Force*, 4th ed., rev. (New York: Benjamin Bloom, 1971): this includes an entire essay on interrogatory torture.

_____. *History of the Inquisiton of the Middle Ages* (New York: Harbor Press, 1955).

_____. *History of the Inquisition of the Middle Ages*, abridged ed., intro. by W. Ullmann (London: Eyre and Spottiswoode, 1963).

_____. *The Inquisition in the Spanish Dependencies* (New York: Macmillan, 1908).

_____. *History of the Inquisition of Spain* (New York: Macmillan, 1922).

J. H. Lipsius, *Das attische Recht und Rechtsverfahren* (Leipzig: O. R. Reisland), III (1915).

Theodor Mommsen, *Römisches Strafrecht* (Leipzig: Dunekar und Humblot, 1899).

Sir James Fitzjames Stephen, *History of the Criminal Law of England*, (London: Macmillan, (1883), I.

James L. Strachan-Davidson, *Problems of the Roman Criminal Law* (Oxford: Clarendon Press, (1912), II.

L. Tanon, *Histoire des tribunaux de l'Inquisition en France* (Paris: L. Larose et Forcel, 1893).

Gabriel Tarde, *Penal Philosophy*, trans. R. Howell (Boston: Little, Brown, 1912).

Articles

G. Cardascia, "*L'Apparition dans le droit des classes d'honestiores et d'humiliores*," *Revue Historique de Droit Français et Etranger* 27 (1950): 305; 461.

R. Ishi, "The History of Evidence in Japan," *Recueils de la Société Jean Bodin* 18 (1963): 521.

J.-Ph. Lévy, "*L'Evolution de la preuve, des origines à nos jours*," *Recueils de la Société Jean Bodin* 17 (1965): 9.

Jacques Pirenne, "*La Preuve dans la civilisation de l'Egypte antique*," *Recueils de la Société Jean Bodin* 16 (1964): 9.

INDEX

The names of causes and cases are entered in italics. The parenthetic numbering of namesakes is chronological, but ad hoc only. Particular papal bulls and particular statutes are entered under Bulls *and* Statutes, *respectively.*

Abbot, Robert: *Antilogia,* 155-57, 288, 289
Abington, Thomas, 276
Accomplices. *See* Torture, to discover accomplices
Accursius, 13
Accusatorial procedure, 15, 18
Adason, Peter (Petrus filius Adae), 24-27
Admiralty: courts of, 70, 111-13, 275, 293; jurisdiction, torture and, 70, 293
Advocate-General (pro tempore), 176
Aland, Charles, 172
Alexander IV (Pope), 29
Alfield, Thomas, 111
Algeria, torture in, 243
Anderson, E., 281
Andrews (suspected murderer), 94
Anglo-Saxon Chronicle, 199
Anglo-Saxon kingdoms, 14
Anglo-Saxon praxis, 18
Aquaviva, Claudio, correspondence of, 138, 197, 198, 282, 286
Archer, John, 154, 155, 159
Arden, Edward, 126
Arden, Marie, 126
Arlington, Earl of. *See* Bennet, Henry
Armada, the, 114, 192
Arrow, torture with an, 89
Arson, 119
Articles of War. *See* War, Articles of

Arton, William, 172, 176, 177, 178, 183, 294
Arundel, 141
Arundel, Charles, 126
Arundel, Earl of. *See* Fitz Alan, Henry
Ashe (Counter Reformation courier), 117
Asheton, Roger, 114
Ashley, Anthony, 118, 139
Ashton, Ralph, 58
Askew, Ann, 65-67, 196, 295
Atkinson, Clinton, 112, 275, 276
Attorney-General (pro tempore). *See* Law Officers
Aubrey, Dr. (quaere, William), 111
Augustine (Bishop of Hippo): *De civitate Dei,* 253
Aunger, Richard, 120
Azo, 17, 250

Babington, Anthony, 127-28, 276; plot attributed to, 114, 127-28
Bacon, Francis (Viscount Verulam), 119, 120, 134, 137, 152, 153, 164, 288
Bagshaw, Dr., 134, 277
Bagshaw(e) (Counter Reformation courier; quaere, George, of Marsh Green), 117, 277)
Bailly (Bayley), Charles, 98-101, 190, 194
Baker, John, 77
Baldus (of the Ubaldi), 261
Bale, Bishop, 66
Ballard, John, 127-28
Bankruptcy, torture and, 70-71, 266
Bannister, Lawrence, 94-95, 101-3
Barbaro, Daniel, 269

309

322

About the Author

JAMES HEATH is Lecturer in Law at the University of New-
castle-upon Tyne. His earlier works include *Eighteenth Century
Penal Theory*.